In the Face of Death

"In this exhaustively researched and carefully developed study Fabian Grassl uncovers the experiential roots of Helmut Thielicke's theology. In particular, Thielicke's experience of life-threatening illness as a young man and his constant encounters with death during the years of Nazi rule left an indelible mark on the shape of both his theology and his preaching. Grassl examines these influences in detail, offering an appreciative but also critical assessment of a theology marked deeply by the experience of suffering and death. Both those who have a particular interest in Thielicke's work and those who want to think about the strengths and weaknesses of a theology shaped so strongly by experience will profit from Grassl's excellent work."

—**Gilbert C. Meilaender**, Senior Research Professor at Valparaiso University and the Paul Ramsey Fellow at the Notre Dame Center for Ethics and Culture

"In the middle decades of the last century Helmut Thielicke was likely the most quoted German-Lutheran theologian in North-American Protestant churches, more so than Bonhoeffer or any of the other 'big names.' Translations of Thielicke's best-selling sermons and other writings were regular fare for many American clergy and laity, while his academic work in systematic theology and ethics were routinely studied by U.S. seminarians and graduate students. Dr. Grassl here unveils in a masterful way those life experiences of Thielicke that had a profound impact on his thinking, preaching, and pastoral care. Dr. Grassl not only provides insights into Thielicke's biography—frequently on the basis of previously unexplored archival material—but he also helps the reader to understand more clearly the principal themes in Thielicke's complex theology. This is now the best introduction in English to this important theologian's life and work."

—**Matthew L. Becker**, Professor of Theology, Valparaiso University

"Theologian, ethicist, and preacher Helmut Thielicke lived in death's shadow from an illness in his youth that nearly claimed his life to his experiences ministering to those who lost loved ones in World War II. Thielicke's theology, especially his eschatology, bears the indelible imprint of his own biography. Grassl carefully examines both Thielicke's life and his theology in the context of his times. His research is rich with illuminating insights for those who seek to understand one of the most significant theologians of the last century."

—**John T. Pless**, Assistant Professor of Pastoral Ministry and Missions; Director of Field Education, Concordia Theological Seminary

"After a period of relative neglect, Helmut Thielicke and his theological legacy are receiving renewed attention. With its well-researched and closely argued account of the formative interaction between Thielicke's personal life and the central themes of this theology, Grassl's fine study sets an important benchmark for future work."

—**Philip G. Ziegler**, Professor of Christian Dogmatics, University of Aberdeen

"As a pastor who often faced danger, suffering, war, and death, Thielicke is well-equipped to give us wise insight yet today. Not only has Grassl made Thielicke—long one of my favorite authors—a living, breathing human being, but he has also provided a comprehensive and profound perspective on this amazing, durable, and complex pastor and theologian who still has so much to say to us today."

—**Daryl McCarthy**, Director, European Academic Network and Cambridge Scholars Network

In the Face of Death

Thielicke—Theologian, Preacher, Boundary Rider

Fabian F. Grassl

FOREWORDS BY
Timothy J. Wengert
AND
Wolfram Thielicke

☙PICKWICK *Publications* · Eugene, Oregon

IN THE FACE OF DEATH
Thielicke—Theologian, Preacher, Boundary Rider

Copyright © 2019 Fabian F. Grassl. All rights reserved. Except for brief quotations in critical publications or reviews, no part of this book may be reproduced in any manner without prior written permission from the publisher. Write: Permissions, Wipf and Stock Publishers, 199 W. 8th Ave., Suite 3, Eugene, OR 97401.

Pickwick Publications
An Imprint of Wipf and Stock Publishers
199 W. 8th Ave., Suite 3
Eugene, OR 97401

www.wipfandstock.com

PAPERBACK ISBN: 978-1-5326-5547-0
HARDCOVER ISBN: 978-1-5326-5548-7
EBOOK ISBN: 978-1-5326-5549-4

Cataloguing-in-Publication data:

Names: Grassl, Fabian F., author. | Wengert, Timothy J., foreword. | Thielicke, Wolfram, foreword.

Title: In the face of death : Thielicke—theologian, preacher, boundary rider / by Fabian F. Grassl ; foreword by Timothy J. Wengert ; foreword by Wolfram Thielicke.

Description: Eugene, OR : Pickwick Publications, 2019 | **Includes bibliographical references and index.**

Identifiers: ISBN 978-1-5326-5547-0 (paperback) | ISBN 978-1-5326-5548-7 (hardcover) | ISBN 978-1-5326-5549-4 (ebook)

Subjects: LCSH: Thielicke, Helmut,—1908–. | Death—Religious aspects—Christianity.

Classification: BT825 .G76 2019 (print) | BT825 .G76 (ebook)

Manufactured in the U.S.A. 05/10/19

To my mother and father,
whose love and example led me to Christ,

&

in grateful remembrance of my great-grandfather,
Josef Hunger (1889–1967),
who had the mind—but not the opportunity—to become a scholar

> Even though I walk through
> the valley of the shadow of death,
> I will fear no evil,
> for you are with me;
> your rod and your staff,
> they comfort me.
>
> —Psalm 23:4 (ESV)

Contents

Foreword by Timothy J. Wengert | ix
Foreword by Wolfram Thielicke | xi
Acknowledgments | xiii
Key to Primary Source Abbreviations | xv
Introduction | xxi

Part I	Life
Chapter 1	Setting the Stage: Thielicke's Biography as Key to His Theology	3
Chapter 2	Existence in the Face of Death: Thielicke's Childhood and Sickness as Key to His Theology	16
Chapter 3	Existence in a Culture of Death: Thielicke's Experiences during the Nazi Regime as Key to His Theology	36
Part II	Theology
Chapter 4	The Lutheran Way: Thielicke's Conversion and Thought in Historical Context	73
Chapter 5	The Pneumatic Theologian: The Spirit's Regenerative Work as Theological Starting Point	88
Chapter 6	The Triune God: Divine Personhood and the Origin of Evil	117
Chapter 7	The Crucified God: Borderline Situations and the Cross of Christ	149

Part III	Proclamation
Chapter 8	*Orator sub specie existentiae:* The Making of a Preacher Man in a Culture of Death | 179
Chapter 9	*Homo sub specie malis:* Pastoral Challenges in the Face of Death | 187
Chapter 10	*Homo sub specie aeternitatis:* The Pastoral Commission in the Face of Death | 206
	Conclusion | 232

Bibliography | 237
Index of Names | 257
Index of Scripture Passages | 265

Foreword by Timothy J. Wengert

MARTIN LUTHER ONCE NOTED that experience makes a theologian. This trenchant remark is the guide through which Dr. Grassl has viewed the life and work of one of the most important and yet (now) least known German theologians of the twentieth century.

I first learned about Helmut Thielicke and his remarkable sermons as an undergraduate at the University of Michigan—active in the Lutheran student congregation—an interest that continued through my years at Luther Seminary in St. Paul, Minnesota. Now, over four decades later, few Lutherans, let alone other Protestants or Roman Catholics, have even heard the name, let alone read anything by this remarkable twentieth-century theologian. Yet Helmut Thielicke, alongside other far-better-known German theologians such as Dietrich Bonhoeffer or Karl Barth, demands attention, especially for the unique way he blended theology, proclamation, and life. That is the unique contribution of Grassl's book: an analysis of Thielicke's theology and proclamation from the perspective of his life, especially his personal experiences of death (between the late 1920s and 1933) and living in a culture of death (from 1933 to 1945).

By grounding Thielicke's work in his life, Grassl has found a way to give new perspectives on this remarkable theologian and preacher of the 1930s through the 1960s. Reading this careful study ought to motivate every reader at very least to purchase and devour Thielicke's sermons (about which he once said that his translator, John W. Doberstein, made them better in English than in the original German). But Grassl has also done a great service to theology by bringing this highly contextual theologian back to life, thus making a plea for the preeminence of truly existential theology in the Christian church.

In a world where autocrats abound, Thielicke's down-to-earth theology may prove to be the perfect antidote. In any case, from this book, we learn that experience made Thielicke one of the very best theologians of all.

Timothy J. Wengert
Philadelphia, PA, May 2018

Foreword by Wolfram Thielicke

QUITE SOME TIME HAS passed since the death of my father and no one talks about him much anymore. All the greater my surprise and joy when Fabian Grassl got in touch with me one day to find out more about Helmut Thielicke for the purposes of his dissertation. We invited him and his wife, Anja, to our home and spent a lovely and cheerful afternoon together. I was staggered by the knowledge he had acquired about Helmut Thielicke. As a passionate technician who studied mechanical engineering, I could not contribute much to theological subjects, but that was not Grassl's concern anyway: he was rather interested in my relationship with my father.

Our upbringing was very important to my father, but his work made such demands on him that he mainly left it to our mother. Being in the public eye as he was, my poor school performance certainly proved challenging to him. But his distinct humor helped him to make the best of this, too: during a conversation with colleagues and their wives, the topic of their children's school achievements came up. One mother praised the prodigies of her offspring and their excellent school reports. At that, my father responded dryly: "If one of our children comes home with a 'D' in their school report, we hoist the colors."

As his son, I especially liked that he was not afraid of his superiors. He met every traffic policeman with respect, but not "authorities" such as the Gestapo in the Third Reich, who terrorized him greatly. I miss my father's courageous statements on current political affairs and ethical issues, statements that often got him into trouble. What, for example, would he say about the whole process of digitization, with all of its positive and negative consequences? In his day, a quip circulated about my dad that said: "The Last Judgement will arrive so fast that not even Helmut Thielicke could say anything about it."

At any rate, I am pleased about this work: that my father lives on; and not least about the friendship with Fabian and Anja Grassl that has come out of it.

Wolfram Thielicke

Nuremberg, March 2018

Acknowledgments

"Man cannot think of himself as human without
being conscious of his indebtedness."
—Abraham J. Heschel

I am indebted to . . .

The Triune God, for placing me on this journey

My wife, *Anja*, for joining me on this journey

My daughters, *Talitha*, *Yadah*, and *Keziah*, for inspiring me on this journey

My parents, *Hans* and *Marialuise*, for blessing me on this journey

My supervisor, *Professor Stephen N. Williams*, for guiding me on this journey

My editors, *Dr. Charlie Collier* and *Zane Derven*, for assisting me
in the publishing process of this journey

Wolfram and *Karina Thielicke*, for opening their home to me on this journey

&

Professor John T. Pless, for giving me the hint that led to this journey

Soli Christo Gloria

Key to Primary Source Abbreviations[1]

Abbreviation	German Original	English Publication
Abenteuer	Glauben als Abenteuer	*Faith: The Great Adventure*
Anfechtung	Theologie der Anfechtung	n/a [own translation: Theology of Contestation]
B&E	Begegnungen und Erfahrungen	n/a [Encounters and Experiences]
Bergpredigt	Das Leben kann noch einmal beginnen: Ein Gang durch die Bergpredigt	*Life Can Begin Again: Sermons on the Sermon on the Mount*
Bilderbuch	Das Bilderbuch Gottes: Reden über die Gleichnisse Jesu	*The Waiting Father: Sermons on the Parables of Jesus*
"Church and Atheism"		"Can the Church and Atheism Coexist?"
"EdR"	"Das Ende der Religion: Überlegungen zur Theologie Dietrich Bonhoeffers"	n/a [The End of Religion: Some Thoughts on the Theology of Dietrich Bonhoeffer]
Einführung	Einführung in die christliche Ethik	n/a [Introduction to Christian Ethics]
Ernstfall	Der Christ im Ernstfall	*Being a Christian When the Chips Are Down*

1. For full bibliographical information, see the bibliography.

Abbreviation	German Original	English Publication
EvF I	Der Evangelische Glaube, Band I	*The Evangelical Faith*, Volume I
EvF II	Der Evangelische Glaube, Band II	*The Evangelical Faith*, Volume II
EvF III	Der Evangelische Glaube, Band III	*The Evangelical Faith*, Volume III
Fragen	Fragen der Christenheit	*Man in God's World* contains chapter 12
"Frage nach dem Sinn"	"Die Frage nach dem Sinn unseres Lebens"	n/a [The Question of Meaning in our Life]
Freedom		*The Freedom of the Christian Man*
Freiheit	Von der Freiheit, ein Mensch zu sein	n/a [On the Freedom of Being Human]
Gebet	Das Gebet das die Welt umspannt: Reden über das Vaterunser aus den Jahren 1944/45	*Our Heavenly Father: Sermons on the Lord's Prayer*
Gespräche	Gespräche über Himmel und Erde	*Between Heaven and Earth: Conversations with American Christians*
G&E	Geschichte und Existenz	n/a [History and Existence]
GldChr	Der Glaube der Christenheit	*Man in God's World* contains chapters 18 to 32
Humor	Das Lachen der Heiligen und Narren: Nachdenkliches über Witz und Humor	n/a [The Laughter of the Saints and Fools: Some Thoughts on Wit and Humor]
Kanzel	Auf dem Weg zur Kanzel	n/a [Heading for the Pulpit]: contains abbreviated versions of the three English publications: (1) *A Little Exercise for Young Theologians*, (2) *How modern should theology be?*, and (3) *Encounter with Spurgeon*
K&K	Auf Kanzel und Katheder	n/a [At Pulpit and Lectern]

KEY TO PRIMARY SOURCE ABBREVIATIONS   xvii

Abbreviation	German Original	English Publication
K&Ö	Kirche und Öffentlichkeit	n/a [Church and Public Life]
Krauss	Helmut Thielicke im Gespräch mit Meinold Krauss	n/a [Helmut Thielicke in Conversation with Meinold Krauss]
Kulturkritik	Kulturkritik der studentischen Rebellion	n/a [The Cultural Criticism of the Student Rebellion]
LmdT	Leben mit dem Tod	*Living with Death* [revised version of *Tod*]
Lebensangst	Die Lebensangst und ihre Überwindung	Two smaller volumes in English: *Out of the Depths* and *The Silence of God*
Mensch	Mensch sein—Mensch werden	*Being Human—Becoming Human*
MF&T	Glauben und Denken in der Neuzeit	*Modern Faith and Thought*
Nihilismus	Der Nihilismus	*Nihilism*
Notwendigkeit	Notwendigkeit und Begrenzung des politischen Auftrags der Kirche	n/a [The Need and Limit of the Political Mission of the Church]
Offenbarung	Offenbarung, Vernunft und Existenz: Studien zur Religionsphilosophie Lessings	n/a [Revelation, Reason, and Existence: Studies on Lessing's Philosophy of Religion]
Reden	Und wenn Gott wäre . . . Reden . . .	*How to Believe Again*
"Religion in Germany"		"Religion in Germany"
Schuld	Schuld und Schicksal	n/a [Guilt and Fate]
Schweigen	Das Schweigen Gottes: Glauben im Ernstfall	n/a [The Silence of God: Believing in Times of Crisis]: contains parts of *Lebensangst*, *Ernstfall*, and two additional essays
SdA	Die Schuld der Anderen	n/a [The Guilt of the Others]

Abbreviation	German Original	English Publication
Sterben	Wer darf sterben?	*The Doctor as Judge of Who Shall Live and Who Shall Die*
"Strukturen"	"Können sich Strukturen bekehren?"	n/a [Can Structures Be Proselytized?]
Suche	Auf der Suche nach dem verlorenen Wort	n/a [In Search of the Lost Word]
ThDvGl	Theologisches Denken und verunsicherter Glaube	Revised version of *How modern should theology be?* [Theological Thinking and Unsettled Faith]
ThE I	Theologische Ethik, I. Band	Three abridged and edited versions of the *Theological Ethics* in English: (1) *Foundations*, (2) *Politics*, and (3) *Sex*
ThE II/1	Theologische Ethik, II. Band, 1. Teil	
ThE II/2	Theologische Ethik, II. Band, 2. Teil	
ThE III	Theologische Ethik, III. Band	*The Ethics of Sex* represents one subsection of the German third volume
Tod	Tod und Leben	Earlier version of *LmdT* [Death and Life]
Trouble	Leiden an der Kirche	*The Trouble with the Church*
Wayfarer	Zu Gast auf einem schönen Stern	*Notes from a Wayfarer*
Welt	Wie die Welt begann	*How the World Began*
Weltanschauung	Weltanschauung und Glaube	n/a [Ideology and Faith]
WiG	Wo ist Gott?	n/a [Where is God?]
Woran	Woran ich glaube	*I Believe: The Christian's Creed*
Wunder	Das Wunder	n/a [The Miracle]: also contained in *Anfechtung*

Abbreviation	German Original	English Publication
"WuV"	"Wahrheit und Verstehen"	n/a [Truth and Understanding]
Zeitgenossen-schaft	Theologie und Zeitgenossenschaft. Gesammelte Aufsätze	n/a [Theology and Contemporaneity: Collected Essays]
ZG&S	Zwischen Gott und Satan	*Between God and Satan*

Introduction

"Kant's philosophy can be understood apart from the life of its author, but in the case of Schleiermacher, a look into his biography is an essential aid to interpretation."[1] Such is the verdict of Wilhelm Dilthey on the work of the father of modern theology. To show that this intriguing dictum regarding the life of Friedrich Schleiermacher holds equally true in the case of Helmut Thielicke is the *broad* aim of this book. Its *specific* goal is to demonstrate that Thielicke's theological thought is permeated by a particular biographical period which, in turn, was saturated with multiple encounters with definite phenomena that no human being can evade: death and suffering. I will argue that Thielicke's existential default mode, which culminated—to borrow a phrase from Kierkegaard—in his "sickness-unto-death," lasting from 1929 until 1933, should be regarded as constituting if not the very *heart* of his theology, then at least a life-giving organ within the overall Thielickean organism of thought, without which his theological program would not have become what it is.

The fact *that* these encounters are reflected in the theology and proclamation of Thielicke indubitably becomes clear through his own explicit confessions, and even simply by throwing a cursory look at his manifold literary output. To explicate *how* these existential encounters with man's finitude are theologically processed, not just in his obvious publications dedicated to this theme, but rather implicitly, indirectly, and possibly subconsciously, *this* is the exciting question arising out of the "that." It is also the concrete task I aim to fulfill in what follows.

To state the obvious—and quite contrary to the Cartesian mind-set—such an undertaking cannot claim to reach a level of "objective certainty," which is a *contradictio in adiecto*, anyway. As philosopher and theologian

---

1. Wilhelm Dilthey, as rendered by Thielicke in *MF&T*, 166–67. See also *MF&T*, 273.

William Lane Craig points out, science *per se* does not deal with "certainty," the latter being a psychological property neither necessary nor sufficient for knowledge.[2] Instead, the question is whether the premise at hand is more probable than not, given the evidence available.[3] I am thus concerned with warranted belief, i.e., with a justified degree of *probability*.

Correspondingly, in terms of methodology, I subscribe to presumptive or circumstantial evidence—what the Germans call *Indizienbeweis*. I therefore try to ascertain a high degree of probability regarding my central thesis: that major areas of Thielicke's theological thinking were decisively and often subtly impacted by definite "real life" encounters with the phenomena of death and suffering. In other words, I simply apply the exegetical principle that a text is interpreted best in its context to Thielicke's theology. I claim that it is best interpreted when seen against the background of his *Sitz im Leben*, i.e., his existential context. More precisely: in light of his "*eschatological* existence," which will be established in part I. In parts II and III, moreover, my aim will be to make the existential foundations of major theological convictions of Thielicke explicit, while at the same time providing a systematic overview of his theology.

It is worthy of note that this study would not have been possible on just any randomly chosen theologian. This is true not merely because many other theologians have not encountered suffering and death to a "sufficient" extent that could enable them to come to a similar theological focus. Rather, the project at hand became feasible because Helmut Thielicke possessed one specific character trait not shared by many in his field: his passion for autobiographical anecdote and narrative. Whereas outstanding thinkers such as John Calvin[4] or Karl Rahner[5] tended to keep personal things private, Thielicke, in contrast, was quite outspoken about

---

2. See Craig, "Defenders—Doctrine of God, Part 3: Excursus on Natural Theology" (31:05–34:11), and "Part 11: Scientific Confirmation of the Beginning of the Universe" (3:54–6:18). See also Moreland and Craig, *Philosophical Foundations*, 29–30, 80–81. Thiede emphasizes that even in the natural sciences, "certainty" is a myth (see Thiede, *Gekreuzigte[r] Sinn*, 98n20, 102n44).

3. This is one of the claims of Joseph Butler (1692–1752) in *Analogy of Religion*: that probability is the essential guide in life. See also John Henry Newman, who was greatly influenced by Butler in this regard: "Absolute certitude . . . was the result of an *assemblage* of concurring and converging probabilities" (Newman, *Apologia Pro Vita Sua*, 20).

4. See McGrath, *Calvin*, 34, 98. Interestingly, McGrath only uses one brief autobiographical segment from Calvin's foreword to the *Commentary on the Psalms* to draw inferences from his theology (McGrath, *Calvin*, 98–101). How much more should it then be possible to do the same in the case of Thielicke, who provides plentiful material in this regard?

5. See Rahner, *Erinnerungen*, 10, 11, 24, 31–32.

both his inward and outward life. This particular characteristic proved to be indispensable for this study, which seeks to investigate how his life experiences impacted his thinking *in concreto*.

I try to achieve this goal by way of ten chapters, subsumed under three major parts devoted to his life (part I), theology (part II), and proclamation (part III)—the first serving as starting point and basis for the latter two. Whereas part I offers an original and fresh account of Thielicke's life through the lens of his own afflictions and "near-death experiences,"[6] a theological analysis of select aspects of his overall program—in light of the said biographical account—will be attempted in the second and third parts. Those two parts, focusing on Thielicke's theology and proclamation, respectively, were structured on the basis of his early work report, *Auf Kanzel und Katheder* [*At Pulpit and Lectern*], where he differentiates between both tasks in spite of their intrinsic inseparability, more on which is to come later (see especially chapter 8). As will be seen, Thielicke's verdict on Friedrich Schleiermacher, that "the pulpit and the rostrum are the two crucial points in the ellipse of his spirit,"[7] applies directly to himself, too.

In the introduction to his anthropology, *Mensch*, it is telling that Thielicke asks the rhetorical question of how one could write about man without revealing those traces that "the trap of one's own existence" left behind.[8] Indeed, this is the purpose of the second and third parts: to explicate those aspects of Thielicke's massive theological output that disclose the impact of a Wayfarer's life in the face of death, as unfolded in part I. By initially placing his historic-confessional *context* and soteriological starting point under scrutiny, his pneumatological *focus* then leads to the trinitarian and christological *center* of orthodox Christianity, finally moving to the homiletical and pastoral *dimension* of man *sub specie aeternitatis*. In this structural manner, the nucleus of my argument—namely, that Thielicke's "theological work was always only a superstructure placed upon the experiences and sufferings of [his] life"[9]—is to be unfolded with regard to his very specific experiences of death and suffering.

---

6. By "near-death experience," I do not have the conventional use in mind; that is, chiefly, an out-of-body experience after a person's heart has stopped beating and brainstem activity has gone silent. To call such events NDEs, in fact, is a misnomer since we are really talking about death experiences. In contrast, and in the true sense of the term, I simply mean the experience of life-threatening events; of events bringing one *near* death.

7. *MF&T*, 178.

8. *Mensch*, 20.

9. *Wayfarer*, 85 [115].

I commence part II with an analysis of Thielicke's conversion and thought within his denominational *context* in chapter 4. The twofold aim of showing both his basically Lutheran frame of thinking as well as its principal conformity with his own early experiences of life shall thereby be pursued.

I then move on to Thielicke's theological starting point of saving trust (*fiducia*) in Jesus Christ, highlighting not only its deeply existential embeddedness but also that, without it, much of his later system would not have been realized in the way that it was. Afterwards, attention naturally shifts to that "uncontrollable power"[10] without which personal faith could not come into being: by concentrating on Thielicke's pneumatological *focus*, both the Spirit's indispensable role for Thielicke's thought as well as the experiential saturation of his cognitive process are to be acknowledged. Since a person's saving faith and the work of the Holy Spirit go hand in hand, however, both will be treated together in chapter 5. In the sixth chapter, I will take up the task of examining Thielicke's understanding and defense of divine *personhood* in light of his "eschatological existence" and pursue the issue of supralapsarianism, which arises out of the former. In chapter 7, the thematic development segues into Thielicke's *personalistic* answer to the problem of evil.

Part III concentrates on his homiletical and pastoral handling of the problem of theodicy. Whereas chapter 8 highlights Thielicke the preacher, *sub specie existentiae*, chapters 9 and 10 shed analytical light on four main pastoral loci under the aspects of evil, *sub specie malis*, and eternity, *sub specie aeternitatis*, respectively. Despite Thielicke's statement that the relation between life and thought was later to reveal itself more immediately and openly in his sermons rather than in his systematic thought,[11] interest is nonetheless directed slightly more towards the latter.

There are three reasons for this structural move, the first two of which really represent two sides of the same coin. First, the bulk of postgraduate research has focused on Thielicke's prominence as a preacher, a datum to be returned to in chapter 8. Out of the major number of contributions dedicated to Thielicke's preaching, the doctoral dissertation of Michael Calvert (in 2014) has given specific attention to Thielicke's sermonic handling of the problem of evil and suffering.[12]

The flipside of this heightened interest in Thielicke the preacher—and, *ipso facto*, the second reason for the chosen structure—is a corresponding scarcity of research on Thielicke the systematic theologian. Yet, by

---

10. *EvF III*, xxvii.
11. See *Wayfarer*, 85 [115].
12. See Calvert, "Preaching and the problem of evil."

approaching the recognized focal point in Thielicke's pastoral care and sermons via its existential embedment, I hope to make an original contribution in this area whilst avoiding a too-extensive treatment of the same at the cost of Thielicke's worthwhile but undervalued systematic theology.

The final reason is, at least in part, personal: in relation to the proposed thesis, I found it to be a more exciting and innovative challenge to focus on Thielicke's theology as a whole, rather than concentrating on one particular area. It is more challenging to try to discover the hidden dimension than that which, in the words of Thielicke, is "immediate" and "open." That the impact of his "eschatological existence" makes itself felt in a more subtle but nevertheless equal way in his systematic thinking is to be demonstrated in part II.

In terms of the primary sources, this research mainly relies on material published in German, Thielicke's mother tongue. An exception was made for his three volumes of systematic theology, *The Evangelical Faith*, his survey and evaluation of significant developments in modern theology, *Modern Faith & Thought*, and an essay collection titled: *Freedom*. Whereas *EvF* and *MF&T* found their way into the English language in an almost unabridged way by means of experienced translator and theologian, Geoffrey W. Bromiley, the latter collection, *Freedom*, was specifically put together for an English audience and, in this form, is not available in German. In the case of Thielicke's autobiography, *Wayfarer*, both the German original and the English translation were used. Hence, whilst it is the usual procedure to cite from *Wayfarer* with the German equivalent added in square brackets [*Zu Gast*], it occasionally happens that this process is reversed whenever I was dissatisfied with the rendering. All other translations are my own unless otherwise noted. For the sake of simplicity and clarity, Thielicke's own practice of referring to humanity as a whole in masculine terms (e.g., man, his, him) is applied throughout this book as well.

Finally, three motives lie behind my specific choice of "conversation partners" as engaged in each chapter. Not only are theologians and philosophers included (1) who noticeably influenced Thielicke's thought, thereby contributing to his intellectual development, and (2) who (obviously) add to the discussion at hand in a substantial way. But, I have also chosen personalities in and outside the field of theology (3) who tragically, and in varying degrees, experienced personal suffering themselves and whose accounts could therefore serve as a basis of comparison for Thielicke's own attempts at making sense of things.

Part I—Life

Now at the end of this valley was another,
called the Valley of the Shadow of Death,
and Christian must needs go through it,
because the way to the Celestial City lay in the midst of it.

—JOHN BUNYAN, *PILGRIM'S PROGRESS*

Chapter 1

Setting the Stage

Thielicke's Biography as Key
to His Theology

> "My theological work was always only a superstructure placed
> upon the experiences and sufferings of my life..."
>
> —Thielicke, *Wayfarer*, 85 [115]

With this statement, Helmut Thielicke reveals the exegetical key to his theological thought. If Thielicke's theology is to be adequately understood and appreciated, his personal life experience—which was, to a great degree, shaped by encounters with suffering and death—must be taken into account. By "superstructure" [Überbau] he means the theological effects of an inextricable connection between life and thought. It connotes specific theological convictions produced by "the existential drive at work"[1] in his thinking. The Thielickean "superstructure" is a theological outlook shaped by his "eschatological existence"; one that would not have arisen without this "underpinning foundation" [*Tiefenstruktur*][2] that informs his work so uniquely.

For that reason, as the title of this chapter claims, Thielicke's biography constitutes the key to his theological *corpus*. It is, therefore, the purpose of this first part to analyze Thielicke's *Sitz im Leben* (his existential context) and how his personal formation and experience of life—especially his formative years, as a child and young man—served as a hotbed in which his particular theological focus on human finitude was later to flourish. Part I is thereby *not* to be regarded as a comprehensive biographical treatment, but

---

1. *Wayfarer*, 85 [115].
2. A fitting term coined by Langsam, *Konkretion*, 14–15.

rather as a necessarily selective look at Thielicke's life and formation as seen through the lens of suffering and death. Its aim is thus to unlock the door to Thielicke's theological outlook with the biographical key that he himself provides. It is to lay the existential foundation for the subsequent theological analysis. In this process, Thielicke's own words are given priority.[3]

Part One: Biographical Sources

In order to serve the purpose of presenting a reliable and objective biographical presentation, I draw on five different primary sources. The earliest autobiographical source, considered by Thielicke to be a "work report,"[4] first appeared under the title *Begegnungen* (*Encounters*) in 1957. This initial account of his life and work was extended and republished twice, first in 1965 (*Auf Kanzel und Katheder* [*At Pulpit and Lectern*], hereafter *K&K*), and again in 1977 (*Begegnungen und Erfahrungen* [*Encounters and Experiences*], hereafter *B&E*).

The second and at the same time most comprehensive authority on Thielicke's life is his autobiography, *Zu Gast* (*Wayfarer*), which originally appeared twenty months before his death, in August 1984. The latest German edition, which I have used, comprises 542 pages and, if Thielicke had had his way, would not have been so "condensed."[5]

Third, an extensive interview for the German TV documentary *Zeugen des Jahrhunderts* (*Witnesses to the century*), produced by the *ZDF* and later published to its full extent as a book (hereafter *Krauss*), has granted additional invaluable insight and clarification. Lutheran pastor and journalist Meinold Krauss conducted six hours of Q&A over two and a half days in the first half of 1985, less than one year before Thielicke's death.[6]

A fourth indispensable source and helpful corrective to Thielicke's own published words proved to be his massive literary records archived at the University of Hamburg.[7] Thielicke states the obvious in a letter to Paul

---

3. In the interest of substantive clarity, I have judged it better to refer to some relevant secondary literature after I have offered my own exposition and not before it, so I have reserved this for the end of chapters 2 and 3, respectively.

4. *K&K*, 7 [*B&E*, 7].

5. See the comment of his wife, Marieluise Thielicke, in "Freundesbrief Juni 1985," (*NHT*). The "Freundesbrief" was the couple's annual newsletter to friends.

6. See Marieluise Thielicke, "Freundesbrief Juni 1985," (*NHT*).

7. Handschriftenlesesaal der Staats- und Universitätsbibliothek Hamburg, Carl von Ossietzky, Von-Melle-Park 3, 20146 Hamburg, Germany. As of February 2019, the number of archived manuscripts comprises 842; the number of archived letters written by Thielicke amounts to 221; and the number of archived letters received by him account for 347. The total number of pages exceeds 8,000.

Althaus on March 27, 1945, namely that "in a letter, one can write more openly than in a public polemic."[8] This openness—along with unpublished material and other miscellaneous personal documents—has, without doubt, furthered the cause of this book.

Finally, a fifth source consists of scattered biographical notes throughout Thielicke's theological writings. Thielicke sometimes refers to events in his life for illustrative purposes—especially in his homiletical works. In rare cases, these references reveal something new. Most commonly, however, they serve as a means of comparison, either strengthening or undermining statements made elsewhere.

The most helpful *secondary* source of a biographical nature proved to be the PhD project of Holger Speier, published in 2009.[9] Speier dedicates a lengthy first chapter to outline significant events in Thielicke's life in chronological order, making auxiliary use of the material archived in Hamburg. One other secondary source which was particularly important to consider in connection with this study (and therefore deserving of explicit mention) is a collection of four commemorative speeches. They were delivered by theological companions at an academic memorial in honor of the late Thielicke at the University of Hamburg on December 4, 1986.[10] Moreover, Helmut Thielicke's oldest son, Wolfram Thielicke, added some valuable detail to his father's biographical representation on the occasion of a personal meeting at his Nuremberg home on September 29, 2016.

This first part is made up of three chapters, each subdivided into several subsections. In addition to the methodological remarks, the present chapter serves as a first guide to Thielicke's complex personality. Chapter 2 focuses on Thielicke's childhood and sickness, whereas his encounters with death and suffering during the Nazi regime gain center stage in chapter 3, closing with an overview of other encounters with the same phenomenon beyond 1945.

The major twofold impact upon his life and thinking of sickness and the Nazi regime are well recognized by Thielicke himself, as well as among secondary sources. In what follows, his sickness is given especially extensive consideration for two major reasons: first, Thielicke's stance under the Third Reich has generally been granted much stronger academic and popular

---

8. The letter quoted is archived under the label *NHT : Ba : 2a*. *NHT* stands for *Nachlass Helmut Thielicke* (*Nachlass* meaning "papers" or "literary estate/remains"). Hereafter, I will not cite serial numbers of Thielicke's archive files but only indicate such material by adding (*NHT*). For full bibliographical information, I refer the reader to the bibliography at the end.

9. Speier, *Initiator*.

10. Lippert, *Zum Gedenken an Helmut Thielicke*.

attention than his even more crucial "sickness-unto-death" (to use Kierkegaard's phrase somewhat freely here). Consequently, by way of a detailed analysis of the said illness in chapter 2, I offer a new perspective in a fresh biographical account, as a secondary original contribution in its own right, within the framework of the primary original contribution of this book as a whole. In doing so, I draw on unpublished or no longer published secondary sources (archived at the University of Hamburg) to which English-speaking readers not familiar with German might have no other access. The second reason is that the seriousness and persistence of Thielicke's condition must be explicated clearly and in detail—not only as a major turning-point in his life, but also since without it, as to be shown in the course of this work, many aspects of his theology would not have emerged as they did.

It is therefore substantial to unfold *both* influences systematically for the first time—as far as I am aware. By entering the house of Thielicke's theological system via his existential main entrance, specific pieces of furniture in the mansion's various rooms shall be examined, thereby determining whether those pieces were brought in through the same doorway.

Part Two: A Musical Analogy

"Ours is the century of death, and Mahler is its musical prophet." These penetrating words of Leonard Bernstein,[11] widely considered as one of the great composers of the twentieth century, illuminate the essence of his era in a few words. As composers generally seem to display a heightened sensitivity towards culture and its accompanying *Zeitgeist*, one might look at a theologian's favorite musician in order to gain a first insight into the theological inclination typically embedded within and consequently arising from his or her personal formation and development, i.e., one's *Sitz im Leben*.

Before attention turns to the musical pointer, however, it is noteworthy that Thielicke himself stresses the undeniable importance of a theologian's existential circumstances, for "a theologian's work . . . is even more strongly related to one's life and existence than in other faculties."[12] Elsewhere, he reiterates that "the lives of those who do theology can never be ignored. They play a part. They have a major role. They are the battlefield between eternity and time. In them the decision is taken who or what rules and who or what serves as an instrument."[13]

---

11. Bernstein, *Unanswered Question*, 313.

12. *K&K*, 8. Not contained in *B&E*.

13. *MF&T*, 5. See *MF&T*, 176; and *Wayfarer*, 73 [99], where he comments on the homiletical style of his teacher, Althaus: "There was nothing artificial about him. The truth he preached was *part of his life*." Emphasis added.

In addition to his own personal approach to this persuasion, Thielicke most likely found further theological justification in Luther's understanding of "the subject of theology." For "subject," according to Luther, "refers both to *the one who does theology* and also to its theme."[14] The truly Lutheran stance of Thielicke's thinking is further discussed in the fourth chapter. In any case, for now, the "essential connection between theology and existence"[15] represents—in Thielicke's eyes—a "truism"[16] whose emergence within Thielicke's consciousness is inseparably connected with his experiences of sickness and near-death, as will be shown later on. It is therefore not surprising when he states that one of his "constantly recurring theological tasks [is] to reveal the dogmas' existential relevance."[17]

In this fundamental conviction, he is joined by a number of notable theologians, such as Dietrich Bonhoeffer, according to whom "insight cannot be separated from the existence within which it is won"[18]; Bonhoeffer's famous teacher, Adolf Schlatter, who contends that "the state of life establishes the act of thinking"[19]; Jürgen Moltmann, who "found theology . . . a fascinating adventure" since "one can only stand up to it by exerting all one's heart and all one's soul and all one's strength"[20]; and two of the outstanding Roman Catholic thinkers of the twentieth century: Karl Rahner, stating that "the personal life essentially plays itself out in the theological work,"[21] and Joseph Ratzinger, who opines that "the mark of a great teacher of the church . . . is that he teaches by his life, since thought and life penetrate and define each other in himself."[22] Likewise, yet more strongly, Lutheran theologian Helmut Gollwitzer proclaims "the blaze and blood of a living heart and a keenly lived life" to be a component of the very substance of theology: "Theological existence demands . . . will, passion, spontaneity,

---

14. *EvF I*, 15n2. Emphasis added. "Luther's line 'Persona facit opera,' i.e., 'it is the person who does the works,' became my leitmotif. In everything man does, wills, and accomplishes . . . he fulfills himself" (*K&K*, 16 [*B&E*, 15]).

15. *ThE I*, §502. "Insight and existence belong together" (*Gespräche*, 162). Compare two statements of Barth in this regard: "There is no avoiding the fact that the living object of theology concerns *the whole man*" (Barth, *Introduction*, 84) and "since the concern which claims the theologian even in his private life is total, his commitment is also total" (Barth, *Introduction*, 85). See also Romans 6:13.

16. *Kanzel*, 12, 38.

17. *Suche*, 150.

18. Bonhoeffer, *Nachfolge*, 38.

19. Schlatter, *Rückblick*, 102. See also Schlatter, *Einführung*, 36.

20. Moltmann, *Experiences*, 9.

21. Rahner, *Erinnerungen*, 63. On page 105, Rahner makes the same point in relation to the Pope.

22. Ratzinger, "Einführende Worte," 16.

and tendency. Somebody claims something within theology, for within it somebody is claimed. That is why the intricacies and the incalculable of the personal life belong particularly to this very science."[23]

Returning to the discussion on musical inclination as a theological pointer within his personal life, Thielicke's "trusty friend and colleague Dr Rainer Röhricht,"[24] in the commemorative speech for his former teacher, highlights the idea that a human being's preferences in the aesthetic realm are almost always representative of his or her character (and consequently, it might now be added, of his or her theology).[25] The very same idea is expressed by Alan Torrance, who evaluates Karl Barth's conception of Christian experience, for example, as seeming "predominantly to be a joyful and optimistic one." Torrance concludes that this conception is reflected in "Barth's at times almost embarrassingly extravagant praise and adulation of the music of Mozart."[26]

Jürgen Moltmann, in contrast, "cannot stand Mozart longer than one hour." He prefers Beethoven's compositions, the tensions in his music, instead of the omnipresent harmony and absence of conflict in Mozart.[27]

Karl Rahner, again, had no favorite composer at all.[28] Perhaps this, I might add—with tongue in cheek—explains his vast number of essays and monographs on a great variety of themes without presenting a singularly prodigious, systematic work in the Barthian or Thielickean sense.

Helmut Thielicke's favorite musician, finally, was not Gustav Mahler,[29] as might have been expected in light of his experiences, nor Johann Sebastian Bach, "the one composer whose music forms a perfect mirror of Lutheran theology,"[30] but Joseph Haydn. The calmness, sobriety, and reasonableness

---

23. Marquardt, "Helmut Gollwitzer," 558–59. Compare Clark's statement: "The predispositions or desires of the knowing subject need not decisively control genuine knowledge of God and thus obscure God. As theologians, we can allow the subject of investigation . . . to exert a dominant influence on our knowing process" (Clark, *To Know and Love God*, 215). Similarly, Polanyi states: "Into every act of knowing there enters a passionate contribution of the person knowing what is being known . . . this coefficient is no mere imperfection but a vital component of his knowledge" (Polanyi, *Personal Knowledge*, viii).

24. *EvF I*, 17. See *B&E*, 218.

25. Röhricht, "Thielicke," 21.

26. Torrance, "Christian Experience and Divine Revelation," 111. Thanks to Stephen N. Williams for providing me with this source.

27. Moltmann, "Look Forward!," reply to second last question.

28. See Rahner, *Erinnerungen*, 66.

29. Mahler was greatly admired by the one politician who became the unprecedented epitome for Bernstein's "death-ridden century," Adolf Hitler. See Hamann, *Hitlers Wien*, 94–95, 499.

30. Herz, "Bach's Religion," 129.

of the Austrian composer obviously appealed to Thielicke's own nature, with its disgust of fanaticism and enthusiasm [*Schwärmerei*],[31] a nature "by no means" tending towards optimism.[32]

It is therefore telling to observe how he describes his own theological position in light of this (without wanting to imply, by way of the previous paragraph, that the following positions are to be classified as "fanatic" or "enthusiastic"). When asked by a student where he puts himself theologically, Thielicke once responded: "I am sailing in line, astern Barth and Brunner, but trying to steer my own course."[33] In a letter to Hermann Diem on May 16, 1947, he delineates this in more detail: "Every serious theologian of our generation is somehow rooted in that place where Barth had his Romans breakthrough. Now this place as starting point . . . yields different directions to proceed, of which Barth and his people only represent one. I sit on another branch of the same tree."[34] On this basis, it is possible to locate Thielicke firstly and roughly as a second-generation dialectical theologian, finding his own particular focus within the said parameter.[35]

---

31. Röhricht, "Thielicke," 21. Thielicke's preference for these special characteristics was certainly already predisposed by the influence of his mother, who "was a sober woman who treated herself with puritanical strictness . . . Her piety was sincere and profound, though stamped with a Calvinistic sobriety" (*Wayfarer*, 15 [26]). See *Krauss*, 15–16.

32. *Wayfarer*, 419 [535].

33. Cited in Quest, "Thielicke," 549. That Thielicke was sailing more in Brunner's wake than Barth's will become clearer as we proceed. For now, see Brunner's comment in *Wayfarer*, 131 [174], and the following remarks of Brunner in the same personal letter to Thielicke on September 25, 1947 (*NHT*) (not published in *Wayfarer*): "In my eyes you are a big-time hope on the theological field. Not just because of your extraordinary prowess, but also because *I have confidence in your overall alignment.*" Emphasis added. A few lines earlier, Brunner states: "That Barth makes you responsible for the 'hardening' of the theologians I find amusing and at the same time saddening, for it shows how definitely he identifies matters with KB. Whoever is not with me [KB] is hardened towards God." Here, Brunner probably refers to the issue of Germany's collective guilt, over which Thielicke plunged into great controversy with Barth after 1945. See Greschat, *Die Schuld der Kirche*; Besier and Sauter, *Wie Christen ihre Schuld bekennen*, esp. 9–61; and the dissertation of Richter-Böhne, *Unbekannte Schuld*.

34. *SdA*, 23. See *KuÖ*, 40–41, where he states his own commitment to the nature and task of the original dialectical theology, not without making some reservations concerning the later development of the movement.

35. For a helpful secondary source to approximate Thielicke's overall position, see the comprehensive work of Boa and Bowman Jr., *Faith Has Its Reasons*, Part five. Although the authors do not concentrate on Thielicke, his thinking principally matches the basic fideist criteria presented here. See esp. 409–12 for a brief overview of the central *loci*, and 361, where a quotation from Bloesch refers to him as a neo-Lutheran in the fideist strand.

Part Three: Thielicke's Personality —An Introductory Sketch

Taking this musical analogy as a starting point, a first introductory sketch of Thielicke's nature may be attempted. The already mentioned Röhricht places his former friend's personality type between moods of dejection and a radiant zest for life. Thielicke was able to unfold a kind of "Dionysian joy of the self," and yet, at the same time, he was always aware of the dark depths of human life—with its basis in guilt and death.[36]

Röhricht's appraisal of Thielicke's antipodean nature—swinging between melancholy and sanguinity, misery and joviality—is in full accordance with Thielicke's own description of the "crass difference" of his parents' tempers. Whereas his mother had a very withdrawn and sober personality, merely pouring out her feelings in many letters,[37] his father, in stark contrast, tended to the other extreme, displaying uncontrolled emotions as well as an inclination to overdo things.[38] Hence, both sides already provided a predisposition for characteristic manifestations in their son.

This initial predisposition is further played out in Thielicke's life as described in his autobiography, which, in different places, endorses the supposition that his psychology was pendular. As to the first, "low" end, Thielicke paradigmatically remembers a "foolish error" of his youth. After recognizing his ignorance in this particular situation, Thielicke "fell into great despondency."[39] Later on, during his first post-war professorship, Thielicke recalls: "My Tübingen period was also marked by periods of severe depression." Due to difficulties, defamations, and denunciations, Thielicke discloses "a range of sharply differing moods with which I had great difficulty in coping. . . . I often suffered periods of extreme despair."[40]

Perhaps even more serious fits of dejection can be ascribed to the time when one of the "saddest phases" in his life began, namely, the student revolt in the late sixties.[41] Thielicke's personal letters from his literary records, archived at the University of Hamburg, reveal a much gloomier and more desperate inner state during this particular period—*inter alia* leading to a

---

36. Röhricht, "Thielicke," 26–27. Some parallels to certain character traits of his favorite composer, Haydn, do in fact appear. See Kavanaugh, *Spiritual Lives*, 37–43.

37. See *Wayfarer*, 16 [26–27].

38. See *Wayfarer*, 16 [27].

39. *Wayfarer*, 59 [82]. See *K&K*, 13 [*B&E*, 12].

40. *Wayfarer*, 226 [291].

41. *Wayfarer*, 377 [483]. For Thielicke's account of the student revolts, see *Wayfarer*, 377–99 [483–511]; and *B&E*, 173–91. In his monograph, *Kulturkritik*, he analyses the movement's philosophical roots.

temporal hospitalization, due to exhaustion[42]—than is expressed in his autobiography.[43] The same conclusion can be reached regarding his existential struggle during the Nazi period, which will be discussed shortly.

Asked about this specific characteristic, Thielicke's oldest son, Wolfram, cautiously affirms that one cannot speak about his father's dejection in the sense of being manic-depressive but rather as having an awareness of the dark depths of human life, as mainly experienced through the three life phases: sickness, war, and student revolt.[44] Wolfram remembers one specific and recurring situation where he personally witnessed "a constant concern" of his father: for a while, he and his brother Berthold accompanied their dad in the car on his monthly trip to St. Michaelis church, where Thielicke delivered his famous sermons. The crowds wanting to hear him were so great that six policemen had to be placed around the building as parking-assistants to help with the traffic. Wolfram reports that every time they left home, one hour before the service began, his father became greatly frightened in the car at the prospect of no one (or merely a few people) turning up to hear him preach. Each time, those fears were only allayed by Thielicke finally sighting the policemen, whose presence promised the appearance of many listeners.

This deeply personal insight also reveals how much Thielicke identified himself with his success as a preacher—the role that, after all, he was mainly known for. Apparently, for him, failure in this area would have meant the loss of public status, of being appreciated.[45] Overall, however, Wolfram concludes

---

42. See *Wayfarer*, 388–89 [498]. See also Thielicke's letters to the Minister of Justice, Gustav Heinemann (1966–69; and Germany's president from 1969–74), on February 17, 1968 (*NHT*), and to Dr. Wulff on June 12, 1968 (*NHT*).

43. I am indebted to Speier, *Initiator*, 67n166, for originally drawing my attention to this fact.

44. Wolfram Thielicke in a personal meeting at his Nuremberg home, September 29, 2016.

45. A certain general disposition to crave acclaim is also detectable in the partly heroic portrayals in his autobiography. For Thielicke's somewhat self-aggrandizing undertone, see the paradigmatic depictions in *Wayfarer*, 88–89 [119–20], 105 [141], 112 [149–50], 117–19 [156–58], and 121–23 [161–63]. For his emphasis on being acclaimed, compare the following statements, for example: "The audience pointedly received us with seemingly neverending applause" (*Wayfarer*, 88 [119]); "They received me with thunderous applause and were clearly inspired and delighted by my protest" (*Wayfarer*, 92 [124–25]); "It was a source of some embarrassment that virtually every student preferred my lectures to his" (*Wayfarer*, 111 [148]); "Afterwards, I received a small ovation from my comrades" (*Wayfarer*, 122 [160]); and "My lecture took place and . . . was met with 'loud applause'" (*Wayfarer*, 343 [439]). For similar boastful tendencies during his childhood and youth, see *Wayfarer*, 27, 59 [41, 81]. For Thielicke hereby strongly taking after his father, see *Wayfarer*, 12, 14–15 [22, 25–26]; see also chapter 3, part one.

that the joy of living predominated in the life of his father, thus directing our attention to the second, "high" end of his personality.[46]

Thielicke's general *Lebensfreude* is already expressed by the German title of his autobiography, *Zu Gast auf einem schönen Stern* (literally: "Visiting a beautiful star").[47] Although he describes his nature as "by no means" tending towards optimism,[48] Thielicke nevertheless presents the crucial theological justification for his *joie de vivre* in God's promise after the flood (Genesis 6), as symbolized by the rainbow.[49] Accordingly, in a letter congratulating Thielicke on his sixtieth birthday, his former colleague and friend in Heidelberg, Lutheran church historian Hans von Campenhausen refers to the honoree's appeal which can not only be grasped in his books, but, above all, in his "lively persona." Von Campenhausen remembers an "always open, uninhibited, and intimate Thielicke."[50]

Rudolf Haas, another companion, likewise comments on Thielicke's zest for life permeating the whole of his preaching,[51] and his son, Berthold, confirms the Dionysian spirit by stating his father's enjoyment of life until the very end.[52] This latter assertion is well illustrated by Berthold's older

---

46. See Chesterton's anthropological insight: "Man is more himself, man is more manlike, when joy is the fundamental thing in him, and grief the superficial. Melancholy should be an innocent interlude, a tender and fugitive frame of mind; praise should be the permanent pulsation of the soul. Pessimism is at best an emotional half-holiday; joy is the uproarious labour by which all things live" (Chesterton, *Orthodoxy*, 138).

47. *Wayfarer*, 418–19 [534–36].

48. *Wayfarer*, 419 [535].

49. "Indeed, I have encountered no darkness above which it [the rainbow] does not shine and no valley, no matter how gloomy, which some of God's greetings [i.e., blessings] have not reached" (*Wayfarer*, 419 [535]). For the rainbow as a "hint from another world whilst . . . cross[ing] the dark valleys and cry[ing] out from the depth," see esp. *Welt*, 14, 196, 317–18.

50. Letter from Hans von Campenhausen on November 8, 1968 (*NHT*). For Thielicke's characterisation of Campenhausen, see *Wayfarer*, 99–100 [132–34]. For another "real-life-example" as to his *Lebensfreude*, see *B&E*, 210. See also *Welt*, 21, and esp. 34–38.

51. Haas and Haug, *Thielicke*, 28. Thielicke was "very unhappy," however, about the first contribution of Haas to this sixtieth-birthday surprise in book form, since Haas portrays him as a "shadowless-docetic ghost." "Fortunately," Haug's second portrayal "makes up a lot." See Thielicke's letter to Rudolf Augstein on October 15, 1968 (*NHT*).

52. Berthold Thielicke, "Vorwort," in *Schweigen*, 7. Thielicke and his wife, Marieluise, née Herrmann, to whom he got married in October 1937 (see *Wayfarer*, 106 [142]), had four children: Wolfram, Berthold, Elisabeth, and Rainer. See *Wayfarer*, 126–27, 149, 280–84 [167, 194, 359–64]. From all accounts, they enjoyed a happy marriage, a fact Campenhausen also refers to in his letter. Eight years after her husband's death, Marieluise Thielicke published her childhood memories under the title *Aus meiner Kinderzeit*. In 2010, she died in Nuremberg, where she spent the final year and a half of her life near her oldest son, Wolfram, and daughter-in-law, Karina.

brother, Wolfram, who reports that two weeks before Thielicke's actual death on March 5, 1986, he travelled from his Nuremberg home up to Hamburg, prompted by the news that his father would not make it through the night. Against all odds, however, Thielicke recovered and, according to Wolfram, was full of joy the next morning—in light of the fact that he had cheated death.[53]

Correspondingly, Thielicke, in spite of being German (I might say with tongue-in-cheek), was known for his outspoken sense of humor. In addition to family and friends explicitly referring to this side in his nature,[54] as well as Barth's specific comment,[55] Thielicke also published a book in 1974 titled: *The Laughter of the Saints and Fools: Some Thoughts on Wit and Humor*, thus expressing the importance of humor to his life and theology. In Thielicke's eyes, humor is essentially a means and "a sign of overcoming this world" [*ein Zeichen der Weltüberwindung*].[56]

This significant insight is echoed by at least two other great theologians of the twentieth century. Whereas Dietrich Bonhoeffer specifically states that "final severity never lacks a dose of humor,"[57] the broader stance of "joyful overcoming" (within which the specific characteristic of humor is embedded) is well explicated by Joseph Ratzinger. Focusing on how the Beatitudes are played out existentially in the life of the Apostle Paul, Ratzinger emphasizes that "in the midst of suffering, Jesus alone provides [deep, real] joy" (as opposed to the shallow, surreal "happiness" the world offers). Paul experiences "infinite joy precisely by being delivered [up to suffering and persecution], by giving himself up, in order to bring Christ to men."[58]

53. Wolfram Thielicke in a personal meeting, September 29, 2016. Thielicke's attitude regarding death during his final days thus differs to such as that of seventeenth-century Scottish Covenanter martyr, John Nesbit, who gladly welcomed death along with God's ensuing immediacy. See Rusten and Rusten, *One Year Christian History*, 678–79.

54. In the same conversation, Wolfram recounts how, upon his return home from a voyage, Thielicke locked himself away for several hours with his longtime foster-son (who had lost both parents and, as a student, became a full member of the Thielicke-family). In that time, he told the son all the (partially dirty) jokes that he had collected in written form from the sailors during the voyage. Their broad laughter could be heard throughout the house. See also Haas and Haug, *Thielicke*, 23, 102.

55. See *Wayfarer*, 241–42 [310]. In passing, Zahrnt, *Sache*, 127, in the context of criticizing Barth's monistic tendency and "a-historicalness" [*Geschichtslosigkeit*], highlights the theologically questionable facet of the Swiss's wit. I leave it to the reader's judgement whether Barth's comments on Althaus (see *Wayfarer*, 70–71 [95–97]) amount to social inappropriateness or a great sense of humor.

56. Krauss, 66; *Humor*, 96–101. See also *K&K*, 50–51, 168 [*B&E*, 44, 119–20].

57. Bonhoeffer, *Widerstand*, 201.

58. Ratzinger, *Jesus I*, 101–3. Ratzinger particularly bases his observations, amongst other passages, on 2 Corinthians 4:8–10; 6:8–10.

This phenomenon of deep, Pauline-like joy amidst agony, potentially unloaded in what Thielicke calls "eschatological laughter," was also experienced, for example, by Roman Catholic priest Johann Lenz during his internment in Gusen concentration camp,[59] as well as by Thielicke himself during an air raid.[60] While cynical skeptics might judge such happenings as an overreaction of the nerves to the existential borderline, followers of Christ recognize in this the peace of their master, which the world cannot give.[61]

Thielicke's elliptical personality, finally, is also reflected in his preaching methodology. Friedrich Langsam, focusing his PhD-research on Thielicke's homiletical methodology, compares the Thielickean approach with "a kind of [intended] zig-zag course . . . oscillating from one extreme to the other." This "serpentine-like" preaching style enables the advancement of knowledge by getting to the bottom of both extremes of human experience, thereby finding the solution somewhere in the middle.[62] Again, Thielicke himself endorses this analysis existentially by speaking, for example (in the context of deciding to go for an operation in 1929), of "my delight in dramatic and quick solutions."[63]

Several secondary sources further endorse the conclusion that Thielicke's biography provides the *key* to his theology.[64] In the correct words of Langsam, Thielicke and his work can only be fully understood in a retrospect of his life.[65] Likewise, Röhricht proclaims, in the memorial speech for his late friend and teacher, "from now on, we can evaluate Thielicke *sub specie aeternitatis* . . . Then one will be able to evaluate him more justly than the polemics and enthusiasm during his lifetime."[66]

Thus, one of Thielicke's favorite quotes, the words of Joseph Wittig, certainly applies to his own life as well: "a biography really should not begin with a man's birth, but with his death . . . for only there can one see the

---

59. See Lenz, *Christus in Dachau*, 62–63.

60. See *Humor*, 177–80.

61. See John 14:27.

62. Langsam, *Konkretion*, 122–23. Remember also his locating himself between Barth and Brunner earlier.

63. *Wayfarer*, 59–60 [82]. See *K&K*, 13 [*B&E*, 12–13]. The same disposition comes to the fore after his operation failed and he was faced with one final chance to take a yet untested medicine: "I wanted to force a decision: either this maximum dose of the medicine would help me or the 'poison' would kill me" (*K&K*, 65 [*B&E*, 89]). See also chapter 2, part two.

64. See Röhricht, "Thielicke," 19–20; Langsam, *Konkretion*, 5–6, 12; and Speier, *Initiator*, 16.

65. Langsam, *Konkretion*, 6.

66. Röhricht, "Thielicke," 28.

whole of his life in its fulfillment."⁶⁷ Thielicke's life and work was completed on March 5, 1986. As tempting as Wittig's suggestion may seem, however, our investigation must commence in his childhood, for it is here that the foundations for his later theological inspiration were first laid.

---

67. *Freedom*, 167. See also *EvF II*, 449; *Ernstfall*, 76; *Lebensangst*, 200; *Nihilismus*, 73; *GldChr*, 413; *Gebet*, 67; *Mensch*, 330; *Woran*, 253; and *K&K*, 237.

Chapter 2

Existence in the Face of Death

Thielicke's Childhood and Sickness
as Key to His Theology

Part One: Thielicke's Childhood
—"First Shadows of Death"

HELMUT FRIEDRICH WILHELM THIELICKE[1] was born on December 4, 1908, the very same year which, according to Bernstein, also marked the turning-point towards "a life-and-death crisis in musical semantics," thereby already hinting at the overall social and existential collapse still to come.[2] His hometown was Barmen, at that time a heavily industrial urban area, situated north of Bonn and Cologne in the western central part of Germany. In 1929, Barmen was united with other towns to form the new city of Wuppertal. This general area of Germany has long been known as an area of religious ferment and development. The German *Brethren Movement*, for example, took root in the neighboring town of Elberfeld in the 1840s (later on, this town would be the birthplace of the well-known *Elberfelder-Bibel*, one of the first alternative Bible translations to the Luther translation).[3] In May 1934, Barmen also hosted the First Synod of the Confessing Church, where the famous *Barmen Declaration* was adopted.[4]

---

1. Friedrich and Wilhelm are Thielicke's two rather unknown middle names. See his "Ariernachweis" (Aryan certificate) in (*NHT*).

2. Bernstein, *Unanswered Question*, 264–65 (see chapter 1, part two). 1908 was also "a year of death" for C. S. Lewis, witnessing *inter alia* his mother's tragic death from cancer.

3. See Holthaus, *Konfessionskunde*, 192–93.

4. For Thielicke's description of the religious atmosphere of his birthplace and its effect upon him, see *Wayfarer*, 37–38 [53–56]. For his evaluation of the *Barmen Declaration*, see Krauss, 26–27.

As early as when he was a little boy, Thielicke had his first experience with finitude. On the very first pages of his autobiography, he recounts the death of his beloved grandfather. As he—together with his three-year-old sister, Elisabeth—illicitly entered the half-dimmed bedroom where the loved one was laid out, the sudden sight of the eerily flavescent corpse "triggered a trauma from which I suffered for a long time."[5] Sobbing and screaming in bewilderment, they rushed out of the room. Thielicke quite dramatically concludes, "These were the first shadows of death and finitude reaching for me."[6]

A *thanato*-psychological study on young children ascertains that, from the beginning of language-acquisition onwards, "death is of such importance to a child that it [the child's attitude towards death] is hardly distinguishable from that of a grown-up."[7] Yet, at once it is even more complex since it is additionally challenged by the burden of parental mourning[8] as well as the fact that children under eight years of age are not readily capable of expressing their grief in words.[9] Moreover, "the younger the child is, the greater the trauma's repercussions are."[10] At that time, Thielicke was most likely five, perhaps six years old,[11] and the caring environment he experienced to cope with his shock—especially well wrought from the maternal side—certainly helped matters.[12]

Thielicke praises his mother's emotional way of dealing with his subsequently recurring fears and screaming fits in contrast to his father, who chose the informative method, instructionally trying to appeal to his mind.[13] As Thielicke concludes that his mother's way always appeared to

---

5. *Wayfarer*, 2 [8].

6. *Zu Gast*, 9 (for Law's translation, which does not capture the German meaning well enough in this case, see *Wayfarer*, 3).

7. Raimbault, *Kinder*, 154, 157.

8. Raimbault, *Kinder*, 162. In this particular context of increased complexity, the study speaks about the specific death of a sibling. To a lesser degree, it also applies to wider family like grandparents.

9. Brocher, *Wenn Kinder trauern*, 59. For the child's greater helplessness in general, see Brocher, *Wenn Kinder trauern*, 59–61; for the difference between the death of a grandparent and other relatives, see Brocher, *Wenn Kinder trauern*, 96.

10. Raimbault, *Kinder*, 154.

11. He reports that this event took place at the beginning of the First World War.

12. See Raimbault, *Kinder*, 154. "When a child . . . has lost a family member, it wants to understand. The importance of its environment [herein] is clear from the beginning" (Raimbault, *Kinder*, 155–56). Thielicke's experience confirms both.

13. Compare Brocher: "A common misconception . . . is the idea that didactic knowledge sufficiently helps . . . to understand the child. . . . And yet it is not the words or learned concepts of adults which help the child in the experience of death . . . but

him as the right one in later life, it is certainly more than an intriguing side note to see how he applies this earliest experience with both parental methods *mutatis mutandis* to the section of sex education in his *Theological Ethics*.¹⁴ This event thus provides us with a first glimpse of Thielicke conceptually connecting experience and ethical deliberation.

On account of these psychological studies—as well as his own, rather extensive treatment of this incident—Thielicke's earliest conscious encounter with death should not be underestimated, especially in view of two further occasions around that age in which he "felt death's cold breath" again: "A classmate who sat near me and who often played with me and visited me at home, died of diphtheria. Because of the risk of infection, we were not allowed to accompany his coffin to the cemetery. The result of this was that his death had something oppressively unreal about it for us."¹⁵

The other (chronologically earlier) event was triggered by his innermost wish for a ladder-wagon. Thielicke's grandmother finally succumbed to the "heart-rending pleas" and bought the desired vehicle for her grandson. Bursting for joy, little Helmut was welcomed by his father back home. Following him into the house, his happiness suddenly evaporated and he burst into tears. Upon the indignant questioning of his father as to why he was crying, Thielicke replied, "One day it's bound to get broken anyway!" Looking back, Thielicke interprets his boyhood feelings in the following words: "In the midst of my greatest happiness, the terror of life's transience had come over me. This was a child's first foreboding that the happy moment does not last."¹⁶

In his "Little Biography of Faith,"¹⁷ he lists this incident next to three other major episodes in his life, calling it "my first religious experience."¹⁸ Elsewhere, in a sermon titled, "Of the end of all things," Thielicke says about

---

emotional expressions and the behavior of [the child's] environment" (Brocher, *Wenn Kinder trauern*, 59–60).

14. Along with the negative experience of his father's attempts (*Wayfarer*, 12–14 [22–25]), see esp. *ThE III*, §1995, §1998–99.

15. *Wayfarer*, 10 [19].

16. *Wayfarer*, 3 [10].

17. Originally written for the book of Frazier, *Theologians and their Faith*; German reprint in *Ernstfall*, 148–54.

18. *Ernstfall*, 148. The other three being his "sickness-unto-death," his enforced preaching ministry during the Third Reich, and the late "Faith Information Project Group" [*Projektgruppe Glaubensinformation*], an evangelistic task force whose fellowship turned out to be the couple's "wealth of our late years." See *Wayfarer*, 403–6 [515–20]; *B&E*, 193–97. Thielicke states that this "work and life partnership with my young friends ranks among the most beautiful that I experienced" (*B&E*, 207).

the same experience: "In the face of a great fulfilment the transitoriness of the beautiful became clear to me; *I experienced the shock of finiteness.*"[19]

The importance that this event occupies within Thielicke's thinking is underscored once more by the somewhat astonishing fact that he reiterates it, again, in the extensive interview with Krauss shortly before his death:

> Thielicke: At six years of age, I got a little ladder-wagon . . . Precisely because I was so attached to this wagon and because it made me so happy, I was thinking of the end. This fundamental feeling [*Grundgefühl*] has stayed with me ever since.
>
> Krauss: So already very early you experienced that . . . the whole of life consists in one episode of dying [*das ganze Leben aus einem Stück Sterben besteht*].
>
> Thielicke: Yes, that is how I felt.[20]

But is this *Grundgefühl* unique to Thielicke's existence? And if not, might it therefore generally point to a deeper reality transcending this world? To some lost reality that somehow still evokes this apparently intrinsic yearning of human nature?[21] C. S. Lewis intriguingly seems to answer these questions via his fictional character, Psyche, who confides in her sister, Orual, as to this mysterious mixture of joy and finitude which, like Thielicke—and perhaps even the Apostle Paul[22]—also haunts her:

---

19. Emphasis added. In *Ernstfall*, 148, he calls it the "knowledge of transience." This quote serves as an apt example for certain confusing publication practices in Thielicke's German works: sermon and citation first appeared in 1967, in his work *Wie modern darf die Theologie sein?*, 77 [*How Modern Should Theology Be?*]. *Wie modern* was then revised and republished in 1974 under a different title, *ThDvGl*. Here the quote is on page 106. Finally, a shortened version of *Wie modern* was once more included in *Kanzel* (1983), with the quote appearing on page 127. *Kanzel* is a republication of four of Thielicke's earlier and shorter works. The translation I use is taken from Dirks, *Laymen*, 71 (based on *Wie modern*, 77). Dirks personally heard this specific sermon preached in St. Michaelis on February 11, 1967. See Dirks, *Laymen*, 85–86n3.

20. *Krauss*, 64. See "Traum vom gnädigen Ende," 3 (*NHT*), where Thielicke uses this story as an illustration for the fact that "from my youth onwards, the thought of the end has consistently beset me."

21. See Augustine's masterful synopsis of the human predicament as expressed at the very beginning of his *Confessions*, 21: "You made us for yourself and our hearts find no peace until they rest in you." See also Pannenberg, *Systematic Theology II*, 202: "Basic to the personality of each individual is the destiny of fellowship with God." See further Lewis, *Problem of Pain*, 40, 150–52; Thielicke, *Wayfarer*, 78 [106–7]; and *Mensch*, 394.

22. See Philippians 1:18–26.

> I have always—at least, ever since I can remember—had a kind of longing for death. . . . It was when I was happiest that I longed most. It was on happy days when we were up there on the hills . . . with the wind and the sunshine . . . Do you remember? The colour and the smell, and looking across at the Grey Mountain in the distance? And because it was so beautiful, it set me longing, always longing. Somewhere else there must be more of it. Everything seemed to be saying, Psyche come! But I couldn't (not yet) come and I didn't know where I was to come to. It almost hurt me. It felt like a bird in a cage when the other birds of its kind are flying home.[23]

If Psyche's inability to come (not yet) and her disorientation as to where to come to were applied to Thielicke's early life, then his impending terminal illness would soon clarify both aspects in a most unexpected and certainly undesired manner. At any rate, C. S. Lewis's literary character, Psyche, beautifully renders young Thielicke's mental state. Whilst comparison with her implies that his subconscious awareness of death—occasionally forcefully breaking out in the midst of joviality—is by no means limited to Thielicke's own subjective consciousness,[24] it was nonetheless certainly furthered by those specific *Thanatos*-experiences that are unique to his early biography and which proved to be especially defining on grounds of his elliptical nature as outlined above. The underlying existential drive behind Thielicke's theological thinking can thus be traced back to his earliest childhood memories: "This sense of the imminent end of all things has *always* accompanied me, even in sickness and when I was close to death, and it occupied my thoughts and many pages of my diary *long before my later publications on the subject.*"[25]

---

23. Lewis, *Till We Have Faces*, 74. The general theme of longing [*Sehnsucht*] is, of course, central to Lewis's thinking.

24. See also Becker, *Denial of Death*, who argues that the terror of death is an innate fear which haunts man from birth.

25. *Wayfarer*, 3 [10]. Emphasis added. Thielicke's "passionately written" diaries would have been a rich treasure of primary source-material: "During the many difficult times in my life I helped myself a little by writing a diary. . . . Whenever I was hard up, the notes in my diary piled up" (*Krauss*, 65). Unfortunately, he ordered to have them burnt after his death. To overcome crises in life by way of writing was Thielicke's "tried and tested remedy for life's problems" (*Wayfarer*, 399 [510–11]). See also *Wayfarer*, 121 [160]. This habit was *inter alia* also shared by C. S. Lewis and Roman Catholic martyr Franz Jägerstätter, executed for his conscientious objection to National Socialist military service. See Coren, *C. S. Lewis*, 57, 121; Putz, *Jägerstätter*, 131.

Part Two: Thielicke's Sickness
—On the Border to Death

In the first part of the second volume of his German work, *Theological Ethics*, Thielicke commits to paper his existential conclusion that "the . . . knowledge [of man's own impending death] . . . is only set free in its immediacy when man is acutely confronted by it; thus his having to speak [about it] in the first person."[26] Roman Catholic philosopher Dietrich von Hildebrand goes one nuanced step further in his book on death when he differentiates between an "instinctive fear of death" and a "fully conscious grasping of the phenomenon of death."

The first naturally arises when man finds himself in danger of his life— such as during soldiering or air raids, whilst in a burning house, on a sinking ship, or situated in any other life-threatening situation.[27] But this awareness of death is more of a mortal danger, often taking on an animal-like character. The second, fully cognizant realization of death, however, does not happen to most men until "they fall sick or get imbued with anxiety because certain symptoms seem to indicate a fatal illness."[28]

Applied to Thielicke, this means that his earliest preoccupation with this theme (outlined above) was of more indirect concern, experiencing the finitude of creation via beloved, albeit not too intimate, second-person encounters. Moreover, his later, manifold experiences during the war (to be outlined below) were more a kind of "instinctive fear of death." Yet, the immediate and thorough first-person perspective of which he and von Hildebrand speak was forced upon him when he reached the tender age of twenty-one. For at this juncture, in 1929, his character's early disposition was crucially deepened by his taking a decision with almost fatal consequences:

> I had suffered for some years from a massive swelling of the thyroid gland (goiter), which impeded my breathing. This problem could have been treated medicinally with some chance of success. Although I was warned by various doctors against having an operation . . . I employed all my cunning and energy to force them to give me one. It was not only my delight in dramatic and quick solutions which drove me to this decision . . . but above

---

26. *ThE II/1*, §623. See also *ThE II/1*, §623–25, 631; *ThE III*, §1981; and *Tod*, 26, 72. Brocher states: "Surely, no one can imagine his own death, for it is always the death of another which we have experienced until one's own death becomes reality" (Brocher, *Wenn Kinder trauern*, 61).

27. "In peaceful times . . . we could hide the questioning character of death, of course" (*GldChr*, 18).

28. von Hildebrand, *Tod*, 17–18.

all, the desire, through pain and the dulling of consciousness, to distract me from the horrible emptiness and dreadful lack of direction I was feeling.[29]

According to Thielicke's attending doctor, Paul Martini, the director of the medical clinic of the University of Bonn, his patient had always been healthy until 1929. From then, "minor ailments" ensued from a swelling of the thyroid gland (goiter). The medical clinic of the University of Greifswald recommended an operation, which took place on February 21, 1929. Three days later, the first symptoms indicating a nascent tetanus appeared. From the sixth day onwards, increasingly severe cramps emerged, soon followed by difficulty in breathing.[30]

The cause of these severe complications was a "deficient function or complete absence of the epithelium corpuscles."[31] Martini tentatively made the operating surgeon responsible, since the chronological nexuses do not allow for "inevitable coincidences" as an explanation: "The occurrence of severe tetanic conditions already on the third day after the operation prompts the conclusion that by unfortunate accident indeed all epithelium corpuscles were removed."

At the beginning of October 1929, after a five-month improvement due to transplantation, the cramps returned, turning into tetany once more. The alleviative injection of calcium into the veins was no longer possible because of Thielicke's inflamed arms—caused by the very same procedure. Peroral ingestion of a calcium and ammonium chloride mixture solved this problem, but occasionally, insignificant overdosage led to life-threatening signs of paralysis. A more precise dosage was found in November 1930, avoiding both the emergence of tetany and paralysis. This treatment made Thielicke "capable of work" until the first half of 1932. Within this productive period of about a year and a half, he gained his doctorate in philosophy under Eugen Herrigel with *summa cum laude* in 1931[32] and embarked on

---

29. *Wayfarer*, 59–60 [82].

30. See Martini, "Gutachten der Medizinischen Klinik in Bonn" (*NHT*).

31. See Dirks, *Laymen*, 75, who explains that "the very small 'para-thyroid' glands, which produce a hormone preventing tetanus type disease, were damaged in the operation. A substitute for this hormone had not been found at the time of the operation." Thielicke's sister confirms this conclusion in a conversation with Langsam, *Konkretion*, 13n43.

32. *Wayfarer*, 61 [84–85]. See Eugen Herrigel, "Referenz für akademische Laufbahn" (*NHT*). Thielicke's philosophical dissertation, *Das Verhältnis zwischen dem Ethischen und dem Ästhetischen* (*The Relation between the Ethic and the Aesthetic*), appeared in book form in 1932.

his theological dissertation under the supervision of Paul Althaus.[33] As to why Thielicke immersed himself so zestfully into his academic work in spite of his fatal circumstances, he reminisces that "focusing on creative labor offered a soothing distraction from my excruciating condition."[34]

Thielicke's sister, Elisabeth von Loewenich, offers yet another reason. In a personal conversation with Langsam, she confided that her brother did not earn his PhD in spite of, but *because of*, his sickness. For after Thielicke's failed operation and his ensuing physical breakdown, the rumor circulated in his hometown, Barmen, that Thielicke had lost his mind—not an uncommon accusation in relation to thyroid disease at that time. In order to produce evidence to the contrary, Thielicke made every effort to finish his philosophical dissertation under Herrigel.[35]

This period, however, did not last, and between spring and autumn 1932 Thielicke suffered again from ever-increasing pain. By November, he was completely unable to walk and stoop, a deterioration caused by the high dosage of ammonium chloride taken over the years.[36] Now eking out his existence in a wheelchair, he was not able to dress himself and had to be brought to and medically supervised during his first theology examination at Koblenz University, taking place in Bonn.[37] Thielicke nevertheless passed his exams with the overall grade of "good" [*gut*].[38]

Attempts to counter these renewed medical complications by returning to intravenous administration of calcium, thereby dropping the ammonium chloride, was again made impossible by Thielicke's arms and veins once more becoming infected. Another attempt to transplant the epithelium corpuscles from a deceased new-born also failed, making a return to

---

33. See Althaus, "Zeugnis" (*NHT*). In *Wayfarer*, 74 [101] (see *Wayfarer*, 72 [99]), Thielicke incorrectly states that he came to study under Althaus in 1934. In addition to the date provided by Althaus's "Zeugnis," see *Wayfarer*, 77–78 [105]: "When I was writing up a large section of my thesis [supervised by Althaus] in the summer semester of 1933 . . . " See also *Wayfarer*, 79 [108], where Thielicke refers to himself as a "twenty-five-year-old student." If this specification is correct, the year must have been 1933.

34. *Zu Gast*, 84 [*Wayfarer*, 61]. See *K&K*, 14 [*B&E*, 13].

35. See Langsam, *Konkretion*, 13–14n44. As Langsam rightly observes, Thielicke's statement in *Wayfarer*, 64 [88], that the doctors did not take him for sane, gains meaning in light of this.

36. See Martini, "Gutachten" (*NHT*).

37. See *Wayfarer*, 62 [85]; *K&K*, 14–15 [*B&E*, 13–14].

38. See "Prüfungszeugnis (11. Oktober 1932)" (*NHT*). This final examination certificate further attests to the following grades in *Systematische Theologie* (systematics): "rather good" [*recht gut*]; *Predigtprobe* (homiletics): "good" [*gut*]; and *Altes Testament* (Old Testament): "not completely passed" [*nicht völlig bestanden*]. Now we know why Thielicke did not become an Old Testament scholar.

the calcium and ammonium chloride mixture necessary—which, in turn, led back to severe muscle pain.[39]

This exceptional—and, at that time, therapeutically hopeless—status resulted in a sad notoriety in the medical world.[40] Within the four years of his sickness (between 1929 and 1933), Thielicke was continually moved from one university hospital to another to no avail. Once he had to suffer an implantation of the glands into the peritoneum without any anaesthetic,[41] another time he fell into the infamous hands of the then well-known specialist for internal medicine in Cologne, Dr. Hans Eppinger, who was later responsible for the so-called "seawater experiments" on Romany prisoners at the Dachau concentration camp[42] and whose bestial treatment of patients Thielicke experienced in person.[43]

The medical world's heightened interest in Thielicke is further reflected in the research of Johann Sebastian Preuss on *latente Tetanie*, leading the medical doctorand to an engagement with Thielicke's case in the context of his dissertation in 1937. Preuss's analysis helpfully expands on the observations of Martini and Thielicke:

> Three days after [the strumectomy due to Basedow], appearance of severe tetany with the involvement of the limbs—laryngeal, nuchal, and pectoral muscles—and fierce choking fits. The tetanic seizures, which are preceded by ungrounded feelings of anxiety, occasionally last for about five hours with harrowing pains in the limbs and trunk. Thereby vibrating of the eyelids, occurrence of double vision, paraesthesia. Over the years, severe destruction of nails and teeth, hair loss up to baldness, depressions, complete invalidity. For four years application of current scientific therapy, partly unsuccessful, partly with otherwise disruptive side-effects with little success . . . As a first indication of the commencing decline of calcium entirely unfounded states of anxiety appear each time . . . The patient cannot think of any cause for their emerging; he does not know why or from where they come.[44]

---

39. See Martini, "Gutachten" (*NHT*); *K&K*, 14 [*B&E*, 13].

40. See *Wayfarer*, 59 [82].

41. *Wayfarer*, 61 [83].

42. Born in Prague on January 5, 1879, Eppinger operated in Cologne from 1930 until 1933. He committed suicide on September 25, 1946, in Vienna. See Klee, *Personenlexikon zum Dritten Reich*, 138.

43. See *Wayfarer*, 62–64 [86–88]. This incident occurred after Thielicke was already discharged by Martini in April 1933 whilst waiting at his Barmen-home.

44. Preuss, *Die latente Tetanie (relative Nebenschilddrüseninsuffizienz)*, 7–8 (*NHT*).

These insights cast additional light on the mental as well as physical anguish Thielicke had to go through. In his own words:

> I would fall into terrible and painful tetanic paralysis, which spread to the respiratory center and each time brought me to the point of death. These attacks were preceded by a feeling of animal anxiety. When, in later years, I often had to speak and write on the phenomenon of anxiety, I always had these fits in my mind's eye.[45]

In the meantime, a medical cure, the "Collipian Para-T-Hormone,"[46] had been developed in the USA, which, according to Thielicke, "was supposed to work veritable miracles in cases like mine." As certified by Martini, Thielicke now depended with his life on this new *Para-Thor-Mone-Medikation*, whose procurement, in turn, was dependent on the raising of adequate funds. The monthly cost of this hormone amounted to 1200 *Reichsmark*, then an unaffordable sum for any health insurance company.[47] Thus, Martini filed a written request for funding, embedded within the medical report cited thus far, to the *Preussische Kultusministerium* (the ministry of education and cultural affairs) with the concluding words also rendered in Thielicke's autobiography: "Your decision in this matter will determine whether this . . . young man may continue to live or whether he faces severe agony and certain death in the near future."[48]

Thielicke's doctoral supervisors, Herrigel and Althaus, supported their (in Herrigel's case, former) student's plea for funding—indeed, for life—with well-intended references. Herrigel states that he has not had a student ever since who could be put on a level with Thielicke.[49] He even "strongly advised" his "considerably above average talented" former student to pursue an academic career,[50] as did Althaus.[51] The latter, who, despite theological differ-

---

45. *Wayfarer*, 60 [82–83]. In *K&K*, 14 [*B&E*, 13], Thielicke states that the pains of these hours served as a model for the chapter on fear in his book, *Nihilismus*.

46. According to Martini, "*Para-Thor-Mone*, an American compound obtained from animal epithelium corpuscles" ("Gutachten" (*NHT*)).

47. See *Wayfarer*, 62 [85–86]. Martini figures the monthly cost to be about 705 *Reichsmark* (23.50 *Reichsmark* per day)—not nearly as high as Thielicke's allegation, yet still expensive.

48. *Wayfarer*, 62 [85–86]. See also Martini, "Gutachten" (*NHT*).

49. This statement is somewhat relativized by the fact that less than a year had passed since graduation under Herrigel, as well as Thielicke's statement that he hardly saw his doctoral supervisor nor heard from him during his research. See *Wayfarer*, 61 [84].

50. Herrigel, "Referenz" (*NHT*).

51. See *Wayfarer*, 82 [111].

ences, was to become Thielicke's fatherly friend and confidant in later life,[52] praised his student as "one of the most talented and significant young theologians I have ever met. . . . His retirement from the young academic generation would, in my judgement, be a total loss to theological science."[53]

All three references—Martini's, Herrigel's, and Althaus's—had one common goal: to prove Thielicke's "worthiness" [*Würdigkeit*] for funding.[54] In cruder language: to show that his life was worth the money. This requirement and their assessments, respectively, already testify to the looming advent of Germany's darkest era, with Nazi dictatorship just around the corner.

At the beginning of April 1933, Thielicke was discharged by Martini, awaiting the government's decision at home in Barmen.[55] The existential intensity of this latency must be imagined: Thielicke, fully aware of being in "permanent mortal danger"[56] ever since his ordeals became life threatening, finally expected his warrant of death or life:

> Paul Martini . . . fought doggedly for government money to pay for this medicine, which, by the way, I would have to use for the rest of my life. I thought very highly of him for never leaving me in the dark about the seriousness of my condition. We spoke quite openly about this being my very last chance.[57]

52. Thielicke appreciated that his criticisms of Althaus's theology did not affect their personal relationship (see *Wayfarer*, 72 [98]). In their lifelong correspondence, Althaus regularly addressed his former student with "My dear Doctor . . . " whilst Thielicke sought his advice on the important career moves of his life, such as on the question as to whether to leave Tübingen for Hamburg in a confidential letter dated November 27, 1953 (*NHT*): "You already advised me in such a touching and comforting way on the issue of the main pastorate in Hamburg (see *Wayfarer*, 119–20 [159]). Like no one else, you know my work and my plans and also my situation in Tübingen. What do you think? At this stage I can't ask anyone else . . . if it goes wrong I will be disgraced." In his response on December 6, 1953 (*Wayfarer*, 119–20 [159]), Althaus advised Thielicke to make the move to Hamburg. For a critical account of Althaus's life and work, see the third chapter of Ericksen, *Theologians under Hitler*. See also *Wayfarer*, 74–75 [101–2]; Krauss, 29; and *EvF II*, 26–27.

53. Althaus, "Zeugnis." Although these superlative comments, due to their dramatic circumstances, cannot be taken as sober evaluations, they nevertheless show that Thielicke was not completely off the mark in his choice of career.

54. Prof. D. Hermann of Greifswald and Dr. Heinrich Frick of Marburg provided two further references.

55. See *Wayfarer*, 62 [86]. In the interim (Thielicke's "resurrection" took place on April 14), the aforementioned incident with Eppinger occurred.

56. Martini, "Gutachten" (*NHT*).

57. *Wayfarer*, 62 [85]. Out of this experience followed Thielicke's later thoughts on the "truthfulness of a physician at the patient's bedside." See *Sterben*, 65–75; *ThE II/1*, §567–641; and *Zeitgenossenschaft*, 42–52.

The government turned down his appeal. Yet, the same message from Martini informing Thielicke about this also raised another instant hope, for it contained news about a recently developed German medicine which, although it had not yet been tested, was at his disposal, in case he wanted to make one last attempt.[58] Surprisingly, Thielicke had to be persuaded by his mother to have one more go, as the failure of a large number of different medicines taken during the years before had worn down his motivation.[59]

Upon arrival at the clinic, he was given a small bottle classified as "AT 9" (*antitetanicum*)[60]—and additionally marked as "poison." Thielicke assumed that this warning meant that the medicine had not yet been tested and thus led the doctors to administer only the "very smallest dose" to him. Preuss confirms that for fourteen days, Thielicke had to take 5ccm daily.[61] But when that did not help, Thielicke drank the whole bottle in despair. He wanted to force a decision: "Either this maximum dose of the medicine would help me, or the 'poison' would kill me."[62]

In the observational tone of Preuss, the small doses remained ineffective until "he took in desperation over 40ccm at one go."[63]

> That evening, I bid farewell to my life. I sat there gazing constantly at the crucifix opposite my bed. . . . When I awoke the next morning, I was at first astonished at the mere fact of being alive and felt happy in a way I cannot explain. I had the feeling that I had been saved and could feel a sense of euphoria running like an electric current through my limbs.[64]

Preuss is once more an independent witness to this fact: "The next day, a sense of well-being and less calcium requirement. Within four weeks, disappearance of cramps, eventually also [disappearance of] incipient mutual cataract."[65]

---

58. See *Wayfarer*, 64–65 [88].
59. See *Wayfarer*, 65 [89]; *Ernstfall*, 149.
60. According to Preuss, *Latente Tetanie*, 8, it was called "AT 10."
61. See *Wayfarer*, 64–65 [88].
62. *Wayfarer*, 65 [89].
63. Preuss, *Latente Tetanie*, 8.
64. *Wayfarer*, 65 [89]. See also *Krauss*, 21.
65. Preuss, *Latente Tetanie*, 8.

Thielicke's Evaluation of His Sickness

Thielicke's "resurrection," as he calls it, took place on April 14, 1933, Good Friday, and was regarded by him as a miracle.[66] In an extensive interview shortly before his death, he states that this life-threatening sickness "was perhaps the most drastic intervention in my life. . . . This feeling, to be finished at just twenty years of age and to have had an experience usually only known by elderly people, this incredible, creaturely *Angst*, has shaped me very much."[67]

Within this context, a significant question arises: from which point onwards did Thielicke consider himself to be a genuine Christian? For in his autobiography, he states that when he was asked in school what career he intended to take up, he replied that he wanted to become a theologian, but not a pastor, "because I was not in fact a Christian. Despite this I was attracted to theology."[68] In his "Little Biography of Faith" he reiterates: "Back then I was not a Christian; much more a fatalist who had accepted his fate."[69] Further, "despite my Christian upbringing, I was not a Christian. The Greek gods . . . were closer to me than the Father of Jesus Christ."[70]

Thielicke points out two reasons for his attraction to theology: in addition to his being utterly impressed by Karl Barth, whom he witnessed as a boy at a church conference in Wuppertal ("This was when I totally lost my boyish heart to theology"[71]), he also felt that theology was concerned

---

66. *Wayfarer*, 65 [89]; *GldChr*, 345–46; and *Ernstfall*, 150–51. In 1939, Thielicke published his book, *Wunder*, in which, motivated by his own experience, he unfolded his convictions as to this theme. An abridged version can be found in *Anfechtung*, 94–134. Just prior to his death, Thielicke reaffirmed that he still regards the way he was healed as a miracle. See *Krauss*, 17.

67. *Krauss*, 17.

68. *Wayfarer*, 35 [52]; *K&K*, 11–12 [*B&E*, 11–12]. In spite of him recalling a pietistic conversion experience as a fourteen-year-old (see *Wayfarer*, 41–42 [59–60]), he reasserts that originally, he was not a Christian (*Wayfarer*, 118 [157]).

69. *Ernstfall*, 149.

70. *Ernstfall*, 151.

71. *Wayfarer*, 36 [52]. See also *Krauss*, 23. However, this initial impression did not last very long (see the further course of this work, esp. chapter 3, part one). On a personal level, intensified by differing theological and sociopolitical viewpoints, Barth and Thielicke had a rather tense relationship, too—as revealed by their personal correspondence. In the context of their controversy over Germany's collective guilt, for example, things got fairly personal when Thielicke inappropriately attacked Barth's friend, Martin Niemöller. Whilst Thielicke saw himself "greatly dishonored" and "deeply ashamed" by Niemöller (letters to Niemöller, April 5, 1950 [*NHT*] and to Karl Handrich, February 7, 1950 [*NHT*]), he was sternly rebuked by Barth for his dealings with Niemöller in a letter on April 1, 1950 (*NHT*). Within the same context, Karl Handrich, a friend (!) of Thielicke, asked him in a letter (February 3, 1950, [*NHT*]) whether he had become a

with the eternal or last questions. In contrast to philosophy, which had the same concerns, there was a theological community, however, "which was prepared to risk its life for what it believed in."[72] In a different context, he confirms that "the God-question is a cipher for the question about ultimate meaning. It has impressed me that human beings have suffered for the sake of this question. There were martyrs, people risked their lives."[73]

Accordingly, in an essay engaging with some themes raised by Bonhoeffer, Thielicke testifies how fulfilling his first encounter with Bonhoeffer's *Widerstand und Ergebung* (*Letters and Papers from Prison*) proved to be, "with this emergency-laden language of a man who lived and suffered on the cusp of martyrdom."[74] This particular fascination with *Martyrium* serves as another instructive pointer to Thielicke's existential drive outlined thus far.

Consequently, in light of the importance Thielicke later ascribes to being a committed Christian in order to be a proper theologian,[75] he must have had a change of heart—i.e., a conversion[76]—at some stage in his life. As just seen, he did not consider himself a Christian during his schooldays. The same can be said for his time of sickness and undergraduate studies, for not only did his

---

victim of his "Barth-complex." In his response (February 7, 1950 [*NHT*]), Thielicke negated this, adding that he would "fundamentally establish" his theological criticisms in his forthcoming *Theological Ethics*. Furthermore, see Barth's letter from April 22, 1956 (*NHT*): "You know (in part from my own mouth) that I hold quite a bit against you." See also Barth's cynical remark to Thielicke in a letter from November 7, 1967 (*NHT*): "I have always been prejudiced as to your great ability to explain to your fellow man anything and everything in such an absolute, edifying way, which I could not do. But this simply has to do with your bestowed gift for wide-spanning perception and with your amazing temper." Despite this comment, about one year before Barth's death, their relationship improved somewhat with age, thanks to the mediation of their mutual friend, Eduard Thurneysen. For Thielicke's portrait of Barth, see *Wayfarer*, 66–72 [90–98].

72. *Wayfarer*, 35–36 [52]. See also *Ernstfall*, 151.

73. Krauss, 16.

74. "EdR," 72–73. Although the earliest possible encounter with *Widerstand* could only have been in 1951 (the year of its first publication) and thus does not fall into Thielicke's formative time as a theologian, this statement still indicates his general inclination, very likely rooted in those years.

75. This crucial point of personal faith as a decisive prerequisite for a theologian to "do" theology reveals a significant theological thought directly impacted by his life experience. It will be further unfolded in chapter 5, part one.

76. By "conversion" I mean a person's deliberate, volitional turning towards God under the repentant impression of his or her own shortcomings in light of God's perfect nature. For Luther's usage of the term, see Rieger, *Luthers theologische Grundbegriffe*, 36–37.

ordeals not bring him to faith[77] but he also went through "serious theological crises" during his time of hospitalization.[78]

But there is one crucial event that must indeed be considered as the turning-point for Thielicke's personal journey of faith, namely, his miraculous recovery on Good Friday, 1933, after he "bid farewell" to his life and took the overdose of "AT 10." Speier must be corrected when he states that there is no specific hint of such sort in Thielicke's autobiographical writings.[79] For the entirely unexpected recovery from his sickness leads Thielicke to the conclusion that "I now knew what faith meant and everything that had previously fascinated me about theology was swept away by completely new impulses."[80]

In citing these words, Speier only *speculates* whether Thielicke's sickness and recovery might have been the key leading to his inner change. Interestingly, Thielicke's earlier autobiographical sketch contains two crucial words omitted in the *Wayfarer* quote: "Everything that had previously *only intellectually* fascinated me about theology."[81] The immediate context in both sources (*Wayfarer* and *K&K/B&E*) does not advance the reader's understanding as to the concrete meaning of this statement. Yet, on the occasion of the extensive Krauss interview shortly before his death, Thielicke clarified his thought, a clarification not taken into account by Speier:

> The night I took the medicine I kind of set my life in order. I prayed. In my [hospital] room hung a crucifix. . . . In the face of the crucified, I thought of the forgiveness of sins, simply to straighten my life out. Subsequently, this very evening has become tremendously important to me. Thus, *my way to faith was not destined by theoretical considerations, but by the superior power of this event.* Tonight your life comes to an end; or you will live entirely anew.[82]

In his "Little Biography," he remembers that night with the following words:

> After I had finished the bottle, I looked at the crucifix . . . Back then, Christ was still foreign to me, but in that picture of the cross, I recognized his own and his fellow-suffering

---

77. See *Krauss*, 17.

78. *Kanzel*, 63. The main motivation he gives for having an operation in the first place is "the horrible emptiness and dreadful lack of direction I was feeling" (*Wayfarer*, 60 [82]).

79. Speier, *Initiator*, 19–20n4.

80. *Wayfarer*, 66 [90].

81. *K&K*, 15–16 [*B&E*, 14]. Emphasis added.

82. *Krauss*, 22–23. Emphasis added.

[*Mit-Leiden*]. I recognized him as a brother and companion and I talked to him. . . . It meant a lot to me that he too was in mortal danger. Beneath that cross, I settled my affairs. I remember that I asked for forgiveness. . . . I thought: Perhaps you will not wake up again; or you might recover. At that moment I had committed it into another hand and let myself go. This was my first encounter with Christ.[83]

Whereas Thielicke evaluates the all-crucial decision of taking the yet untested medicine as "bordering on attempted suicide,"[84] his "euphoric" awakening the very next morning was experienced by him as "a new birth [*eine Neugeburt*]," like "high voltage power inside me [*es war wie ein Kraftstrom in mir*]."[85] The immediate context does not clarify whether Thielicke's use of the term "a new birth" implies conversion in the Christian sense or merely serves as an illustration pointing to the initiation of his physical restoration. The account in his "Little Biography" seems to negate the former: "Surely it is understandable that this miracle, which—considered from the outside—happened in quite a normal and nomological way, constituted a deep caesura in the history of my faith. Still, I could not call it a conversion which chronologically would be definable."[86]

In spite of Thielicke's unwillingness to fix this event chronologically as his conversion, the immediate context still reveals its incisive importance. For just prior to this statement, he relates that in the moment, he was hardly aware that after "touching the hem of his garment," Christ felt the touch and turned to him.[87] But the fact that Thielicke can state that he was not yet fully aware that night implies his realizing it *in retrospect*. Thus, even his belated, *subjective* realization of the importance of the event does not invalidate but, to the contrary, establishes its *facticity*.

Irrespective of the precise meaning of "new birth [*Neugeburt*]" in the specific usage of the Krauss-interview outlined above, however, earlier, in the same context, Thielicke emphasizes once more that his regaining of life after this near-death experience was indeed the situation which existentially led him to the Christian faith: "At first, this experience [of sickness and almost certain death] had not . . . let me find the faith. . . . *The relation to faith* came much later *when I was healed* after a number of years."[88]

---

83. *Ernstfall*, 150.
84. In *Ernstfall*, 149, he calls it "an act of desperate determination."
85. *Krauss*, 21. See *Wayfarer*, 65 [89].
86. *Ernstfall*, 150–51.
87. See Mark 5:25–34.
88. *Krauss*, 17. Emphasis added.

Although Thielicke again does not pin down his conversion chronologically, he nevertheless connects it *causally* with his miraculous recovery. This finds confirmation in a sermonic note during the war. After having illustrated the miraculous convergence of the final stage of his sickness and the medical discovery of the life-saving medication "AT 10," Thielicke proclaims to his listeners in Stuttgart: "You will understand how strongly I was under the impression back then: 'This was the Lord's doing.'"[89]

In other, analogous words, this event might therefore be illustrated with the gradually opening bud of a flower called "faith"—not yet out entirely, but already there. It therefore appears well justified to speak of an if not necessarily fully conscious conversion at that very moment, then at least of the entering wedge of an embryonic faith, without which the later emphases of the mature theologian would hardly be thinkable; without the embryo, there can be no fully-fledged man! Thielicke calling man's depths "the very nurseries where *the vital germs of our faith* grow and prosper" adds further weight to this thesis.[90]

The tremendous theological implications of his existential turnaround will be picked up again in the following chapters. For now, the insight must be made clear that, although Thielicke elsewhere appears adamant not to make "fancy" or "cheap conversion stories" out of certain other episodes,[91] he nonetheless explicitly and decisively highlights this experience as his key to a personal faith. He just does not want to use the term "conversion" for it. The four years of suffering might herein be regarded as his personal *Via Dolorosa* by which he approached this turnaround. As Timothy J. Wengert points out, according to Luther's *theologia crucis*, "the sufferer . . . driven by suffering, comes to the realization . . . of [his] true neediness."[92] The intriguing overlap of Thielicke's specific experience and Martin Luther's view of coming to faith will be further shown in chapter 4, thereby explicating how Thielicke's Lutheran conversion experience lays the foundation for his subsequent theological work.

By all means, his sickness was instrumental in helping him cope with all the suffering he lived through later on: "During the severe air raids, it became very important to me that I had experienced this death threat.

---

89. *GldChr*, 346.

90. *Freedom*, 199. Emphasis added.

91. "Fancy" as to his suffering (see *Krauss*, 17); "cheap" as to the overcoming of a theological crisis during hospitalization (see *Kanzel*, 63–64).

92. Wengert, "Peace, Peace," 205.

Whatever dreadful thing happened then, it was not comparable with the terrible fear which I had already undergone."[93]

In light of von Hildebrand's differentiation outlined at the beginning of chapter 2, part two, it can also be added that it provided Thielicke with the "mature" basis of thorough reflection on the phenomenon of death, thus helping him in his "instinctive fear of death," particularly as experienced during the war.

The Evaluation of Thielicke's Sickness by Secondary Sources

Several secondary sources explicitly refer to the impact of Thielicke's illness. In order to substantiate my central claim further, other authorities' thoughts and interaction with this crucial event will be documented within this subsection.

In his introduction, Meinold Krauss highlights two occasions that decisively shaped the thinking and feeling of his interlocutor. One, the takeover of the National Socialists, shall be discussed shortly. The other event Krauss highlights is the operation on Thielicke's thyroid gland and its disastrous consequences: "For years, he lived at the threshold of death. Since then he has never taken life for granted."[94]

In his doctoral thesis, published in 1972, Marvin J. Dirks stresses the importance of Thielicke's disease in order to understand him as a man, before he goes on to describe it in some detail.[95] He concludes that "through the suffering and darkness of those years, Thielicke came to a new understanding of the meaning of faith."[96]

In his foreword to Thielicke's autobiography, translator H. George Anderson observes:

> Thielicke's ability to speak directly to the inner needs of his hearers came from a life that had felt many of those doubts and pressures. His academic career was plagued by a progressive illness that rendered him weak at times and finally became life-threatening. . . . It was all he could do to cling to life itself. . . . Thus death became a reality to him, as did the possibility of miracle.[97]

93. *Krauss*, 19.
94. *Krauss*, 8–9.
95. Dirks, *Laymen*, 73.
96. Dirks, *Laymen*, 76.
97. Anderson, "Foreword," xix.

Furthermore, Holger Speier, focusing on Thielicke's apologetics in his doctoral thesis, stresses the meaning of sickness and suffering for Thielicke's theological work: "The impulse emanating from Thielicke's illness and thus affecting his theological work *can hardly be overestimated*. Thielicke falling ill was for him a borderline situation by which he learned that the border is always a prolific place for gaining knowledge."[98] Strangely enough, during the remaining course of his thesis, Speier does not lay any further emphasis on this experience or the consequences it might have had for Thielicke's theological or apologetic program.

Moreover, whereas Speier refers to the impact of Thielicke's sickness on his theological work generally, Michael Calvert, who specifically directed his research towards the subject's homiletical treatment of the problem of evil, concludes that "it seems most apparent that both the power and the passion of Thielicke's preaching ministry flowed from his personal experiences with suffering (e.g., his early experiences of death, his life-long sickness, and his numerous tribulations during and immediately following the war years) and from his close pastoral interaction with fellow sufferers."[99] Especially in regard to Thielicke's illness, Calvert, relying upon Thielicke's autobiography, *Wayfarer*, and Dirks as a secondary source, describes it as "perhaps the greatest test of Thielicke's faith,"[100] without drawing any further specifics out of this event.

Finally, Friedrich Langsam accentuates and interprets Thielicke's suffering in his thesis, published in 1996, highlighting it, most poignantly, as one of three formative experiences.

> Those four years of illness, having death constantly before his eyes, shaped his life and thought decisively. The continually recurring engagement with the theme of death in Thielicke's later work stands in closest connection with this experience; and yet it cannot be limited to it. Upon closer inspection, one recognizes that this experience and the subject matter emanating from it are always present in the background. In a certain sense, it is the *underpinning foundation* [*Tiefenstruktur*] permeating his work.[101]

---

98. Speier, *Initiator*, 20n4. Emphasis added. As indicated by Speier, the idea of the "borderline" would finally acquire immense ethical importance in Thielicke's thought (see chapter 7, part one). In the present context, Speier thinks of the existential border between life and death and rightly establishes a connection between this specific episode in Thielicke's life and his later thinking.

99. Calvert, *Preaching*, 356.

100. Calvert, *Preaching*, 15.

101. Langsam, *Konkretion*, 14–15.

Langsam is right, of course, that Thielicke's theological program can by no means be restricted to those insights gained from his encounters with death and suffering. However, to use one of Thielicke's own illustrations,[102] they must be considered to constitute if not the very *heart* of his theology, then at least a life-giving organ within the overall Thielickean organism of thought. Just as the heart pumps blood into the different parts of the whole body and thus animates it, Thielicke's theological program is better analyzed—and, in fact, appreciated—by explicating both the specifically existential as well as eschatological implications establishing the inner logic of his thought. To appreciate Thielicke's existential awareness of death and suffering fully, however, one must not stop at his near-death experience caused by this fateful operation in 1929, but must also take into account his encounter and dealing with the fate of the German people during their darkest hour—between 1933 and 1945.

---

102. See *Einführung*, 10; *Mensch*, 293; *Notwendigkeit*, 14; *Suche*, 28, 224; and Zahrnt, *Sache*, 203.

Chapter 3

Existence in a Culture of Death

Thielicke's Experiences during the Nazi
Regime as Key to His Theology

As mentioned earlier, the second major occasion that decisively shaped the thinking and feeling of Thielicke was the National Socialist seizure of power [*Machtergreifung*] on January 30, 1933, just a few months before his recovery.[1] Krauss is correct in his assertion that Thielicke cannot be understood without prior knowledge of this particular period in his life.[2] In order to gain this knowledge, it is helpful to differentiate between *Thielicke's specific conflict with the Nazis* (and his consequent fears and anxieties) and *his manifold experiences of death and suffering* embedded within the *overall turmoil of war*. By applying this structure, I follow Thielicke's own differentiation between "The Threat from the Regime" and "The Burden of the Air Raids."[3] The first part is again subdivided into two subsections: first, I will present Thielicke's own published accounts, before analyzing them on the basis of his literary remains.

---

1. See *Krauss*, 9–10. For the Austrian martyr Jägerstätter, Austria's annexation by German troops in March 1938 was of similar effect, constituting the great caesura in his life. See Putz, *Jägerstätter*, 284.

2. *Krauss*, 10. As noted previously, Dirks, *Laymen*, 73, ascribes the same importance to Thielicke's illness.

3. *Wayfarer*, 161 [210].

Part One: Thielicke's Experiences during the Nazi Regime

Thielicke's Conflict with the Nazis: "The Threat from the Regime" in His Own Words

Thielicke's encounter with the Nazi regime is more complex than generally assumed. From the Nazis' *Machtergreifung* in 1933 onwards, he struggled with a growing inner conflict as to what course to take, for his academic future depended on his political stance. Yet, his political stance was clearly anti-fascist.[4]

Thielicke lists four reasons for his opposition to the Nazis: (a) he found the "fuss" surrounding Nazism and the type of people it attracted physically repugnant[5]; (b) he was one of the few people who had actually read *Mein Kampf*, and the style and content of Hitler's manifesto had "to a certain extent" immunized him against Nazism; (c) in the early beginnings of the Third Reich, he had to attend an "ideology course" for prospective lecturers, and this experience "exorcised any susceptibility to this political gospel that was left in [him]"[6]; and finally, (d) in his first "work report," he mentions the fellowship of his brothers and comrades within the Confessing Church as another reason.[7] Bonhoeffer, by the way, also appreciated the value of this kind of trusting friendship in his resistance.[8] All in all, Thielicke's opposition "was at first based not so much on the fact that [he] had fully understood the depravity of Nazi doctrine as on the sum total of many individual experiences that had disgusted [him]."[9] His ensuing convictions, though, gave rise to another deeply existential quandary:

> I thus found myself in the dilemma of being a young man pursuing a much-desired career while living under a dictatorship. This continually confronted me with the problem of either being consistent and refusing to compromise, which would mean giving up the goal I had set my heart on; or of pursuing my chosen profession and seeing to it that, without selling out, I maneuvered myself past the obstacles in my way.[10]

---

4. See *Wayfarer*, 86–87 [117]; *K&K*, 19 [*B&E*, 16–18].

5. "I always followed the impressions I had of humans and in this case [regarding the Nazis], they were negative" (*Krauss*, 42).

6. See *Wayfarer*, 85–86 [116]; *K&K*, 18–19 [*B&E*, 16–17]; and *Krauss*, 40–41.

7. *K&K*, 18 [*B&E*, 16].

8. See Bonhoeffer, *Widerstand*, 19–20, 28, 43.

9. *Wayfarer*, 86–87 [117]. See *Krauss*, 41.

10. *Wayfarer*, 89 [120–21]; *K&K*, 19–20 [*B&E*, 18].

Thielicke chose the latter and justifies his decision as follows:

> I wanted to become a university lecturer and longed fervently to devote all my energies to the truth and to pass this truth onto young . . . people. I had a great passion for teaching. . . . Should all of this come to nothing? And if it did come to nothing, what was then to become of the deserted lecterns? . . . [The young students] were a flock that had to be led. Should not the shepherds do something to avoid being picked off too easily by the marksmen waiting to discover a chink in our armor?[11]

In his anthropology, Thielicke justifies his rationale by referring to Matthew 10:17: "They [the disciples] have to ensure how to pull through, avoiding easy loss of life. For if they are dead, they cannot proclaim anymore. On the other hand, they are not allowed to behave only tactically, thereby regarding their self-preservation higher than their calling."[12] In light of this, it is more than just a side note to acknowledge the importance Thielicke ascribes to the idea of compromise with regard to man's political and ethical acting in this aeon. Whilst the "spirit of compromise" [*Kompromissgeist*] must be rejected by all means, the compromise *per se* is nonetheless an "essential feature" of the ontological structure of this fallen world.[13] Yet again, this particular ethical concept seems to be deeply entrenched in his "eschatological existence."

At any rate, to keep his integrity and credibility, Thielicke decided that there were certain things he would not do under any circumstances, such as (a) swearing an oath to the Führer,[14] (b) joining the party, and (c) expressing any support—whether orally, in writing, or in print—for the regime.[15] Thus, he came into increasing conflict with the Nazis, initiated by the contents of his theological thesis, *Geschichte und Existenz*, published in 1935 under the supervision of Paul Althaus,[16] which ran counter to the National-Socialistic worldview.[17] Several further incidents led to his being sacked from the Uni-

---

11. *Wayfarer*, 90 [121]; *K&K*, 20 [*B&E*, 18–19].

12. *Mensch*, 298.

13. *ThE* II/1, 6. For Thielicke's notion of compromise, see *ThE* II/1, §147–687; *ThE* I, §1839–1851. For a concise summary, see Zahrnt, *Sache*, 208–11. For a more detailed analysis, see van Bentum, *Grenzsituationen*, 127–70, 174.

14. See *Wayfarer*, 86 [116].

15. See *Wayfarer*, 90 [122]; *K&K*, 21–22 [*B&E*, 21–22]. See chapter 3, part one, for an appraisal.

16. *G&E*, republished thirty years after its original publication.

17. "Because it was diametrically opposed to the Nazi understanding of life and history, it was later one of the reasons for my dismissal in 1940" (*Wayfarer*, 77 [105]). Compare the Nazi comment that "an understanding of history in which the fall played

versity of Heidelberg in 1940 and finally, to being banned from his theological profession altogether. According to Thielicke, "the beginning of the end of my teaching career" took place in the summer of 1939. He gave a special lecture at the University fiercely attacking a student leader's speech that had taken place the day before in which the theology students were publicly discriminated against.[18] This speech, however, rather than playing a major role in the process of his dismissal, only gave the Nazis the needed official justification for it.

For Thielicke, already aware of his pending removal from office, subsequently wrote a letter to Prof. Schmidt of Halle, at that time president of the Lutheran faculties in Germany, asking for help. Schmidt's response[19] clarifies that the reason the party wanted to have Thielicke out of the way was his book, published in 1938, *Jesus Christus am Scheidewege* (*Jesus Christ at the Crossroads*).[20] In the eyes of the Nazis, it revealed a negative attitude towards the state. Thielicke comments that as a way of helping him to keep his integrity and credibility, he studied the temptations of Jesus. The work on this book "helped me and some other people to strike the right balance in the confusion of the times."[21] Additionally, according to Schmidt, the party knew of an incident supposed to have taken place between Thielicke and the Gestapo. This occasion may refer to Thielicke's protest against the "despicable excesses" of the publisher of *Der Stürmer*, Julius Streicher.[22]

In summary, the main reason for his conflict with the Nazis, *as presented to the public by Thielicke*, was his essentially Christian stance. This seems to be confirmed by Thielicke trying to gain a hearing (some kind of protestation) at the national headquarters of the National Socialist Party ("the Brown House") in Munich, shortly after his dismissal, on October 1, 1939. He succeeded in getting access to the "National Head of Lecturers"

---

such a dominant role and which refused to predicate a 'hierarchy of creation' for nation and race is unacceptable to National Socialism" (*Wayfarer*, 117 [155]).

18. *Wayfarer*, 111–12 [150]. See *Krauss*, 43, where Thielicke recalls this incident as one of the reasons leading to his dismissal. The lecture was published after the war under the title, "Eine Rede im Dritten Reich vor Heidelberger Studenten zur Eröffnung der Vorlesung am 15. Juni 1939."

19. See Speier, *Initiator*, 34.

20. The book was later republished under the title *ZG&S* (*Between God and Satan*).

21. *Wayfarer*, 91 [123].

22. *K&K*, 23 [*B&E*, 21]. Thielicke's somewhat ostentatious description of his "public and very sharp protest against the despicable excesses of *Stürmer* publisher Julius Streicher" might be relativized by a personal letter to Prof. Schmidt on March 23, 1940, however, where he downplayed the whole event as "a harmless inspection of a Streicher-quote which I used." Cited in Speier, *Initiator*, 34n49. It is not absolutely clear, though, whether Thielicke refers to the same event in both cases.

[*Reichsdozentenführer*], Walter Schultze, who informed him of the main reason for his dismissal:

> As long as theology faculties still exist—and that won't be for much longer, I can tell you!—I will make sure that only suckling pigs and no wild boars are appointed to professorships. You belong to the younger generation of lecturers *who have most influence with the students* [my correction: *who fight for their convictions*]. We don't want lecturers like that. *We'll deal with the older lecturers later* [my correction: *We'll soon wear down the old ones*].[23]

A comparison of this passage with the original transcript, preserved in the literary remains, reveals that Thielicke's meeting with the *Reichsdozentenführer* took place on May 24, 1940, and that he made some modifications for publication. The original reads as follows:

> Thielicke: For the time being, I am inclined to think that as a Christian, I have permission to exist in the Third Reich. Otherwise, not I would have to be singled out . . . but the theological faculties, and these still exist . . . the church would have to be forbidden.
>
> Schultze: Certainly, the theological faculties still exist—unfortunately!—and I myself am convinced not for much longer. [Thielicke adds in brackets: "in Hess's staff, I came across another view."][24] But if we still have to grapple with them, then at least I want the chairs to be staffed with—crudely put—piglets and not wild boars. [Thielicke adds in brackets: "the latter [sentence] is, in all circumstances, exactly literal."]
>
> Thielicke: . . . Why am I a wild boar?

---

23. *Wayfarer*, 119 [158]. Emphasis added. See *K&K*, 23-24 [*B&E*, 21]; *Krauss*, 31. See Dirks, *Laymen*, 76-77.

24. Siegele-Wenschkewitz, "Die Theologische Fakultät im Dritten Reich," 504-5, shows that from 1938 onwards, the Nazis pursued plans concerning the systematic dismantlement of the theological faculties, finally aiming to eliminate them completely. Since the National Socialist worldview and Christianity were "fundamentally incompatible," it was a matter of "to be or not to be" for the faculties of theology during the Third Reich. In the words of notorious Nazi-judge, Roland Freisler, to the defendant and member of the resistance, Helmuth James von Moltke, the only commonality between Nazism and Christianity is that both "claim the whole man" (Von Moltke, *Abschiedsbriefe*, 478).

Schultze: ... You have to admit that you fight for your views, and to me, you are the exponent of theological fighters within the younger generation, and they are no good to us.[25]

Thielicke's Conflict with the Nazis: "The Threat from the Regime" Reappraised

As convincing as Thielicke's presentation might seem, it is not the whole story. His private correspondence, archived at the University of Hamburg, sheds a different light upon the main reason for his dismissal. For the real driving force behind his termination was not so much his essentially Christian stance, but rather a denunciator who accused him of allegiance to Barth.[26]

When the charge of being "a student and follower of the emigrant professor Dr. Barth and, as such, for the party, not bearable,"[27] was repeated by

---

25. "Gespräch mit dem Reichsdozentenführer am 24. Mai 1940" (*NHT*). Thielicke reminisces that Schultze ended the meeting by prophesying that in ten years, Thielicke would be one of them, closing this episode by saying that nobody knows what became of the *Reichsdozentenführer*. Walter Schultze, born on January 1, 1894, in Hersbruck, was a surgeon and participant of the *Hitlerputsch* in 1923 (Hitler's first and failed attempt to seize power in Munich; this explains Schultze's autonym: "old fighter of the Führer" [*alter* Kämpfer des Führers]). He was a co-drafter of the NS-euthanasia law [*NS-Euthanasiegesetz*] and responsible for the murder of invalids [*Krankenmord*] in Bavaria. Several lawsuits after the war were finally discontinued in 1960 due to his inability to stand trial. He died on August 16, 1979, in Krailing near Munich. See Klee, *Personenlexikon zum Dritten Reich*, 567–68.

26. This denunciator was a German Christian theologian, Wolf Meyer-Erlach (1891–1982), rector at the University of Jena from 1935 until 1937. See Thielicke's letter to Prof. Dr. Schultze on May 27, 1940 (*NHT*). See also Speier, *Initiator*, 36. Another bitter antagonist in Thielicke's struggle for employment was Werner Elert (1885–1954); see *Wayfarer*, 80–81 [109–10]; 92–93 [125]; and Thielicke's letters to Althaus on March 7, 1945 (*NHT*); October 3, 1939 (*NHT*); and to D. Dibelius on October 1, 1939 (*NHT*).

27. Letter from *Generalmajor a. D.* Friedrich Haselmayr on March 28, 1940 (*NHT*). See also the letter from the "former German Christian but now long since 'converted' Bishop of Hamburg, Franz Tügel" (*Wayfarer*, 120 [159]), on May 24, 1940 (*NHT*), who rants against Barth: "Well, I am an old Barth-opponent and nowadays I still rejoice that in 1933 I thrust this man a not-all-that-genteel spear in the ribs.... To me, he is and remains a theologian of the battlefield of the defeated. Thus, he can now celebrate his resurrection in Finland, Norway, Holland, Belgium, and France; and after a short time also in England; [but] he has no place in Germany anymore." Tügel could not believe that Thielicke was accused of "Barth dependence" [*Barth-Hörigkeit*] and concludes his letter by sending him "many loyal Uttenruthia greetings." That Thielicke's alleged Barthianism was the real reason for his dismissal is confirmed by a letter from Gustav Adolf Scheel, leader of the National Socialist German Students' League and the German

Schultze in their meeting, Thielicke tried everything in his power to convince the "Head of Lecturers" of his clear stand against the Swiss. Upon Schultze's suggestion, Thielicke produced a report in which he outlined—by means of four articles—the apparently unmissable differences, each time listing several witnesses to confirm his "attitude and polemics against Barth." The letter not only lists theological reasons but also condemns Barth's "unqualifiable attitude towards Germany," at the same time emphasizing Thielicke's own "decent character." *Inter alia*, his explanation concludes with the following remark: "I passionately and with a vengeance defend myself against an accusation [of Barthianism], which would rob me of nothing less than my honor."[28] Not only this report but also all the numerous letters addressed to Nazi officials—by means of which he tried to secure his position—were signed by Thielicke with "Heil Hitler!"

Whilst one might connive at such a Nazi salute in light of the existential pressure, Thielicke's *Hitlergruss* nonetheless becomes a relatively delicate issue. Not only did he recall others who made that specific greeting,[29] but also presented in his publications a high standard of Thielickean resistance against the regime:

> I could not give in [to the Nazis] because, as a theologian and even more when I held a chair in Heidelberg, I was of the opinion that a professor stands or falls with his word, and that therefore, his word must be authentic, lest it becomes untrustworthy.[30] That is why I placed enormous value on my words, and actually *I am proud . . . that no one can prove any utterance of mine during the era of the Third Reich with which I would have betrayed my own principles. . . .* I would consider it really bad if a professor were nowadays convicted of paying homage to the regime back then, even if he was not a member of the party.[31]

Student Union, on April 24, 1940 (*NHT*), and by a letter of Scheel's father on April 17, 1940 (*NHT*), who tried to help Thielicke in this matter.

28. See letter to Prof. Dr. Schultze on May 27, 1940 (*NHT*). Thielicke also emphasizes the "anonymous defilement of my honor" in his letter to "Regierungsrat" Bechtold on April 7, 1940 (*NHT*). See further the letter of "Kreisleiter" Seiler, June 1940 [no day given] (*NHT*): "You assure me on your honor that you are neither Barthian nor hostile to nation or state. This is confirmed by the decisive public bodies of the University and the [National Socialist] University Teachers' League in Heidelberg."

29. In *Wayfarer*, 120 [159], Thielicke, in a slight undertone of sensationalism, highlights the fact that after his dismissal, he received a letter of refusal from the Hamburg parish council signed, "Heil Hitler."

30. See the Latin etymology: *profiteri*, "to profess." See also *Freiheit*, 13.

31. *Krauss*, 42. Emphasis added. See *Wayfarer*, 90–91 [122]; *K&K*, 21–22 [*B&E*, 19–20]. In *Bergpredigt*, 31, implicitly, and in *Wayfarer*, 89–90 [121], explicitly, Thielicke

But what sort of behavior is defined as "paying homage to the regime"? And where does "resistance" to a totalitarian system begin? Speier contends that the way Thielicke struggled to keep his lectureship must lead one to reconsider and, indeed, categorically deny his status as a "resistance fighter." According to Speier, Thielicke had first and foremost one thing in mind: to show that he, as a citizen and as a member of the faculty, had acted in conformity with the system, thereby trying to secure his position in Heidelberg.[32]

An analysis of Thielicke's literary remains shows that he did not succeed in keeping his integrity and credibility by living up to his third point listed above, namely, to express any support for the regime either orally, in writing, or in print. It also demonstrates a certain degree of duplicity when compared with his own moralistic judgements.[33] Furthermore, his own presentation (especially in *Wayfarer*) leaves the reader with a strange aftertaste of self-aggrandizing flavor.

At the same time, however, Speier's conclusion throws out the baby with the bathwater. First of all, Speier fails to define what he means by a "resistance fighter," simply applying the term to Thielicke's case—and then negating it.

Israeli historian, Saul Friedländer, for example, asks for actual criteria by means of which "resistance" in a totalitarian regime can be measured. According to Friedländer, one such criterion can be found in the "danger" that certain behavior brings upon someone when one turns his or her critical attitude into (potentially dangerous) action.[34] His German colleague, Martin Broszat, generally defines "resistance" as "effective defense, limitation, stemming of NS-dominion or its aspirations, regardless of motifs, reasons, and forces." Broszat even considers an individual's "inner preservation of NS-opposing principles, resulting in one's [mental] protection

---

articulates uneasiness regarding his overall stance between 1933 and 1945: "Although I have undeservedly come to acquire the reputation of advocating the policy of no compromise towards the Nazis," [Law's translation] "I was not at all that unambiguous in my stance." [My own translation of the second part of the sentence, since Law's rendering misrepresents Thielicke's intention.] Interestingly, in *K&K*, 20 [*B&E*, 18], Thielicke writes: "*Perhaps* I was not that unambiguous in my stance." Emphasis added. He thus switches from the *subjunctive* mood, applied in his earlier account, into the *indicative* mood, applied in his late autobiography. Without reading too much into it, this may nevertheless indicate a heightened degree of conviction as he grew older.

32. Speier, *Initiator*, 35n52.

33. "Conversely, I despised those who, though they avoided giving public support to the Nazis, were unscrupulous opportunists as far as their principles were concerned" (*Wayfarer*, 91 [122]). Is this judgement, as now seen in light of his private correspondence, not dangerously falling back on his own struggle to keep his lectureship?

34. See Friedländer, *Gerstein*, 196.

against National Socialist ideology and propaganda" as a form of effective resistance. For such immunity to become historically demonstrable, however, it must empirically stand the test of having had some restrictive impact upon NS-ideology. Broszat concludes that oppositional behavior was usually strongly conditioned by a person or group's protection of interests or power [*Kompetenz- oder Interessenwahrung*], such interests defining the scope of resistance in each particular case.[35] This definition is helpful insofar as it shows that Thielicke, in spite of his strongly interest-driven behavior, nonetheless exhibited historically verifiable opposition to the Nazis, thus rebutting Speier's unfounded conclusion.

But, second, Thielicke, on the basis of his Christian and anti-fascist stance, nonetheless clearly exhibited behavior that ran counter to the state, making a categorical negation of his resistance further untenable. The mere fact that he was loosely connected with Goerdeler and the Freiburger Kreis—thus putting his life at risk—bears witness to this.[36]

In the following point, though, Speier is right: for in the context of discussing Thielicke's part in the student rebellion of 1967–68,[37] he concludes that Thielicke was basically unable to engage in a truly critical evaluation

---

35. Broszat, "Resistenz und Widerstand," 697–99.

36. See *Wayfarer*, 174–79 [226–32]; and his letter to Goerdeler on June 16, 1944 (*NHT*).

37. Speier sees Thielicke's high regard for authoritarian structures to be the primary reason for his lack of understanding of the rebellious students (see Speier, *Initiator*, 69n174, 72n184, 74–75n192). However that may be, Speier's observation as to Thielicke's authoritarian thought structure is corroborated on the corporate political level by his response to Schultze that "as a Christian, *I have permission to exist* in the Third Reich" (emphasis added); by his manifold efforts *to prove to the Nazi authorities* that he was not a follower of Barth; and by his emphasis in several letters on "the duty of the state" to him as a lecturer or, after the war, by a letter to the Minister of Justice, Gustav Heinemann, on February 17, 1968 (*NHT*), in which Thielicke appealed for governmental protection of his Michaelis church services, which the students threatened to disturb: "We still do not understand why the attorney is . . . not intervening. . . . This passiveness of state and legislation grieves me more than the few radicals." See also his letter to Heinemann on September 14, 1968 (*NHT*). On the personal level, this sort of thinking is revealed in his view of the university as an "aristocratic institute" (*Krauss*, 71) and his regarding himself to belong to this elitist circle. See, for example, his remark in *Wayfarer*, 121 [161]: "It was a very enjoyable change to be able to associate with ordinary people." See further his letter to the imprisoned Colonel-General Eberhard von Mackensen on February 14, 1946 (*NHT*): "It very much touched me . . . that I . . . [hurt] the generals [with my essay], of all people, who I can only revere and with whom I am so close as a soldierly man. . . . By nature, I wholeheartedly live in the traditions of Christian Prussianism." Besides, see *SdA*, 24, where he refers to himself as a "militaristic theologian," and Zahrnt, *Sache*, 213, who observes Thielicke's gusto for "military analogies." Finally, see his controversy with the Free University of Hamburg, evaluated by Montgomery, "Thielicke On Trial," 57.

of Germany's National Socialist past.[38] Speier's verdict is sadly confirmed not only by Thielicke's telling criticism of the Malmedy massacre trial as a "show trial,"[39] but also by a significant—and yet, so far, unnoticed—remark in Thielicke's "Foreword to the Book of the Fallen of the Students' Fraternity Uttenruthia in Erlangen."[40] Thielicke begins this foreword by asking a rhetorical question: "What did [the students] die for?" He gives the obvious answer, i.e., Nazism, immediately linked, though, with another question: "We know ... that our brothers fought for symbols which *appear* despicable to us today [note: he does not say "are" but "appear," emphasis added]. Is, for this reason, their sacrificial death [*Opfertod*], their honest idealism ... not gruesomely devalued?" Again, Thielicke merely uses this question as a plug for his own negative reply, which proves to be highly dubious. Whilst earlier generations could remember their dead soldiers in more harmless and comforting ways because of the unproblematic values for which these men fought and died, Thielicke reassures his audience that they, likewise, must not be intimidated in the mourning for their dead:

> They [the fallen] stored this great [ideal] in their hearts, for which they sacrificed themselves, *even if they were part of the SS* [emphasis added]. Even if they were willing in their youth and at the beginning of the war to die for the "Führer," they did not mean the "Führer" himself, whom they did not know at all ... No: the Führer was for a countless number of our youth ... what a picture puzzle or a cheap advertising brochure is for a child: he [the child] projects his childlike world, his dreams and ideals onto that.

On this conceptual basis, Thielicke now puts forth his comfort for the bereaved: "That is why we shall not needlessly agonize over the idea that they died for National Socialism. The ideas and shapes of tyranny ... are only ciphers under which the real values were buried: ... father and mother, wife and child ... they believed to be in danger and for whom they fought." Thielicke concludes this specific line of thought with a statement which carries the dubiousness of his position to extremes: "With these values,

---

38. See Speier, *Initiator*, 68n171. This is further confirmed by the analysis of Richter-Böhne, *Schuld*, esp. 108–14, 136–37, who, *inter alia*, focused his research on Thielicke's problematic "Good Friday Sermon" [*Karfreitagspredigt*] of 1947. For Thielicke's account of the sermon, see *Wayfarer*, 232–36 [297–302]. For Thielicke's epistolary dispute with Hermann Diem on this issue, see *SdA*.

39. *Nihilismus*, 94–95, 212n9. For the highly controversial role of the German Lutheran Church in defending the culprits who stood trial for the massacre, see Klee, *Persilscheine*, 57–60, 83–93.

40. For Thielicke's connection to the fraternity, see *Wayfarer*, 91–92 [123–24].

they ultimately join the ranks of the loneliest of all: the . . . men of [the] July 20 [plot]. In the face of death, only the greatness and purity of the sacrifice is worth something."[41]

This passage raises serious doubts with regard to his perspective on Germany's guilt and responsibility. Without any differentiation, Thielicke *includes*—if only in the subjunctive—members of the worst Nazi henchmen, the SS, in his already questionable honoring of the fallen soldiers' ideals; he *camouflages* the real nature of their deaths by religiously calling them a "sacrifice"; he *downplays* the young men's capacity for critical thinking in order to excuse their support of the regime;[42] he *strengthens* his audience's self-righteousness by leaving out any mention of guilt and repentance, at the same time exhorting them not to worry about the "trifling" fact that the fallen died for National Socialism;[43] and finally, he even has the nerve to *put* the death of soldiers who uncritically followed the "Führer" in the Wehrmacht and SS *on a level* with those men and women of resistance who knowingly gave their lives for a completely antithetical set of convictions.

It seems almost ironic when Thielicke brings this passage to a close by calling his remarks "a hard but liberating truth" for the bereaved. At the end of the foreword, he finally drops a line for the "nameless multitude" of all those who had to suffer in the gas chambers in Theresienstadt, in Auschwitz, and in all the other camps of terror. That the millionfold victims suffered and died because those whose ideals he previously praised backed a regime which put them there obviously does not occur to him.[44]

---

41. "Vorwort zum Totenbuch der Erlanger Uttenreuther," May 24, 1964 (*NHT*).

42. It is acknowledged, of course, that on the basis of differing social, hierarchical, intellectual, and other preconditions, not the same amount of insight, critical thinking, and (thus) resistance could be expected of all groups or individuals alike, as highlighted by Broszat, "Resistenz und Widerstand," 698. Nonetheless, Thielicke's general levelling down of the students' (!) cognitive and moral prowess to excuse them without differentiation is spurious.

43. See Richter-Böhne's similar evaluation regarding Thielicke's staunch criticism of the Allies in his infamous "Good Friday Sermon" of 1947: "[In this sermon], the Germans almost entirely disappear as doers and responsible people" (Richter-Böhne, *Schuld*, 112). He concludes that "Thielicke's sermon is an example of a preached impenitence: the preacher distances himself and his church from guilt and judgement. All the more clearly, he judges the others" (Richter-Böhne, *Schuld*, 135). Richter-Böhne aptly speaks of Thielicke's virtually exclusive focus not so much on Christ's, but on "Germany's Passion." For the strategy of certain representatives of the post-war Lutheran Church to list, first and foremost, the "crimes of the Allies," see also Klee, *Persilscheine*, esp. 89.

44. Yet, it occurred to the ordinary but perceptive farmer, Franz Jägerstätter, whose admirable courage to live accordingly by saying "no" to National Socialist military service put him above his contemporaries, making him thus *extra*ordinary.

Returning to the actual reason for his removal, the following can be concluded: Thielicke's Christian stance, as occasionally expressed in public, undoubtedly contributed to his collision with the Nazi agenda, which aimed at significantly reducing any Christian influence on public life.[45] The *real* driving force behind his dismissal, however, not mentioned in his publications, was his alleged following of Karl Barth. In spite of the fact that Thielicke compromised his own principles in order to convince the Nazi superiors that he was "politically clean" [*politisch sauber*],[46] and despite his manifold efforts to refute such allegation, he had to give up his much-loved teaching position at the University of Heidelberg.

Part Two: Thielicke's Experiences during Wartime

Germany's Downfall: "The Burden of the Air Raids"

As a result of his struggle for an income, Thielicke time and again experienced the kind of emotional reaction which he had had after he lost a briefcase containing secret notes about a meeting of the resistance movement, *Freiburger Kreis*, to which he was loosely connected: the lives of him and his family were darkened by a debilitating, paralyzing fear.[47] In addition to this psychological pressure, he increasingly underwent the horrors of the home front as the downfall of the Third Reich was closing in.

---

45. Consequently, for example, "religion was no longer taught in the schools" (*Wayfarer*, 134 [177]). See *Wayfarer*, 137 [181]. See also Cornelius, *Genese und Wandel*, who analyses the National Socialist restructuring and reinterpretation of mainly Christian festivals for the sake of an all-embracive "Führer cult" instead, based on ancient Germanic-pagan tenets. Thomas Schirrmacher states that "the extermination of Judaism and Marxism was a part of Hitler's worldview and therefore relieved of tactical considerations. The extermination of Christianity was not a part of Hitler's worldview and came about only gradually, as Hitler realized that the churches could not really be brought into line" (Schirrmacher, "Zur religiösen Sprache Adolf Hitlers," 17). This is confirmed by historian Rissmann, *Hitlers Gott*, 89, who points to Hitler's announcement that after the war he will consider it to be his "life's final task to sort out the church problem. Only then will the German nation wholly be secured." Both Rissmann and Schirrmacher agree that Hitler preserved his "day of reckoning" with Christianity for the time after Germany's victory in World War II (Schirrmacher, "Zur religiösen Sprache Adolf Hitlers," 5–6). For another careful analysis of Hitler's anti-Christian worldview (and its possible roots), see Hamann, *Hitlers Wien*, 18, 32, 164–65, 238, 296–97, 305, 308–9.

46. See his letters to Viktor von Weizsäcker on March 16, 1940, and esp. to "Regierungsrat" Bechtold on April 7, 1940 (*NHT*).

47. See *Wayfarer*, 179 [232].

Thielicke is right, of course, that for someone living nowadays it is no longer possible "to comprehend these apocalyptic hopes and fears," as they are unrecoverable.[48] Nevertheless, in order to—at least partially—picture and thus appreciate the shaping of his outlook, a brief and summarizing account of Thielicke's published portrayal must be given. This is necessary even if this rendering of events is garnished by his "inclination to fabulate" [*Lust zu fabulieren*],[49] thus giving his accounts some undercurrent of imagination and heroism.[50] Whereas this characteristic trait does not substantially shake the essential truth of his narrative *per se*, it must be kept in mind to sustain a sober distance so as not to take every single detail literally, especially regarding his rather heroic depictions of his stance during the Hitler regime.

With this in mind, it is important to begin with two events, which—although not directly connected with the events of the war—still took place during it. Both occasions concern men with whom Thielicke was, in differing ways, warmly involved.

The first one, Emil Christians, was his mathematics teacher and, to Thielicke, "the epitome of manhood." Praise and criticism from this reserved yet warm-hearted man had a major impact on the young Thielicke.[51] They remained in contact until shortly before Christians's death: "He confided to me in our last conversation how frightened he was not of death itself but of dying, and asked me to pray for him. That this restrained man should request this of me *shook me considerably*."[52]

The second encounter with death occurred just before the outbreak of the war, when Thielicke's friend from his youth, Horst Erbslöh, committed suicide in April 1939. This "greatly distressing" event was intensified

---

48. *Wayfarer*, 167 [217].

49. *Zu Gast*, 28 [*Wayfarer*, 17]. See Marieluise Thielicke's confirmative comment in her "Freundesbrief Juni 1985" (*NHT*).

50. See his introductory comment in a brief sermon titled: "Jesus Christus im vordersten Graben" (*NHT*) ["Jesus Christ in the Front-Line Trenches," in *Christ and the Meaning of Life*]: "How often at the sight of ruins . . . did I recover by letting my fantasy go on the tramp." Thielicke owes this disposition to his father, who possessed a "tendency to exaggerate" and an "overactive imagination" which, in the course of time, "repelled" him and led to his estrangement from his father. See also *Wayfarer*, 12, 14–15 [22, 25–26]. Thielicke "always fought those aspects" of his nature, which he realized he had inherited from his paternal side (*Wayfarer*, 17 [28]). Thielicke's oldest son, Wolfram, in a personal meeting on September 29, 2016, evaluated his father's relationship to his [Wolfram's] grandfather as "critical." For example, after his father's retirement, Thielicke was not able to understand how he could just throw away his great intellect by solving crossword puzzles.

51. *Wayfarer*, 27 [40–41]. For an earlier account, still during Christians's lifetime, see *K&K*, 227–32.

52. *Wayfarer*, 28 [42]. Emphasis added.

by Thielicke having a precognitive dream in which he stood, suntanned, in front of Erbslöh's coffin, holding a funeral oration in his honor.[53] Shortly afterwards, he received the friend's farewell letter in which he was thanked for all the friendship and instructions on faith, as well as being urged not to search for him as he was about to die "at the most beautiful place on earth." After recovering from the paralyzing shock of this news, Thielicke remembered that Erbslöh once sent him a postcard from Berchtesgaden on which he had highlighted a spot in the Watzmann massif as the most beautiful place on earth, further noting that "this is where I would like to die."[54] Upon this revelation, Thielicke rushed to Berchtesgaden, persuading the mountain troops to send out a search party for his friend. The corpse was found at the exact spot Thielicke had predicted. Back in Barmen, tanned by the mountain sun, he conducted the funeral service, just as it had appeared to him earlier in his dream.[55] Thielicke dedicated his book *Wo ist Gott?* (*Where is God?* [*WiG*]), published in 1940, to "the remembrance of my friend Horst Erbslöh."

From this time on, death was a constant, as Thielicke would receive regular news that former students died in the war;[56] he would encounter young and entirely antagonistic Nazis about to die[57]; and he would conduct numerous funerals for war-related fatalities.[58] Once he had to comfort a group of sixteen-year-old boys who were part of an anti-aircraft company and to whom he was allowed to give religious education alongside their cannons once a week. During the visit of one of the boys' fathers, an Ameri-

---

53. *Wayfarer*, 108 [144–45].

54. *Wayfarer*, 109 [146].

55. *Wayfarer*, 110 [146–47]. See also *Wayfarer*, 28–29 [42–44], where Thielicke recounts another dream of the same foretelling nature. Regarding the phenomenon of precognitive or prophetical dreams, Thielicke finds himself in famous company. Resistance fighters Franz Jägerstätter and Sophie Scholl also experienced them (for both, see Putz, *Jägerstätter*, 83–85), as did Nietzsche; the latter dreaming the deaths of his brother Joseph and of his grandfather ten years beforehand. See Thiede, *Gekreuzigte[r] Sinn*, 68.

56. "One Saturday I received news that *four* of my former students, to whom I was particularly close, had been killed in action" (*Wayfarer*, 132–33 [175]). See also *Wayfarer*, 91 [123–24]. Compare Bonhoeffer's similar situation in *Widerstand*, 49, 63.

57. Such as a twenty-year-old member of the SS, who had thrown a hot water bottle at the crucifix hanging opposite his deathbed. Thielicke states that the encounter with this man and his mother (who asked Thielicke to visit her son) carved itself particularly deep into his memory (*Wayfarer*, 139 [183]).

58. See, for example, Thielicke's grim and yet emphatic recounting of the funeral of a young student and soldier which took place amongst other mass burials (*Wayfarer*, 168–70 [219–21]). Earlier, he states that "these smells of burning, cold sweat, and decay from mass burials heightened our horror . . . and increased our fear" (*Wayfarer*, 165 [215]).

can aircraft attacked their position and killed the father: "They crowded around me, some crying, others stunned. I put my arms around those who stood closest to me. A long time passed before I could bring myself to say a word."[59] When he and his family finally left their bombed-out home in Stuttgart, making their way to a temporary shelter in the nearby town of Korntal,[60] he once more had a brush with death:

> When we were near the main railway station, the drawer containing our china . . . toppled from the van. I leaped down and began to brush the pieces to the side . . . At that moment, a bomb exploded a few hundred metres further up the road we were travelling, leaving a large crater. If it had not been for our mishap with the china, we would probably have been at exactly that spot when the bomb exploded.[61]

Some time later, in the final stages of the war, his lecture in Stuttgart's borough Bad Cannstatt was suddenly interrupted by an air raid. Thielicke had arranged with the organist that, in case of evacuation, he should play a few quiet evening chorales in order to calm down the crowd. After the attack was over, he learned that two of the people attending the lecture were killed, one of them being the organist, "who had continued to play right up to the last moment."[62] On his way home from this very lecture, Thielicke passed the botanical garden of Bad Cannstatt, which was ornamented with miniature temples:

> A young girl was squatting in front of one of these little temples, which had collapsed into a pile of stones. Beckoning to me, she said, "A mother and her four children are buried beneath this rubble. The children are already dead. The mother is still alive but is trapped and suffering dreadful pain." I could hear the whimpering and screaming, and I doubted that she would last much longer. The girl shouted touching and comforting words to her while I tried in vain to lift the heavy ashlars away. I cried for help at the top of my voice but there was no other human being for miles around. While we squatted despairingly and helplessly on the stones, the dreadful moaning grew quieter

---

59. *Wayfarer*, 173 [225]. See also *Welt*, 130–31.

60. Thielicke and his family lived in Stuttgart from 1942 until 1944. Their time as refugees in Korntal lasted from 1944 until 1945.

61. *Wayfarer*, 183 [237].

62. *Wayfarer*, 186–87 [241–42]. See K&K, 49 [B&E, 43]; *Lebensangst*, 119; and *Man in God's World*, 9–10, where he recounts the same event in his "Preface" to the English translation.

and quieter and eventually ceased altogether. There was nothing more for us to do.[63]

Early in the morning, Thielicke finally arrived at home. Yet, just after having crawled into bed, sirens began to announce the next air raid, forcing him to get his family and himself down into the cellar. "Feeling very cold from exhaustion, it was then that I noticed that I was almost on the edge of a nervous breakdown."[64]

These select examples provide a significant glimpse of Thielicke's *Sitz im Leben* during his thirties. For this specific time of gloom, he concludes that "wherever we looked and whatever questions we asked, the result was the same—we were surrounded by precipices and a future so dark that no eye could pierce it."[65]

Thielicke's Evaluation of His Experiences

In light of such despairing encounters with human suffering, one wonders how Thielicke coped with all of this. The first major key to him enduring these years of despair was already given above, with Thielicke contending that the death threat and suffering during his sickness prepared him for what was to come.[66] Second, recalling that Thielicke tried to overcome crises in his life through writing,[67] he authored his first book on the theme of death, written "under the impression of the war."[68] Third, he states that he gained his most profound comfort from "the spiritual core of his job." In 1942, a relaxation in the prohibition against him travelling and speaking was achieved by Lutheran Bishop Theophil Wurm. Thielicke was therefore able to hold theological courses for ministers in and around Stuttgart and popular lectures on Christianity, attracting large crowds. This even took place during the bombings of the city by the Allied forces. After one

---

63. *Wayfarer*, 187 [242].

64. *Wayfarer*, 187 [243].

65. *Wayfarer*, 188 [243–44]. For his description of "the general mood" of this time, see *Wayfarer*, 166 [216–17].

66. See *Krauss*, 19; and chapter 2, part two.

67. See *Wayfarer*, 399 [510–11]; and chapter 2, part one.

68. *Zu Gast*, 209 [*Wayfarer*, 160]. *Tod* was published anonymously in Switzerland during the war, along with Thielicke's second literary output at that time, *Fragen*. Law's translation of this book title, *Man in God's World*, is misleading, however, for it only contains one chapter (chapter 12) from *Fragen*, whereas the remainder of the book is a translation of chapters 18–32 of *GldChr*, thus presenting the "public dogmatics" held during the war in Stuttgart. See also *Wayfarer*, 149–55 [195–202], 185–86 [240–41].

such lecture, an underground anti-aircraft battery near Thielicke's home, manned by an officer and about fifty female auxiliaries, suffered a direct hit during one bombing.

> Not a single corpse could be found in the huge crater, just scattered pieces of human limbs. Severely shaken, I stood before this enormous hole of total annihilation. A woman with a string bag then approached me . . . She said, struggling to maintain her composure, "My husband was the officer in charge of this anti-aircraft battery. They couldn't find a single trace of him, nor could they find anything left of the girls. All they gave me was this cap of his [she pointed to her bag]. While he was still alive, we both attended your lecture last Thursday. I would now like to thank you before this hole for preparing him for his death."[69]

Thielicke, stating that it was now his turn to struggle to maintain his composure, concludes that scenarios like this one, in spite of their cruelty, gave him moments of consolation in the midst of chaos. He refers to this as "the spiritual core of his job." In the foreword to the English translation of his "public dogmatics," after depicting the same incident, he stresses that "what we were doing there was *teaching theology in the face of death*."[70]

This crucial phrase was used by Thielicke as early as November 1944. In his annual *Freundesbrief* (a sort of newsletter for friends) under the heading "Korntal bei Stuttgart, Mitte November 1944,"[71] Thielicke first described the events listed above (the organist killed during an air raid and the officer inadvertently prepared for death in his lecture). At first publication, Thielicke chose the title "Theology in the Face of Death—A letter to friends on the battlefield"[72] for this specific *Freundesbrief*.

In it, Thielicke ponders that as he goes over the shorthand notes of his sermons during this time, he comes under the strong impression of how all of this was drafted and presented as a "theology in the face of death."[73] He further assumes that this theology's "emphasis on extreme emergency

---

69. *Wayfarer*, 168 [219]. See *K&K*, 47–48 [*B&E*, 41–42]; *Lebensangst*, 117–18.

70. *Man in God's World*, 10. Emphasis added.

71. The original manuscript, which is identical in content to the published versions in *K&K* and *B&E*, is stored in (*NHT*), 15–21.

72. *Lebensangst*, 115. The letter first appeared abridged 1954 in *Lebensangst*, 115–21. The book presents a collection of sermons and addresses between 1942 and 1951. The extended and thus original version was published in *K&K*, 45–52 [*B&E*, 39–45]. In English, *Lebensangst* was published in form of two smaller volumes. The first one, *Silence of God*, contains a selection of ten titles. The second one, *Out of the Depths*, covers the remaining nine titles of *Lebensangst*, including "Theology in the Face of Death."

73. *K&K*, 49 [*B&E*, 44]; *Lebensangst*, 119.

[*Akzent des äußersten Ernstfalles*]" will still be felt in later times, hoping that those words spoken on broken pulpits will not have lost but rather gained substance through "the vicinity of death" and "the nearness of eternity."[74] Thielicke closes this reflection with the following verdict:

> We all have to go through this "theology in the face of death." For too long we have thought in terms of stages. Yet, all the great experiences of the church matured in this close and threatening proximity [to death]. (Can one imagine Luther's theology of the cross having originated under the rosebush of a rural peace, whilst "far away in Turkey, the nations strike against each other"?) Whoever goes through this is later enabled to pass on some secrets. And certainly God must have some people who know about this.[75]

Significantly, the final sentence suggests that Thielicke considered himself to be one of those "know[ing] about this." But what does he "know"? What does he mean by "secrets"? The following may prompt an answer.

In the immediate context, just before he reaches his "verdict" above, Thielicke ascertains that such a "theology in the face of death" is bound to a specific time which, in turn, in a threatening and yet comforting way, is bound to eternity. Such a theology "cannot tolerate minor matters." It therefore helps to gain precisely the right sense of proportion for both the significant and irrelevant.[76] Yet, although this theology is *time bound*, it nevertheless unfolds questions and insights that are *timeless*. Thielicke thus speaks of "the fruitful moment of insight [*der für die Erkenntnis fruchtbare Augenblick*]"—i.e., the one prolific instant that makes insight possible. The *way* in which the insight occurs is time bound, but the *result* is timeless.[77] Thus, in addition to Thielicke's momentous "Maundy Thursday experience" in 1933, this "theology in the face of death" likewise furthers his theologically outstanding albeit not exclusive focus on "the borderline" or "frontier situation" [*Grenzsituation*], to be returned to in chapter 7.

This understanding is further confirmed by a statement in a sermon that was part of Thielicke's "public dogmatics," held during the time Stuttgart

---

74. *K&K*, 49–50 [*B&E*, 44]; *Lebensangst*, 119–20.

75. *K&K*, 51 [*B&E*, 45]. The second part, beginning with brackets, is not contained in *Lebensangst*, 120.

76. *K&K*, 49–50 [*B&E*, 44]; *Lebensangst*, 119–20. In light of this, Krauss's question as to whether it is fair to state that Thielicke—in contrast to Barth—is not so much concerned with dogmatic subtleties but rather with the fundamental approach to living and dying, gains meaning. See *Krauss*, 24–25, 55, 61.

77. See *Gebet*, 8; and *GldChr*, 7: "The one terrible hour of our history contains all hours."

was under bombardment, just before the *Freundesbrief* above was dispatched in November 1944.[78] This passage summarizes the purpose of the "public dogmatics" which took place under such exceptional circumstances:

> Everything that we do on these nights . . . can be summarized under one formula, [namely,] that we want to learn to differentiate between the big and the small . . . "Eternity, shine forth brightly into the times, so that the small might become small in our eyes and that the grand might appear grand."[79] If we know this, then we will also only recognize God's mighty arm through the terrible catastrophes of our time . . . *God is suffered. We have to suffer God.*[80]

That God "has to be suffered" seems to be the "secret" Thielicke speaks about above.[81] Furthermore, this crucial insight *precisely* coincides with Thielicke's own conversion experience and with Luther's emphasis on God being hidden in suffering, i.e., Luther's *theologia crucis*. Just as faith "can only be received and suffered . . . suffer[ing] its coming from [God],"[82] so the initiator of that faith must be suffered just as well. This insight is not granted to everybody but only to "some people," amongst whom Thielicke does not fail to include himself. The close interconnectedness of his *sickness experience and own conversion* on the one hand and *the war experience and sustenance and conversion of others* on the other becomes clear at this point. It is further illuminated by the already-cited statement that "during the severe air raids, it became very important to me that I had experienced this death threat.

---

78. According to *K&K*, 38 [*B&E*, 34], the "public dogmatics" commenced at the beginning of May 1944, only suspended during school holidays. The said statement was made on the eleventh evening, which might have happened on July 27, 1944 (if Whitsun holiday took place back then and lasted for two weeks). The sermon definitely took place before the beginning of the summer holidays on August 8, 1944.

79. Here, Thielicke quotes the fourth stanza of a then well-known hymn in East Westphalia, *Brich herein, süsser Schein*, by Marie Schmalenbach (1835–1924).

80. *GldChr*, 140. Emphasis added. "God instils into *our generation of death* a sharp eye for . . . the relative . . . and for the other, . . . God's rock" (*Gebet*, 63). Emphasis added. See also *Lebensangst*, 44 [*LmdT*, 297]: "From all possible illusions . . . one has to wake up again for the last, true realities: death and God." Regarding the cosmic dimension of "eschatological existence," see *EvF III*, 431: "To be realistic here [i.e., the Lord's Parousia] is not to confuse the transitory with the eternal, the little with the big, the useful with the 'one thing needful' (Luke 10:42). It is not to treat the relative absolutely." See also *Bergpredigt*, 93; *Mensch*, 354: "The values of our life get transvalued if illuminated . . . by the light of his arrival."

81. For the use of "pathos" as a powerful theological motif in a broader pneumatological-ecclesiological regard, see Hütter, *Suffering Divine Things*.

82. Bayer, *Luther's Theology*, 43.

Whatever dreadful thing happened then [during the air raids], it was not comparable with the terrible fear which I had already undergone."[83]

The study of Thielicke's own evaluation of his wartime experiences is to be concluded, however, with several consequences that he draws from his "eschatological existence" during that time. These experiences and insights not only intensified his life in general, but also naturally impacted his theological thinking.

First, resulting from Thielicke's existential proximity to death, he experienced not the eschatological dissipation of the moment but an enormous increase in intensity of life. The "beautiful moment," which he nevertheless still experienced in the midst of suffering and despair, "acquired a heightened luminosity."[84] In the words of Jürgen Moltmann, "after we have experienced what death is like, we experience life more intensely every moment, because every moment seems unique."[85] Thielicke calls this condition "eschatological existence."[86] As such, it does not diminish but rather intensifies life: "Every siren preaches: 'Tonight your life will be required of you!' And every all-clear signal states: 'The time of favor is still on! Repent, for the kingdom of heaven is near!' Anyway, I have the feeling that I have never before lived so saturated with reality [*wirklichkeitsgesättigt*]."[87]

In this particular context, Thielicke employs the term "eschatological existence" (or, a few lines later, "eschatological life") in a very specific sense, focusing on the personal end of an individual. As such, it must be differentiated from the cosmic, universal, and supra-individual dimension of the eschaton as characterized by Christ's Parousia.[88] In the third volume of *The Evangelical Faith*, Thielicke demarcates the individual from the cosmic level (the grander second level thereby obviously including the first). Regarding the cosmic level, he states that "we are already surrounded by his coming and do not know from what direction he himself will come. Hence waiting means extreme vigilance: . . . The nearness of the Lord gives to each moment an unconditioned accent and confirms . . . that the coming end does not empty our time but fills it."[89] Thus, both levels of "eschatological existence," cosmic

83. *Krauss*, 19.
84. *Wayfarer*, 162 [211]. See also *Woran*, 265.
85. Moltmann, *Experiences*, 79.
86. *K&K*, 34 [*B&E*, 30].
87. *K&K*, 34 [*B&E*, 30]. "The question raised by death is whether the world or God is the binding force in our lives" (*EvF III*, 389).
88. In his seminal work, *Eschatologie*, Ratzinger provides a fine analysis of the eschaton's individual (chapter 2) and cosmic dimension (chapter 3).
89. *EvF III*, 430. See also *EvF III*, 431n2. "[The nearness of the Parousia] does not make the present moment of life less important but it takes away from both our own end and that of the world the fear of sinking into nothingness" (*EvF III*, 439).

and individual, are alike in their effectuating an intensification of life, segueing into "a form of soberness which demands extreme realism."[90]

Two examples of Christian resistance to the Nazi regime, both laying their lives down for their convictions, at once confirm and further inspirit the individual dimension of such existence as expressed by Thielicke. The first one, Dietrich Bonhoeffer, explicates in his *Letters and Papers from Prison*: "All that is left to us is the very narrow and sometimes hardly traceable path of *taking each day as if it were the last*, and yet to live in faith and responsibility as if there were still a great future."[91] In a letter to his parents on the first Sunday in Advent, he reflects similarly as he remembers former Christmas celebrations within the family circle: "Probably everything is done more intensely now since you don't know for how long you still have it."[92] In the same vein he claims: "The daily threat of life . . . uniquely spurs you on to appreciate the moment, to make the most of your time."[93] That this sort of "eschatological existence" should really be one's essential approach to life is an elementary insight gained by another light in the darkness, the imprisoned Helmuth James von Moltke, whilst realistically yet peacefully awaiting his death sentence:

> It is a strange feeling to see the evening approach in which the messenger might arrive with the death warrant and to say to yourself: this time tomorrow I am perhaps already dead. You should actually always remind yourself of this [that tomorrow you might be dead], but if you are not coerced like me right now then you just don't do it.[94]

Thus, Thielicke, Bonhoeffer, and von Moltke vividly exemplify what Janine Goffar perceives to be an essential component of the worldview of C. S. Lewis:

> Lewis loved life immensely, yet he retained a sober awareness of its dangers and sufferings, at times even flirting with a desire for death. This is not quite the paradox it seems. His hearty relish of life was precisely because he realized its potential for pain and

---

90. *EvF III*, 431. See *Mensch*, 354.

91. Bonhoeffer, *Widerstand*, 23. Emphasis added.

92. Bonhoeffer, *Widerstand*, 58.

93. Bonhoeffer, *Widerstand*, 122. Unsurprisingly, this eschatological dimension shines through regularly in Bonhoeffer's letters and papers from prison. See Bonhoeffer, *Widerstand*, 65, 109, 147.

94. Von Moltke, *Abschiedsbriefe*, 53. See Bonhoeffer, *Widerstand*, 107–8, who makes a similar point in relation to prayer: that one is often and regrettably only driven into prayer by a state of emergency.

horror, and therefore he more fully cherished all its loveliness, as one might treasure a rose garden on prison grounds.[95]

Goffar goes on to suggest "Tragicism" as a new term for such a view. Yet, it appears that "eschatological existence" expresses this potentially rich dimension of being more aptly, which became a reality in the lives of the four men just listed.

Second, in light of these experiences, which were too immense to cope with immediately, routine Christian statements or clichés were no longer sufficient: "Everything gained in specific weight, in substance. The events we experienced were . . . tailored for long-term effect and only bore fruit after a long process of maturation. But whatever grew in such a way was never forgotten, not even in a long life."[96]

Elsewhere, he states that during those times they were living merely upon the substance of their faith. But these desperate hours especially helped to find that very substance.[97] Accordingly and as a direct result of this, Thielicke is able to express in his introduction to *Lebensangst*: "Basically our lives are moved by very few elementary questions. Likewise, we subsist on a few, yet fundamental, truths. What these questions are, and whether those truths are able to comfort and uphold us, comes to the fore in the crises of our existence . . . when we are presented to the borders of death."[98]

The same notion of "gained substance" is likewise expressed slightly differently in his emphasis on setting the right priorities. In the context of speaking about the *Analogielosigkeit* (i.e., the absence of analogies) of the future world, Thielicke opines as to eternity that "everything will be completely unlike." The last will be first and all that "we living consider as necessary will recede behind the one who is necessary." Whatever "is big and

95. Goffar, *C. S. Lewis Index*, xi.

96. *Wayfarer*, 170 [221]. Ignoring its historical context for a moment, this very evaluation intriguingly can also be applied to Thielicke's own coming to faith on the evening of Maundy Thursday. See my analogy of a flowering bud and embryonic faith, respectively, in chapter 2, part two.

97. See *Man in God's World*, 10; *Reden*, 233; and chapter 7, part two. Likewise, Bonhoeffer, *Widerstand*, 26, states that "personal suffering is a more fitting key . . . to the reflective . . . opening of the world than personal fortune," in spite of Bonhoeffer wanting to look for God not on the borders of human life but in the middle of it. See also *EvF II*, 100–1; *EvF III*, 332.

98. *Lebensangst*, 7–8. See also *EvF III*, 349 (fully cited in chapter 7, part one); *Wayfarer*, 417 [533], where Thielicke strikes the same chord by stating that "there are only very few gospels that endure"; and his interpretation of John the Baptist's imprisonment in his sermon "When Nothing Makes Sense" in *Reden*, 231–32 (see chapter 7, part two). See also Bonhoeffer, who, surrounded by prison walls and threatened by heavy air raids, reaches a similar conclusion (*Widerstand*, 41, 86).

small is now [in eternity] looking entirely different."[99] That is why those apocalyptic times contain such substance, because they precisely teach man "to differentiate between the big and the small."[100] Thus, what Martin Haug calls the "passion for substance" in Thielicke's preaching[101] and, at the same time, Thielicke's aversion towards any overuse of method at the expense of substance can be traced back to this period in his life.[102]

Third, due to this specific time of immense suffering, "light was shed on many questions of faith, human nature, history, and life in general with *a profundity that is scarcely possible in peacetime.*"[103] Looking back at the overwhelming crowds of up to three thousand people gathering around his pulpit every week, many of them walking for hours to hear him, Thielicke concludes that "it is very difficult to grasp this intellectual hunger in our comfortable and overfed age."[104]

In total, those three elements, *intensity, theological substance,* and an *existential yearning for profundity,* seem to be the reflective outcome of Thielicke's proximity to death as he evaluates their manifestation in his own life. As indicated especially by the second point, theological substance, these experiences triggered a long process of theological maturation.

The same verdict propagated by Thielicke in his *Freundesbrief* outlined above is also already present in slightly different wording in the said sermon a couple of months earlier. It aptly brings Thielicke's own evaluation to a close:

> In retrospect, we will be able to know that all things really and literally work together for good to those who love God. The greatest insights of our church and the richest hymns of our hymnbooks have always been thought and versified *in the face*

---

99. "Traum vom gnädigen Ende," 6 (*NHT*). For the "inconceivability of the hereafter," which Thielicke likes to illustrate via the legend of the two medieval monks (*totaliter-aliter*), as well as for his personalistic overcoming of this inconceivability, see *EvF III*, 406–9; *Mensch*, 386.

100. *GldChr*, 140.

101. Haas and Haug, *Thielicke*, 60. Thielicke speaks of his listeners' "thirst for tangible substance," hoping to "understand these mad times sub specie aeternitatis" (*K&K*, 40 [*B&E*, 36]).

102. See Haas and Haug, *Thielicke*, 19.

103. *Wayfarer*, 151 [197–98]. Emphasis added. See also *GldChr*, 7.

104. *Wayfarer*, 186 [241]. See *K&K*, 38–39 [*B&E*, 34–35]. Billy Graham had a similar experience during the Korean War: "It seemed that everywhere we went there was despair and fear and danger. And yet every meeting . . . was packed with eager, enthusiastic audiences" (Graham, *Just As I Am*, 195–96).

of death. There is no terror out of which God could not create a spring of mercy.[105]

The Evaluation of Thielicke's Experiences by Secondary Sources

If one looks at the following variety of comments made about Thielicke's involvement with death and suffering, along with his own accounts, it might come as a surprise that—as far as I can see—this important feature of his life and work has thus far only found specific treatment in relation to Thielicke's sermonic handling by Michael Calvert as late as 2014. The explicit and significant references of Langsam and Speier have already been referenced above (see chapter 2, part two) and shall therefore be left out at this stage.

The one person who arguably knew Thielicke best, Marieluise Thielicke, briefly portrays her husband in the foreword to Thielicke's book on humor (!) as a man who knew about the depths of human existence through his own suffering.[106] The translator of his more academic works, Geoffrey W. Bromiley, extends this initial observation further:

> Thielicke himself believed that in the last resort, life may be reduced to a few elementary questions and a few fundamental truths. These emerge when we are plunged into the deep crises of existence and peripheral concerns and comforts lose their point. They are the result not of study or reflection but of contact with exhaustion, terror, hunger, sickness, and death.[107]

Bromiley's appropriate analysis could not better summarize the findings presented under the previous subsection. His voice thus serves as a fine secondary theological confirmation of Thielicke's own evaluation.

A similar line of thought is picked up by Richard Higginson whose PhD, earned in 1982, was titled: "The Contribution of Helmut Thielicke to Theological Ethics." In an article six years earlier, Higginson very briefly comments on Thielicke's "sensitive handling of the problem of suffering, an experience which Thielicke has obviously tasted first-hand—as a young man, he suffered for many years from serious illness, and Nazism could not

---

105. *GldChr*, 141. Emphasis added. Bonhoeffer agrees: "Every event, however ungodly it may be, offers access to God" (Bonhoeffer, *Widerstand*, 93). The life of Joseph is paradigmatic in this regard (Gen 37–50).

106. Marieluise Thielicke, "Vorwort," in *Humor*, 7.

107. Bromiley, "Thielicke," 545. See *EvF III*, 349.

but leave its traumatic marks on one so opposed to it."[108] Higginson already anticipates what interviewer Krauss later also highlights as the same two circumstances crucial to the understanding of Thielicke.[109]

In another doctoral thesis on the reception of Thielicke's preaching by laymen, Marvin J. Dirks provides a comment similar in nature. After giving a brief overview of Thielicke's book, *Tod*, he contends that "from this time on, in his preaching, Thielicke is never to be unaware of the fact of suffering and death."[110] Whereas Dirks's observation is mainly accurate, he must be corrected in his chronological assumption. For Thielicke states in his autobiography (not yet available to Dirks in the early seventies) that "this sense of the imminent end of all things . . . occupied my thoughts and many pages of my diary long before my later publications on the subject."[111] Also, Thielicke's awareness of death did not restrict itself to the area of preaching, as Dirks implies, but permeates all of his work, as shall be shown in parts II and III.

One more significant yet different clue pointing to the underlying presence of the proposed theme in Thielicke's work is the *Festschrift* in honor of his sixtieth birthday. The mere title illuminates the main emphasis of his whole theological outlook, namely, *Living in the Face of Death* [*Leben angesichts des Todes: LadT*]. The similarity to Thielicke's own periphrasis, "Theology in the Face of Death," hints at the inextricable interrelatedness of experienced life and theological thought. This "existential drive at work in [his] thought"[112] was recognized and honored by his former students and colleagues as they published their own *Beiträge zum theologischen Problem des Todes* ("Contributions to the theological problem of death," the publication's subtitle) in honor of his sixtieth birthday. In the foreword, Bernhard Lohse and Hans P. Schmidt justify their choice of title by two reasons. They chose *Living in the Face of Death* (a) for its systematic relevance and (b) because it was at the center of Thielicke's studies in Christian anthropology from the very beginning.[113]

Probably the most extensive treatment of the case in point (within an English-speaking context) was given by Michael Calvert in his dissertation on Thielicke's sermonic treatment of the problem of evil and suffering. As to Thielicke's preaching, he notes:

108. Higginson, "Thielicke," 179.
109. See chapter 2, part two; *Krauss*, 8–9.
110. Dirks, *Laymen*, 91.
111. *Wayfarer*, 3 [10].
112. *Wayfarer*, 85 [115].
113. *LadT*, vi.

> Even a cursory examination of his upbringing and early years of life . . . will demonstrate that Thielicke's preaching was but a more eloquent reflection of his own persistent struggles with the reality of suffering and death. As a consequence, much of what he preached over five decades of sermons in one way or another addressed life's most daunting questions and perplexities.[114]

Thielicke's focus on the personal and universal eschaton was also recognized five years earlier, in an introductory article by John T. Pless. Pless highlights Thielicke's encounters with death during the different stages of his life, beginning from childhood, with one of his earliest memories, the death of his grandfather, which "would leave its imprint on Thielicke." Moreover, "The death of a primary school classmate and later on, the wartime deaths of numerous . . . students as well as members of the Stuttgart congregation would focus and sharpen his writings on death as well as his preaching, which often engaged eschatological themes."[115]

While Pless only picks up on Thielicke's "sickness-unto-death" in a dependent clause,[116] he pays more attention to his experiences during the Third Reich. By invoking the continual death of students and conducting numerous funerals, Pless concludes that for Thielicke "death was a constant": "Thielicke's existential awareness that human life is always lived on the borderline between life and death *permeates both his academic and pastoral work*."[117] Furthermore, Pless contends that "his early encounters with death as a child and these wartime casualties would leave a deep and abiding imprint on Thielicke *that would show itself throughout his career*. His sermons would reflect an *eschatological edge*, setting the hearers' own lives in the context of eternity."[118] He ends his portrayal of Thielicke's engagement with suffering and death with the dictum that "this awareness that life is lived in the presence of death never left Thielicke," as it is—citing *Death and Life*—"something that leaves its mark upon his entire life."[119]

Besides, Pless endorsed this study in a personal email. In his words, "this would be a promising study [not only as it relates to death, but also] as it would draw on Thielicke's work in systematic theology, ethics, and

---

114. Calvert, *Preaching*, 10.
115. Pless, "Thielicke," 439.
116. "After multiple hospitalizations and surgery . . . " (Pless, "Thielicke," 440).
117. Pless, "Thielicke," 441. Emphasis added.
118. Pless, "Thielicke," 442. Emphasis added.
119. Pless, "Thielicke," 442.

apologetics (as exemplified in his preaching)."[120] I am thus indebted to Prof. Pless for initially drawing my attention to this area of research.

Finally, by looking at the commemorative speeches held during Thielicke's memorial at the University of Hamburg on December 4, 1986, the recognition of this central theme in Thielicke's theology by his colleagues once more approves the overall proposal outlined thus far. Wulf-Volker Lindner opened the *Akademische Gedenkfeier* by thanking Gerhard Ebeling for choosing the title of his paper so appropriately: "'Death's death: Luther's theology of the confrontation with death.' In accordance with Helmut Thielicke, with this memorial, and with theology [as a whole], I could not think of any other theme being more appropriate [for this occasion]."[121]

Röhricht subsequently gave an overview of Thielicke's life and work. As his former student and friend, he lists three factors elementary to the shaping of Thielicke's personality: (a) his resistance to political violence, (b) his experience of death, and (c) the horrors of war.[122] Even more importantly, Röhricht describes two ways leading into the person of his former teacher:

> One way is the way of suffering, which, physically and mentally, scarred him for life. He talked little about this . . . but his theology was also a *pathei mathos*, a learning in suffering. And parenthetically, he could frequently say that a preacher should never give a sermon without using the word "Angst" [fear/anxiety] at least once. This was no negative methodology, this was experience.[123]

This application of *pathei mathos* to the personality of Thielicke most aptly sums up the main concern of part I. Röhricht's observation is further confirmed by the fact that Thielicke's autobiographical expositions pale in comparison with the sort of intense anxiety conveyed in his letters: "Countless letters testify to the existential fear Thielicke went through during this time [i.e., the Third Reich]. One does not get this impression by reading his autobiography."[124]

Last but not least, Gerhard Ebeling[125] concludes Thielicke's memorial by discussing Thielicke's book, *Life and Death*, in light of Luther's under-

---

120. Personal email correspondence on October 19, 2013.
121. Lindner, "Eröffnung," 9.
122. Röhricht, "Thielicke," 20–21.
123. Röhricht, "Thielicke," 27.
124. Speier, *Initiator*, 27n22.
125. Of Ebeling, Thielicke states: "I have never since met a person who worked as intensely as he did." For the quote and his portrayal of Ebeling, see *Wayfarer*, 205–6 [264–65]. As an intriguing side note, Emil Brunner, in a personal letter to Thielicke

standing of death. His introductory remarks are also highly indicative of the implicit substance behind his former colleague's theological output:

> Had the faculty not suggested the topic "Life and Death" to me as a title for this lecture, Helmut Thielicke's leitmotif would have pointed me in the same direction. The book *Life and Death*, written before his time as a professor during the war and only published in Germany in 1946, was revised by him again, in 1980, under the slightly different title, *Living with Death*. Thus, it frames Thielicke's major works: the Ethics, the Dogmatics, and the Anthropology; it reveals the necessary connection to their respective origin and, at the same time, indicates the experiential background as well as the proclamatory aim of his theology.[126]

These secondary voices, showing a well-balanced mixture of theological expertise and/or personal acquaintance with Thielicke, strengthen my thesis substantially and round off, in a satisfactory way, what has been the purpose and aim of this first part: to reveal what Ebeling aptly calls the "experiential background" of Helmut Thielicke's theology. To make this task complete, however, it remains to touch on Thielicke's further encounters with death and suffering beyond the war. Although no significant *formative* character might be ascribed to these post-war experiences, they nevertheless show that the "eschatological life," as he calls it, did not end in 1945.

Part Three: Beyond the War—Further Encounters with Death and Suffering

In this final part, I present significant examples of Thielicke's further encounters with death and suffering beyond 1945, thereby completing my exposition on his existence "in the face of death." These post-war encounters with *events and symbols of explicit finitude*[127] can arguably be subdivided

---

on September 25, 1947 (*NHT*), writes of Ebeling: "I would have thought of Ebeling as being capable of great things, had he not got lost to church history. His Barthianism would certainly have disappeared in time." About Brunner's relief as to Ebeling becoming Thielicke's successor in the chair of systematic theology at Tübingen in 1954, one can only speculate.

126. Ebeling, "Todes Tod," 31–32.

127. In contrast to implicit or indirect (and thus more ambiguous) pointers, which might include a far broader range of events, such as the extremely stressful effect on Thielicke of the student revolts in the late sixties. Although not directly confronting him with death, one might still reasonably argue that the mental agony experienced at that time nevertheless confronted him with the finitude of humanness. Due to both

into three, broadly thematic blocks, which I would like to classify as "third-person observations," "second-person encounters," and "first-person experiences," thus signifying Thielicke's respectively heightened degree of personal involvement.

Beyond 1945: Thielicke's Third-person Observations of Death and Suffering

The first and most general block of "third-person observations" would include certain media reports, news, events, etc. which triggered an empathetic—yet still rather uninvolved—commitment of various sorts on the part of Thielicke. The continuation of a car race in Le Mans after a terrible crash claimed twelve casualties, for example, provoked a strong public response, as he branded this act as an "expression of Western materialism."[128] Similarly, Thielicke strongly opposed the film portrayal of a *real* pastor conducting a wedding ceremony or a *real* judge cinematically sentencing a victim to death. Whereas he criticized the former for misusing his position purely in the interests of providing some solemnity, thus toying with the Word of God, the latter was accused of downplaying the existential matters of life and death: "But the gospel is also about life and death. And if people do not see this anymore, then we emphatically have to inculcate them with it."[129]

His travels to the USA in particular provided Thielicke with several pointers of such sort. For example, he begins a reflective journey induced by the informal way of American greetings, finally arriving at thoughts on individual death.[130] A visit to Hollywood's graveyard,[131] his observance of the desperate attitude towards ageing of America's older people,[132] his speech at Harvard University two days after John F. Kennedy's assassination,[133] and—back in Germany—his commemorative speech on the occasion of a freighter-disaster[134] also repeatedly provided Thielicke with opportunities to elaborate more or less extensively and formally on this key issue.

---

the lack of space and the fact that such a widening of scope does not seem necessary in light of the evidence documented thus far, this subsection restricts itself to a number of explicit examples.

128. *K&K*, 75 [*B&E*, 64].
129. *K&K*, 75–76 [*B&E*, 64–65].
130. *K&K*, 98–102 [*B&E*, 73–76].
131. *K&K*, 198 [*B&E*, 143].
132. *K&K*, 112–15 [*B&E*, 81–82].
133. *Wayfarer*, 361–62 [463–64]; *K&K*, 208–9 [*B&E*, 151–52].
134. *Schweigen*, 69–78.

Certainly, the most upsetting illustration for Thielicke's involuntary yet recurrent engagement with death and suffering was the abrupt ending of their holidays in 1981. On the isle of Juist, a little girl of eight, whose family was about to return home the next day, was raped and murdered by a sex offender. Marieluise Thielicke reports that "this horrendous deed shook us to the bones . . . At the same hour as the little girl was buried in her home church . . . we distraught spa guests and locals gathered in a church for a commemorative service."[135]

Beyond 1945: Thielicke's Second-person Encounters with Death and Suffering

The second block of "second-person encounters" mainly consists of the death and suffering of people with whom Thielicke had a close relationship, i.e., trusted friends and loved ones. The passing of his teacher, Emil Christians, has already been mentioned earlier. Similarly, the loss of his "fatherly friend," Eduard Spranger, on September 17, 1963—with whom Thielicke carried on a correspondence on the last questions—affected him deeply. He bemoans the fact that due to his stay in the USA, he was neither able to comfort Spranger on his deathbed nor to bury him as continually promised during his final years.[136]

Moreover, the tragic death of the above-mentioned Hans P. Schmidt, a former student, assistant, and lifelong friend of Thielicke, who died in a car accident together with his youngest son at Christmas 1980, serves as another case in point. Thielicke dedicated his *Modern Faith and Thought* to the memory of his "late friend" and further commemorates Schmidt in the preface to this concluding volume of his systematic theology.[137] In his autobiography, he closes the description of the festive week in celebration of his seventieth birthday (in 1978) with the remark that, in retrospect, this day was likewise branded by a "sign of pain," since on that day he saw Schmidt for the last time.[138]

Finally, the question of mortality tragically arose once again due to the severe cancerous condition of one member of their close circle, *Projektgruppe Glaubensinformation*.[139] Marieluise Thielicke reports on how

---

135. Marieluise Thielicke, "Freundesbrief Februar 1982" (*NHT*).

136. See *K&K*, 204–5 [*B&E*, 148–49].

137. *MF&T*, xvii–xviii. A mistake occurs in his autobiography as he wrongly dates the year of Schmidt's death as 1981 (see *Wayfarer*, 222 [285]).

138. See *Wayfarer*, 408 [522].

139. For information on the *Projektgruppe*, see chapter 2, part one.

painful it was when this forty-year-old wife and mother of three had to die after months of deep suffering, "wavering between anxiety and hope, finally passing away peacefully, safe in the knowledge that God would take care of the family."[140]

These "second-person encounters" become heightened in intensity as Thielicke pondered on his changed view of the future amidst the encroachment of old age, with such rumination usually triggered just before milestone birthdays. The future is no longer in front of him like a panoramic countryside but rather has become the "temporal symbol of our finitude, of our limited life-span; it now presents the tense of death. Suddenly I start counting my days from the end."[141]

Whilst thinking about his earliest possible retirement in December 1973, he comes to the very same conclusion, adding that "one calculates the remaining time."[142] Marieluise Thielicke speaks for them both when she reflects on the fact that they have by now reached "an age in which we soon receive more obituaries than engagement notices."[143] Eleven months later, she repeats and further elaborates on this comment, aptly summarizing the concern of this second block:

> We are now in a biblical age which means, amongst other things, that we have to experience many people from our big circle of friends, with whom we had been connected for decades, die. Every death leaves a painful void and makes us meditate on our own end inevitably approaching. Every so often, with regard to time, I find myself trying not to waste this precious good.[144]

Beyond 1945: Thielicke's First-person Experiences of Death and Suffering

Lastly, the third and final block of "first-person experiences" represents Thielicke's most intense post-war reminder of human finitude, as it signifies his personal involvement with the theme at hand.[145] In his own words: "I

---

140. Marieluise Thielicke, "Freundesbrief Februar 1984" (*NHT*).

141. *Zu Gast*, 514 [*Wayfarer*, 402].

142. *B&E*, 206. Not contained in *K&K*. Adolf Schlatter underwent the same reflection after the premature death of his wife, Susanna, then unaware that he would still be given three decades within which he would complete some of his greatest works. See Neuer, *Schlatter: A Biography*, 117.

143. Marieluise Thielicke, "Freundesbrief März 1981" (*NHT*).

144. Marieluise Thielicke, "Freundesbrief Februar 1982" (*NHT*).

145. See *ThE* II/1, §623–25, 631; *Tod*, 26, 72.

only recognize what death 'is' as a dying man."[146] This third area is rooted in his decisive experience of sickness between 1929 and 1933. However, Thielicke's medical problems were not over with his sudden recovery on Good Friday, 1933, but really left its "eschatological mark" on his entire life. Three brief examples of his failing health, each time bringing him devastatingly close to death, are representative thereof.

The first instance took place just after his birthday in 1972. Not for the first time, Thielicke collapsed due to a pulmonary infarction [*Lungeninfarkt*] with him consequently being "carted" into hospital "with blue light and siren." He somewhat dramatically concludes this episode in his *Freundesbrief* that if it had not been for his neighbour, friend, and surgeon, Lindenschmidt, this current greeting would perhaps not have come about.[147]

The second occasion of Thielicke's health dangerously letting him down came in 1975. As the year's low-point, he describes a "severe ailment, exposing me to most extreme dangers," caused by a wrong dosage of medication. Thielicke reminisces that the chief physicians "did everything humanly possible to snatch me away from the abyss." That he nevertheless forced himself to make a train journey down to Freiburg, just before hospitalization, because he did not want to cancel a speaking engagement and thus disappoint his listeners, did not help matters: "During both nights, I was not able to sleep in bed due to pain but wandered through the night sleeper. *Once again, as so often in my life, I experienced in borderline situations mercy and preservation.*"[148]

The third incident is testified to by Thielicke's wife, Marieluise, who grants valuable insight into a severe complication at the beginning of 1984. In the couple's final *Freundesbrief*, written in June 1985, she reports that "Helmut fell so seriously ill that for weeks I was in the greatest distress for his life; it was literally only hanging by a thread."[149] The cause this time was Thielicke's medication, which had to be taken for a lifetime to keep his post-operative tetany under control. His body suddenly started to produce the missing *parathormone* roughly fifty years after the additional medication had begun to poison Thielicke's organism. Due to this previously medically unknown process, he was once again hospitalized for weeks, with the medical staff finally succeeding in "snatching him from death." After he had slightly recovered, he had to undergo yet another operation which delayed his convalescence. Her concluding words on

146. *ThE III*, §1981.
147. *B&E*, 207.
148. *B&E*, 220. Emphasis added.
149. Marieluise Thielicke, "Freundesbrief Juni 1985" (*NHT*).

this matter reveal an additional aspect of the "eschatological existence" unfolded above:

> In all those weeks of sorrow, it was comforting for us to experience how much family and friends supported us, not least with their intercession. I sometimes think about how people who have never been ill in life must feel. They are envied by all ... and yet: they never experience the feeling of happiness from newly given health. We are daily *thankful* for the span of time that is given to us once again.[150]

In a manuscript titled, "[My] dream of a merciful end," Thielicke *inter alia* chimes in with his wife on this. Reflecting on his own dying, he not only desires a joyous vision of the one who is expecting him on the other side but also hopes for a grateful retrospect, bringing near once more both the most beautiful moments and the most beloved people in his life: "This dream [of a merciful end] is a hope: that at the end I want to be thankful for the life lived."[151] ... Thankfulness really is the only therapy for the pains of parting."[152]

This aspect of thankfulness becomes—if not exclusively, then at least especially—clear to people who are consciously confronted by their immediate death and are thus "existentially helped" in becoming aware of this "eschatological existence" within which every human being lives, moves, and has his or her being. A study of farewell letters, written by members of resistance groups sentenced to death in the Third Reich, proves to be particularly rewarding in this regard, especially as many of them were committed Christians, able to consider their freely chosen fate *sub specie aeternitatis*.[153]

In conclusion, these tripartite "post-war reminders of suffering and transience," namely, "third-person observations," "second-person encounters," and "first-person experiences," all attest to the fact that Thielicke's painful encounters with the dark side of human existence were by no means restricted to the time of his youth, but much more traversed the whole of his life. The final encounter with death occurred on March 5, 1986, at a place

---

150. Marieluise Thielicke, "Freundesbrief Juni 1985" (*NHT*). Emphasis added.

151. "... and that I am spared the agony that suppresses any other thought but that of pain and breathlessness." These two aspects (being surrounded by loved ones and a painless end) are also mentioned in reply to the same question by Krauss as to how he imagines "a merciful end." See *Krauss*, 21. The first is furthermore expressed in *LmdT*, 90.

152. "Just like love and sacrifice are the only cure for depression." See "Traum vom gnädigen Ende," 4 (*NHT*); *Reden*, 154; and *Lebensangst*, 39.

153. See, for example, the moving compilation of farewell letters in Gollwitzer et al., *Abschiedsbriefe*.

where he spent a considerable time of his life: aged seventy-seven, Thielicke dies at a Hamburg hospital.[154] He was certainly well prepared.

---

154. Lundin, "Helmut Thielicke Is Dead at 77," 42.

Part II—Theology

So teach us to number our days
that we may get a heart of wisdom.

—Psalm 90:12 (ESV)

Chapter 4

The Lutheran Way

Thielicke's Conversion and Thought
in Historical Context

LIKE ROMAN CATHOLIC PHILOSOPHER von Hildebrand, Thielicke emphasizes death as a human determinant: "Death is feared because it lies like a shadow over the whole of life, characterizing it as a 'being for death.'"[1] I have shown in the first part that different events in Thielicke's life in general, and his "sickness-unto-death" in particular, enforced his contemplative confrontation with the phenomenon of death. Hence, Thielicke's recognition of the power of death was a deeply existential matter. His literary engagement with it became reality by his finally being able to say in the first person: "I die." That is, the focus on death and suffering biographically "grew" inside Thielicke.[2]

With respect to his book, *Living with Death* [*LmdT*], one reviewer aptly states that "the overriding accomplishment which renders this text so highly significant is that Thielicke has placed awareness of death at the very heart of Christian living."[3] To document that this awareness is the fruit of Thielicke's specific *Sitz im Leben* was the aim of part I. To show how it plays itself out in his theological thought will be the purpose of parts II and III.

Although I draw from his homiletical, pastoral, ethical, and dogmatic sources equally, I will nonetheless have a stronger focus on ethical and especially dogmatic themes in chapters 4 to 7 (part II), whilst his homiletical

---

1. *EvF III*, 389. "Death is not life's endpoint but its essence" (*Tod*, 161). See also *Woran*, 173–74; *Suche*, 150; and von Hildebrand, *Tod*, 14: "Every man lives in the shadow of death, *in umbra mortis*."

2. See *ThE II/1*, §631; *LmdT*, 17. Thielicke further likes to quote Rilke's differentiation between little and big death in this regard. See also *EvF III*, 391; *ThE II/1*, §635; §1205–6; *Mensch*, 399; *Tod*, 76–77; *LmdT*, 71; and *Sterben*, 32.

3. Walker Jr., "Living with Death," 414.

and pastoral emphases will be examined in chapters 8 to 10 (part III). Since Thielicke himself, in truly Lutheran fashion,[4] considers the ethical task to be of dogmatic rank,[5] it can likewise only be proper for any investigation of his work to avoid setting up a false divide between the primary material. His *Theological Ethics* is thus treated with the same systematic importance as his three volumes of *The Evangelical Faith* and his anthropology, without setting the first apart conceptually.

Chapter 1 began with the key words of Thielicke that "my theological work was always only a superstructure placed upon the experiences and sufferings of my life."[6] If Thielicke's statement is true, then we must expect to find a processing and explicit outworking of such experiences and sufferings in his theological work. I will begin my analysis in this chapter by trying to show the truly Lutheran embeddedness of Thielicke's "sickness-unto-death." This will provide us with a theological framework within which his specific life and work is to be located, thus serving as a basis for our subsequent chapters.

Part One: The Lutheran Thought-form of Relation —Man *coram Deo* and the Analogy of Faith

In the second chapter, the principal analogy between Thielicke's Good Friday experience and Martin Luther's understanding of coming to faith was initially implied. In the same context, it was further indicated that Thielicke neither subscribes to a pietistic manifestation of conversion, nor indeed applies the term itself to his own experience.

As to the former, Thielicke somewhat derogatively describes a pietistic conversion he experienced as a fourteen-year-old in his autobiography.[7] Although in retrospect he regards "the dense, pietistically saturated atmosphere" of the religious circle within which his adolescent, "ardent love for Jesus à la Zinzendorf" was first ignited as "pretty extravagant," he nevertheless expresses thankfulness for this "exuberance of piety which was so elementary

---

4. See Althaus, *Luther*, 27.

5. He states that his "*Theological Ethics*, especially the first volume, is already in large part a dogmatics" (*EvF I*, 13). Furthermore, a theological ethics "must at first itself be a part of the dogmatic doctrine of principles" (*ThE I*, vii). See also *Mensch*, 21: "The *Theological Ethics* . . . is virtually already conceived as an anthropology."

6. *Wayfarer*, 85 [115].

7. *Zu Gast*, 59–60 [*Wayfarer*, 41–42]. For a closer look at the soul of classical pietism, see Spener, *Pia Desideria*. For a helpful secondary source, see Brown, *Understanding Pietism*.

that it almost made one's heart burst, filling it with bliss."[8] That this specific impression had deeply engraved itself on Thielicke became clear to him only much later, when he participated in the ecstatic Afro-American church services during his visits to the USA.[9] Nonetheless, Thielicke concludes that he learned to see that "all this was rather psychological [*seelisch*], with the secret of faith being at home in quite another dimension."[10] Yet, that the pietistic influence never really left him will become clearer later on.

As to the latter, Thielicke, in spite of avoiding the term "conversion," regards his "resurrection" on Good Friday, 1933, as shown in chapter 2, part two, to be the key moment in his life at which he came to a personal, trusting faith in Jesus Christ. His coming to faith thereby falls under the first of two ways via which man—according to Thielicke—can arrive at religion, defined by him as "the transparency of final reality." This first access route he calls the "ecstasis of experiencing the absolute" [*Ekstasis des Unbedingtheitserlebnisses*].[11] To be clear, Thielicke's Maundy Thursday experience should not be equated with the conventional meaning of the term "ecstasis" (Greek *ek*, out of; *stasis*, a standing), i.e., a sort of trance. But in his eyes, he certainly experienced the absolute, final reality that night, without, however, any trance-like "condition in which ordinary consciousness and the perception of natural circumstances were withheld."[12] And whereas he rejects, not unlike Barth, religion as *human reaction* to such an encounter by which man distorts God, it is still important to note that Thielicke does not negate the two above-mentioned ways of encounter, which may or may not lead to this religiously distorting reaction.[13]

This comes into sharper relief if we draw a parallel to Martin Luther himself, to whose line of thought Thielicke confessionally subscribes. Gerhard Ebeling, in his memorial speech in honor of the late Thielicke, discusses Luther's own early encounter with death via mishap and storm, which provided Luther with his unusual power to speak about the theme of death.[14] Ebeling thus subtly and without explicit mention puts Thielicke's

---

8. *Zu Gast*, 59–60 [*Wayfarer*, 41–42]. This is my own translation.

9. With his pietistic roots, he joins the ranks of two thinkers he held in high esteem: Kant and Schleiermacher. For the former, see Geier, *Kants Welt*, 21–27, esp. 23–25. For the latter, see Clements, *Schleiermacher*, 15; and Dyrness, "The Pietistic Heritage of Schleiermacher," 15–17. See also *MF&T*, 168–73.

10. *Zu Gast*, 59–60 [*Wayfarer*, 41–42].

11. "EdR," 65. The second way consists of "the rationality of metaphysical reflection." It is noteworthy that in this context, Thielicke seems to grant both ways validity.

12. "EdR," 44. See Vine, *Expository Dictionary*, 1160.

13. "EdR," 68.

14. Ebeling, "Todes Tod," 41.

experiential background on a par with the great Reformer's own existential key event.

Indeed, the intriguing similarities between Luther and Thielicke do not stop there but segue into their subsequent reflections as to (a) what makes one a theologian and (b) what theology actually is. By briefly unfolding Luther's answers to these questions, one might almost get the impression that Thielicke's experience and ensuing thought-process follow Luther's "existential-theological blueprint." As this is, of course, impossible, it is all the more intriguing considering how much like "chalk and cheese" Thielicke and Luther are in their existentially-founded replies to the above-mentioned questions.

Regarding the first question (as to what a theologian is made of), Oswald Bayer highlights Luther's deliberate prioritization of this question over the second one, concerning the essence of theology. For the unique life story of each individual is constitutive for answering the second question of what theology is.[15] The existential context cannot be left out.[16] More precisely, in light of the fundamental importance of temptation (*tentatio*) for the theologian's life, the essential nature of theology as a "theology of the cross" is anticipated already.

The theological reason for this is to be found in Luther's and Thielicke's personalistic view of man's existence *coram Deo*.[17] According to Ebeling, the Latin preposition *coram* is "the key word to Luther's understanding of being."[18] Translatable into the English *before* (German: *vor*), "it implies a determination of place which as such is a determination of time. Its precise meaning . . . is 'before the face of,' 'in the sight of.'"[19] Luther's—and subsequently, Thielicke's—anthropological conviction of man's existence "in the presence of" God,[20] thus defining man not in himself "but . . . in terms of the

---

15. Bayer, *Luther's Theology*, 15–16.

16. See Thielicke's own as well as other noted theologians' remarks presented in chapter 1, part two.

17. By "personalistic" I do not mean Thielicke's adherence to a certain strand of philosophical Personalism (for an overview, see Williams and Bengtsson, "Personalism"). Rather, it is to highlight (a) Thielicke's Lutheran-anthropological conviction of man's existence *coram* the tri-*personal* God; and (b) his almost exclusive focus on the *person* of Jesus of Nazareth, especially when dealing with the question of theodicy (see chapter 7).

18. Ebeling, *Luther*, 193. Gloege, "Personalismus," 25, confirms: "Luther thinks in concretely personal terms. Concretely, i.e., as man who receives his life 'coram Deo.'"

19. Ebeling, *Luther*, 193.

20. "God is the basis, goal, and meaning of my existence and to that extent of my thinking, willing, and acting, of my capacity to think, and also of my freedom" (*EvF I*, 367).

relationship of something else with [him],"[21] thereby also determines their rejection of any ontological schema of thought in favor of a personalistic, relational one:

> [For] the profundity of the situation to which the *coram*-relationship leads is naturally only manifested in an encounter between one person and another. The most important element in the situation that is implied by the preposition *coram* is ... the way that I myself am before someone else and exist in the sight of someone else, *so that my existential life is affected.*[22]

The whole of man's existence is involved in this encounter between the divine and the human person. In his whole being, man is either disposed towards God in faith or against God in unbelief; and, for that reason, exists either towards God or away from God.[23] Thus, Thielicke enunciates that "Luther is right to allow only two attributes to remain: belief and unbelief. Herein the whole relational character of man is being expressed most consistently."[24]

For Luther, the person is "always only an *actus* [hence: *actuality*], namely, either of positive relationship or . . . negative relationship with God."[25] Gloege traces the early form of such personal thinking beyond Luther and via Augustine back to Plato. Thielicke supports his own personalistic understanding by referring to the latter in his essay, "Truth and Understanding." On the basis of equating the question of truth with the question of meaning,[26] Thielicke defines the human condition ultimately as being related to meaning or meaninglessness, either upholding man in case of the former or destroying him if the latter.[27] Agreeing with Heidegger that the being of man is "ontically distinguished" by being concerned with being whilst being [or: whilst man is/exists],[28] he concludes that being itself

---

21. Ebeling, *Luther*, 194.

22. Ebeling, *Luther*, 196. Emphasis added.

23. See Ebeling, *Luther*, 200–1.

24. *ThE I*, §873. See also *ThE I*, §268, 275–76; *EvF II*, 200, 310; and *Offenbarung*, 153: "The I is a relational term." Emil Brunner shares the same view. See his *Dogmatics II*, 58–59; and *Letter to the Romans*, 17.

25. Luther cited in Gloege, "Personalismus," 32.

26. "The question of meaning is the most urgent of all. [It] is identical with the question of truth, which determines life. Truth, enquired about in the question of meaning, decides whether we can stand reality. [Truth] would thus be reality's absolute carrying principle" ("WuV," 115).

27. Hence, Thielicke, *Mensch*, 443–44, strongly objects to Sigmund Freud seeing a sign of sickness in the very question of meaning and value.

28. "WuV," 118. ["*Dass es diesem Seienden in seinem Sein um dieses Sein selbst geht.*"] That is, man, by virtue of his self-awareness, is enabled to concern himself with the question of being.

is a relation, i.e., that man in his being relates to the essence of being via a relation of being [*Seinsverhältnis*], which is the truth.

Thielicke states that this was already Plato's understanding, as Plato regards man's essence as originating from his relation to that which truly has (or is) being.[29] That is why "meaning and meaninglessness always incarnate themselves in persons,"[30] for "man 'is' his relation to God."[31] Man's "Godlikeness is a relational concept [*Relationsbegriff*]."[32] Thielicke expands this, saying that "personhood . . . is and is present [*ist und west*] within man's relation to the divine ground of being which, in turn, determines him."[33] His relational understanding of man is thereby given classical expression in the parable of the prodigal son[34] as well as in Thomas Carlyle's "tadpole-illustration."[35] According to the latter, man's essence is not defined by his evolutionary relation to the below (illustrated by the tadpole), but by his heavenly relation to the above (illustrated by Psalm 8:6).[36] This illustration, according to Thielicke, boils "anthropology's crucial problem"[37] down to its very relational essence.[38]

---

29. In *EvF II*, 106–7; and *Mensch*, 158, Thielicke acknowledges the ancient Greek endowment of man with the *humanum* since man is defined as theonomous by virtue of his relation to the gods. Gloege contraposes the "metaphysically founded" "platonic-augustinian type" of personalism with the "aristotelian-thomistic" understanding of person, the former thereby providing Luther with the philosophical foundation upon which he developed his concrete personalism (Gloege, "Personalismus," 23–26).

30. "WuV," 118.

31. *EvF I*, 15. See also *ThE I*, §317.

32. *ThE II/1*, §1251.

33. *ThE II/1*, §1260. Correspondingly, in *EvF III*, 412, Thielicke defines the soul as "the epitome of the relation to God." "Soul is man as he is addressed by God's Word." He concludes: "The one firm point is that the concept of the soul cannot be abandoned when we have to speak of bodily death . . . Soul is thus a term for partnership in this history. It denotes the I in fellowship with God's Thou. It thus remains relational." In *EvF III*, 414, Thielicke declares the convergence of his view with "what Ratzinger has in mind when he refers to 'dialogical immortality.'" Ratzinger, in the afterword to the sixth German edition of his *Eschatologie*, 205n27, states that "Thielicke, subsequent to my eschatology, refined his position, largely aligning it with my own."

34. See *EvF I*, 146–51; *EvF III*, 174; *ThE I*, §817–18, §837–42, §871; *ThE II/1*, §1308–9; and *Mensch*, 237–38, 394.

35. See *Mensch*, 430–31; *GldChr*, 335–36; *Anfechtung*, 7; *Sterben*, 61; and *Welt*, 92.

36. "The immanent continuity of man's evolution merely constitutes a biological medium within which man's actual humanness emerges as an underivable factum" (*ThE II/1*, §1260).

37. *Mensch*, 62, 431.

38. *ThE II/1*, §1272–73. See also *Kulturkritik*, 46, where he classifies his conviction of man being a relation as "a basic law of every anthropology."

Consequently, Thielicke rejects both the *analogia entis* mode of thought[39] and, along with Luther, any ontological definition of God's image in human nature in favor of a purely relational characterization: "The *imago Dei* does not express humans' substantial attributes in themselves, but [is the expression of] an external quality [*Außenschaft*] of a co-relation [*Gemeinschaftsbeziehung*]."[40] By "external quality" he simply means, in contrast to Schlatter, for example,[41] that man's God-likeness is not intrinsically grounded in a human quality like reason, will, freedom, etc., but rather is extrinsically based on God's relation to man, on his being "Immanuel": God's image in man is not "essential potency" [*inhaltliche Potenz*], but a relation.[42] It is furthermore the *imago's character indelebilis*[43] that constitutes the indispensable worth of human life, thus establishing Thielicke's tireless stress not on the intrinsic, but on the *alien* dignity of man: "Man 'is' something because God thinks of him, because God has this imago of him," man's essence thereby being "secured and hidden as an alienum in the heart of God."[44]

Thus for Thielicke the *imago Dei*, constituting man's alien dignity, and the term "person" are interchangeable,[45] leading him time and again to render Luther's phrase variedly that "God does not love us because we are of

---

39. From his theological dissertation (*G&E*: his "theological firstling" completed in 1934. See *G&E*, 19; and *Wayfarer*, 77–79 [105–7]) onwards, Thielicke, like Barth, rejects all forms of natural theology and *analogia entis* modes of thinking in favor of the *analogia fidei*. See *EvF I*, 310, 370; *Anfechtung*, 39, 58; and *LmdT*, 315n1. One's respective preference is, according to Thielicke, rooted in the schema of thought to which priority is given: either ontological (analogy of being) or personal (analogy of faith). See *EvF III*, 224.

40. *ThE I*, §785; *ThE III*, §1865. See *Abenteuer*, 223; *Welt*, 93; *ThE I*, §793; and §763–828 for his general systematic unfolding of the *imago Dei*. Nordlander, *Gottebenbildlichkeit*, dedicated his PhD thesis to Thielicke's understanding of man's God-likeness. Furthermore, see Thielicke's anthropological work, *Mensch*, published five years after Nordlander's thesis, esp. 62, 101–2, 107, 138, 158–59, 161, 227–29, 236, 396, 425–31.

41. Schlatter evaluates man's essence as an intrinsic God-likeness which, contrary to the interpretation of Protestant Orthodoxy, did not get entirely lost but characterizes empirical man, too. See Neuer, *Schlatter: Ein Leben*, 169.

42. *ThE I*, §781. In this regard, Thielicke commends the same perspective which Melanchthon took regarding the being of Christ: the Son of God is not recognized in his metaphysical attributes but rather in his *beneficia*, in his salvation-historical [*heilsgeschichtlich*] efficacy. See Ebeling, *Luther*, 194, 200–1.

43. See *Mensch*, 429–30; *Gespräche*, 54–55; *ThE I*, §792, §823; and *ThE II/1*, §1262–63: Man's relation to God, his *imago Dei*, cannot get lost for "even a broken relation still is a relation."

44. *ThE I*, §821. See also *ThE I*, §462, 868–69.

45. See *ThE I*, §1410; Nordlander, *Gottebenbildlichkeit*, 93.

such worth but we are of worth—we bear the alien dignity—because God loves us."[46] Although Thielicke, unsurprisingly, finds philosophical support in Pascal and, especially, Kierkegaard,[47] his espousal of man's alien dignity is firmly rooted in Luther's doctrine of justification "as the act through which God grants a man value in relationship to him."[48]

Being primarily concerned with the divine-human *relation*—and not with a purely transcendent God taken theistically in and for himself[49]—Thielicke not only concludes that talk of God is merely possible in such a way that one speaks of God's *relation* to man,[50] but also that "man cannot understand himself so long as he does not know God and understand himself *in relation to him*."[51] In addition to the names listed above, this personalistic view is well grounded in Augustine[52] and shared by, for example, Emil Brunner[53] and Joseph Ratzinger,[54] two theologians to whom Thielicke generally—in spite of their differing confessional affiliations—considers himself close. Thielicke and Brunner, by the way, besides theological affinity,[55]

---

46. *EvF III*, 57. See Luther's explanation of thesis 28 as rendered in Moltmann, *Crucified God*, 214: "For sinners are beautiful because they are loved; they are not loved because they are beautiful." See further *ThE II/1*, §1679; *ThE III*, §1866, 2082; *GldChr*, 129; *Tod*, 205; *Lebensangst*, 53; *Fragen*, 253; *Ernstfall*, 45, 60; *Nihilismus*, 131; and *Welt*, 109–10.

47. See *ThE I*, §459–61; §823–25; *MF&T*, 487; and *Mensch*, 151, 159. Gloege, "Personalismus," 26–29, highlights both as representatives of a "rational" (Pascal) and "categorial personalism" (Kierkegaard).

48. Althaus, *Luther*, 227. "Righteousness comes to a man from outside himself and is not a quality of his heart" (Althaus, *Luther*, 229). See the whole subsection: "Alien Righteousness," in Althaus, *Luther*, 227–33, for further unfolding.

49. *EvF I*, 15. See also *EvF I*, 172, 224–25, where he compliments the death-of-God theologians for bringing the specific concept of a "God of the theistic tradition" to an end. See *EvF II*, 99.

50. *EvF I*, 167–68. See *EvF I*, 15–16, 40, 49. Yet, likewise, "one cannot talk about God without the world being present in some way" (*EvF II*, 128).

51. *EvF I*, 15. Emphasis added. See *ThE II/1*, §1587; *Gebet*, 111; *K&K*, 16–17 [*B&E*, 15]; *Freiheit*, 25. See Althaus's rendering of Luther in *Luther*, 10: "We men can know our essential nature only when we view ourselves 'in our source, that is, in God.'" See also Bromiley, "Thielicke," 548.

52. See *Mensch*, 394; *Wayfarer*, 78 [106–7].

53. "Man is only truly human when he is in God. Then, and then only, is he truly 'himself'" (Brunner, *Dogmatics II*, 58). Barth agrees: "True man . . . exists not in his independence but in his union with the one true God" (Barth, *Introduction*, 202).

54. "Man only knows himself if he learns to understand himself in relation to God, and he only knows fellow man if he recognizes God's secret in him" (Ratzinger, *Jesus I*, 327).

55. For instance, Nordlander, relying on the work of Roessler, *Person und Glaube*, points out that Thielicke shows close affinity to the basic existential-ontological

also got along well on a personal level, the latter thereby prospering on the basis of the former, a fact testified to by a warm-hearted correspondence.[56]

It follows that "the question 'Who am I?' can be answered adequately and appropriately only when I speak of God as the author of my life history . . . so that one certainly must start not with speaking about him, but to him, must start with answering him."[57] The theological task thereby *follows* as a response to the divine address, which in turn determines one's existence.

What, therefore, according to Luther, makes one a theologian? Human nature! For every human being is already a theologian simply by virtue of man's capacity to ask himself the question "Who am I?"—which must be answered either in relation to God or without God, but always in the presence of God, i.e., *coram Deo*.[58] Accordingly, Thielicke, in truly Lutheran fashion, replies to the question of identity: "Who am I? . . . I am the man I am before God. My form of being is thus expressed in a relation. I am the one who is taken up into this relation."[59]

That is why, for Thielicke, man is "incurably religious,"[60] and why he considers atheism akin to faith.[61] What then, according to Luther, makes one a *Christian* theologian? Answer: the affirmative response to God's ad-

---

structure of Brunner. In Brunner, all forms of personal thinking show five essential features: personality, relation, actuality, verbal capacity [*Verbalität*], and dialectic. They present the formal terms by which Brunner describes the indicative [*Wirklichkeitsform*] of the divine-human relation. See Nordlander, *Gottebenbildlichkeit*, 30–31, 43, 190n17, 195–96n86. Gloege, "Personalismus," 32–33, highlights three basic elements of personal thinking: subjectivity (or: personality), relation, and actuality.

56. See, for example, Brunner's letters to Thielicke on September 25, 1947 (*NHT*); July 25, 1964 (*NHT*).

57. Bayer, *Luther's Theology*, 16.

58. Bayer, *Luther's Theology*, chapter 1, "Every Person is a Theologian: Luther's Understanding of Theology," esp. 15–17. See also Ebeling: "The fundamental situation of the *coram*-relationship is existence *coram Deo*" (Ebeling, *Luther*, 199).

59. *EvF I*, 189.

60. *EvF III*, 335. According to Pannenberg: "For the pioneers of modern secular culture in the seventeenth-century religion . . . was a part of human nature" (Pannenberg, *Christentum in einer säkularisierten Welt*, 26). Similarly, Martin Heidegger, just like one of his theological interpreters, Macquarrie, *Heidegger*, 60, is convinced that "no man is without religion." See Heidegger, "Martin Heidegger: Ein Porträt," (25:08).

61. One of the world's leading scientists, Francis S. Collins, intensifies Thielicke's point made in *Fragen*, 32–33, and calls atheism "a form of blind faith" as "it adopts a belief system that cannot be defended on the basis of pure reason" (Collins, *Language of God*, 165). For Thielicke's view, see *EvF I*, 233, 249; *EvF II*, 292; *Anfechtung*, 256; and *Mensch*, 48–49, 317. Within the context of discussing Bonhoeffer's notion of "religionless Christianity" in "EdR," 75, Thielicke reasserts that "I can never break out of my ontic God-relationship," but submits, however, that it remains questionable to define man's negative relationship to God as "religion," for then the term "religionlessness" [*Religionslosigkeit*] would become absurd.

dress and promise.⁶² This reply, which will be taken up again in the following subsection, already anticipates the concern of chapter 8, viz., the theological grounding of Thielicke's prioritizing of proclamation over theology. Like Luther, he is convinced that "the creed needs to come after its gospel preamble and must be related to it."⁶³ In any case, just as every human being is a theologian, every person putting his sole hope and trust in Christ is a *Christian* theologian, for "faith causes one to reflect: not only the professional theologian."⁶⁴

Part Two: The Lutheran Touchstone of *tentatio*—Encountering Christ Personally via Suffering

In light of this, Luther's answer to the second question of the nature of theology becomes clear. According to Bayer, Luther's famous three rules for studying theology, *oratio* (prayer), *meditatio* (meditation on the text), and *tentatio* (agonizing struggle) not only take "into account the historical nature of theological existence," but also give "due recognition to the fundamental importance of temptation (*tentatio*)."⁶⁵ Hence, in the eyes of the Reformer, the subject of theology naturally includes "the one who does theology"—as Thielicke himself makes clear.⁶⁶ Whereas Thielicke's application of Luther's *oratio* and *meditatio* will be returned to below, explicit focus must now shift to the outworking of the "touchstone"⁶⁷ of the tripartite rule in Thielicke's life, namely, *tentatio*.

Luther's favored German translation for this Latin term is *Anfechtung*, finding its English equivalent in a number of possibilities such as temptation, trial, test, contestation, or—as used by Bayer—agonizing struggle or spiritual attack.⁶⁸ As such, it is the deepest existential, practical expression of Luther's *theologia crucis*, playing itself out in the life of the followers

---

62. For Barth, likewise, "Faith is the *conditio sine qua non*, the indispensable condition of theological science. . . . Without this event, a man . . . cannot become and be a theologian" (Barth, *Introduction*, 100).

63. Bayer, *Luther's Theology*, 15. Again, Barth agrees: "Without the *precedence* of the creative Word, there can be not only no proper theology but, in fact, no evangelical theology at all!" (Barth, *Introduction*, 18).

64. Bayer, *Luther's Theology*, 16. See also Bayer, *Lutheran Way*, 83, 212.

65. Bayer, *Lutheran Way*, 34.

66. *EvF I*, 15n2.

67. Bayer, *Luther's Theology*, 35.

68. For "spiritual attack," see *Lutheran Way*, 96, 212. The Greek root for all these equivalents is πειρασμός (*peirasmos*). See Bayer, *Luther's Theology*, 20; and Vine, *Expository Dictionary*, 1129. For an analysis of Luther's usage of *Anfechtung*, see Rieger, *Luthers theologische Grundbegriffe*, 21–23.

of Christ.[69] Luther's "theology of the cross" thereby does not denote one theological aspect amongst others, but determines the very being, nature, essence, *Wesen* of Christian theology.[70] It is *the* theology of the cross, or it is nothing.[71] Therefore, what appears to be the most pressing point regarding the present Thielickean context is best outlined by Paul Althaus:

> Luther's statement "God is known only in suffering" . . . points to the deep correlation between the suffering Christ . . . and *the suffering man, who is the only man able to enter into community with God*. Luther's transition from the cross of Christ to the suffering of the Christian . . . means that the knowledge of God is not theoretical knowledge but rather a matter of man's entire existence. We cannot view the cross as an objective reality in Christ without at once knowing ourselves as crucified with Christ. The cross means: *God meets us* . . . *in the death of Christ, but only when we experience Christ's death as our own death*. . . . *Contemplating the death of Christ necessarily becomes a dying together with him*.[72]

In recalling Thielicke's very own experience, it looks like an existential realization of Althaus's words, almost serving as a blueprint for Thielicke: "That evening, I bid farewell to my life. I sat there gazing constantly at the crucifix opposite my bed."[73] Likewise: "The night I took the medicine I kind of set my life in order. I prayed. In my [hospital] room hung a crucifix. . . . In the face of the crucified, I thought of the forgiveness of sins, simply to straighten my life out."[74]

Thielicke, as a "suffering man," was enabled that night "to enter into community with God." In "contemplating the death of Christ," Thielicke "died together with him." By experiencing "Christ's death as [his] own death," he met God. Thus, Thielicke underwent precisely what Lutheran theologian, Werner Thiede, encapsulates as follows: "Anyone who meditates on the cross discovers his own death in it."[75] Via this personal encounter with the divine, Thielicke experienced that above-mentioned

---

69. See Althaus, *Luther*, 33. For Thielicke's systematic reflections on the cross, see chapter 7.

70. See Ebeling, "Todes Tod," 32; Wengert, "Peace, Peace," 190–91.

71. Helpful publications on Luther's *theologia crucis* are Althaus, *Luther*, chapter 5; Forde, *On Being a Theologian of the Cross*; and McGrath, *Luther's Theology of the Cross*.

72. Althaus, *Luther*, 28. Emphasis added. In passing, the emphasis "that the knowledge of God is not theoretical knowledge" but transforming, existential knowledge is also laid by Ratzinger, *Jesus I*, 232, as well as Brunner, *Divine-Human Encounter*, 139.

73. *Wayfarer*, 65 [89].

74. Krauss, 22–23.

75. Thiede, *Gekreuzigte[r] Sinn*, 195.

Lutheran transition from being merely "a theologian" to becoming "a *Christian* theologian." This comparison between Thielicke's actual experience and the delineation of Luther's thought by his fatherly friend and former supervisor, Althaus, is rounded off well by Thielicke reporting that he was allowed to take the crucifix in his hospital room home after his recovery and henceforth had it placed above his office desk.[76]

Luther's experiential understanding of the coming to and meaning of faith, however, deserves yet another look, thereby further revealing the closeness between Thielicke's concrete experience and his confessional patron's thoughts. Althaus states that "the cross makes itself available only to experience; more accurately: only to the suffering of God prepared by him for us through and with Christ."[77] Althaus herein emphasizes two components likewise strongly surfacing in Thielicke's decisive four-year episode of illness—namely, the already-mentioned *experience* and *passivity*. While Wengert qualifies the first, saying that "it is not any old experience that makes a theologian, but precisely the experience of having been stretched out on Christ's cross,"[78] Bayer connects both aspects, emphasizing Luther's understanding of faith as *vita passiva*: "Theology is practical in the sense that it is an experience. . . . In this experience, God is the active subject. He works at shaping and molding us. And we are the passive recipients who 'suffer,' who undergo his work. For that reason, Luther calls theology the receptive life (*vita passiva*)."[79]

Bayer's further elaboration on this elsewhere draws out the existential parallel to Thielicke even more clearly:

> The decisive aspect of the *vita passiva* is that it is linked to a specific experience: to an experience for which I am not the prime initiator, but which instead I suffer: "He becomes a theologian . . . in that he dies and delivers himself to hell, not in that he knows, reads, or speculates." The righteousness of faith is passive, . . . "we ourselves . . . do not do anything." . . . Faith is thus the work of God, . . . it can only be received and suffered. . . . We

---

76. See *Wayfarer*, 65 [89]; *Krauss*, 22–23.

77. Althaus, *Luther*, 28.

78. Wengert, "Peace, Peace," 196. Bayer, *Luther's Theology*, 21–22, 37, however, favors a wider interpretation. In his eyes, the term "does not advocate . . . some principle of pure experience, which could offer instead the principle of some indeterminate openness and openendedness. It is not experience as such that makes the theologian a theologian, but rather experiencing Holy Scripture."

79. Bayer, *Lutheran Way*, 96. See also the work of Reinhard Hütter, *Suffering Divine Things*, as well as Rieger, *Luthers theologische Grundbegriffe*, 23, who renders Luther's words: "Whoever experiences fear and vileness and in this process becomes a new man: just keep still and let God have his way; he will do it well without any human help."

can only receive it. We do nothing, but instead suffer its coming from another, who works in us: God.⁸⁰

Once more, the similarity to Thielicke's "specific experience" on Maundy Thursday, 1933, is striking. He was not the "prime initiator"; on the contrary, he "received and suffered passively." It is certainly no coincidence that later, during the war, Thielicke reminded his listeners in a bombed out *Stiftskirche* in Stuttgart that *"God is suffered. We have to suffer God."*⁸¹ He further "died"—as already shown above—a soulish death by giving himself up (or, in Bayer's words, by "delivering himself to hell"). His "way to faith was not destined by theoretical considerations," not by knowing, reading, or speculating, "but by the superior power of this event," thus, by what Luther terms *vita passiva*. Yet, while Bayer footnotes that here "Luther is clearly exaggerating, for he does not want to exclude knowing and reading,"⁸² Thielicke, at least in the literal formulation of his principle, seems to reject both in this process when he declares in 1943: "How little can one be taught by theological thoughts! God has to put you into the eschatological life in order to realize at last with thirty-four years and as an 'old theologian' that it is about life and not about thoughts."⁸³ At any rate, Wengert's emphasis, that according to the theology of the cross "the sufferer . . . driven by suffering, comes to the realization . . . of [his] true neediness,"⁸⁴ fully applies to Thielicke himself.

Finally, just as "the reformational turning point in Luther's own life and theology did not happen all at once . . . [but] instead . . . happened in the midst of 'meditating day and night,'"⁸⁵ so it can be said that Thielicke's existential turnaround must not be reduced to the final climactic events of Maundy Thursday (him sorting his life out) and Good Friday (his miraculous recovery). Rather, by recalling von Hildebrand's distinction outlined in chapter 2, part two, the whole four-year period of

---

80. Bayer, *Luther's Theology*, 42–43. See Ebeling, *Luther*, 200. For the passive process of justification, see Althaus, *Luther*, 228; and Adam, *Dogmengeschichte*, 155–56, who contrasts Luther's passive understanding of how perfection in Christ is to be achieved with Thomas à Kempis's active view.

81. *GldChr*, 140. Emphasis added. For this "crucifying form of knowledge," see Moltmann, *Crucified God*, 212; *Experiences*, 64.

82. Bayer, *Luther's Theology*, 42n34.

83. *K&K*, 34 [*B&E*, 30–31]. Obviously, at that moment, it does not appear to Thielicke that the latter might be an inseparable part of the former, i.e., Thielicke writes as though no (theological) thought were required to arrive at such a conclusion.

84. Wengert, "Peace, Peace," 205.

85. Bayer, *Luther's Theology*, 22.

Thielicke's "sickness-unto-death"—including going through severe theological crises[86] as well as fighting through his dissertation in the midst of great agony—came to be not only the period in which he acquired a fully conscious understanding of the phenomenon of death. In fact, in light of the *vita passiva*, it might now also be regarded as Thielicke being led to his personal encounter with Christ via passive suffering. It was "the way of suffering" through which he endured God's work in him. He was thus shaped and molded in order to arrive at the great soteriological insight, namely, "the one thing essential [which] *must convey itself to me in its essentiality*," as he himself states in one of his last books.[87]

Before this background, the already-quoted and profound analysis of his friend and former student, Röhricht, gains additional weight. It is worth recalling that, according to Röhricht, one of two ways into Thielicke "is the way of suffering which, physically and mentally, scarred him for life. He talked little about this . . . but his theology was also a *pathei mathos*, a learning in suffering. . . . This was experience."[88]

Thus, Althaus's Lutheran recognition that "all men, including the Christian, must endure before the miracle of faith can occur,"[89] indeed, that "the theology of the cross views man as one who has been *called to suffer*,"[90] could probably not be more applicable than in the case of Thielicke's coming to faith. Wengert fittingly summarizes the Lutheran understanding of suffering as "God's alien work, opposed to God's very nature," within which Thielicke's experience precisely must be located:

> The cross reveals that the senseless suffering of this sorry existence has a point in God, and that this point is penultimate—God's first, alien work that clears the way in us for God's proper work of salvation. Thus, the cross reveals human suffering for what it truly is—a curse—and thereby opens us up to receive God's own, proper work and blessing in the resurrection.[91]

This theological interpretation seems rather appropriate in the case of Thielicke, especially in recalling his own words that the time of sickness and almost certain death did not let him find faith at first (it was a "curse," and

---

86. See *Kanzel*, 63.

87. *Suche*, 150. Although I am not aware of such an assessment by Thielicke, he might even have been able to see death, just like Luther, as "a father's rod used to punish his child" (Luther cited in Althaus, *Luther*, 407).

88. Röhricht, "Thielicke," 27. The other way is "the way of friendship."

89. Althaus, *Luther*, 31.

90. Althaus, *Luther*, 27. Emphasis added.

91. Wengert, "Peace, Peace," 200.

yet, still "God's first, alien work that clear[ed] the way in [him]"). Rather, "the relation to faith came . . . when I was healed after a number of years . . . "[92] ("God's own proper work . . . in the resurrection"). In light of this, it might not come as a coincidence that Thielicke himself called his miraculous recovery on Good Friday, 1933, a "resurrection." For with Luther, Thielicke can say: "Hitherto, I have heard that Christ is my Savior . . . Now my experience bears this out. For I was often in the agony of death and in the bonds of the devil, but He rescued me and manifested Himself."[93]

It was the purpose of this chapter to show the truly Lutheran embeddedness of Thielicke's "sickness-unto-death." To unfold a first major systematic theological consequence of it—namely, that Thielicke, like Luther, considers theology to be "identical with faith"[94]—will be the aim of the next.

92. *Krauss*, 17.
93. Luther cited in Althaus, *Luther*, 62n59.
94. Bayer, *Lutheran Way*, 93.

Chapter 5

The Pneumatic Theologian

The Spirit's Regenerative Work
as Theological Starting Point

WHILE THE PREVIOUS CHAPTER revealed the Lutheran context of Thielicke's "sickness-unto-death," in this one, I aim to demonstrate that both his soteriology and pneumatology were significantly influenced by his "eschatological existence." Part one concentrates on the "that" and "how" of Thielicke's own salvific experience bearing immediate fruit in his soteriological thinking, with him, like Luther, regarding "theology [as being] identical with faith."[1] Part two highlights the specific *suffering* context of Thielicke's existence from which his understanding of the *pneuma* emerged. Since orthodox Christianity, in general—and Thielicke, in particular—regard man's salvation as brought about by the Spirit of God, it is only proper to deal with both aspects in one chapter.

Part One: Thielicke's Soteriological Starting Point —*fiducia* as Key to the Theological Task

Knowledge, Assent, Trust: The Three Components
of Faith and Thielicke's Ordering of the Same

The year was 1928.[2] Thielicke, the nineteen-year-old high-school graduate, had been asked by his professor what career he intended to take up. Thielicke replied that he wanted to become a theologian, but not a priest, because he did not consider himself a real Christian.[3] Five years later, on Good Friday,

---

1. Bayer, *Lutheran Way*, 93.
2. See *Krauss*, 16.
3. See *Wayfarer*, 35 [51–52]; *K&K*, 11–12 [*B&E*, 11–12]; and *Ernstfall*, 149–50.

1933, Thielicke miraculously recovered from a fatal illness that had plagued him for four years and which was originally brought upon him by a desire to distract himself from the horrible emptiness and dreadful lack of direction he was feeling at the time.[4]

Without this biographical guideline, extensively laid out in part I, it is difficult—if not impossible—to understand Thielicke's conception of faith as, first and foremost, trust. In addition to his later disposition—like Martin Luther and Philip Melanchthon—to regard faith in this way,[5] Thielicke's mother had already laid the grounds for such a personalistic understanding.[6] Yet, as his accounts make clear, it was only through his own crisis of sickness and near-death experience that he existentially began to embrace his mother's understanding of faith as trust—*fiducia*—for himself.[7]

Traditionally, the differentiation between *the act* of faith (*fides qua creditur*: faith by which it is believed) and *the contents* of faith (*fides quae creditur*: faith that is believed) has always been recognized within Christianity. Furthermore, at least since the posthumously published *Loci theologici* (1591) of Lutheran theologian Martin Chemnitz, who drew on his teacher, Philip Melanchthon,[8] in this respect, it became the rule for post-Reformation theology to dissect faith into the three components: *notitia* (a notion, conception, knowledge of some person or thing), *assensus* (assent, approbation), and *fiducia* (confidence, trust, reliance).[9]

Following Augustine's tripartition of man into intellect, emotion, and will, Augustus H. Strong, the great Reformed Baptist theologian, relates *notitia* to the first element, *assensus* to the second, and *fiducia* to the third.[10] What is problematic about this view, however, is the fact that emotion—as Schlatter stresses—neither is nor was meant to be an *explicit* part of Chemnitz's

---

4. See *Wayfarer*, 59–60 [82]; chapter 2, part two.

5. In the eyes of Luther, believing in Christ means "recogniz[ing] and grasp[ing] the love of God the Father in the history of Jesus Christ," faith hence being "an intellectual" as well as "an effective act of trusting" (Althaus, *Luther*, 230–31; see Bayer, *Luther's Theology*, 240–41). For Melanchthon, see Pannenberg, *Systematic Theology III*, 146.

6. *Wayfarer*, 16 [26].

7. Whilst Matthew Rueger, "Individualism in the Christology of Helmut Thielicke's Sermons," 82, is thus correct in stating that "for Thielicke, personal wrestling leads to the personal decision which defined faith," he does not take note of the existential grounding of that view.

8. Thanks to Timothy J. Wengert for pointing out that Chemnitz is standing here on the shoulders of Melanchthon.

9. See Pannenberg, *Systematic Theology III*, 146n152. See also Simpson, *Cassell's Latin Dictionary*, 19, 396–97, 731, 749.

10. Strong, *Systematic Theology*, 465.

trichotomy. Rather, feeling *constantly* accompanies man's inward processes,[11] and by relating emotional confidence to faith, one implicitly acknowledges that the act of faith goes beyond (not against!) mere logical assent, thereby determining the act of life. But there is no confidence without an act of the will. Rather, the latter is constitutive of the former.[12] Strong's separation of the "awakening of the sensibilities" from a "fundamental decision of the will" therefore seems—at least in the eyes of Schlatter—invalid.[13]

R. C. Sproul and his fellow-authors apparently hit the proverbial nail more centrally on the head when they refer the second component, *assensus*, not to emotional but to intellectual assent, namely, assent to the truth of the first constituent, *notitia* (referring to the data, *notae*).[14] According to Schlatter, data—or facts—can only determine man's personal life if he or she can form an idea about them in the mind. It is by this very act, i.e., by cognitively imagining the data (*notitia*), that one can fulfill the element of agreeing to the data (*assensus*). Assent, therefore, logically involves *notitia*, and both, in turn, are essential to the third aspect, *fiducia*—the personal, volitional trust dimension of faith by which redemption stands or falls.

This finds confirmation in Thielicke's telling exhortation to young students in his well-known book, *A Little Exercise for Young Theologians*. Here, he differentiates between a mere educational experience [*Bildungserlebnis*] and the crucial primal experience [*Urerlebnis*]. Whereas the first consists only of an intellectual understanding of theological data (*notitia*) and perhaps even rational assent (*assensus*),[15] the second experience is the decisive one, which the individual has to undergo existentially (*fiducia*).

Like Brunner,[16] he emphasizes that having the former does not mean that one is seized by the latter.[17] Herein lies, according to Thielicke, the great danger for the young student: for one can be aesthetically mesmerized by the beauty of Christian thought (that is, the student, in addition to recogniz-

---

11. C. S. Lewis seems to imply the same when he says of love that in this life it is always attended with emotion, "not because it is itself an emotion . . . but because our animal souls . . . have to respond to it in that way" (Lewis, *Grief Observed*, 87).

12. See Schlatter, *Dogma*, 568n74.

13. Walldorf, in his dissertation on Schlatter's philosophical concept, *Realistische Philosophie*, 228n11, points out that although Schlatter explicitly refers to three human functionalities (intellect, emotion, will), he implicitly prioritizes intellect and will whilst emphasizing emotion's passivity (or, to rephrase it for the current context, emotion's dependence on intellect and will).

14. Sproul et al., *Classical Apologetics*, 21.

15. See James 2:19.

16. See Brunner, *Divine-Human Encounter*, 139–40.

17. See *Kanzel*, 17–18, 30–31 [*Exercise*, 11, 29–30]. Thielicke does not mention, however, that the latter, in turn, cannot be had without the former.

ing the objective data—*notitia*—may even be drawn to it intellectually—*assensus*) without, however, having understood what it means to live willingly (concerning man's *voluntas*) within the power of the risen Lord.¹⁸ The same applies to the contested, doubting teacher who may present his dogmatic architecture without "living" in that very "house."¹⁹

Ratzinger provides a similar metaphor when he—based on the Apostle Peter's confession that Christ is the Messiah²⁰—differentiates the disciple's [*fiducia*-like] declaration from the mere and timeless opinion of the rest of the people who somehow have got to know Christ, and may have even studied him academically (*notitia, assensus*), but have not encountered him in his very own and yet wholly other (*fiducia*).²¹ This existentially new faith-dimension is finally brought out by Jesus when he alludes to the mere teacher of the law (*notitia, assensus*) who has now become a disciple (*fiducia*) in the kingdom of heaven (Matt 13:52). Jesus as well as Ratzinger both apparently refer to the distinction between *notitia/assensus* and *fiducia*, at the same time stressing the latter's key-function on the basis of the former.²²

Thus, in light of the post-Reformation tripartition of faith—as well as his admonishing differentiation between *Ur-* and *Bildungserlebnis*—Thielicke's early autobiographical statement that he "now knew what faith meant and everything that had previously *only intellectually* fascinated [him] about theology was swept away by completely new impulses,"²³ appears in a new and richer light. It also provides a first hint as to how Thielicke's pivotal experience is reflected in his theological thinking. The Christian message, according to him, "is music which must be played at sight—by interpreters who are seized by its notes, who let [the notes] pass through the medium of their faith experience, in this way reaching out to others with that which has reached themselves."²⁴

It is therefore significant to highlight Thielicke's basic understanding of faith as one of volitional trust, only viable within a personal relationship to another *person* (see chapter 6, part one). This conception of trust, just

---

18. *Kanzel*, 30 [*Exercise*, 29].

19. See *Anfechtung*, 56; *Suche*, 142. The metaphor is taken from Kierkegaard (see Rohde, *Kierkegaard*, 110).

20. Mark 8:27–30; Matt 16:13–20; Luke 9:18–21.

21. Ratzinger, *Jesus I*, 339. "Intellectual transliteration [of the Christian faith into a secular world] presupposes existential transliteration" (Ratzinger, *Licht der Welt*, 84–85).

22. See also 2 John 9 for the importance of the *notitia/assensus* aspect.

23. *K&K*, 15–16 [*B&E*, 14]. Emphasis added.

24. "Der Glaube kommt vom Lesen" (*NHT*).

like the coming into existence of such faith "by the superior power"[25] of the divine, perfectly corresponds to both his own conversion experience *and* his broader Lutheran frame of thinking. For Thielicke—as for Luther—faith is, first and foremost, an attitude of *Vertrauen*,[26] and the places where he refers to it as such are abundant.[27]

Thielicke's Idea of the Theological Task: Difficult *intra fidem*, Impossible *extra fidem*

Unsurprisingly, in light of Thielicke's own conviction regarding the "existential drive" at work in his theology,[28] as well as his Lutheran, personalistic understanding of man outlined above (see chapter 4), his own soteriological experience bears immediate fruit in his theological thinking: *fiducia* becomes the methodological key to the theological task. It especially comes to the fore in an exemplary way in *EvF II*, where he systematically engages with the doctrines of God and Christ.[29]

In the second part of chapter 28, within the context of surveying christological methods, Thielicke outlines the tragic historical choice between either an Alexandrian or Antiochene type of Christology. On the one hand, the Alexandrian type "proceeds deductively from the supernatural divine sonship of Christ," with Barth being a modern representative (the method "from above"). The Antiochene type, on the other hand, "proceeds inductively from the man Jesus of Nazareth," with Bultmann as a modern example (the christological approach "from below").[30]

Here it may be noted that Wolfhart Pannenberg, although theologically as far removed from Bultmann as the sun is from the earth, is another exemplar of the christological approach "from below." Pannenberg, in an essay delivered to different audiences on December 3, 1960, and November 24,

---

25. *Krauss*, 22–23.

26. "The attitude of trust" (*EvF III*, 16) and "faith given by the Spirit means the commitment of trust" (*EvF III*, 29). For Luther, see Rieger, *Luthers theologische Grundbegriffe*, 116.

27. See the following examples in *EvF II*, 35, 82, 186, 268, 270, 375; *EvF III*, 12, 29, 152, 258, 361–62, 417; *Anfechtung*, 201, 205–6; *Gespräche*, 19, 116, 154; *Woran*, 25, 59, 87, 97, 163, 183, 216, 244, 282, 285; *Bergpredigt*, 124; and *Mensch*, 493.

28. *Wayfarer*, 85 [115].

29. See also *Kanzel*, 26, 34–35 [*Exercise*, 24, 36–37], 58–59: without personal, existential trust, no "proper" theology.

30. *EvF II*, 265–66. "Faith never starts from above, not with . . . divine sonship or even predestination. . . . Faith rather always starts from below . . . where we are familiarized with the facts of this [Christ's] unique life" (*Abenteuer*, 187).

1961, strongly criticizes Barth's "proceeding from above to below, from God to man," in light of Feuerbach's gauntlet thrown at religion: "Theology has to learn that after Feuerbach, it can no longer mouth the word 'God' without offering any explanation . . . as if the meaning of this word were self-evident; that it cannot pursue theology 'from above,' as Barth says, if it does not want to fall into the hopeless and, what is more, self-inflicted isolation of a higher glossolalia, and lead the whole church into this blind alley."[31]

Barth, in a personal letter to Pannenberg on December 7, 1964, returned the favor, censuring the addressee's "way from the general to the specific . . . from below to above," calling it a "severe relapse into a mode of thinking . . . which substantially I have to regard as inappropriate and overcome and which I cannot join." Barth concludes his detailed letter expecting the surpassing of Pannenberg's as well as his own position by yet "an even more vigorous and cannier pursuit of the way from above to below, from the particular to the general, whilst I can regard yours [Pannenberg's] only as—pardon the harsh phrase!—reactionary."[32]

Thielicke, after briefly referring to the "mental acrobatics" needed in both types, asks why it is so difficult to make christological statements. It appears that he offers a twofold but closely interwoven reply to this question. Whereas the first strand highlights the existential impossibility of knowledge of God for man *extra fidem*, the second focuses (in truly Kierkegaardian fashion) on the difficulty faced by the decidedly Christian theologian due to the fact that God is *qualitatively different* from man.[33]

As to the latter, Thielicke stresses that even *intra fidem* "reflection cannot master the contradiction of the divine and the human in Christ, but faith must believe it all the same."[34] Drawing on an analogy from microphysics, Thielicke tries to show that the behaviour of the contents observed (namely, Christ in the case of theology) "is related to the process of observation." As "the schemes of thought impinge on this reality and alter it . . . the reality in itself cannot be the object of our knowledge and reflection."[35] Here Thielicke's personalistic thinking—as already outlined above—lurks in the background. Since, ontologically, man *is* his relation to God,[36] sinful man, after the fall, *post lapsum*, has qualitatively been disconnected, so to

---

31. Pannenberg, *Basic Questions II*, 189–90.

32. (*NHT*). The letter is labelled "Strictly confidential!" It is not clear how Thielicke got hold of it.

33. See esp. "WuV," 123, where Thielicke highlights the importance of the Dane's focus on the "wholly other."

34. *EvF II*, 267.

35. *EvF II*, 267–68.

36. "I can never break out of my ontic relationship to God" ("EdR," 75).

say, from the "wholly other." It follows that the contents (true God and true man) in themselves, i.e., ontologically, cannot be known due to man's preconceived schemes of thought.[37]

Thielicke further clarifies this in the third volume, stating that "God cannot be located in the sphere described by man's self-produced postulates, world-views, and ideologies. . . . We have to do with the Wholly Other . . . from whom man is separated *not only* by the diastasis of Creator and creature *but also* by the alienation of the fall."[38] Only when man "encounter[s] the reality of Christ in faith" is he met by this reality "in undivided form."[39] But as soon as the faithful believer "tries to get closer to the . . . christological reality in itself does it break up into heterogeneous aspects which form a contradiction on the logical level."[40]

Thielicke concludes that the difficulty of making christological statements therefore does not lie in faith, but in reflection on faith[41]—i.e., even in his redeemed status, man is not able to comprehend logically the "wholly other." This thinking leads Thielicke *inter alia* to the inference that the theologian "must give up trying to think together what [he] believes together,"[42] a separation between *notitia/assensus* and *fiducia* which is open to criticism (see chapter 9, part one).

The believer's difficulty in reflection segues straight into the first strand of Thielicke's reply. For if the component of personal faith is not a given for the one who studies theology, then it follows even more strongly that "the man who is unaffected by faith in Christ will not be able to understand christological reflection."[43] Hence, faith must be "the fixed point around which reflection circles." This fundamental conviction that "knowledge of Christ is imparted to us only as we achieve a personal relation of trust in

---

37. See *EvF II*, 267. "The will of God . . . cannot be clearly known and fixed because we are alienated from this will of God" (*Freedom*, 150).

38. *EvF III*, 12. Emphasis added. The second line also explicates the twofold strand of Thielicke's reply, introduced in the last paragraph. "Since I can know only what is analogous, but God is not analogous to me in virtue of *his own alien being* and *my alienation*, he is closed to me" (*EvF III*, 23). Emphasis added.

39. Brunner and Barth agree: "Only he can actually speak the Word who has himself been gripped by it and thereby has also been transformed" (Brunner, *Divine-Human Encounter*, 139). "The peg on which all theology hangs is acquaintance with the God of the Gospel" (Barth, *Introduction*, 32).

40. *EvF II*, 268.

41. *EvF II*, 268.

42. Ratzinger, without following Thielicke's inference, also underlines reason's difficult task of explicating the connection-of-being [*Seinsverbindung*] between God the Father and God the Son (Ratzinger, *Jesus I*, 368–69).

43. *EvF II*, 268.

him,"[44] that "faith precedes theology,"[45] reappears in all three volumes of his *Evangelical Faith* (especially the second) and in the first part of the second volume of his *Theological Ethics*.[46] Only in retrospect, *after* this personal relation of trust has been initiated, can the individual's implantation into the *Heilsgeschichte* be grasped by the believer: "I encounter the figure of Christ ... in a direct, pre-theoretical way."[47] Only later, after this encounter, is there a transition from immediacy to reflection.

This, of course, bears tremendous epistemological consequences for the *un*believer. Along Barthian lines, the individual *extra fidem* is not at all able to arrive at God's truth.[48] Neither nature nor history assist fallen man in being reconciled with the "wholly other." Thielicke grants the validity of this early phrase of Barth on the condition that it is not separated from Kierkegaard's original idea of the moment, since, apart from this connection, the "wholly other" takes on a Docetic thrust.[49] Thielicke believes that the Apostle Paul makes the same link to the "wholly other" in Romans 1, but not out of ontological interest. According to Thielicke, Paul instead refers to the *actuality* of an event of revelation and concealment. It is the *actuality* of man in the here and now, his rejection of God's revelation, which causes him no longer to understand or even hear God's Word. The problem therewith is not that God is not present in his creation, for he is. Rather, man *subjectively* refuses to accept him and therefore God's *objective* creative presence: "As man opposes truth, God withdraws from his revelation in creation. He delivers him up (*paredoken*, Romans 1:24, 26)."[50]

---

44. *EvF II*, 268. Note once more the epistemological similarity to Barth here: "Christian faith occurs in the *encounter* of the believer with him in whom he believes" (Barth, *Introduction*, 99).

45. *EvF II*, 306. The same applies, of course, to proclamation itself. See *Fragen*, 237; chapter 8.

46. See *EvF I*, 105; *EvF II*, 94, 237, 305, 317, 337, 349; *EvF III*, xix, 12, 30, 141; *ThE II/1*, §300-1.

47. *EvF II*, 304. See also *EvF II*, 318; *Gespräche*, 51; and *Abenteuer*, 230-31.

48. Baillie emphasizes Barth's "fundamental premise that no knowledge of God exists in the world save in the hearts of regenerate Christian believers" (Baillie, *Our Knowledge of God*, 17). In contrast, see Moreland and Craig, *Philosophical Foundations*, 275: "Before the new birth, the spirit is real and has certain abilities to be aware of God." Again, differing schemas of thought underlie each view, entailing disparate views regarding the epistemological consequences of total depravity.

49. *EvF II*, 45n53.

50. *EvF II*, 7. In *ThE I*, §1304-7, he refers to "the christological meaning of all knowledge of nature." See also *Weltanschauung*, 19: "[God's transparency in] nature is of no use whatsoever to man."

Thielicke's rationale is again negatively rooted in his criticism of the ontological schema of thought and positively in his relational and personalistic view of man. The crucial problem rests in the fact that man has surrendered himself to untruth (his key passage in this regard is Romans 1:18–32): "This folly, which has its basis in a flaw in existence, cannot . . . be overcome . . . by epistemological manipulation, but only by dealing with the flaw that causes the folly." For Thielicke, it is "decisive that epistemological folly has its basis in an existential state. The blindness of reason . . . rests on a blinding of existence itself."[51]

Thielicke subscribes to the conviction of Protestant Orthodoxy according to which reason is indissolubly interwoven with the fate of fallen human existence. Reason is not a timeless, a priori phenomenon, as per Kant, but rather a historically grounded and existential phenomenon. Reason depends on existence.[52] Depravity, however, affects the whole of existence,[53] and since man *coram Deo* ontologically *is* his relation to God, there is no ontological side-path on which to return. The all-decisive analogy between God and man, the necessary analogy between knower and known, has broken down.[54] Consequently, loss of analogy is also loss of the possibility of knowledge of God.[55] Bloesch is therefore right when he highlights Thielicke's doctrine of sin as that which "separates him from the Roman Catholic position on natural law,"[56] since, due to man's total depravity, there is no such thing as natural theology or a natural moral law.[57] Rather, "only

---

51. *EvF I*, 95. See also *EvF I*, 194; *Anfechtung*, 26.

52. See *ThE I*, §1938 ("I am my rationality"); *Anfechtung*, 28, 38, 55–56; *KuÖ*, 50–51. Whereas Thielicke is in agreement with Schlatter as to the historical grounding of reason, the latter comes to an essentially differing understanding as to its role within and outside faith.

53. See *EvF II*, 88; *ThE I*, §735, 2080, 2144; *ThE II/1*, §144a, 695, 709, 1130; *ThE III*, §2329; and *Sterben*, 35.

54. *EvF I*, 207.

55. *EvF II*, 19. See also *EvF II*, 76; *Gespräche*, 55.

56. Bloesch, "Thielicke's Ethics," 310.

57. In the final part of *ThE I*, Thielicke critically engages with the natural moral law. On sin making natural knowledge of the moral law impossible, see *ThE I*, §1902–3, §1914. See also *G&E*, 188; and *EvF I*, 211: "There is no such thing as natural theology. No analogy exists because of man's fate, i.e., sin." See further *EvF I*, 310, 355, 366. Nonetheless, he argues for the preservation of the natural law for the sake of the common good. See *ThE I*, §2128–37; Bromiley, "Thielicke," 551–52. However, he seems to display a similar state of mind to Barth regarding the idea of moral personality: despising (but nonetheless tolerating) it in a heuristic interim. See *EvF III*, 426. For a concise juxtaposition of Roman Catholic natural law with its orders of creation [*Schöpfungsordnungen*] and Reformed teaching with its emergency regulations [*Notverordnungen*], see *ThE III*, §2756–57. See also Ratzinger, *Jesus I*, 183.

in the retrospective glance of faith is the dialectic of the relation of the self and [general] revelation set up."[58]

Equally, *extra fidem*, nothing can be known about Christ from history. To be sure, the salvation event is part of earthly history and can be documented as such. Words and works of Christ are firmly grounded in history: "By nature, faith is not characterized by its element of consciousness, but by the *extra se* to which it relates, namely, the [earthly] history of Christ into which we are adopted."[59] Against Bultmann, who does not abandon historicity as such but rather regards it as irrelevant,[60] Thielicke holds that "he does not reckon with the fact that . . . the salvation history of the years AD 1–30 . . . that facticity outside me, has *ontic priority* over the later fulfilment of dying and rising again in me."[61]

Yet likewise—and this time, contra Pannenberg[62]—the true theme, viz., its character as salvation history, is not an object of ordinary historical study. Only faith can see Christ as the Lord.[63] Thielicke thus places himself—along with other thinkers, such as his fatherly friend Paul Althaus[64] or his Lutheran contemporary, Helmut Gollwitzer[65]—under the umbrella

---

58. *EvF II*, 25. See the whole subsection, "Natural theology only in retrospect of faith," in *EvF II*, 21–27, esp. 25–26. Thielicke critically engages with Althaus's doctrine of primitive revelation in particular, but also accuses Brunner and Schlatter of following this concept along different lines. See also *Mensch*, 358; *Bilderbuch*, 7; and *EvF III*, 433: "We do not move from history to God (as all natural theology does); we move from God to history."

59. *EvF I*, 63. By this adoption, Thielicke means the "implantation into the continuity of the salvation event."

60. See *EvF I*, 57.

61. *EvF I*, 59. Emphasis added.

62. Thielicke explicitly opposes Pannenberg in *EvF III*, xxvi–xxvii. See Pannenberg, *Basic Questions I*, chapter 2, esp. 15–16: "[The historical] presupposition . . . must be defended today . . . on two sides: . . . against Bultmann and Gogarten's existential theology . . . [and] against the thesis, developed by Martin Kähler in the tradition of redemptive history, that the real content of faith is suprahistorical. . . . The historical character of redemptive event must therefore be asserted today . . . with the methodological principles of critical-historical investigation." For two brief, secondary summaries of Pannenberg's program in this regard, see Zahrnt, *Sache*, 316–17, 321; Grenz and Olson, *Twentieth-Century Theology*, 189.

63. See *EvF I*, 209–10; *EvF II*, 280.

64. Althaus and Pannenberg entered into a constructive and insightful dialogue over this issue. See Pannenberg, *Basic Questions II*, chapter 2, "Insight and Faith."

65. See Marquardt, "Gollwitzer," 559: "God's existence discloses itself only to the confession of faith." For a criticism of Gollwitzer's (and thus implicitly Thielicke's) theocentrism, see Pannenberg, *Basic Questions II*, 203–7.

of the so-called *heilsgeschichtliche Theologie*, established by Martin Kähler (1835–1912).⁶⁶

Thielicke's Appreciation for Kähler's *Heilsgeschichte*: "Love at Second Sight"

Intriguingly, Thielicke's passionate support for Kähler's perception of the impossibility of subscribing to historicity apart from faith (Kähler's *Übergeschichte*⁶⁷) was once more evidently reinforced by his own life-experience. Thielicke reports how his final decision to put his main academic focus not on philosophy but on theology was *decisively* impacted by a fascination with his theological teachers in Greifswald during his first semester and a half in 1928: "There I realized how crucial, especially for a young man, the [teacher's] person is. A truth *in abstracto* does not hit home, but a truth incarnated in a person comes vividly and concretely up to one."⁶⁸

Elsewhere, in the very same vein, he states that "all the really vital questions that touch the depths of existence enter man's consciousness *through the medium of persons* in whom these questions are, as it were, incarnated."⁶⁹ The following subsection will focus in more detail on Thielicke's personalistic understanding of truth. For now, the question arises of where the existential connection to Thielicke's subscription to Martin Kähler's concept of salvation history is to be found.

The answer resides precisely with his favorite teacher of his youth, the New Testament scholar Julius Schniewind. Schniewind was born in Elberfeld—the neighboring town of Thielicke's own birthplace, Barmen—in 1883. Thielicke dedicates several pages in his autobiography to this "outstanding figure among our teachers": "He was for me *the* great religious teacher."⁷⁰ Schniewind, intriguingly, was one of Kähler's most important students and subsequently active in line with Kähler's spirit,⁷¹ thus furthering the legacy of his deeply beloved teacher.⁷² Consequently (and

---

66. However, as Pannenberg notes, "the loss of history . . . had not yet happened in Kähler," but "a curious process" was initiated with Kähler's problematic distinction between 'historical fact' and 'revelatory value'" (Pannenberg, *Basic Questions I*, 85–86).

67. See Kantzenbach, *Programme der Theologie*, 125.

68. *Krauss*, 17. See *Freiheit*, 13.

69. *Trouble*, 15. Emphasis added.

70. *Wayfarer*, 56 [77]. For Thielicke's overall "portrayal of this much-loved teacher," see *Wayfarer*, 55–59 [76–81].

71. See Lohse, "Martin Kähler," 23.

72. See Kraus, "Julius Schniewind," 220.

most likely via the existential link of his favorite mentor, Schniewind), Thielicke became not only familiar but also, by all accounts, most impressed with Kähler's concept of *Heilsgeschichte*.[73]

However, since Thielicke did not yet consider himself to be a committed Christian at the time of his studies under Schniewind—and, therefore, probably did not have much use for statements like "every theological effort has to be enclosed within the act of faith"[74]—it must be assumed that his appreciation for Kähler's construct came only after his own existential turnaround. In other words: "the revelatory side of history,"[75] perceptible only by saving *fiducia*-faith, dawned upon Thielicke retrospectively. In his own phraseology, he learned to "recite" the doctrinal statement prior to perceiving its miraculous dimension existentially. Already anticipating the next subsection, the context-of-being (*Seinszusammenhang*, the ontological *fiducia*-aspect) and the context-of-understanding (*Erkenntniszusammenhang*, the epistemological *notitia/assensus*-aspect) followed different sequences.[76]

Finally, as to the existential embedment of his personalistic/relational mode of thought, the empirical data available suggests on balance that Thielicke was *subsequently confirmed* but not *initially grounded* by his early life circumstances in his philosophical inclination as a young man. By travelling back once more to Thielicke's first theological semester in Greifswald, a very early manuscript, dating from November 20, 1928, titled, "How one can explain and imagine Christianity's paradoxes," intriguingly still seems to favor the *analogia entis* mode of thinking. In this manuscript, he uses the curved mirror [*Hohlspiegel*] for a theological metaphor:

> The attributes of the concave mirror and the fact of a small [but] real part of the object reflecting itself [in the curved mirror] safeguard the expert in assuming that the rest of the object's picture is not pointless (or even non-existent) but only formally distorted and thus paradoxical. [Next to this, in the margin, Thielicke has added in handwriting: "That is faith."] Thanks to the mirror's curious style, it cannot reflect the real object.[77]

73. See *Kanzel*, 25–26 [*Exercise*, 22–24]; *EvF II*, chapter XX (esp. 290, 302), 337; *EvF III*, 196; *Offenbarung*, 161–62; and *KuÖ*, 40n13.

74. This is Thielicke's phrase within the context of unfolding his own indebtedness to Kähler in *Kanzel*, 26.

75. Althaus as rendered in Bloesch, *Essentials of Evangelical Theology II*, 268. See also *Offenbarung*, 162.

76. See *Gespräche*, 106; *EvF I*, 196: "I can understand the truth of God only through the Holy Spirit . . . This analogy, however, is an analogy of being before it is one of understanding."

77. "Wie man sich das Paradoxe im Christentum erklären und vorstellen kann" (*NHT*).

The curved mirror obviously stands for fallen humankind, with the descriptive adjective "curved" in the English translation (the German original, *Hohl-*, only implies the bent shape) finding itself again in Thielicke's later and more theologically matured description of man *post lapsum*, i.e., man's *incurvitas in se* (see chapter 5, part two). Although in later years Thielicke speaks of the *total* loss of analogy between God and man,[78] here he still grants at least a minimal—but nevertheless real—part of divine reality ontologically reflecting itself in man, despite his fallenness.

However, the theological influence of Luther and the philosophical impact of Kant and Kierkegaard (Kant influencing him especially through his first and philosophical dissertation written during his time of sickness),[79] indicate that he was already personalistically grounded before his existential turnaround over Easter 1933. Regarding Kierkegaard Thielicke's exclusive stress on the primacy of God's revelation and regeneration in Christ is a Lutheran characteristic he shares with the Reformed Barth as early as in his second—and this time, theological—dissertation,[80] likewise written during his illness. Thielicke calls this solely theocentric starting point "non-Cartesian" (or "Theology B"), whereas any theology starting from man's religious consciousness or self-understanding is anthropocentric, "Cartesian" (or "Theology A").[81] The distinction itself does not originate with Thielicke but can be traced—via Barth and Schlatter[82]—back to Kierkegaard.[83]

By all means, and quite in the *heilsgeschichtliche* spirit of Kähler, according to Thielicke, the Christian truth as such is historically grounded and existent *extra me*, but it is not an objectifiable truth recognizable *extra fidem*.[84] God's truth is epistemologically veiled *extra fidem* and becomes

---

78. See *EvF II*, 19, 76; *EvF III*, 312.

79. See *Wayfarer*, 61 [84]; Röhricht, "Thielicke," 21. Nordlander, *Gottebenbildlichkeit*, 196n87, considers Kant and Kierkegaard as the two philosophers influencing Thielicke the most, with the Dane also being held in the highest regard by Brunner. See Zahrnt, *Sache*, 76.

80. See *G&E*, 30–31, 34.

81. The first part of *EvF I* is committed to outlining and contrasting both theological approaches. For Thielicke, the constructs of Spener (who is "the first theologian in the German Church to try to do justice to subjectivity and individuality in the sphere of theological conviction"), Lessing, Schleiermacher, Bultmann (whose theology is "the climax of the Cartesian inquiry"), and Tillich represent historical examples of the Cartesian approach. See *EvF I*, 40–49.

82. See Karl Barth, *Kirchliche Dogmatik I/1*, §6/3, esp. 223–39; and Schlatter, *Philosophische Arbeit*.

83. See *EvF II*, 40, 80. Higginson, "Thielicke," 180, is therefore incorrect in granting Thielicke originality in this respect.

84. See *EvF II*, 308; *Offenbarung*, 161–62.

only valid and effective *intra fidem*, by *being existentially seized* (note the "Lutheran passive voice"[85]) by the *fiducia*-aspect of faith. This monergistic emphasis leads to the second part of this chapter, namely, Thielicke's focus on the work of the Holy Spirit in light of his "eschatological existence."

Part Two: Thielicke's Pneumatological Focus —"Being in the Truth"

Thielicke's Pneumatological Focus: Theologically Predisposed and Existentially Reinforced

Sometimes theologians quip that for a long time in church history, the Holy Spirit took on the role of Cinderella within the Trinity. While the two sisters went to the theological ball, the Holy Spirit had to stay at home.[86] This *bon mot* does not apply to Thielicke.[87] To the contrary, according to Speier, Thielicke's pneumatology is "possibly . . . the truly innovative [feature] of his theology," principally differentiating him from Karl Barth.[88] Without putting too much weight on Speier's questionable distinction between Barth and Thielicke in this regard,[89] the latter not only tries to develop his three volumes of *The Evangelical Faith* pneumatologically but also criticizes some contemporaries for their decisive lack of the *pneuma* in their theological constructs.

As to his pneumatological focus, Thielicke's intention is "to pursue every theological discussion *sub specie* of the third article."[90] As to his criticism

---

85. "Faith is not the power which makes him present; it is the point at which his presence breaks through" (*EvF II*, 40). See also chapter 4.

86. See McGrath, *Christian Theology*, s.v. "Holy Spirit." For a similar evaluation, see Zahrnt, *Sache*, 84.

87. See, for example, his rhetorical question in *Kanzel*, 47: "Should it not chasten us that and why the doctrine of the Holy Spirit leads such a shadowy existence nowadays . . . ? Has this pneumatic vitamin deficiency of our theology not been the very reason for the coming into existence of the scurvy of an enthusiastic Pentecostalism which separates the Holy Spirit from the Word?" N. T. Wright raises a similar (albeit more soberly put) question with regard to Spirit-baptism in *Surprised by Hope*, 283–84.

88. Speier, *Initiator*, 242–43.

89. See, for example, Barth, *Introduction*, 55: "It is clear that evangelical theology itself can only be pneumatic, spiritual theology." See also Barth, *Introduction*, 58: "*Veni creator Spiritus!* . . . Even the best theology cannot be anything more or better than this petition made in the form of resolute work." Zahrnt, *Sache*, 71, highlights Barth's "sole reliance on the Holy Spirit," too, thus relativizing Speier's assessment.

90. *EvF II*, xiii. Without, however (and contrary to Bromiley's phraseology in "Thielicke," 555), offering a "theology of the Spirit," since, in Thielicke's eyes, it is "a

of some contemporaries, for Thielicke, the antithetical theologies of Bultmann and Pannenberg both serve as a case in point. For "the final secret" of Bultmann's theology is "that he has no doctrine of the Holy Spirit," whereas Pannenberg's system equally "falls short pneumatologically."[91] In contrast, it is Thielicke's "own task to understand the Spirit as the uncontrollable power of presentation or making present."[92]

Right at the outset, the existential must once more be seen as the beating heart of Thielicke's pneumatological focus. Two key events are to be noted—the first already outlined earlier and the second to be returned to later—so that a brief recapitulation and anticipation, respectively, suffices.

First, without Thielicke's "sickness-unto-death" and his subsequent coming to a personal saving faith (*fiducia*), it is hardly thinkable that he would have arrived at placing such a strong emphasis on the Holy Spirit. As his own words testify, before being healed, he was "only intellectually" fascinated by theology; that is, he recognized and possibly understood the data (*notitia*) and may have given assent to it (*assensus*). However, the third and most crucial aspect of trusting, *fiducia*, for Reformed and Lutheran alike—namely, the monergistic work of God the Holy Spirit—had not yet affected him.[93] For Thielicke this pneumatic dimension was clearly "activated" by his four years of sickness, culminating in "the superior power of this event,"[94] when he settled his affairs beneath the crucifix on Maundy Thursday, 1933, combined with his subsequent recovery from the next morning onwards.

The other crucial experience, to be turned to in detail in chapter 8, was his enforced acceptance of a pastorate after being dismissed by the Nazis. It was here that he practically (and at first, unwillingly) learned about the Spirit, about "God in action,"[95] via the kerygma. It is because of this specific time in his life that Thielicke began to acknowledge the primacy of the Spirit's work

---

serious mistake" to link any nominative theology with a genitive. See *EvF III*, xxiii. For his criticism of a theology of genitives, see *EvF III*, xvi.

91. *EvF I*, 60 (Bultmann); *EvF III*, xxvii (Pannenberg). Thielicke criticizes Pannenberg in spite of the latter's central attempt to develop a new pneumatology. See Grenz and Olson, *Twentieth-Century Theology*, 193–95.

92. *EvF III*, xxvii.

93. For a prominent example on the Reformed side see, Barth, *Introduction*, 73; but not Brunner, who, in the words of Olson, *God in Dispute*, 221, "radically rejected monergism" and whose theology was closer to Arminianism. See also Olson, *God in Dispute*, 230. Thus, whereas the human heart must be opened by the power of the Holy Spirit (Brunner, *Dogmatics II*, 20; *Divine-Human Encounter*, 16), Brunner does not regard God to be the sole active agent in salvation. For the Lutheran emphasis on monergism, see chapter 4.

94. *Krauss*, 22–23.

95. *EvF I*, 180.

in proclamation, it being the movement of the Word to man in which the Creator Spirit does the real work.[96] Theology is but "a reaction of the existence already smitten by this Word,"[97] i.e., a secondary human *fiducia*-based response initiated by divine, pneumatic, kerygmatic action.

This experiential anchorage reinforced Thielicke's theological predisposition as expressed in his negative anthropology. His pessimistic view of the human and cosmic status *post lapsum*, with the total loss of analogy (due to total depravity) between God and man,[98] leads him to an exclusive emphasis on the pneuma's work in the believer. Thielicke's pneumatology hereby strongly affects his anthropology. Langsam points out that Thielicke's view of the new, spiritually regenerated man along with his capabilities to change this world is—in contrast to his pessimistic view of man *extra fidem*—very optimistic.[99]

Apart from God's pneumatic action, however, there is no given point of contact in the reality of fallen man.[100] Revelation solely unfolds via the Spirit's testimony, not via human (rational) insight.[101] As Thielicke regards the epistemological to be grounded in the existential, the former can only function with regard *to* God if the latter is *in* God: "The ontic state of man shatters his noetic possibilities. His knowledge, and with it his relation to the truth, can be corrected only as his being is corrected."[102]

That is why he repeatedly talks about "being in the truth," since theological reflection on the truth is tied to this existential pre-condition.[103] Thielicke originally even wanted to call his systematic work "Being in Truth," according to John 18:37, but due to the title's strong echo of Heidegger's philosophical catchphrase ("being"), he refrained from it.[104] Conversely,

---

96. See *EvF I*, 213.

97. *EvF I*, 212. For the parallel to Luther, see Bayer, *Luther's Theology*, 15–17.

98. See *EvF I*, 211; *EvF II*, 19; *EvF III*, 312; and Langsam, *Konkretion*, 21–22.

99. Langsam, *Konkretion*, 235. Speier, *Initiator*, 217, confirms Langsam's observation.

100. See *EvF I*, 144; *Anfechtung*, 49.

101. *EvF III*, 337.

102. *EvF I*, 194. As to Thielicke's "theological epistemology" being grounded in a "new creation by the Spirit," see *EvF I*, chapter XI.

103. *EvF I*, 196. See *EvF I*, 16, 200, 202, 306; *Offenbarung*, 167; and "WuV," 121. He also believes that this is what Anselm had in mind at the beginning of his *Proslogion* (*credo ut intelligam*): understanding only follows faith.

104. See *EvF I*, 14. Although, given Thielicke's strong pneumatological focus, and Ratzinger calling the Gospel of John the "pneumatic gospel" (*Jesus I*, 277), such a title would certainly have been apt. For the Spirit's role in the Gospel of John, see Emery, *Trinity*, 40–43.

epistemological blinding or folly has its basis in man's existential state *extra fidem*, in an act of rebellion.[105]

Thielicke's "Epistemological Aporia" Pneumatically Solved: The Spirit's Call into the Trinitarian Circle

Yet, Thielicke regarding personal faith (*fiducia*) as the controlling factor for studying theology, seeing the theological task as solely based on the *intra fidem*, leads his thinking into a hermeneutical circle which he recognizes and accepts. More accurately, he does not consider it to be a problem due to his pneumatological anchorage: "Entry into this circle of theological knowing is not via an epistemologically comprehensible way . . . but rests on an act of calling. The doctrine of the Holy Spirit has its doctrinal place in the attempt to make this act of calling predicable."[106]

For Thielicke, the epistemological circle is not only "indissoluble," calling this the "epistemological aporia,"[107] but "eventually rests on the doctrine of the Holy Spirit," i.e., "the miracle of divine self-disclosure,"[108] as certainly as the act of faith is in itself revelatory since it is induced by God's Spirit.[109] He recurrently illustrates this by referring to the stained glass windows of a cathedral, for such windows remain dark and dull when looked upon from the outside of the building.[110] As soon as one enters the sanctuary, however, they begin to glow. Only then do the paintings on the windows start to make sense in all their beauty. Correspondingly, whoever is "seized by the Spirit of Pentecost" will be moved into the sanctuary,[111] where the windows shine.[112] Thielicke considers Jesus's encounter with the two disciples on their way to Emmaus as paradigmatic in this regard, as a "prelude" to Pentecost itself: "This act of opening, this escape from the circle of our human confinement is what the Bible conceives of as the act of the Holy Spirit."[113] For Thielicke,

---

105. See *EvF I*, 95.
106. *Anfechtung*, 5. See *Gespräche*, 56; "WuV," 121.
107. "WuV," 124.
108. "WuV," 124.
109. *ThE I*, §1071–72.
110. See *EvF I*, 370; *Anfechtung*, 115; *Abenteuer*, 101; *Ernstfall*, 110; *Lebensangst*, 221–22; *Gebet*, 161–62; *Reden*, 250; and *Bilderbuch*, 33.
111. *Abenteuer*, 101.
112. *Ernstfall*, 110.
113. *Abenteuer*, 103. See also *Anfechtung*, 4–5, 11.

God's Spirit is thus the "Spirit of actualization" who "performs the miracle of making the blind see."[114]

This specific understanding can once more be traced back to Thielicke's personalism. As God is a tri-personal being, he can never be reduced to an object, a fact that sets theology apart from all other sciences.[115] Moreover, as every subject area requires its very own approach, it follows that—given theology's necessarily *relational* methodology, as it rests on the subject of God's tri-personal (and hence relational) being—man can only know something of God if he becomes a relational partner in the divine self-knowledge.[116] Referring to Kierkegaard's notion of subjectivity, Thielicke can even go so far as to state that truth does not rest in its object, but in the relation to this object: "It does not matter if something is objectively true, but whether I relate truthfully . . . to it, whether I am in the truth. Christianly speaking, this relation is faith."[117]

Thielicke's understanding of the Trinity must therefore also be seen through his personalistic mode of thinking:

> The communion of love between the three persons is . . . understood as . . . a being from and being to the other. . . . God's being is self-giving. . . . The I of Christ . . . lives by its basis, i.e., the Father. Hence, it cannot be defined as self-grounded entelechy in Aristotle's sense. Its basis is a relation . . . Christ does not seek his own will but the will of the Father. . . . This is his primal uniqueness which distinguishes him from every human creature and in face of which every human I is seen to be an alienation, a fall from its own origin.[118]

The similarity to Ratzinger at this stage is striking. A little later, within the same context, Thielicke confesses his indebtedness to the Bavarian Pope-to-be regarding a reference to Augustine. Moreover, when it comes to personalistic implications drawn from the Trinity, the Lutheran theologian and the Roman Catholic theologian likewise agree.

For Ratzinger, sonship [*Sohnsein*] equals relatedness [*Bezogensein*]. It is a relational term with Jesus being "wholly relational," being nothing but relation to the father in his whole being. Jesus's [human] prayer is thus

---

114. *Ernstfall*, 111.

115. See Barth, *Introduction*, 16, 90–92. See also Schlatter, lucidly explicating theology's "academic uniqueness" in his essay, "Atheistic Methods in Theology," in Neuer, *Schlatter: A Biography*, Appendix D.

116. Thielicke makes this specifically clear in *Anfechtung*, 11.

117. *Offenbarung*, 167.

118. *EvF II*, 165–66.

"the dialogue of love within God himself—the dialogue which *is* God."[119] Consequently, sonship means the giving up of one's own autonomy that cloisters itself away in itself [*die sich in sich selbst verschliesst*].[120] Thielicke similarly speaks of the I as a relational term, a fact revealed by the meaning of childship [*Kindschaft*].[121]

Furthermore, whereas Thielicke—like Brunner and Ratzinger, albeit in different wording—repeatedly speaks of man's *incurvitas in se* after the fall (Brunner uses *cor incurvatum in se*), that is, man being curved in upon himself due to the sinful loss of analogy between God and man,[122] C. S. Lewis equally does not mince his words in this matter. Lewis, who in *Out of the Silent Planet* speaks of fallen man as a "bent creature," calls this very condition "hell."[123] Like his Lutheran and Roman Catholic contemporaries,[124] the Anglican lay theologian draws epistemological conclusions as to this human state of mind after the fall[125] but also has the eternal state of the post-mortem soul in mind, for "good beats upon the damned incessantly as sound waves beat on the ears of the deaf, but they cannot receive it."[126]

The *premortal status post lapsum*, man's *incurvitas in se*, his loss of immediacy, however, can only be undone by Christ.[127] More precisely, given Thielicke's (and Brunner's) relational understanding of the Godhead, it can

---

119. Ratzinger is truly Augustinian in this regard: love constitutes the relational factor within the Trinity. The Augustinian-Anselmian interpretation of defining the triune being as inner-trinitarian relations was dogmatized by the Council of Florence (1439–1445). See Horn, "Augustinus," 79–80; Adam, *Dogmengeschichte*, 166–67.

120. See Ratzinger, *Jesus I*, 394–95, 400.

121. See *Offenbarung*, 153.

122. See *EvF II*, 19, 76; *EvF III*, 312; and Rieger, *Luthers theologische Grundbegriffe*, 43.

123. "Every state of mind, left to itself, every shutting up of the creature within the dungeon of its own mind—is, in the end, Hell" (Lewis, *Great Divorce*, 63, 113). See Thielicke's similar definition of hell as "utmost loneliness" in *Woran*, 157.

124. According to Ratzinger, "our will must become the Son's will. Only then we can see" (Ratzinger, *Jesus I*, 394). Thielicke quite agrees: "God's Spirit takes care that God's will . . . becomes our will" (Thielicke, *Abenteuer*, 104).

125. However, Thielicke's view regarding the degree of sin's epistemological impact significantly differs from Lewis and Ratzinger. See the discussion in part one of this chapter.

126. Lewis, *Great Divorce*, 113. He further illustrates this damned state of mind in a literary way through the character of the dwarfs in the final Narniad (Lewis, *Last Battle*, 135–40, esp. 140). If applied to the *premortal* life, one might find exemplary and pitiful expression of such a state of mind in any denial of personal guilt and lack of remorse on the part of former SS-henchmen after 1945, who went berserk in the Nazi concentration and extermination camps.

127. See *ThE I*, §865.

only be undone by a pneumatic calling, by being spiritually drawn into God's self-knowledge.[128] This, in turn, can only come to pass via man giving up on himself, by "the giving up of one's own autonomy" (Ratzinger), viz., by *spiritual martyrdom*, which might be circumscribed as the *volitional* dying of the proud, autonomous self,[129] leading straight back to Luther's *theologia crucis* touched upon above: "Only when I die and rise again with Christ can I appropriate noetically his death and resurrection."[130]

The pneumatic and anthropic dimensions of the salvific event "mysteriously" (as Thielicke would label it) intersect at this point. According to Thielicke, the basic and primary "trinitarian reality," i.e., God's pure relationality, monergistically calls and adopts the human "outsider *extra fidem*" into their circle: "This calling . . . is [a humanly] inaccessible experience . . . ";[131] it is faith "won by the power of the One who encounters us";[132] a theological conviction strongly resonating with his very own experience as Thielicke's "way to faith [on that night he took the medicine] was . . . destined . . . by the *superior power* of this event."[133]

Thus, only God himself can again set up the broken analogy and undo the rebellious act against the divine,[134] leading to the fact that knowledge of God is always christological and pneumatic—never anthropic:

> I have the world only as God gives it to me and lets me see it. I have God only insofar as he condescends to me . . . and gives me the light in which I can see him. Thus the relation between God and the world can be described only in trinitarian terms.

128. See *Anfechtung*, 11. See *EvF I*, 196: "I can understand the truth of God only through the Holy Spirit." For Brunner, see *Divine-Human Encounter*, 16: "The human heart must be opened in faith through the power of God's own Spirit if that on which everything depends is to come to pass: the knowing of God."

129. This is to be differentiated from the state of "suffering" which can be (and usually is) an aspect of martyrdom without necessarily having to be so. As to the idea of "spiritual" or "soulish suffering," see Bonhoeffer, *Widerstand*, 125–26, who criticizes this notion, *inter alia* emphasizing that the *physical* dimension must be a crucial part of suffering in order to be real. One cannot help but wonder what "spiritual sufferers" like C. S. Lewis or Friedrich von Bodelschwingh would have replied contra Bonhoeffer, given the loss of their deeply beloved spouse and four children, respectively. Earlier on, however, Bonhoeffer seems to concede the reality of spiritual suffering (Bonhoeffer, *Widerstand*, 101–2).

130. *EvF II*, 437. For Thielicke's attraction to the idea of martyrdom—being one of the reasons why he chose to study theology—see his confession in *Krauss*, 16, also cited in chapter 2, part two.

131. "WuV," 122.

132. *EvF I*, 211.

133. *Krauss*, 22–23. Emphasis added.

134. See *EvF II*, 325; *Gespräche*, 56; and "WuV," 121.

> God the Creator establishes the world. God the Redeemer condescends to the world and comes into it in the incarnation. *God the Holy Spirit provides the conditions and means by which God may be known.*[135]

Correspondingly, Thielicke can state that "our process of understanding in relation to the gospel has a highly dialectical structure. For we learn who he [Christ] is precisely from his words and works, from what happens to us through him."[136] Thus, following Calvin's lead, Thielicke's Christology is conceived in functional terms: who Jesus is follows from his functions for man as prophet, priest, and king, the *munus triplex Christi*.[137] Thielicke's position, therefore, finds cogent expression in Melanchthon's christological thesis of 1521 to which he continually refers throughout his works: to know Christ is to know his benefits (*beneficia*),[138] polemically adding the question of how else he should be known.[139] In other words, Christ is known by his existential effects upon the believer, not according to dogmatic knowledge. Once more, Thielicke's own conversion experience shines through.

Yet, here it seems that Thielicke succumbs to a narrowing down of faith to the subjective component of *fiducia*, much to the detriment of the objective *notitia* and intellectual *assensus*. He justifies this by a strong reliance on the pneumatic dimension of the kerygma theology. But why should the Holy Spirit not be able to use *notitia*, moving through metaphysical reflection and intellectual testing?[140] Why can the Spirit not use the tenets of natural theology, for example, in drawing the fallen sinner to the unfathomable love of the trinitarian God?[141]

---

135. *EvF I*, 367. Emphasis added. The "Spirit is imparted to me to give me a share in God's analogy" (*EvF I*, 195).

136. *EvF II*, 301. In this "christological epistemology," Thielicke is thoroughly Barthian. See Zahrnt, *Sache*, 73.

137. See *EvF II*, chapters XXVI, XXVII, and XXX. For Calvin, who follows the tradition of Eusebius of Caesarea, see McGrath, *Calvin*, 210; see also Moltmann, *Crucified God*, 257.

138. See *EvF II*, 116, 268. See also Althaus, *Luther*, 62; Moltmann, *Crucified God*, 237–39. Characteristic of his relational approach is Thielicke's extending of Melanchthon's phrase to the Holy Spirit (*EvF III*, 9), the Lord's Supper (*EvF III*, 299), and the devil (here, of course, related to his attacks; *EvF III*, 451. See also *Fragen*, 177n1).

139. *EvF II*, 301.

140. In the words of Pannenberg: "Argumentation and the operation of the Spirit are not in competition with each other" (Pannenberg, *Basic Questions II*, 35).

141. See Pannenberg's criticism: "An otherwise unconvincing message cannot attain the power to convince simply by appealing to the Holy Spirit" (Pannenberg, *Basic Questions II*, 34).

Inter alia basing himself on Romans 1:18-32, Thielicke would counter, in typical dialectical fashion, that this is due to the total loss of analogy, due to God's whole otherness: "There is, between the reality of God and that of the world, an ontological distinction which does not permit us to understand them as dimensions of one and the same reality. The basis is distinguished ontologically from what is based on it. . . . The constant error of natural theology is to erase this distinction."[142] For Thielicke, it follows that since God's "truth comes to us in an event and is not attainable in our own reason or strength, it claims a monopoly, refusing coordination with other truths that arise within this sphere of our own reason and strength."[143] He continues that "claiming the Pneuma for a revelation outside the Word comes under the suspicion (or the verdict) of confusing our own spirit with God's Spirit and doing something that is a characteristic mark of radical enthusiasm."[144]

But, in this connection, it may be worth noting the kinds of critical questions which can be put to Thielicke. For example, is the basis, ontologically speaking, really "wholly other"? Is Thielicke's Occamist conception in this regard the right one?[145] And might the same accusation of pneumatological confusion not be directed against his limiting the Spirit's radius of action to the preached Word and to the subjective realm of the individual? According to Thielicke, the Word of God becomes solely apparent in the act

---

142. *EvF I*, 366.

143. *EvF III*, 305.

144. *EvF III*, 305. In his writings, Thielicke repeatedly refers to his dialectical interpretation of Romans 1, which Schlatter polemically calls a "dialectical abuse" (see Neuer, *Schlatter: Ein Leben*, 659). For two examples, see *EvF III*, 6-7; and *Anfechtung*, chapter II. Besides, see *EvF III*, 369, where he criticizes the Roman Catholic concept that the *pneuma* is not bound to the Word but also works in active tradition. See Moreland, *Love Your God with All Your Mind*, 59-60. Furthermore, see (in paradigmatic contrast) C. S. Lewis's view of the Holy Spirit as unfolded by Ward, *Planet Narnia*, 32-39, esp. 38-39. In this regard, see also Macaulay and Barrs, *Being Human*, 53-55.

145. Standing in the Thomistic tradition of analogical predication, C. S. Lewis strongly negates this question: "To say 'God is good,' while asserting that His goodness is wholly other than ours, is really only to say 'God is we know not what.' And an utterly unknown quality in God cannot give us moral grounds for loving or obeying Him. [This basic view, by the way, preserved Lewis from coming to see God as a *genius malignus* after his shattering experience of Joy's cancer-death; see Lewis, *Grief Observed*, 35-38.] . . . The doctrine of Total Depravity—when the consequence is drawn that, since we are totally depraved, our idea of good is worth simply nothing—may thus turn Christianity into a form of devil-worship" (Lewis, *Problem of Pain*, 28-29). For Lewis's take on total depravity, see also *Problem of Pain*, 61, and the third chapter on Divine Goodness in general, esp. 28-33. Finally, see Baggett and Walls, *Good God*, 80-81. For the "analogical mode" of Thomism, see Emery, *Trinity*, 94-100.

of proclamation; in other words, in its subjective effect upon the hearer.[146] In doing so, however, he withdraws theology's truth claims from the objective sphere to the inner dimension of the subject,[147] therefore putting his theological enterprise at risk of an unchecked enthusiasm or, as Speier suitably paraphrases, an "occlusive self-sufficiency" which can become blind to any criticism from outside.[148]

Not only does Thielicke thus fail to distinguish between the logic of faith and its psychology, as helpfully outlined by Pannenberg,[149] but one also wonders whether his view of the Spirit's *scope of action* is still as non-Cartesian as his robust focus on the *person* of the Holy Spirit. Regarding the former, Thielicke's tendency to subjectivization appears more Cartesian than he himself would probably dare to admit. I shall return to this problematic aspect of Thielicke's theology in chapter 9.

At any rate, this is one of the implications of Christ's incarnation: one can only speak of God in his condescension to man.[150] Thielicke thus approaches the first article of the Apostles' Creed, God the Father, in a purely christocentric way. The creator is only recognized via the savior, an approach putting him in line with Schleiermacher.[151] God's relation to man in Christ, in turn, cannot be systematized "but discloses itself only to the faith which posits this relation";[152] in other words, via the divine *pneuma*. Thielicke

---

146. "God's Word creates its own hearer" (*EvF I*, 150). On the creative work of the Spirit, see also *Anfechtung*, 49; *Woran*, 114–15, 118, 148. Accordingly, he can state that "we can never know a priori what might yet prove to be canonical in the course of future proclamation" (*Kanzel*, 56–57). See *Kanzel*, 48, 63; Bromiley, "Thielicke," 558.

147. This becomes particularly obvious in his essay, "WuV," where he unfolds his understanding of the place of theology within the secular university. See the criticism of Pannenberg in this regard: "If the moment of decision becomes foundational for the structure of faith, then the bond with truth 'outside myself' [*extra me*] is irretrievably lost" (Pannenberg, *Basic Questions II*, 34). See also Pannenberg, *Basic Questions II*, 194–95, where he criticizes the "decision of faith" *if* conceived as a "leap into supranatural truth."

148. See Speier's appraisal in *Initiator*, 237–39 (for the phrase "occlusive self-sufficiency," see 238).

149. See Pannenberg, *Basic Questions II*, 32–34.

150. See *EvF I*, 293. For Calvin's principle of accommodation, see McGrath, *Calvin*, 172–75, 326–27, 336.

151. Among many places, see the first part of *Woran*, esp. 43–44. For a criticism of the exclusively christocentric method, see Lütgert, *Die theologische Krisis der Gegenwart*, 22, 30; Neuer, *Schlatter: Ein Leben*, 169.

152. He calls this "a christological secret . . . grounded in the incarnation" (*EvF I*, 371). God's higher thoughts "cannot be imprisoned in human systematizations" (*EvF III*, 164). For him, this is one reason to reject the ontological schema of thought, as it "carries with it a temptation to systematize the mystery of the incarnation" (*EvF I*, 371).

himself states his conviction that Christology generally—and, in his own work, especially—"contains an implicit doctrine of the Holy Spirit."[153] Man being thus incorporated into God's relational being by the creative and transformative work of the Holy Spirit[154] on the basis of Christ's incarnation not only makes the task of theology possible, but also dissolves, in his view, the alleged problem of the hermeneutical circle.

Finally, Thielicke's pneumatological focus is further illuminated by his differentiating between Gotthold Ephraim Lessing's and the New Testament's understanding of the Spirit. In brief, Thielicke interprets Lessing's view as the intellectual seizing of a timeless truth of reason,[155] the spirit thereby being understood as the comprehensive capacity for meaning.[156] Because Lessing regards the relation between spirit and truth as one to be seized by man, so that man has or possesses the truth, he actually knows nothing of the Holy Spirit in the biblical sense. For man can never arrive at the truth of the gospel rationally and possessively on his own, but only via the bestowed possibility of God's love.

While both the New Testament and Lessing want to make man the subject, leading him back to his authenticity, it is only the first that succeeds. The Holy Spirit, being God in loving action, authorizes and executes the proclamatory Word that calls man into a living relationship with the truth.[157] This is possible since for Luther (as well as Thielicke), truth is a person.[158] It can only to be understood if man stands in a very specific relationship to this person, if man *is* in the truth,[159] and if he approaches truth existentially

---

153. *EvF II*, 453.

154. See *Gespräche*, 165; *EvF I*, 150. The Word "is rather an active word, which posits a new creation by the power of the *pneuma*" (*EvF II*, 34). See also *ThE II/1*, §1083: "The power of reality that makes me become a subject of love . . . is the Holy Spirit." In his culture-critical work, *Culture of Interpretation*, 243, 252–53, Lundin also refers to Thielicke's specific emphasis on the creative, pneumatic power of God's Word.

155. See *Offenbarung*, 152.

156. See *Offenbarung*, 149 [*Aufnahmevermögen für Sinngehalte*].

157. See *Offenbarung*, 154–55.

158. Unsurprisingly, due to their mutual dependence on Kierkegaard's *Wahrheit des Verhältnisses*, certain similarities to Brunner ("truth as encounter") open up again.

159. *Offenbarung*, 152–53. For Thielicke's existential understanding of truth (as he negates both Jaspers's and Galileo's concepts), see *EvF II*, 307–10. See also his essay "WuV," esp. 119–24; *EvF I*, 202–5; *EvF III*, 361–64; *Anfechtung*, 4, 11; and *Offenbarung*, 152, 166. For truth-as-person, see Bromiley, "Thielicke," 560. For his encounters and discussions with Jaspers, see *Wayfarer*, 100–2 [134–36]. Thielicke uses the analogy of motherly love to illustrate that one only understands the other person if one is in a specific relationship with that person: "I only experience motherly love as a child" (see *Offenbarung*, 152; *Anfechtung*, 4; and *Woran*, 19).

from the inside,¹⁶⁰ leading back to the Spirit's act of calling into the truth (and hence "being in the truth," *intra fidem*) outlined above.

Lessing and Scripture therefore entertain different notions of truth and spirit. The first treats truth as insight and the spirit as emancipating the subject from the Word. The second understands truth as love and the Holy Spirit as leading the subject into the Word, the gospel, which is Christ, revealing the otherness of both worlds.¹⁶¹ Here, Thielicke's Lutheran intellectual context comes to the fore once more since, like the German *Reformator*, he inextricably links the Spirit to the external Word.¹⁶² This theological insistence already sheds anticipatory light upon Thielicke's prioritization of proclamation (see chapter 8).

The Dogmas' "Existential Relevance": Pneumatological Commitment Biographically Rooted

This existential understanding of truth, rooted in the grander framework of Lutheran relational thought—which, in turn, is embedded within and confirmed by Thielicke's own crucial experience of "sickness-unto-death"—leads him to proclaim that "the one thing essential must convey itself to me in its essentiality. If one does not arrive at this insight, then every elementary access to the deposit of the faith is blocked."¹⁶³

By "the one thing essential," Thielicke means the dogmas' "existential relevance," their pneumatic dimension, the fact that dogmatic statements claim man's existential context, one's *Sitz im Leben*, personal, spiritual, *fiducia*-like faith.¹⁶⁴ That is why Thielicke can almost programmatically explain to his listeners in Stuttgart's *Stiftskirche* during the final stages of World War II: "I do not want to present the basic truths of Christianity historically [*notitia/assensus*-like]. . . . Rather . . . I want to uncover something which illuminates our immediate existence and which approaches us life-sized and in a way that grasps us [*fiducia*-like]."¹⁶⁵

Not only does Thielicke's understanding of truth-as-person shine through in these lines but also the unambiguous embeddedness of both quotation and understanding within his own biography. For, as already cited in the previous subsection, it was via his first theological teachers in

---

160. See *ThE III*, §1982.
161. See *Offenbarung*, 155.
162. See Bayer, *Lutheran Way*, 54–55; *Luther's Theology*, 34–35.
163. *Suche*, 150. See *ThE III*, §1982.
164. *Suche*, 149–50. See "WuV," 121–22.
165. *GldChr*, 114.

Greifswald that he "realized how crucial, especially for a young man, the [teacher's] person is. A truth *in abstracto* does not hit home, but a truth incarnated in a person comes vividly and concretely up to one."[166]

Now he applies this adolescent experience to his epistemological thinking, concluding that "I can only speak of the truth if I see it incarnated in a person, [incarnated] in the 'king of truth' (John 18:37)." It is the truth "understanding us before we understand it [or, more adequately, 'him']."[167]

Moreover, in this very agenda, Thielicke's indebtedness to Kierkegaard and Kähler reappears. Thielicke thinks that Kierkegaard's legitimate focus on the "wholly other," on the *totaliter-aliter*, is best expressed symbolically, in the doctrine of the Holy Spirit. Therefore, along with Kähler, he wants to secure the independence of faith from historical research by centralizing the kerygmatic Christ "from above," rather than the so-called historical Jesus "from below."[168]

According to Kähler, faith "is not focused on a historical figure of the past, but on a present figure proving his presence by effecting faith."[169] The parallel to Thielicke's own *heilsgeschichtliche*, kerygmatic aim appears striking, further undergirded by Thielicke seeing an illustration of man's pneumatic transformation in the Tanakh. Already in Jeremiah and Ezekiel, God promises to put his law into man's heart. Thielicke interprets this as the Spirit's transformation of the command "Thou shalt"—as expressed symbolically, through the tablets of stones or Christian dogmas—into man's own

---

166. *Krauss*, 17.

167. "WuV," 119. Compare Ratzinger and Brunner in this regard: "We never own [the truth]; at best we are owned by it" (Ratzinger, *Licht der Welt*, 69). "If the Word of God meets me in faith . . . I do not have something like property . . . but I myself become property" (Brunner, *Divine-Human Encounter*, 61). For a brief comparison of the classical (especially Hebrew) and the modern way of knowing—the former classified as an act of participation, which transforms the perceiver, and the latter as an act of possession and domination, as symbolized by Francis Bacon's *scientia potestas est*—see Moltmann, *Experiences*, 58–59; *Crucified God*, 238. See also Wilson, *Father Abraham*, 287–89.

168. "WuV," 123. See Pannenberg, *Basic Questions II*, chapter 2, esp. 43, strongly opposing Thielicke's fatherly friend, Althaus, on this issue.

169. *Offenbarung*, 146. "Not focused" but nevertheless still *based* on the historical Jesus. This goes for Kähler himself, despite his problematic distinction (Pannenberg, *Basic Questions I*, 85–86) as well as for Thielicke. "Faith is only a subsequent act by which what took place then is appropriated to me now. . . . If I today die and rise again with Christ . . . , this presupposes that Christ has already died and risen again" (*EvF I*, 129). See *EvF I*, 111, 158, 179, and esp. 130: "We were saved nineteen hundred years ago." See also *EvF II*, 41: "Christian theology is always a theology of facts." Likewise, see Brunner, *Dogmatics I*, 30, for whom the *historical revelation* that took place in Christ becomes a *personal encounter* in the "Word of the Holy Spirit . . . *Deus dixit* [God spoke] becomes *Deus dicit* [God speaks]."

will. In other words, Christianity's dogmatic statements become existentially relevant by God's "Spirit having won a bridgehead on the territory of my I . . . so that now it [the I] . . . can will what God wills."[170]

Therefore, as Speier points out, in Thielicke's eyes, the only permanent, methodological commitment theology should make is the commitment to the Holy Spirit as the *Christus praesens*.[171] Thielicke basically offers two ways in which such a commitment might manifest itself in practice.

The first way consists in the "continual engagement with Holy Scripture" (Luther's rule of *meditatio*) as well as prayer (Luther's *oratio*).[172] The second way follows from both *meditatio* and *oratio* and comprises the gifts of the Spirit (*charismata*) according to 1 Corinthians 12–14.[173] Thereby typical of Thielicke's relational mode of thought—and, at the same time serving as a safeguard against possible "excesses"—is his strong emphasis on the Spirit's personhood.[174] Man can never "have" the Holy Spirit in the same way that man cannot "have" another human being. Indeed, the abuse of the charismata has always been the greatest temptation for spiritual man, prompting Thielicke to highlight the safeguarding importance of the earliest dogmatic formulations (such as the Athanasian Creed) or its later expressions (like the first article of the Augsburg Confession). Those creedal formulations clarify the truth that man's relation to the Holy Spirit is never determined by the possessive-verb but rather always expressed by waiting and pleading.[175] This personal/relational understanding also extends to the spiritual gifts themselves: "These gifts are never detached from the giver. . . . Gifts are bound up with the attitude of the heart toward God. . . . They are not qualities of man . . . but qualities of this relation between God and the heart. They come and go with this relation."[176]

---

170. *Abenteuer*, 104–5. See Ratzinger's similar emphasis above, further implying this to be the Spirit's doing in *Jesus I*, 391–92, 401.

171. Speier, *Initiator*, 234.

172. For both Holy Writ and prayer, see *Anfechtung*, 12–13. For prayer in particular, see *Anfechtung*, chapter IX; *EvF III*, chapter V. For the importance of regular engagement with Scripture, see *Kanzel*, 36–37; *GldChr*, 47; and *Ernstfall*, 154. See also Bayer, *Luther's Theology*, 33n11.

173. See *EvF III*, chapter IV, where Thielicke lists and comments on the various charisms. Probably by accident, Thielicke leaves out miracles. He mentions this gift in the heading but does not engage with it. See *EvF III*, 79.

174. For a concise survey of current discussions as to the Spirit's personhood, see Nitsche, "Der Heilige Geist als trinitarische Person?," 333–39. See also Emery, *Trinity*, 36–43; and chapter 6, part one.

175. See *Gespräche*, 128–31; *EvF II*, 48; and *EvF III*, 75–76.

176. *EvF I*, 179.

Much more could be written about Thielicke's specific focus on the third person of the Godhead. As to the primary concern of this book, however, all that remains to be said is that the existential rootedness of his theological aspect is explicated once again. More specifically, Thielicke's theological exposition of the Spirit's ministry on the Emmaus-disciples, as well as during Pentecost, uses a phraseology that radiates in all its "experiential grandeur" if seen against the background of Thielicke's own "death and resurrection" on Maundy Thursday and Good Friday, 1933.

In his pastoral work, *Abenteuer*, under the subsection heading "Stale news begins to shine," Thielicke commences by emphasizing the age-old familiarity of Peter's message to his listeners on the day of Pentecost: "It really was old stuff which Peter preached."[177] Suddenly, however, "the past turned into the present." Peter's addressees underwent the famous "aha-" or "eureka-experience": "They always knew the Writ of old [*notitia/assensus*-like] and yet they did not know it [*fiducia*-like]." But Peter obviously had a key available by which he unlocked the salvation story of the old covenant: "It was just as though until then they had possessed God's Word only in cipher . . . as if the tremendous plaintext was just revealed."[178]

Here, Thielicke changes gear and tries to apply the text to his own readers' situation:

> We can experience something similar first-hand. Early in life we learned Psalm 23, "The Lord is my Shepherd." We had it memorized [*notitia/assensus*-like], and yet we did not know it [*fiducia*-like]. For life had not yet thrown us into those dark valleys where fear and loneliness reach for us and where the comforting voice, the guiding hand . . . would have meant anything to us. Only later, as the terror of the borderline situation reached for us, did those old words come back to us and found the way from . . . our memory, where we had them heedlessly stored, to our heart; there they began to glow and to warm.[179]

Yet again, Thielicke, in highlighting the importance of the "dark valleys" in relation to the decisive *fiducia*-aspect of faith, is truly Lutheran. Like Luther, Thielicke emphasizes the desirable *effects* of suffering: that God begins to mean something in our lives. The cross and *Anfechtung* must come so that our faith might grow, that God might become existentially relevant, because faith (in its *fiducia*-dimension) can be strongest when exposed to

---

177. *Abenteuer*, 100.
178. *Abenteuer*, 100–1.
179. *Abenteuer*, 101.

the strongest *Anfechtungen*.[180] That is why, paradoxically, according to Luther, it is the greatest *Anfechtung* not to have *Anfechtung* since without it, man is in danger of forgetting God.[181] Thielicke continues this sermon with the "stained-glass window" illustration outlined above. He concludes that "whoever is seized by the Spirit of Pentecost will be moved into this interior . . . [and] will be addressed by something as alive that till now had remained silent and had only been dead possession."[182]

In addition to this passage vividly illustrating Thielicke's programmatic explanation regarding his kerygmatic aim, it can furthermore intriguingly be applied *one-to-one* to his own coming to faith at Easter, 1933. Simply by substituting the first-person-singular "I" for the first-person plural "We," the segment begins to read like his own "stepping up," so to say, from *notitia/assensus* to *fiducia*. It thus not only shows the general inextricability of Thielicke's life and thought but also unambiguously highlights the specific *suffering* context of his existence upon which his understanding of the *pneuma* "bloomed." This is as Lutheran as it can get since, for the German reformer, one of the wonderful consequences of successfully overcoming *Anfechtung* consists in being filled with the Holy Spirit.[183] *Anfechtung* is charged with pneumatological potential; a potential Thielicke experienced first-hand. His strong emphasis on the Holy Spirit very likely arose out of a strongly contested life.

---

180. For those aspects in Luther, see Rieger, *Luthers theologische Grundbegriffe*, 22.
181. See Rieger, *Luthers theologische Grundbegriffe*, 21; and *ThE II/1*, §1146.
182. *Abenteuer*, 101.
183. See Rieger, *Luthers theologische Grundbegriffe*, 22.

Chapter 6

The Triune God

Divine Personhood and
the Origin of Evil

THUS FAR, THE IMPORTANCE Thielicke ascribes to the concept of the personal has been made clear. He rejects any ontological schema of thought in favor of a personalistic, relational one (see chapter 4). He does not tire of stressing the importance of the personal *fiducia*-aspect of faith at which he himself arrived through illness and recovery (see chapter 5, part one). Consequently, he strongly stresses the work of the Holy Spirit, whose power draws man back to his origin, back to fundamental reality, back into the communion of love between three divine persons from which the human person has alienated himself (see chapter 5, part two).

Because (a) the notion of divine personhood has been strongly contested in recent intellectual history; (b) it has taken center stage in Thielicke's overall thought in general—and in his reply to the challenge of theodicy in particular (see chapter 7); and especially because (c) it has its origin in the experience of Thielicke's "sickness-unto-death," the following subsections must now explicitly focus on his understanding and defense of God being a (tri-)personal being. As to the third reason, Thielicke clearly states that he decisively experienced the dialogical dimension of prayer at the time of his sickness, when he found himself in the midst of severe spiritual crises with regard to God's personhood. Yet, by reluctantly giving in to the desperate prayer requests of his roommate in hospital who was also seriously ill, Thielicke was exposed to the personal dimension of the divine. Thus, it was "in action" [*im Vollzug*]—and not in theoretical contemplation (see chapter 4)—that he was first personally encountered by Christ.[1] That this "in action"

---

1. See *Kanzel*, 63.

reached its climax on the night he thought to bid his farewell to this world will be shown in the final subsection of part one.

Part two concentrates on one significant implication of God being (tri-)personal, namely, the question of in whose *voluntas*, divine or human, the ultimate root for man's "three great problems" of guilt, suffering, and death[2] is to be found. By way of such specific structure, the ground is finally prepared for Thielicke's personalistic answer to the problem of evil, which will be turned to in the next chapter.

Part One: God's (Tri-)personal Being—Safeguarding Divine *agape* and *actuositas*[3]

In his commemorative speech on Thielicke in December, 1986, Ebeling states that "the phrase 'Theology of confrontation with death' [*Theologie der Konfrontation mit dem Tode*] adumbrates... the criterion for true theology."[4] This applies, once again, to the case of Thielicke when the specific question of God's personhood is addressed.

Within the same commemorative context, Röhricht, his former student and lifelong friend, confesses that for some time he had difficulties with Thielicke's "habit of speaking about the relation between God and man in an almost exclusively plain and unabatedly personal manner, like about a relationship between two friends." Röhricht continues to muse that this might have been due to Thielicke's own "simplicity," such as displayed by "the children of God."[5] Without disagreeing with Röhricht, one nevertheless wonders whether there might be more to it than mere *simplicitas*.

Indeed, in a marginal note, Thielicke reveals that during his "sickness-unto-death" and period of hospitalization, he went through severe theological crises. One of the doubts he wrestled with concerned the personal notion [*Personbegriff*] of God, which he was not able to resolve at that time. Consequently, this led him to question the whole possibility of prayer and with it the associated expectancy of miracles.[6] Deprived of understanding

---

2. "Bin ich blöd, wenn ich glaube [Am I dumb if I believe]?" (*NHT*). Thielicke recurrently uses the tripartite formula "sin/guilt, suffering, and death." See *EvF II*, 384; *ThE I*, §527; *Freedom*, 210, 211; *GldChr*, 452; *Lebensangst*, 40; and his "Kurze Antwort auf die Frage, warum ich ein Christ bin [Brief answer to the question: why am I a Christian]" (*NHT*).

3. Thielicke uses the term "personal," rather than "tri-personal"; thus, I thus follow his lead.

4. Ebeling, "Todes Tod," 32.

5. Röhricht, "Thielicke," 28.

6. See *GldChr*, 348.

God as a personal being, Thielicke, like Paul Tillich,[7] came to understand prayer as monological meditation instead of dialogical communication.[8]

Thielicke's Understanding and Defense of Divine Personhood

In his adolescent struggle with the personal concept of the Godhead, Thielicke was by no means on his own. On the contrary, the concept of divine personhood has been in crisis since at least Johann Gottlieb Fichte's[9] critique, "On the Basis of Our Belief in a Divine World Government," written in the context of the atheistic controversy in 1798[10]—or so it seems: "[Fichte's] declaration seals the end of theism and its concept of God as a conscious being who, as self-conscious, was also a person."[11] With its implications of individuality and limitation, the term is opposed to the absolute, that is, the all-encompassing, unlimited. In the eyes of left-wing Hegelian David Friedrich Strauss, "absolute person" is thus a *non ens*, meaning nothing.[12] In the twentieth century, theological uneasiness as to God's personhood did not vanish but, if anything, remained strongly palpable amongst thinkers such as Paul Tillich,[13] Herbert Braun,[14] and Hans Küng,[15] who tried to develop alternative models of speaking about God.

---

7. Asked shortly before his death if he prays, Tillich, consistent with his theological criticism of the I-Thou-relation to God and his favoring, instead, of a transpersonal mysticism, is reported to have answered, "No, but I meditate." See Schaeffer, *How Should We Then Live?*, 178; Thiede, *Gekreuzigte[r] Sinn*, 117–18. Thielicke and Tillich thus aptly illustrate C. S. Lewis's recognition in *Letters to Malcolm*, 49, that faith in prayer is based upon having a certain idea of God's character. Abraham Heschel makes exactly the same point. See Young, *Jesus the Jewish Theologian*, 171, 179n2.

8. *Kanzel*, 63. See *ThE I*, §1308; *Lebensangst*, 157; and *Gebet*, chapter 1, where he tackles this notion in the first part of his sermon on the Lord's Prayer.

9. Fichte's basic concern can already be found in Spinoza and Aristotle. See Pannenberg, *Basic Questions II*, 227; McGrath, *Christian Theology*, s.v. "Defining person."

10. Fichte's publication was *inter alia* initiated by Forberg's essay "*Entwicklung des Begriffs der Religion*." For both, see Esser, *Atheismus*, 57–69 (Fichte), 70–84 (Forberg).

11. Pannenberg, *Basic Questions II*, 197. See Pannenberg, *Basic Questions II*, 202; "Person," 231.

12. Strauss, *Die christliche Glaubenslehre I*, 504–5. According to Thielicke, Strauss was "one of the great and tragic heretics" in the shadow of Hegel ("Über die Tübinger Theologie" [*NHT*]). See §§33 [502–24] of Strauss's work, originally published in 1841, for his criticism of the concept of divine personhood; and *MF&T*, 424–40, for Thielicke's appraisal of his life and work.

13. See Tillich, *Systematic Theology I*, part II.

14. See esp. *EvF II*, 107. A concise overview of Braun's theology is given by Zahrnt, *Sache*, 297–314; and Lorenzmeier, "Herbert Braun," 500–4.

15. Küng's idea of a "transpersonal" [überpersönlich] God is challenged, for

According to Thielicke, it ought to be clear that making the human blueprint of personal being the theological basis for *defining* divine personhood is doomed to ephemerality.[16] More to the point, the question arises whether Fichte's criticism in this regard validates the abandoning of this analogy altogether. Should his concerns not also be seen within his very specific existential and historical context of culminating "Enlightenment" thought[17] with the doctrine of the *homo mensura* at its very center?

Thielicke himself seems to point in that direction when he critically engages with Tillich's proposal of speaking of the ground of being instead of the personal God.[18] Whereas he grants Tillich's eschewal of God's personhood a certain legitimacy in view of the term's theological abuse in the past, Thielicke nevertheless asserts Tillich to be mistaken when he allows the abuse to abolish the proper use (*abusus non tollit usum*):[19] "Tillich may well be right when he says that God was first called person only in the nineteenth century on the basis of Kant's distinction between nature . . . and personality." However, Thielicke adds that this was only possible because the intra-trinitarian relations as such were called persons well before Kant's distinction. Without this earlier trinitarian use of the concept, it would therefore not have been possible to call God a "person."[20] In light of this, whilst heeding Tillich's concerns (as well as, implicitly, Fichte's criticism), Thielicke states that understanding

---

example, by theistic analytical philosopher, von Wachter, *Kausale Struktur*, 245–46; and by atheistic philosopher, Mackie, *Miracle of Theism*, 242.

16. "If God's personal character is defined by the model of man the verdict of anthropomorphism cannot be averted" (*EvF II*, 103). "The inadequacy is always apparent when, instead of being defined by God, the term is used to define God" (*EvF II*, 111).

17. The term "Enlightenment" is used hesitantly here. J. C. D. Clark points out that in English discourse, this term was only coined in the late nineteenth century, subsequently projected back onto the eighteenth (Clark, "Thomas Paine," 580, 586). In a seminar at QUB on May 19, 2015, Clark expressed his great antipathy for the "E-word." For the German context, von Wachter is even more critical of the term, speaking of "the myth of the Enlightenment [era]" with the coinage first used in the 1770s. Kant's essay, "*Was ist Aufklärung?*," eventually appeared in 1784 (von Wachter, "Der Mythos der Aufklärung I," 3). In contrast, see Thielicke's almost romantically naïve usage of the term in *GldChr*, 437.

18. Ward, *God*, 230, also subscribes to Tillich's "personal ground of being." For an overview of the issue, see Ward, *God*, 228–37.

19. See *EvF II*, 164.

20. *EvF II*, 163–64. According to Adam, *Dogmengeschichte*, 117–18, Personalism as such was first established in principle by John Duns Scotus, who linked it to the structure of the Trinity. Going back further, Thielicke might also allude here to Leontius of Byzantium's concept of *enhypostasis*. See Pannenberg, "Person," 231–32. The use of the Greek term *hypostasis* developed in the East under the notable influence of Leontius's teacher, Origen. The first systematic use of the word "person" can be traced back to Tertullian. See Emery, *Trinity*, 60–61, 101.

God as person is not modelled on the understanding of human personhood with its implications of individuality and limitation. Rather, "the real truth is the very opposite. Our understanding of the human person must be modelled on the prior trinitarian understanding of the person, even though only some of its features may be transferred to man."[21]

Pannenberg, agreeing with Thielicke on this issue, makes the very same point: "[The concept of] God being personal can be reasonably sustained only when the experience of personal encounter is not in its very root limited to humanity, but is always already included within a greater reality which, in turn, endows human personality with its dignity."[22] Whereas religious criticism à la Feuerbach has usually assumed that man first experiences himself as a person and then projects this experience onto his gods, Pannenberg sees it much more the other way round: man's profane self-understanding, as it is taken for granted by such criticism, is only a late product of history.

According to Pannenberg, there are compelling reasons to search for the origin of personhood within the realm of religious experience, namely, by way of the human encounter with divine reality.[23] Only as a result of this encounter was man endowed with personhood; humanity became distinguished by this special relation to the gods.[24] Herein Pannenberg acknowledges "the element of truth in the efforts of modern personalism . . . to understand personality from the side of the claim of the Thou . . . Man is awakened to personality by the Divine Thou, and in this way, first learns to respect the thou of the fellowman as a person."[25]

---

21. *EvF II*, 164.

22. Pannenberg, *Theologie und Reich Gottes*, 15.

23. See also Moltmann: "Man develops his manhood always in relationship to the Godhead of his God" (Moltmann, *Crucified God*, 267).

24. Pannenberg, *Reich Gottes*, 15. Pannenberg also states this elsewhere: "What we nowadays understand by 'person' might have been initially opened up . . . by Christianity" (Pannenberg "Person," 230). "Man only becomes a person by encountering God's personhood as his counterpart . . . God makes man into a person" (Pannenberg "Person," 232). See also C. S. Lewis, who, in his spiritual struggle after the death of his beloved wife Helen Joy Davidman, concludes as to materialism: "If [Helen] 'is not,' then she never was. I mistook a cloud of atoms for a person. There aren't, and never were, any people. Death only reveals the vacuity that was always there. What we call the living are simply those who have not yet been unmasked. All equally bankrupt, but some not yet declared. . . . No, my real fear is not of materialism" (Lewis, *Grief Observed*, 32–33). Von Hildebrand emphasizes the same: "If our personal being . . . were destined to descending into nothingness, [then] our life would be an illusion" (Von Hildebrand, *Tod*, 19, 22). Albert Camus is therefore quite right that on such a view suicide would be a rather compelling option once the chips are down.

25. Pannenberg, *Basic Questions II*, 230n99. For the historical consequences,

Besides Pannenberg[26] and other modern thinkers such as Schlatter,[27] Gloege,[28] or Brunner,[29] Thielicke counters post-Fichtean attempts to do away with the notion of divine personal being in the same vein since "only by encountering God do I become a person, namely, unique, inimitable, and liable for myself."[30] Reminiscent of Nicholas of Cusa's view,[31] Thielicke reasserts that man's alien dignity comes about by man's existence in relation to God, thereby constituting the *humanum*. As this is also the case in Greek antiquity, where man defines himself as theonomous by virtue of his relation to the gods,[32] Thielicke recognizes the Christian West as being "nourished by two springs, Greek antiquity and Christianity."[33]

In light of this, he provocatively asks if it might be more adequate to assume our earthly father to be a theomorphic reflection of our heavenly father, rather than the latter being an anthropomorphic projection of the former.[34] For whenever he speaks of God as person he does not mean this anthropomorphously: "On the contrary, we mean it *theomorphously* when

---

see Siedentop, *Inventing the Individual*; and the first chapter of Maier, *Welt ohne Christentum*.

26. "The personal character of the idea of God precisely in Justin's theology has rightly been defended against all contrary interpretations" (Pannenberg, *Basic Questions II*, 178).

27. "Because it [personhood] is given to us, we have to attribute it first to *the one whose projection we are*" (Schlatter, *Dogma*, 30). Emphasis added. See Schlatter, *Dogma*, 29–32; *Briefe*, 35–36; and Walldorf, *Realistische Philosophie*, 265n129.

28. "The term 'person,' as related to man, is in its truest sense, a theological one, insofar as it always implies the original, archetypal personhood of the triune God" (Gloege, "Personalismus," 25). For a discussion of Luther's use of "person," see Ebeling, *Luther*, chapter 12, esp. 201–9; Rieger, *Luthers theologische Grundbegriffe*, 203–5.

29. See Brunner's anthropological work, *Man in Revolt*, in general; and *Dogmatics II*, 22, in particular: "The fact that man is Person, is an analogy to the Being of God as Person." See also Zahrnt, *Sache*, 76.

30. *Tod*, 167. See further *G&E*, 373; *Fragen*, 249–50; *Anfechtung*, 249; *GldChr*, 68, 284; *EvF I*, 151; *EvF II*, 114; *EvF III*, 348–49; *ThE I*, §462 and esp. §1661; *ThE III*, §2577, §2587, §2875; *Woran*, 241; "Frage nach dem Sinn," 7–8; and "Strukturen," 110.

31. "By looking at man's I, God called it into being as a personal I, which is capable of returning God's look" (Adam, *Dogmengeschichte*, 150).

32. See *EvF II*, 106–7; *Mensch*, 158. See also chapter 4.

33. *Freedom*, 179. See *Freedom*, 125. Moreover, see Chesterton, *Orthodoxy*, 137–38; and von Hildebrand, *Tod*, 24, underlining the crucial difference between the attitudes of ancient Greece (sorrow) and Christianity (joy) regarding man's death and eternal fate.

34. See *EvF III*, 324; *Mensch*, 450. See also C. S. Lewis's allegorical parallel of this response to Feuerbach in *Pilgrim's Regress*, 88; and Viktor Frankl's statement, quoted in Thiede, *Gekreuzigte[r] Sinn*, 121: "In reality God is not a father-imago, but the father is an imago of God."

we speak of man as person," because "the personhood of God has ontic primacy over that of man."[35]

At any rate, true to his personalistic basis of thought, Thielicke understands the concept of person neither to be a self-enclosed entelechy (as in Goethe), monad (as in Leibniz), nor a substance (as in Aristotle),[36] but, by its very nature, "person always includes relation to a Thou, to another personal being."[37] "I always only experience who I am by encountering the Thou."[38] In his foremost concern for the personal and dialogical primacy within the Godhead—and, consequently, between God and man—Thielicke also finds strong support in Ratzinger[39] who, according to Thielicke, "finely" explicates the relational character of the concept of person.[40] Ratzinger, analyzing the Latin term, *persona*, and its Greek equivalent, *prosōpon*, states that relatedness is constitutive—an integral part—of both. He concludes that "person" as an absolute singular does not exist: "If the absolute is person it is not an absolute singular. To this extent the overstepping of the singular is implicit in the concept of person."[41]

Reminiscent of John Donne's "No man is an island," Bonhoeffer and Pannenberg set a similar tone. Whereas the first muses about the interlacement of one's own life with the lives of other people, concluding that man's being-to-the-other, as best expressed in a mother, represents the "natural

---

35. *EvF II*, 114. Emphasis added. Thielicke follows Luther in this, see *ThE I*, §443.

36. Among other references, see *LmdT*, 22; *EvF III*, 451 (Goethe, Leibniz); and *EvF II*, 104–5, 402–3 (Aristotle).

37. *EvF II*, 104. See *EvF II*, 109; *EvF III*, 451; *ThE I*, §433–64; and *Offenbarung*, 153: "The I is a relational term." Further, for Richard of Saint Victor's definition of person as *eksistentia*, a being [*sistere*] out of the other [*ek*], see Pannenberg, "Person," 231. For making a generic case for Social Trinitarianism, drawing on Richard of Saint Victor, see Swinburne, "Social Theory of the Trinity." The ego "is always also beyond itself, ec-centric. It comes to itself in the other than itself" (Pannenberg, *Systematic Theology III*, 562). For Pannenberg's anthropological view of human life's tension between exocentric structure and natural, sinful ego-centeredness, see Pannenberg, *Anthropology*. See also Lewis, *Grief Observed*, 59: "We are 'taken out of ourselves' by the loved one," and Lewis, *Problem of Pain*, 69, defining "a creature" as "an essentially dependent being whose principle of existence lies not in itself but in another."

38. *ThE II/1*, §24. See *ThE II/1*, §19–20.

39. See Ratzinger, *Introduction*, 82–85, 111–13, 117–18, 128–32.

40. In chapter VII of *EvF II*, where Thielicke systematically unfolds his view on "The Personality of God," he refers to Ratzinger's *Introduction* several times, characterizing the Bavarian's thoughts on the relational character of the word "person" as "finely worked out" (*EvF II*, 104n6). Consequently, both likewise interpret the kingdom of God christologically: Jesus himself, his person, *is* the kingdom. See *EvF II*, 364; *Gebet*, 60; and Ratzinger, *Jesus I*, 79, 90, 181, 384.

41. Ratzinger, *Introduction*, 129.

state" of humanity,[42] the latter argues that the essence of person is "to give oneself to the counterpart," the very idea of person thereby including the idea of dependency.[43] This is why Thiede thinks the term "person" to be so elementary for God's being. It is essential to the God who is love to limit himself by entering into a relationship with another and therefore to define and confine himself as a person: first, for the sake of the fundamentally same, namely, his tri-personal relationality, and second, for the sake of the fundamentally other, i.e., creation. Hence the very feature of relationality implies self-limitation, yet also self-transcendence.[44] According to Schlatter, on these grounds it makes an all-decisive difference whether man's faith gives assent [*assensus*] to an object or to a person. For whereas union based on the former [*das Ding*] always remains limited, a complete union, which determines the whole I, is only entered with persons,[45] due to man's essential relationality. Yet, this understanding of the human person finds its basis in the pure relationality existing within the triune Godhead.[46]

It is worth noting that, historically, this understanding of "person" has tragically been confirmed by the infamous isolation-experiments of emperor Friedrich II in the thirteenth century. Determined to find out humanity's original language [*Ursprache*], he ordered a group of children—from their birth onwards—to be brought up in isolation, without any linguistic contact. The experiments failed, for all his test subjects died. In rendering this historical case, Roman Catholic psychologist Manfred Lütz concludes that "man, from his very first breath, is a dialogical existence—and herein in the likeness of the triune God."[47] Indeed, not only from the very first breath

---

42. See Bonhoeffer, *Widerstand*, 50–52, 87, 109.

43. Grenz and Olson, *Twentieth-Century Theology*, 193.

44. See Thiede, *Gekreuzigte[r] Sinn*, 119, 138.

45. Schlatter, *Dogma*, 110–11. The biblical analogy of marital love (Gen 2:23–24; Hos 2:18–25; Matt 19:5–6; John 3:29; 2 Cor 11:2–3; Eph 5:28–32; Rev 19:6–9) is thus to be located within this conceptual context (see Lewis, *Problem of Pain*, 37–40; Pannenberg, *Systematic Theology III*, 363). "There is . . . a sword between the sexes till an entire marriage reconciles them. . . . Marriage heals this. Jointly, the two become fully human. 'In the image of God created He *them*'" (Lewis, *Grief Observed*, 57–58). See also Bonhoeffer, *Widerstand*, 109, 208.

46. See *EvF II*, 104, 106.

47. Lütz, *Gott*, 259. Compare Thielicke: "I always only experience myself via my relations" (*ThE II/1*, §1375). It might also be said that "I *come into being* via my relations," thus already hinting at the meaning of "personality" as well as highlighting the psychological importance of both the toddler period and the family within man's overall development, seriously adding to the dubiousness of the collective upbringing of children under three years old in daycare centers. See, for example, Rabbi Jonathan Sacks's third chapter, "The Fragile Family," esp. 57, in his *Persistence of Faith*; Sherif Girgis et al., *What is Marriage?*, esp. 38; and *EvF I*, 243, 291: "To the degree that the personality of the I is destroyed, to that degree it ceases to be capable of a Thou."

but from conception onwards. As confirmed by recent scientific research, the unborn human is already a dialogical existence, viz., a *person*, within the mother's womb.[48] Trillhaas, Pannenberg, and Thielicke thus rightly differentiate between "person" and "personality": whilst the former denotes man *per se*, from the very beginning, in virtue of his or her (God-given) destiny, the latter represents man's relation to this human destiny—in other words, the development and process of the person's character in the midst of life's challenges.[49] This distinction is further explicated by John D. Zizioulas, another exponent of Social Trinitarianism:

> Being a person is fundamentally different from being an individual or a "personality," for a person cannot be imagined in himself but only within his relationships. Taking our categories from our fallen state of existence, we usually identify a person with the "self" (individual) and with all it possesses in its qualities and experiences (the personality). But modern philosophers recall with good reason that this is not what being a person means.[50]

Personhood as Constitutive of Divine Love and Freedom

Consequently, understanding the divine as tri-*personal* essentially safeguards the biblical understanding of God *being love*, which is at the heart of Christianity. As Thiede aptly encapsulates, God's trinitarian self-distinction, which *ipso facto* establishes his productive distinction from the world, results from the basic understanding of God as love.[51] Thielicke aligns himself with this, since God is not an "atomon substance but a personal communicative We"—the statement "God is love" pointing to the very unity of this communicative We.[52] As "the saying 'God is love' is Christological, in 1 John,

---

48. See, for example, Vonholdt, "Beziehungsraum Mutterleib."

49. See Trillhaas, "Persönlichkeit," 227; Pannenberg, "Person," 233; and Thielicke, *Tod*, 119n1. Therefore, the English title of chapter VII in *EvF II*, "The Personality of God," is—at best—misleading, since God, whilst certainly being personal, cannot be a personal*ity* in view of the term's implication of development and change unless, granted, one subscribes to process theology or open theism, respectively.

50. Zizioulas, *Being as Communion*, 105–6.

51. Thiede, *Gekreuzigte[r] Sinn*, 113n3. See also Moltmann, *Crucified God*, 244–45, who, on the basis of 1 John 4:16 ("God is love"), interprets "the event of the cross [which reveals God as love] in trinitarian terms, as an event concerned with a relationship between persons [and] in which these persons constitute themselves in their relationship with each other."

52. *EvF II*, 164–65.

it tells us that God is in himself the one he is for us in Christ." This means that God is love in his very essence, loving the Son before the foundation of the world. Hence God's love is not "triggered by the world" but rather "He is love from all eternity in himself."[53] This very emphasis finds further elucidation through C. S. Lewis:

> It is against . . . an environment of other selves, that the awareness of Myself stands out. This would raise a difficulty about the consciousness of God if we were mere theists: being Christians, we learn from the doctrine of the Blessed Trinity that something analogous to "society" exists within the Divine being from all eternity—that God is love . . . because, within Him, the concrete reciprocities of love exist before all worlds and are thence derived to the creatures.[54]

In light of this, it follows further that God *being* love (and thus being personal by *necessity*) not only strongly suggests a trinitarian undercurrent[55] but also is thereby clearly distinguished from the Islamic concept of Tawhid.[56] As shown, the very meaning of person necessarily implies the plural. As to human persons, this obviously does not pose a problem. In terms of divine persons, however, it follows that either there is (a) a plurality of gods, as in polytheism; (b) a plurality of persons in one substance, as in Christianity; or (c) a *non*-personal understanding of the divine, as in pantheism. What does not follow is a *personal* understanding, as per Unitarianism, thus confirming Pearcey's conclusion in the preceding footnote.[57] Moreland and Craig clarify the decisive difference between the Unitarian and Trinitarian view, as well:

---

53. *EvF II*, 165.

54. Lewis, *Problem of Pain*, 19–20. See Pannenberg, "Person," 231.

55. For further systematic unfolding, see esp. subsection "a) Love and the Trinity," in Pannenberg, *Systematische Theologie. Band I*, 456–66.

56. This notion also strengthens the proposal as to a non-personal understanding. See Pearcey, *Total Truth*, 387–88, who concludes that the Islamic denial of distinct "Persons" within the Godhead makes the God of Islam "actually more akin to the non-personal Absolute of neo-Platonism and Hinduism than to the God of the Bible."

57. Nevertheless, Muslim attempts to overcome the unbridgeable gulf between Allah and his creation have been undertaken, especially on the part of the Islamic mystics. Siddiqui, "Islam and the Question of a Loving God," 32–47, illustrates such an approach, giving insight into the message of love in Sufi poetry. But even most Sufis do not dwell much on God's love for human beings (see Siddiqui, "Islam and the Question of a Loving God," 45). Moreover, this minority position within Islam has often been harshly attacked by orthodox Muslims, as pointed out by Schirrmacher, *Islamic View of Major Christian Teachings*, 31–32. See also Schirrmacher, *Der Islam*, 48–49.

It is of the very nature of love to give oneself away. Love reaches out to another person rather than centering wholly in oneself. So if God is perfectly loving by his very nature, he must be giving himself in love to another. But who is that other? It cannot be any created person, since creation is a result of God's free will, not a result of His nature.... Contemporary cosmology makes it plausible that created persons have not always existed. But God is eternally loving. So created persons alone are insufficient to account for God's being perfectly loving.... It therefore follows that the other to whom God's love is necessarily directed must be internal to God himself. In other words, God is not a single, isolated person, as unitarian forms of theism like Islam hold; rather, God is a plurality of persons, as the Christian doctrine of the Trinity affirms.[58]

In the eyes of Thielicke, this specific understanding of the Trinity's self-contained love secures God's sovereignty over the world (and thus, implicitly, the attribute of divine aseity), since God's *agape* does not depend on man's partnership or human love.[59] Whereas the human form of love needs the other to inflame, provoke, and complete it (Thielicke classifies this as *eros*[60]), God *is* love; this "is" meaning "that God loves before all ages and before all worlds ... as the triune God."[61] While human love arises only via its counterpart, God creates and therefore precedes what he loves.[62] In other words, God loves into being.[63] That is also why Thielicke regards creation as "a sort of extension of God's goodness"—quickly adding, however, that by this he does not mean emanation.[64]

58. Moreland and Craig, *Philosophical Foundations*, 593.

59. See *EvF II*, 179; *ThE II/1*, §654, §674.

60. However, this is a reductive—and thus not very beneficial—classification, since it equates human love with sexuality. While C. S. Lewis, in his classic, *The Four Loves*, describes *eros* similarly (e.g., *eros*-lovers gazing into each other's eyes, searching for an ineffable something), he does not reduce human love to this one mode of expression.

61. *EvF II*, 179. See *Bilderbuch*, 25; *Schuld*, 34: "It is resolved in an unfathomable secret that God is a Thou and that he loves us." See also "Kurze Antwort auf die Frage, warum ich Christ bin" (*NHT*).

62. See *EvF II*, 179–80. "God's love ... creates [its object]. Man's love, however, begins with its object" (*EvF III*, 57). According to Carnell, "The Christian teaches that there was no antecedent necessity whatever, either from within or from without God, logical or material, which brought on the divine act of creation *ex nihilo*" (Carnell, *Introduction to Christian Apologetics*, 276).

63. 1 John 3:16; 4:7–10, 19.

64. *ThE I*, §722. See *Fragen*, 104–5, where he clarifies this point further. This also expands the Christian answer to the Muslim question regarding how the Christian knows that God essentially loves, as raised by Siddiqui, "Islam and the Question of a

Out of this *agape*-love, which provides humanity with its worth, Christ now enters into full solidarity with broken humankind: "He transfers himself from the shelter of his Logos home to the abyss of guilt, pain, and death."[65] Thielicke thus expresses vertically, in relation to the divine, what Holocaust survivor, Viktor Frankl, experienced horizontally, in relation to fellow man, namely, that "the salvation of man is through love and in love."[66] According to Thielicke, "solidarity of a man with our guilt, suffering, and death does not help us, only the solidarity of God himself, only his loving condescension."[67] The divine essence of *love* herein serves as foundation for the *freely* chosen kenosis of the second person of the Godhead,[68] humanity's need thereby affecting the tri-personal God as though it were his own (see chapter 7).

This further shows that true, divine love is not to be confused with mere emotion, as so commonly assumed nowadays. Rather, for Thielicke (as for Schlatter and Lewis, to name just two further examples[69]) love is not rooted in emotion[70] but in the will, both thereby following the Hebrew line of thinking.[71] Hence, the way Jesus loved is "a movement of being. It simply means being there for the other, entering into his situation, [and] not keeping anything back."[72]

Loving God," 32. The answer consists not only in Christ's incarnation and death but also in the fact of creation and, indeed, in the very fact of personal being. Whereas the former is implied by Thielicke and Moltmann, *Experiences*, 69, the latter is stressed by von Hildebrand in his book on death.

65. *EvF II*, 384.

66. Frankl, *Man's Search for Meaning*, 36. However, Frankl later indicates the danger of a *purely* horizontal experience as exemplified by prisoners after liberation: "Woe to him who found that the person whose memory [or dreams] alone had given him courage in camp did not exist any more [or were so different from all he had longed for]!" (Frankl, *Man's Search for Meaning*, 92).

67. *EvF II*, 325. See Hebrews 7:23–28. In responding to Dorothee Sölle, Gollwitzer makes precisely the same point: "Concerning guilt, there is no substitution between humans; at best only solidarity. . . . Efficacious substitution can only be wrought by someone who is not in the same situation; who enters the place of involvement from the place of non-involvement" (Gollwitzer, *Von der Stellvertretung Gottes*, 104, 105).

68. See, for example, *ThE II/1*, §676: "Jesus Christ is not simply the humiliated one [*der Erniedrigte*], but the one humiliating himself [*der sich Erniedrigende*]." See also Moltmann, *Crucified God*, 243–44, highlighting the conformity of will between Father and Son as to the cross.

69. See Schlatter, *Dogma*, 196; Lewis, *Mere Christianity*, 115, 117–18.

70. As Feuerbach seems to think. See Pannenberg, *Basic Questions II*, 186.

71. See Ward, *God*, 72. For this Hebrew concept as applied to marriage, see Thielicke, *Mensch*, 201, 207, 212; *ThE III*, §2074, 2092–93; and Wilson, *Father Abraham*, 202–3.

72. *EvF II*, 385, 399. "Love is a total movement of the I" (*EvF I*, 182). See also *Woran*, 111; *Abenteuer*, 230; and *Reden*, 40, 181–82.

Conclusively, when Thielicke speaks of God as person, his intention is thus to emphasize God's free movement, address, and disclosure to man[73] on the basis of his being, which is love. God is an *acting* God—not the abstract, timeless God of an idea[74]—and the doctrine of the Trinity fulfills the function of a defensive formula in this regard: it safeguards both God's actuality and His majesty.[75] Scott is right when he states that this "feature of God, his actuositas, is fundamentally important in Thielicke's whole theology." It is "the central attribute which Thielicke is concerned to highlight in his doctrine of revelation."[76]

The term "person," hence, does not refer to God as such, but is used purely instrumentally—namely, relationally and dialogically. From this follows God's ontological non-containment in the concept, which, according to Thielicke, exactly corresponds to what His name Yahweh implies: "I will be what I will be."[77] Yahweh, furthermore, is not known by his name (ontologi-

---

73. See *EvF II*, 111. "God's personal freedom itself is at stake" (*ThE I*, §1210). "It is about the 'decisions' (!) of the personal God" (*ThE II/1*, §887). By doing so, God causes man "to share in the dignity of the personal, making us I to the divine Thou." Thus, man's actual identity consists of an I-Thou-Relation with the one who has designed man in and for Himself (*Mensch*, 394). See chapter 4. According to Pannenberg: "The biblical God is essentially person because he constantly yields new, contingent events, always acts unpredictably and therein proves the infinity of his freedom" (Pannenberg, "Person," 232). "Precisely the God who acts in a personal manner in such deeds is the one who because of his freedom is 'wholly other'" (Pannenberg, *Basic Questions II*, 172, 181). For Pannenberg, it is precisely this biblical concept of God that made Israel's historical consciousness and its bequeathed universal-historical thinking possible. See Pannenberg, *Basic Questions I*, 12, 18.

74. See Bonhoeffer, *Widerstand*, 19, who makes a similar point.

75. See *EvF II*, 135. His concern to highlight the instrumental use when talking about "divine personhood" is simply encapsulated by C. S. Lewis's response to J. A. T. Robinson: God is "a person and more" (Lewis, *God in the Dock*, 185).

76. Scott, "Trinity and Ethics," 7.

77. *EvF II*, 109, 113–14. Thielicke's pupil Röhricht stresses that God is *actus purus*: "God is not, but launches himself [puts himself into action]. And only the name embodies the reality that puts itself into action" (Röhricht, "Der Name Gott," 186). Röhricht then curiously pleads for implementing the theological usage of "name" instead of "person," since it is "the name [that] invokes the unending, intentional will for which the term person is too tight. . . . [Only] the name-bearer can . . . love." But this is a rather questionable proposal, not just in light of what has been discussed thus far, but also in view of Ratzinger's assessment that "the name makes [personal] address, appeal, possible. It establishes relationship" (Ratzinger, *Jesus I*, 177). Röhricht thus wants to make a means to an end, not to mention the fact that his last statement is plainly wrong: for only the name-bearer *who is a person* can love; or has Röhricht ever received love from his cat called Kitty or his favorite toy named Woody? See Ratzinger, *Jesus I*, 310; *Introduction*, 91–92; and Emery's criticism of replacing the category of "substance" with that of "event" in Emery, *Trinity*, 91–92.

cally), but by his blessings (relationally):[78] He is Immanuel, the God who, in his essence, wills to exist for man,[79] leading back to Melanchthon's christological formulae favored by Thielicke (see chapter 5, part two).

Whereas Thielicke's desire to highlight God's nearness and concern for man is thus acknowledged and also justified, it must nevertheless be asked whether his almost purely relational focus, along with his corresponding exegesis of the name Yahweh in this specific instance, does not unintentionally put divine aseity into question. At the very least, his wording bears the possibility of misinterpretation, potentially suggesting not the idea of God's necessary, self-sufficient being—that is, God existing for his own sake—but rather a divine contingency, viz., a being who wills to exist *for the sake of* man.[80]

Whilst Yahweh surely is the most important single definition of God's name prior to Christ, thereby emphasizing his "fundamental inheritance promise" and "testamental nature,"[81] at the same time, it must be taken into account that Christ used the notion of the eternal "I am" to clarify his transcendent existence (see John 8:58). Additionally, in light of other divine names revealed in the Tanakh which highlight divine transcendence,[82] Ratzinger's explication that "the God who 'is' is at the same time he who is with *us*; he is not just God in himself, but our God"[83] appears to be the exegetically more justified and balanced interpretation.

Thielicke's Existential Arrival at the Concept of Divine Personhood

Returning to the existential embedding of the analogy that was hinted at in the beginning paragraphs of this chapter, a few years after his miraculous recovery, Thielicke published an essay on the office of the praying person during the war in 1940. In his opening, he states that the question of prayer touches upon the very question of Christian existence.[84] Prayer presup-

---

78. See *EvF II*, 111. "This name in no way ties God down either in nature or conduct. Everything is left 'open.' . . . The only definite thing . . . is that this self-disclosure and self-impartation will follow" (*EvF II*, 109).

79. See *EvF II*, 35.

80. "God's being as revealed in the name Yahweh is not a being-in-itself (as with the God of the philosophers) but a being-for-us" (*Abenteuer*, 204).

81. Payne, *Theology of the Older Testament*, 147–48.

82. See Payne, *Theology of the Older Testament*, 148.

83. Ratzinger, *Introduction*, 88.

84. See Barth: "The first and basic act of theological work is prayer. . . . Theological

poses a very specific relationship of this existence towards God, "namely, a personal I-Thou-relation between child and father."[85] Thielicke thinks that it is not so much the contents of the prayer that counts, but rather what the person turns into when praying: a loved child of God. Hence with the question of prayer and therein, implicitly, God's personal being, the Christian's very existence is at stake.

The contrast between Thielicke's pre- and post-recovery stance on God's personal being—and, henceforth, the possibility of prayer—is once more striking. *During* his "sickness-unto-death" and period of hospitalization, he went through severe theological crises as to both. *After* his miraculous recovery, however, his deep conviction of God's personal being, of God being the one who essentially loves,[86] reveals itself systematically as well as homiletically. As to the former, systematic focus (outlined above), he critically questions Tillich's transpersonal concept by asking about the bottom line of his construct: "Can the biblical symbol of the 'heart' of God be used for [Tillich's] being? Can the ground of the world as thus described be thought of as love and understanding? Does the depth of being *speak*?"[87]

Likewise, as to Thielicke's homiletical outworking, by taking just a cursory look at his pastoral reprocessing of the very same question of "God's heart," one cannot escape noticing how the personal focus plays itself out even more impressively via his sermons,[88] summarized in the emphatic question: "How can I love fate?" Thielicke answers at once (and as he did with Tillich): "I can only love where I feel a heart."[89] Accordingly,

---

work can be done only in the indissoluble unity of prayer and study" (Barth, *Introduction*, 160, 171).

85. *Anfechtung*, 180. "Prayer is only possible as personal address [*personhafte Anrede*]" (*ThE I*, §1308).

86. Following Barth, he nonetheless stresses the limited use of the analogy since "what must be affirmed is not that God is person but what specific person he is," namely, the One who loves (*EvF II*, 104). For Barth, see *Kirchliche Dogmatik II/1*, 333 [*CD II/1*, 296]. However, as the concept of person is *inevitable* in order to bring out God's love, with the act of love being necessarily tied to a personal agent—and the former, therefore, depending on the latter—one might question such prioritization. Either God is "a person and more" (Lewis) or he is not. The Barthian/Thielickean safeguarding device of prioritizing thus appears to be superfluous.

87. *EvF II*, 113.

88. Thielicke's dictum that Schleiermacher the preacher is needed in order to shed light on Schleiermacher the theologian thus, at least partially, also applies to himself. See *MF&T*, 178; *EvF I*, 365; and *EvF II*, 330, where he includes Luther in a similar reflection.

89. *Gebet*, 75.

references to God's "fatherly heart" or the analogy of divine "fatherhood" in Thielicke's sermons are legion.[90]

In between *pre-recovery doubt* and *post-recovery certitude* falls Thielicke's very own existential encounter with the One whose *personal* feature of loving *actuositas* subsequently becomes so central to Thielicke's whole theology—especially to his doctrine of revelation. Not coincidentally, theological conviction and personal experience decidedly overlap here, too: "The night I took the medicine I kind of set my life in order. I prayed. . . . In the face of the crucified, I thought of the forgiveness of sins, simply to straighten my life out. . . . Thus, my way to faith was . . . destined . . . by the superior power of this event. Tonight your life comes to an end; or you will live entirely anew."[91]

In the existential light of this, Thielicke's belief that with the question of prayer (and hence God's personal being) the Christian's very existence is at stake, gains meaning. On the brink of death, he *prayed*; and in his eyes, the *personal* God—not "the [transpersonal] depth of being" (Tillich)—*spoke*, and thus *acted*. In view of the miraculous convergence of the final stage of his sickness and the medical discovery of the life-saving medication "AT 10," Thielicke calls out to his listeners in Stuttgart: "You will understand how strongly I was under the impression back then: 'This was the Lord's doing.'"[92] Significantly, Thielicke thus evaluates his own recovery from sickness as the personal God's miraculous answer to his own prayer. In other words, in the face of death, Thielicke gave up his *old* existence and consequently gained his *Christian* existence, that is, he turned into a loved child of God[93] via experiencing the *personal, freely,* and *lovingly acting* heart of God on the relational basis of prayerful communication.[94]

Thielicke's emphasis on God's personal being as essentially rooted in his actual love and freedom leads, in turn, to the question of *the origin of evil* and, hence, death and suffering. This shall be turned to in the following subsection.

---

90. For just one example, see his use of "fatherly heart" in the "public dogmatics" held during the final stages of the war in Stuttgart—a time when his listeners had to be especially reassured as to the personal governance of the divine in the midst of chaos (*GldChr*, 59, 72, 107, 113, 239, 248, 254, 269, 286, 304, 391, 459, 461).

91. *Krauss*, 22–23.

92. *GldChr*, 346.

93. See *Anfechtung*, 180.

94. See Matt 10:39; 16:25; Luke 9:24; 17:33. Recall my statement at the end of chapter 4, part one: "What then, according to Luther, makes one a *Christian* theologian? The affirmative response to God's address and promise."

Part Two: The Origin of Evil—Ordained by God or Man?

The Question of *Supralapsarianism:* Death as Part of God's Original Plan?

According to Thielicke's line of thinking, in view of God's omnipotence and omniscience, Christ's freedom to redeem is inextricably interwoven with God's decision to create man. By virtue of his foreknowledge, God knew that man would fall once the "let us create" (Augustine's *posse peccare*[95]) was spoken—a theological conviction masterfully displayed in Michelangelo's fresco in the Sistine Chapel, "The Creation of Adam." God's left arm wraps around Eve and explicitly points to a child, who many hold to be Christ, the second Adam already being in God's mind as he creates the first. Thus, Christ's free choice to atone must be seen simultaneously with God's choice to create: "The creation of the world itself has christological significance; salvation is projected in it."[96] The divine will to create and save go hand in hand, both logically leading to God's freely chosen self-renunciation of his omnipotence in virtue of his lovingly created order.[97] That is why Brunner can state that "the κένωσις . . . began with the Creation of the world,"[98] and why C. S. Lewis makes the point that "when He created the vegetable world . . . He knew already that He Himself must so die and live again."[99]

In relation to God's sovereignty and freedom (which Thielicke does not tire of safeguarding), the question arises whether sin—and, subsequently,

---

95. C. S. Lewis is convinced that "the free will of rational creatures, *by its very nature* included the *possibility* of evil" (Lewis, *Problem of Pain*, 63). Emphasis added. For Lewis's emphasis on "our tiny, miraculous power of free will," see Lewis, *Problem of Pain*, 33; *Great Divorce*, 92, 106, 115: "Freedom: the gift whereby ye most resemble your Maker and are yourselves parts of eternal reality."

96. *EvF II*, 291. See *ThE I*, §751; *Freedom*, 171–72. But does this mean that suffering is an *intrinsic* part of God's divine being from all eternity by virtue of his will to create, by his being-oriented-to-the-other-beyond-himself, as Thiede suggests (Thiede, *Gekreuzigte[r] Sinn*, 173)? Thielicke seems to affirm this when he proclaims that "by shouting like a tormented creature [on the cross], he [Christ] lives in *eternal* dialogue with the father" (*Ernstfall*, 99). Emphasis added. For a criticism of this view, see Weinandy, "Does God Suffer?," §36: "He who is impassible as God was truly passible as man. . . . However, since it was the Son of God who suffered, did He not equally experience such suffering within His divinity? No, for suffering is caused by the loss of some good, and while as man the Son was deprived of His human well-being and life, He was not deprived of any divine perfection or good." See also chapter 7, part two.

97. Thiede, *Gekreuzigte[r] Sinn*, 139, points out Kierkegaard as intellectual source of this implication. In the twentieth century, the idea of God's radical kenosis was picked up, amongst others, by Alexander von Oettingen, Althaus, Brunner, and Moltmann.

98. Brunner, *Dogmatics II*, 20.

99. Lewis, *God in the Dock*, 37.

death—were part of God's original plan, i.e., predestined, as in the Islamic conception of God[100] but also as indicated by the Reformed Barth.[101] The greater historical debate between Reformed and Lutheran theologians, with its roots in Zwingli and Luther,[102] already anticipates Thielicke's Lutheran position on this question.[103] It therefore suffices to outline his stance briefly, at the same time serving as a bridgehead to the succeeding subsection on human suffering and theodicy.

Thielicke commences his criticism of supralapsarianism exegetically, serving as a basis for his ethical reasoning, to which our attention shall turn in a moment. First, as to the Old Testament, by emphasizing God's *creatio ex nihilo* (or *creatio de novo*),[104] he tries to substantiate the claim that (a) God's creation is essentially good; and (b) the origin of sin must be traced back to man.[105] This is the crucial difference between the biblical *ex nihilo* and ancient creation myths. For in the latter, man is always made out of existing material (as in Plato's *Timaeus*, for instance), thus being provided with an excuse and a legitimate right to distance himself from sin.[106] In the former, however, the indicative, God's original and good creation out of nothing, serves as basis for the imperative, God's total claim upon man.[107]

---

100. See Schirrmacher, *Islamic View*, 27–29.

101. See Barth, *Römerbrief*, 153, 159, 232–33, 293; Barth, *CD III/1*, 366; Nordlander, *Gottebenbildlichkeit*, 77, 81; and Gloege, "Zur Prädestinationslehre Karl Barths," 193–217.

102. See Holthaus, *Konfessionskunde*, 91, 96.

103. In spite of Thielicke's vehement emphasis on man's free will being the origin of evil, which I shall discuss below, he does not fit into the philosophical camp of *libertarianism*. Like many theologians and philosophers in the past and present, he adheres to the *compatibilist* position, that is, everything in the universe is caused, whilst equally thinking that human beings are properly held responsible for their nevertheless free actions. See McKenna and Coates, "Compatibilism."

104. Basing himself on Thomas Aquinas, von Wachter prefers *creatio de novo* since it clearly implies the non-existence of matter prior to creation, while this is not unambiguously the case with *creatio ex nihilo* (von Wachter, *Kausale Struktur*, 259n201).

105. See *ThE I*, §712–56. For the implicit rather than explicit presence of *creatio ex nihilo* in Genesis and a brief explication of this article of faith within early Christian theology, see Pannenberg, *Basic Questions II*, 144–46. As to its scriptural basis, Thielicke, *ThE I*, §713, only lists the "very indirect testimony of [Psalm] 33:6 and [John] 1:3," strangely ignoring further references like Romans 4:17 and Hebrews 11:3. Thiede emphasizes the close affinity between this dogma and the modern natural scientific standpoint (Thiede, *Gekreuzigte[r] Sinn*, 107).

106. See *Gespräche*, 172–73; *Freedom*, 19–21; *EvF II*, 53–54, 88; *ThE I*, §730–31.

107. "Therefore, the origin of evil cannot be deduced from the act of creation" (*ThE I*, §719). See *EvF II*, 53–54, 209, 211, 231; *Freedom*, 158.

In light of this, Thielicke's statement is to be understood that "it was God's venture [*Wagnis*] to make man as a free and personal being his counterpart; . . . God 'risked' man,"[108] and this divine risk is made plain by the fall:[109] "No, I cannot deduce sin causally; I have to consider myself to be the first cause. I myself am Adam who broke with God. I have to identify myself with him [Adam]. I cannot . . . give myself back to God the way I received myself from him. Therefore and only on this condition [*creatio ex nihilo*] I am responsible for my *Sosein*."[110]

Second, the overall teaching of the New Testament prohibits such an interpretation since sin, sickness, and spiritual death as conveyed in the medium of biological death are presented there as an unnatural incursion into God's creation.[111] Hence, Thielicke interprets Jesus's miracles as "gracious signs,"[112] as a law exposing evil in all its forms to be of the "crassest perversion, precisely not desired by God. . . . There is no pact between the disorder [of this fallen world] and God."[113]

He further illustrates his conviction that man's spiritual as well as biological death is in no way connected with divine ordinance by repeatedly referring to the diary of a young fighter pilot killed in action. Discovering a half-decayed corpse beneath a lilac, the pilot recoiled under the impression of the obvious contradiction between the dead body and the flowering shrub. The young man intuitively felt this corpse to be an alien element

---

108. *Fragen*, 153; *GldChr*, 111, 400, 435; and *ThE II/1*, §2195. Thielicke sees "man as God's *Wagnis*" preserved in German [Weimar] Classicism, especially in Herder and Schiller (*ThE I*, §796-97). See also his sermon, "Man, the risk of God," in *Welt*, 65-78 [*How the World Began*, 59-71].

109. *EvF I*, 361-62.

110. *Gespräche*, 173. "To the Creator out of nothing I owe myself totally" (*EvF II*, 54). See *Freedom*, 208; *Bilderbuch*, 218; and *ThE I*, §1384: "Adam—c'est moi." *Creatio ex nihilo*'s elementary significance for Thielicke is revealed further in *ThE I*, §1331. "Sin can be understood in a radical way only on the basis of creatio ex nihilo: only from here I can seriously grasp the thought that the origin of sin is 'in me.' Accordingly, creation's rupture (death and suffering) must eventually be traced back to me. . . . In light of creatio ex nihilo the complete . . . inextricability of creation and sin become[s] clear" (*ThE I*, §735). No one, not even the devil, can be made responsible for man's fall but he himself; the idea of evil being personal herein helps that the devil can never be regarded as the cause of evil. See *EvF III*, 450; *G&E*, 371-72; *Anfechtung*, 177-79; and Ratzinger, *Jesus I*, 239, 246. For Thielicke's view of the demonic in general, see esp. *EvF III*, 448-53; *Mensch*, 74-79. Furthermore, see C. S. Lewis's admonition in *Screwtape Letters*, ix; and Kraft, *Defeating Dark Angels*.

111. See *ThE II/1*, §848; *GldChr*, 452; *Woran*, 77, 81-82, 171; *Freedom*, 172; *Gebet*, 21-23.

112. *GldChr*, 452.

113. *Anfechtung*, 118 [*Wunder*, 46-47]. See *Tod*, 27; *Gebet*, 21-22, 75-76; *Welt*, 192; *ThE I*, §529; and *ThE II/1*, §848, §897, §2172, §2200.

within God's flourishing creation, providing him with a premonition of death's abnormality.[114] In at least two contexts, Thielicke then connects this story with Jesus's miracles as finally exposing the truly anti-godly essence of death and suffering.

On this scriptural basis, man's actual sinful suchness [*Sosein*] cannot be excused by embracing it as a divinely ordained status (as further exemplified by the Ten Commandments and the Sermon on the Mount). Rather, man's *Sosein* is rooted in the autonomous, timeless, and emancipatory act of human desire,[115] in the human will.[116] Grounding the fall in God's will rests on the confusion of a permission-to-be-guilty [*Schuldig-sein-dürfen*] with a permission-to-know-oneself-guilty [*Schuldig-wissen-dürfen*], the former presenting the temptation to equate God's mercy with man's sinful origin. If this is the case, that is, if being guilty is interpreted as being the product of God's mercy (since, due to divine predestination, man has no option but to exist in a sinful state), then the whole thought of judgement is not taken seriously.[117] This is precisely the accusation Thielicke directs against Barth—driving the latter towards the doctrine of *apokatastasis*[118]—but also against Schiller and even German Idealism as a whole.[119]

---

114. See *Welt*, 191; *LmdT*, 16; *Woran*, 170; *Ernstfall*, 78. See also the Pauline emphasis on death being the last enemy (1 Cor 15:26; Isa 25:8; Rev 21:4) and the Lutheran theme of Christ's death being "death's death" (Ebeling, "Todes Tod," esp. 39, 41).

115. See *G&E*, 250–51; *Fragen*, 102–3; and *ZG&S*, 30.

116. In addition to man being "God's risk [*Wagnis*]" referenced below, see *ThE II/1*, §654: "God . . . has no share in that world's blame which invoked the split." Not "tragedy" but "original sin" is the "signature" of this world (*ThE II/1*, §770–72). See also *ThE II/1*, §2172. "The question 'How can God let this happen?' . . . reveals man's disastrous talent to look for a scapegoat for his own guilt: God is guilty . . . ! It is always the same way and the same tone" (*Welt*, 273).

117. See *G&E*, 252. "Evil gets essentially distorted when . . . evil . . . itself becomes a carrying principle of salvation history" (*G&E*, 365). "Two things [regarding evil] have to be avoided: The first is . . . [setting] evil over against God in an abstract dualism. . . . The second is . . . [making] it simply the dialectical counterpole of the good [that is, a dialectical necessity]" (*EvF I*, 263). See also *ThE I*, §1345.

118. "There is also a christologically based monism which strips evil of its power and changes it into nothingness. [Thus] . . . theologically [God's] personality is weakened and anthropologically the moment is emptied of its unconditionality" (*EvF III*, 448). In *ThE I*, he speaks of "Barth's monistic tendency towards timelessness, elimination of salvation history, and *Weltanschauung*, as represented in [his] suspension of the antithesis between law and gospel" (*ThE I*, §594). For Thielicke's critical engagement with Barth's view of law and gospel, see *EvF II*, 191, 193–94; *Anfechtung*, 88–89; *ThE I*, §545–96, esp. §596 (a-x). For the Barthian danger of *apokatastasis*, see Zahrnt, *Sache*, 119–22. For Barth's theological monism, see Zahrnt, *Sache*, 124–27. For a broad historical overview as to *apokatastasis*, see Bauckham, "Universalism."

119. See *G&E*, 253, 356, 365; *LmdT*, 323; and *EvF II*, 87.

As to the first, universalism, Calvert must be questioned when he claims that "Thielicke embraced a form of this doctrine [*apokatastasis*], although apparently quite tentatively."[120] Calvert only cites two pastoral passages (from *Gespräche* [*Between Heaven and Earth*] and from the sermon "Descended Into Hell" in *Woran* [*I Believe*]), which, admittedly, make room for the possibility of post-mortem salvation of certain repentant sinners.[121] In both contexts, however, Thielicke only addresses the mere possibility of *individual* cases and not the *universal* dimension of such redemption. Besides, he is much more outspoken about the importance of a personal decision for Christ in *this* life. Post-mortem salvation is only presented in the subjunctive mood: "*Perhaps* God still has some other ways."[122]

The same applies to Thielicke's systematic discussion of universalism.[123] Here, he concludes—with similar conviction as he does regarding the issue of predestination[124]—that "there are some theological truths and circumstances . . . which cannot be the theme of theological statements but [in this case of the position of the lost] only of prayer."[125] Thus, his thoughts in this regard—which, regrettably, not only lack rigor in exploring more orthodox options[126] but also already anticipate his general wariness to dogmatic subtleties (see chapter 7, part two)—must be appreciated within their explicitly *pastoral* context and should be seen against the background of his clearer elucidations in relation to this issue elsewhere.[127]

---

120. Calvert, *Preaching*, 194.

121. See *Gespräche*, 142–47; *Woran*, 165–68. See also *Woran*, 184–86, basically repeating the points of *Gespräche*.

122. *Gespräche*, 146; *Woran*, 166. Emphasis added.

123. See *EvF III*, 453–56.

124. I shall discuss this issue further in the final subsection of this chapter.

125. *EvF III*, 456. Thielicke curiously lists a personal reason too. By entertaining the possibility of universalism, he "seriously [tries] to uphold the communion of saints in the context of a teaching which many contest but some hold in high esteem." See also *EvF III*, 456n35.

126. For example, the lost who never heard about Christ might be judged on the basis of what they *did* know, i.e., on the basis of general revelation. Or, according to the Molinist doctrine of divine *scientia media*, God knows how they would have decided had they had the chance of hearing the gospel, and thus God judges them accordingly. Indeed, God has so providentially ordered the world that any person who would believe in the gospel if he or she heard it will be born at a time and place in history at which they do hear it, so that no one is lost because of a historical or geographical accident. For an excellent discussion, see Craig, "How Can Christ Be the Only Way to God?"

127. See also Bloesch's evaluation in this regard: "Thielicke's sharp differences from Barth appear in his attack upon the doctrine of apokatastasis, the universal restoration of all souls. Barth does not affirm this, and yet the logic of his theology drives him in this direction" (Bloesch, "Thielicke's Ethics," 312). As already indicated, in the

As to Thielicke's criticism of Schiller and German Idealism, Nordlander claims that Thielicke himself is dependent on Idealism as he interprets the fall as the act by which man truly becomes man (not "became," as Thielicke denies any historicity of Genesis 1–3), having left his indifferent state. Thus for Nordlander, Thielicke's personalistic interpretation of creation forces him to equate creation idealistically with the fall,[128] a thesis confirmed by Thielicke's anthropological work published five years after Nordlander's dissertation.[129]

Two Adams and a Missing Link: Thielicke's "Half-hearted Demythologization"?

Nordlander criticizes Thielicke for not explaining, on the basis of his theistic evolutionary view, *the causal connection* between what Thielicke regards as man's purely *a*-historical fall[130] and the actual, historical occurrence of

---

said doctrine Thielicke fears the eschatological dissipation of man's salvific and ethical decision making, creating "a tendency toward indifference" (*EvF III*, 330). See also Graham, *Just As I Am*, 568, concluding that this view "cut[s] the nerve of evangelism." Thielicke even states that, because of this "total ethical blockade," the early Barth was co-responsible for a lack of resistance against National Socialism (*Mensch*, 164–66; Krauss, 26–27). For his outspoken criticism of universalism, see the passages in *ThE I*; *ThE II/1*, §892–905. See also *ThE II/1* §592; *EvF II*, 193–94, 237; *EvF III*, 329–30, 389, 431, 465; *Anfechtung*, 171, 193; *Woran*, 162; *Welt*, 42; *Gebet*, 66; and *Bilderbuch*, 56–60. That Thielicke's theological concerns in relation to Barth were not unfounded is vividly illustrated by Billy Graham's encounter with both Barth and Brunner, as rendered in his autobiography: "When I did hold the meeting in Basel, Karl Barth showed up. . . . I preached on the passage . . . 'Ye must be born again.' . . . 'I agreed largely with your sermon,' he said afterward, 'but I did not like that word *must*. I wish you could change that.' . . . He felt . . . that one should not give an Invitation; one should just declare that God had already acted. . . . When I was in Zurich with Emil Brunner . . . he was warm, friendly, and supportive. He disagreed with Barth's views on this. 'Pay no attention to him,' he said. 'Always put that word *must* in. A man *must* be born again.' And he was in favor of the Invitation" (Graham, *Just As I Am*, 694). For Thielicke's significant encounter with Graham, see *Wayfarer*, 359 [459–60]; *K&K*, 200–1 [*B&E*, 144–45].

128. Like Barth, *Römerbrief*, 151, 231–33, 294; but unlike Brunner, *Dogmatik II*, 113. For Nordlander's criticism of Thielicke in this regard, see Nordlander, *Gottebenbildlichkeit*, 58–59, 172–73.

129. See *Mensch*, 92–93. In doing so, Thielicke follows his favorite philosopher, Kant. "[Kant and the theologians following him] platonically tend to identify creation with the fall" (Bockmühl, *Die Aktualität der Theologie Adolf Schlatters*, 108).

130. See *EvF III*, 394–95; *Tod*, 146–48, 161–62; and *EvF I*, 36. That John Hick did not very thoroughly engage with the work he ought to have reviewed reveals his comment that "a good deal of his [Thielicke's] discussion hinges upon the doctrine of the Fall, which is presented quite uncritically as an event with a before and an after" (Hick, "Theology and Ethics," 23).

suffering and death from the very beginning.[131] Although Thielicke thinks that Christ's resurrection makes death as a value-free, biological law impossible—qualifying it, instead, as an enemy[132]—his existential-relational mode of thinking denies a causal connection between personal/spiritual death and biological death in favor of a mediative, symbolic one, believing that Luther held to the same view.[133]

Indeed, Thielicke's statements as to the precise connection between spiritual and biological death appear to be ambiguous at times. In contrast to Brunner,[134] who opines that biological mortality as a divine ordo is a natural part of life (Romans 6:23 thereby *not* implying physical mortality), Thielicke utters that death is *not* a natural necessity or law but rather "an event which I myself have caused, over against which I am subject, and which I have freely brought about as a responsible person. . . . The wrath of God which comes to expression in death is, in this sense, God's reaction to our personal action."[135] But to conclude, therefore, like Calvert, that for Thielicke "biological death . . . results from man's fall"[136] does not seem to be the full story either. Elsewhere, Thielicke clearly states:

> The misunderstanding that man's biological death is to be regarded as a consequence of the cause "sin" must be eliminated from the outset. Instead, Scripture reveals . . . human death as something taking place within the medium of biological death, which, however, must be differentiated from this medium. Man's death is thus qualitatively different from the "mere" biological dying of animals. The opposite of biological death is biological life. The opposite of human dying . . . is life out of God.[137]

---

131. See Nordlander, *Gottebenbildlichkeit*, 182. See also Nordlander, *Gottebenbildlichkeit*, 172–80, where he moves Thielicke near to a "platonic-idealistic conception," calling Thielicke's move of "the fall . . . into a supra-historical, supra-temporal, and supra-empirical dimension, into a metaphysical 'origin-dimension' [*Ursprungsdimension*]" an "intellectual auxiliary construction" [*intellektuelle Hilfskonstruktion*] (Nordlander, *Gottebenbildlichkeit*, 173–74).

132. See *Freedom*, 172.

133. See *Tod*, 162.

134. See Brunner, *Dogmatik II*, 142–43.

135. *EvF III*, 391. See *Tod*, 106. Likewise, Schlatter and Pannenberg see a causal connection between sin and physical death. See Schlatter, *Dogma*, 255; Pannenberg, *Systematic Theology III*, 560–61. This is also the official Roman Catholic position. See *Katechismus der Katholischen Kirche*, §1008.

136. Calvert, *Preaching*, 182.

137. *LmdT*, 55. See also *ThE II/1*, §1206; *Tod*, 13, 122, 162.

Biological death is merely a "warning" and "reminder" of man's spiritual death. Sin is the "background" and "basis" of biological death, but the latter is *not* a consequence of the former.[138] Accordingly, "the true reality of death through the biological medium is, then, a contradiction of his person, namely, limitlessness."[139]

Interestingly, in a postscript to his lay dogmatics, *Woran*, on "Creation and Natural Science" (not contained in the English translation, *I Believe*), Thielicke appears to hold to a view of theistic evolution which has been associated with James Woodrow and the early Benjamin Warfield: whilst Adam's body was the product of evolutionary development, "his special creation involved the imparting of a rational soul to a highly-developed hominid."[140] Likewise, Thielicke leaves no doubt regarding his view that at some stage within human evolution there must have occurred the all-decisive and final developmental step, when the hominid actually turned into Homo sapiens. This took place when God inbreathed or "ignited" man's antecedent with the "spark of mind" or spirit [*der Funken des Geistes*], a process which, for Thielicke, is well-illustrated by Michelangelo's fresco, "The Creation of Adam": "Michelangelo depicts the last moment of . . . the hominid."[141]

Yet, in spite of making room for the possibility of a historical fall within his theistic evolutionary view, Thielicke nonetheless objects to it. He criticizes Lutheran Orthodoxy for simplifying matters by presenting death merely as the consequence of a first sin committed by an actual first couple.[142] His opposition herein is, mostly, not exegetically motivated, but rather rests in his primary ethical criticism that a historical interpretation depersonalizes man and robs him of his responsibility.[143]

Here Thielicke shares a basic concern of modern theology,[144] and despite widespread theological agreement with Thielicke on the question of the historicity of Adam, it remains worth noting some potential difficulties

---

138. *EvF III*, 394.

139. *EvF III*, 393. "To be sure: biologically, we die the same death as animals, and yet 'for us' it is something entirely different, because we are different. If, for the sake of argument . . . we assume man's death apart from divine judgement . . . then it would indeed be something else entirely, it would merely be 'a sleep' (Luther)" (*Tod*, 148). See Althaus: "Dying is more than a biological phenomenon. It is a human reality; and this distinguishes it from the ending of plant and animal life" (Althaus, *Luther*, 405).

140. "Presbyterian Report of the Creation Study Committee," 73–74.

141. *Woran*, 319–20. See *ThE I*, §1429–30; *LmdT*, 2; *Welt*, 91–92.

142. See *Tod*, 122–23.

143. See *Anfechtung*, 124; *Tod*, 124–26; and esp. *ThE II/1*, §627. This is also the main reason why Brunner objects to a historical interpretation. See Volk, *Emil Brunners Lehre von dem Sünder*, 40–43, 233.

144. See Trueman, "Original Sin and Modern Theology," 180, 183.

with his position which conservative scholarship highlights. For example, in response to Thielicke's interpretation that Luther denied a causal connection between personal/spiritual death and biological death, Nordlander underlines that, for Luther, it posed no problem to keep to the traditional view of a historical Adam and, at the same time, nonetheless, considering present man as immediate [*unmittelbar*] to God.[145] Roman Catholic theologian Hermann Volk criticizes Brunner for the same non-historical interpretation of Adam.[146] Volk's point, that "at the crucial moment of Christian anthropology one must assume an act of ethical decision-making which poses the sole basis for the irrevocable sinfulness of man whilst [present man's] consciousness remains unaware of it,"[147] is also shared by Schlatter[148] and C. S. Lewis.[149] Whereas the latter denies the existence of a literal Adam and Eve, both posit an actual fall for reasons similar to Volk's.

Besides, along with the related "Enlightenment" objection that no person can justly be punished for the sins of another, Thielicke's fear of depersonalization can be rebutted by the Molinist doctrine of divine *scientia media*.[150] In any case, according to Thielicke, one's protology not only

---

145. See Nordlander, *Gottebenbildlichkeit*, 199n32. Here he relies on the work of David Löfgren, *Die Theologie der Schöpfung bei Luther*.

146. In a personal letter on September 25, 1947, Brunner informs Thielicke about a recent and "splendid" meeting with Edmund Schlink: "That is a fine man and not a stubborn Barthian. We got on very well until we got onto the subject of the historical fall. Then it got deeply divided. Am I a man of the last generation or of the future when I say: a theologian who believes in a historical fall, for example Adam as a Neanderthal man, is for me someone who lives in another world than I" (*NHT*).

147. Volk, *Brunners Lehre*, 233.

148. "It is equally certain that the secret of coming into being is neither lit up nor diminished through the long duration of time [between the first historically knowable cultures and the beginning of mankind]. Once there was a creation of the first human I, a first calling by God, a first realisation of the divine norm, its first breaking, a first fall" (Schlatter, *Dogma*, 257).

149. Lewis, *Problem of Pain*, chapter 5, esp. 75–76. According to Chesterton: "Science knows nothing whatever about pre-historic man; for the excellent reason that he is pre-historic. . . . History says nothing; and legends all say that the earth was kinder in its earliest time. There is no tradition of progress; but the whole human race has a tradition of the Fall. . . . Learned men literally say that this pre-historic calamity cannot be true because every race of mankind remembers it. I cannot keep pace with these paradoxes" (Chesterton, *Orthodoxy*, 125).

150. This view of God's "middle knowledge" (as originally advocated by Louis de Molina—Spanish Jesuit theologian, counter reformer, and founder of Molinism—in the sixteenth century) has been reanimated philosophically by thinkers such as Thomas P. Flint and William Lane Craig, trying to show the compatibility of divine foreknowledge and human freedom without robbing either of its full dimension. See Flint, *Divine Providence*; Craig, *Only Wise God*. See also Craig "Defenders—Doctrine of Man, part 15: Original Sin."

already predetermines one's position as to ethics, but also as to the question of justification—and even eschatology.[151] Yet, that he himself displays an essential inconsistency here is precisely the criticism of Nordlander. He questions Thielicke for referring to Christ, the second Adam, as a historical person whilst interpreting the first Adam (like modern theology in general and Schleiermacher and Barth in particular) existentially: "Adam—c'est moi."[152] Therefore, according to this line of criticism, two different perspectives regarding anthropology, on the one hand, and soteriology and eschatology, on the other hand, collide in Thielicke's thinking, dubiously playing themselves out on different levels.[153]

This factum leads Nordlander to the conclusion that Thielicke, quite in the spirit of Bultmann, interprets Genesis 1–3 existentially, but then stops short when it comes to soteriological passages, such as Christ's incarnation, passion, and resurrection. In view of Thielicke denying the first Adam, as the representative of this fallen aeon, historical existence, i.e., by interpreting Adam purely existentially, why should it follow that the resurrection of Christ, the second Adam, as the representative of the new aeon, was physical?[154] Would it not make more sense to proclaim with Bultmann, in an existentialist manner, that it is a mere spiritual resurrection? Nordlander thus concludes that Thielicke "performs half of a demythologization . . . Here Bultmann is more consistent."[155]

I have not tried to enter into all the complexities that would be involved in defending or rebutting Thielicke's position with regard to Adam's historicity and the fall; there is already a great amount being written on this in modern conservative scholarship.[156] My aim in this subsection was

---

151. See *ThE I*, §732.

152. *ThE I*, §1384. See *EvF II*, 247; Trueman, "Original Sin," 171, 177.

153. See Nordlander, *Gottebenbildlichkeit*, 177–80. For the first and second Adam, see also *G&E*, 260–65; *Tod*, 147n1; and *EvF III*, 394–95.

154. Volk points out that Brunner overlooks the fact that Romans 5:12 is not concerned with a physical worldview but rather contains an eminently theological statement, putting man's dependency on Adam on the same level as his dependency on Christ (Volk, *Brunners Lehre*, 232). For Nordlander questioning Thielicke regarding his similar exegesis of Romans 5:12, see Nordlander, *Gottebenbildlichkeit*, 179. Jewett's criticism of Brunner applies to Thielicke, too: "The trouble with Brunner is that he can allow for Christ's righteousness being imputed to the sinner, but not for the imputation of Adam's guilt" (Jewett, *Emil Brunner's Concept of Revelation*, 148).

155. Nordlander, *Gottebenbildlichkeit*, 180. Walters arrives at the same conclusion—namely, that "the modern worldview determines hermeneutic method. The ethics is that of Thielicke, but the hermeneutics is the demythologizing of Bultmann" (Walters, "Thielicke's Ethics," 39–40).

156. See, for example, the collection of essays in Madueme and Reeves, *Adam, the Fall, and Original Sin*. For a discussion of the issue, see Swinburne, *Responsibility and*

merely to outline Thielicke's somewhat ambiguous stance on this matter and to report briefly on the reaction provoked by what Thielicke said, mainly in the person of Nordlander.

Evil and Spiritual Death: Rooted in Man's "Freedom"

On the basis of the above reasoning, Thielicke concludes that "the origin of evil cannot be derived from the act of creation" and hence from God.[157] It follows that the entire responsibility for evil, in spite of its fundamental inexplicability,[158] rests with humanity, constantly realizing its given *posse peccare*.[159] Evil, in stark contrast to educational theories such as Rousseau's,[160] is rooted in the human will.[161] Thielicke uses the image of "wild, hellishly howling wolves suddenly breaking loose in my own cellar" recurrently to get this crucial point across.[162] Indeed, according to Thielicke, in man's freedom, the secret of the suffering God (see chapter 7) is to be found:

> Man is given the chance and the burden to decide for himself... God does not want man to be a marionette.... [God] embraces the possibility of man using that freedom against him.... If this is the case, then our human worldviews, all superstitious

---

Atonement, esp. chapter 9. As a related side note, an increasing number of twentieth-century Roman Catholic theologians (most notably, Karl Rahner) have come to regard biological polygenism as consistent with a historical *status originalis*. See Weger, *Theologie der Erbsünde*, 48–49; Rahner, "Erbsünde und Monogenismus," 202–5.

157. *ThE I*, §719. As he nevertheless seems to equate creation with the fall, Nordlander accuses Thielicke of inconsistency (Nordlander, *Gottebenbildlichkeit*, 174).

158. See *EvF III*, 450.

159. See *WiG*, 33–34; *Welt*, 187, 272: "Have we ever given thought to the possibility that all those sufferings were and are nothing ... but expressions of man's abuse of his gift of freedom?"

160. See Byrne, *Religion and the Enlightenment*, 188. Thielicke criticizes the view of man being a *tabula rasa* in *Mensch*, 263.

161. Thielicke highlights this especially in *ThE I*, §735, §1331; and *How the World Began* [*Welt*, 36, 131, 186–87, 195]. See also his sermon "Thy Will Be Done" in *Gebet*, 68–77 [*Our Heavenly Father*, 68–76]. See also C. S. Lewis: "Man is now a horror to God and to himself ... because he has made himself so by the abuse of his free will" (Lewis, *Problem of Pain*, 63). According to Lewis, the doctrine of man's [volitional] fall protects "against two sub-Christian theories of the origin of evil—Monism ... and Dualism." Recall Thielicke's criticism of Barth's potential monism above.

162. See *WiG*, 34; *Schuld*, 32; *Anfechtung*, 45; *LmdT*, 48; *Woran*, 131; *Welt*, 207; *Bergpredigt*, 79; *K&K*, 17 [*B&E*, 16]; and *Wayfarer*, 79 [107]. Among his many references to the evil of the human heart, see *Schuld*, 31; *Woran*, 147–48; and *ThDvGl*, 118–19: "In the light of eternity ... we find out that what happened in Auschwitz did not happen by chance, but that all this latently slumbers in us and around us."

> haunting created in our heart, even atheism . . . and nihilism are nothing less than possibilities which God provided. . . . If I grant another person . . . certain freedoms . . . then I restrict my own freedom accordingly . . . for I make myself dependent on what the other does with his freedom. At root, this is where the suffering of God starts, reaching its climax in Golgotha. God suffers the consequences of his goodness. . . . This is the secret of the suffering God.[163]

Prima facie, in this specific passage, Thielicke comes intriguingly close to a libertarian standpoint. This seems to find further support in a sermon given during the final stages of the war, as he encourages his listeners to expect miracles when praying: "Logically, we can ask God for certain things only if we assume that not everything is determined yet, that the future is not yet fixed, as expressed in the Mohammedan term 'kismet.'"[164] But this, of course, is only half of Thielicke's compatibilist story, and later, in the very same series of sermons, he states the following: "Ultimately, only God's will happens. . . . We would see things completely distorted if we were to speak of a limitation of God's sovereignty through human autonomy. Quite the reverse is true: Everything men do . . . is included . . . in God's domain out of which no one and nothing can break."[165]

Now it is not impossible that Thielicke's emphasis in the said context is due to psychological reasons, owed to his experience that belief in fatalism, a-personal determinism, or personal predestination noticeably reaches its highest peak during humanity's darker days: "In times of war and terror, I encountered many who gave themselves up to fatalism, muttering the word 'fate' when the ray of destruction hit them."[166] Nonetheless, he can only put more emphasis on something of which he is already convinced.

As he holds to God ultimately being in *causal* control,[167] a systematic unfolding of the doctrine of predestination in view of his compatibilism

---

163. *Welt*, 271. "By making man his partner, God exposes himself to man's freedom and to the events caused by this freedom" (*Mensch*, 352). "God forces no one" (*Bilderbuch*, 17). See further the classic passage in Lewis, *Problem of Pain*, 129–30.

164. *GldChr*, 348.

165. *GldChr*, 449–50. In *Gebet*, 58, he implies that the failed coup d'état on July 20, 1944, was due to God's decreed fate. "All our freedom . . . finally flows into God's aims although no one knows the place of the junction" (*GldChr*, 448). This point is also made by Packer, *Evangelism*.

166. *Reden*, 267. For similar observations during the Second World War, see Bonhoeffer, *Widerstand*, 59, 125; and for the British side, Dummett, rendered in Craig, *Only Wise God*, 14–15. See also the individual example of the Swiss reformer, Huldrych Zwingli, in 1519 (McGrath, *Calvin*, 99).

167. See *EvF I*, 105; *ThE I*, §319, §1087, §2114; *ZG&S*, 94; *GldChr*, 215.

would have been worthwhile. Thielicke, however, considering the subject matter to be "metaphysics's perhaps most difficult problem,"[168] could not recognize any cognitive possibility of delving into this issue more deeply.[169] He therefore basically contents himself with the *pastoral* advice to trust the one in whom this complementarity is secured and hidden.[170]

Yet, one legitimately wonders whether he takes the easy way out in this regard.[171] Thielicke's disdain for metaphysical reflection, along with opting for a purely mediative/symbolical connection between personal/spiritual and biological death, is the reason why, in spite of all his emphasis on evil being rooted in man's will, his position nonetheless remains ambiguous in

---

168. *GldChr*, 455. See *GldChr*, 466; and Ward, *God*, 131, likewise considering it to be "one of the biggest puzzles in the whole history of human thought."

169. See *ThE I*, §1378; *Gespräche*, 144, 152; *Fragen*, 209n1; *EvF I*, 171–72; *EvF III*, 455; and *ThE I*, §1376. For his general thoughts on predestination and free will, see esp. *GldChr*, 454–73; and *Gespräche*, chapters 7 and 8. Where one might most likely expect an exposition (namely, in his sermon, "How Evil Came Into This World," in *Welt*, 129–44 [*How the World Began*, 121–35]), he evades any philosophical answer, merely interpreting the dialogue between Eve and the serpent, thereby reasserting the rootedness of evil in the human will (*Welt*, 131). In his eyes, the question itself is wrongly put since one cannot solve it; one can only be saved from it (*Gespräche*, 144–45). Rather, "I have to ask why *I* am evil. . . . For the secret of personhood is its non-deducibility [*Unableitbarkeit*]." See *Welt*, 177, 273; *ThE I*, §1375, §1389. For his systematic unfolding as to the ethical consequences—esp. with regard to human responsibility—see *ThE I*, §1375–1440.

170. See *Gespräche*, 145, 154. Like Luther and Calvin (McGrath, *Calvin*, 216), Thielicke stresses the importance of the right position of the teaching, viz., always only after the doctrine of justification (*Gespräche*, 160–62, 164; *EvF I*, 171–72; and *EvF III*, 455). See also his implying that the question cannot be solved epistemologically, but only existentially (*EvF II*, 52–55). By giving the pastoral priority over the philosophical, Thielicke bases himself on Luther (*Gespräche*, 151) who, in his struggle with predestination, received the same admonition from his mentor, Staupitz. See Sierszyn, *2000 Jahre Kirchengeschichte. Band 3*, 37–38.

171. In offering a Molinist approach to this issue, William Lane Craig notes: "As I read the treatment of divine omniscience in the standard evangelical works of systematic theology, I am often amazed at their superficiality and lack of clear, logical reasoning" (Craig, *Only Wise God*, 11). He further remarks that "for too many Christians, easy appeal to mystery has become a substitute for the labor of hard thinking" (Craig, *Only Wise God*, 15). In the latter conviction, he is joined by Rahner, *Erinnerungen*, 61. Not only Thielicke—"I am, for example, of the opinion that all problems connected with predestination are principally and theoretically unsolvable" (*Gespräche*, 144)—but also J. I. Packer exemplifies this approach: "What should one do, then, with an antinomy? Accept it for what it is, and learn to live with it" (Packer, *Evangelism*, 21). Moreover, "we ought not in any case be surprised when we find mysteries of this sort in God's Word. For the Creator is incomprehensible to his creatures" (Packer, *Evangelism*, 24).

the end.[172] Hence, in the words of Ward, "an unfriendly critic might say that this is a free-will defense without any free will."[173]

At any rate, for Thielicke, man being the origin of evil, in turn, bears automatic consequences for the "suffering of nature as part of man's history with God in rebellion. . . . [Man's] breach with God has a universal dimension."[174] Thielicke's position thus resonates with the German medieval abbess and "Doctor of the Church," Hildegard von Bingen, for "if man sins, the cosmos suffers."[175] This world is sinister for man because he misappropriated his origin, because he has the fall behind himself,[176] because he has to identify with it: "I am this fallen world."[177] According to Thielicke, this truth finds paradigmatic expression in Francis Thompson's poem, "The Heart," which he interprets for his theological purposes as follows:

> This world is part of the essence of man. He "is" his world. The [evil] structure of this world . . . is only a macrocosmic reflection of his heart. Conversely, the heart is only a microcosmic expression of this world of his. Babylon can only try to be as great and immoderate as our Babylonian heart . . . Man is man in his world and not man apart from his world. He is the one who qualifies this world of his and who objectifies himself in its structures.[178]

This central theological insight similarly grew from a life experience. This time, it was rooted in a conflict with his friend, Wilhelm Schwinn, over the post of being Althaus's assistant after Thielicke's *Habilitation*.[179] In short, without intending to, he had to oust his friend, thereby apparently ruining

---

172. See *Tod*, 161–62, where, in the context of negating any causal connection, Thielicke points out that "I ought not to place myself contemptuously above *death and its originator* but should . . . appreciatively place myself under *him* [God]. . . . Only God himself can heal *the wounds that he has scarred*." Emphasis added.

173. Ward, *God*, 133.

174. *EvF III*, 437. "Much of the sighing of creation is in fact caused by man and is not just a transhuman fate which makes man an uninvolved and innocent victim" (*EvF III*, 437). "The cross of Christ was erected within this aeon because this aeon could not bear God's absoluteness" (*ThE II/1*, §259). "Creation's adversity . . . of this aeon which is rooted in original guilt" (*ThE II/1*, §695, §2172). See also *Bilderbuch*, 20.

175. Cited in Ratzinger, *Licht der Welt*, 68.

176. See *Mensch*, 181.

177. *EvF II*, 257. See also *ThE I*, §2144–46.

178. *EvF I*, 384. See *EvF II*, 247–48; *EvF III*, 420; *ThE I*, §2158–59; *ThE II/1*, §1401; *Mensch*, 35; *Fragen*, 118, 187; *Nihilismus*, 118; *Welt*, 304; *GldChr*, 147, 194; *Gebet*, 110; *Suche*, 97; and *ZG&S*, 5, 34–35.

179. See *Wayfarer*, 82–85 [111–15].

Schwinn's life. This led him to the conclusion that "this conflict was already laid down in the very structure of the world."[180] But if this were correct and it did affect history as a whole, then Thielicke, contrary to his teacher Althaus, could no longer consider the historical world as neutral:

> It would mean that the fall . . . had also come to acquire an objective existence in historical structures. Moreover, . . . [as] a historical being . . . I had to identify myself with it. After all, I myself was and am this history . . . by virtue of my "mere existence." All this resulted in my developing a quite new conception of good and evil, creation and fall, self and history. Virtually everything I have produced in the way of theological theory is based on this conception.[181]

Whilst this specific theological conviction did not directly emerge under the auspices of death and suffering, it nevertheless provides a clear case with regard to my central concern. Thielicke possibly exaggerates when he states that "virtually all my theological problems have emerged not as the result of purely intellectual processes, but have grown from situations in my life—mainly from conflicts."[182] His conflict with Schwinn bears testimony to this.

Finally, besides documenting the case in point, Thielicke's equation of man and world also further clarifies his personalistic thinking. Langsam points out that Thielicke does not represent a "pure" or "principled personalism" à la Buber or Ebner, i.e., only and purely a God-man-relation, but also always thematizes man's relationship to the world.[183] In his relational theology in general (see chapter 4) as well as his focus on man's inextricable interlacement with the created order in particular, Thielicke is firmly grounded in Luther. Indeed, Ebeling highlights that, for Luther, man *coram Deo* cannot be separated from man *coram hominibus* or *coram mundo*, the latter two being "almost identical."[184]

Therefore, by "[detaching] himself from this [worldly] context," the human is not only "reduced to unreality,"[185] but, in Lutheran fashion—and

---

180. *Wayfarer*, 84 [114]. That Schwinn's behavior simply might have been out of the question and thus necessarily led to this conflict is another way of looking at things.

181. *Wayfarer*, 84 [114].

182. *Wayfarer*, 84 [114].

183. Langsam, *Konkretion*, 43n190, 43n191.

184. Ebeling, *Luther*, 199. See Barth: "If the community and the world were not involved, he [the theologian] himself could not be involved. For only in the community and the world is he the one who he is" (Barth, *Introduction*, 82).

185. *EvF I*, 384. Thielicke calls this "anthropological Docetism."

thereby going beyond Buber and Ebner—Thielicke also programmatically states that "I can never have the *coram Deo* without the *coram mundo* within which it actualizes itself."[186] Van Bentum must therefore be corrected when he aligns Thielicke with Ebner's and Buber's thought-form.[187] Like his teacher Althaus,[188] Thielicke not only sees himself grounded theologically in this regard but at the same time wants to make sure that this all-determining relation does not turn into a (philosophical) relational*ism* by testing the personalistic concept each time *ad hoc*.[189]

In conclusion, it was shown in part two of this chapter that in view of divine goodness and perfection it is unthinkable for Thielicke to include evil in God.[190] Moreover, part one revealed Thielicke's positive conviction as to God's personhood, albeit his stressing of the term's instrumental function if applied to the latter. By referring to Camus, however, Moltmann points out that it is the very "concept of the personal God" as derived from the Bible that intensifies the "metaphysical rebellion" in light of this world's miserable state.[191] This intensification of the question of theodicy thus leads to Thielicke's "personalistic solution" with regard to the problem of evil, which I will analyze in the next chapter.

---

186. *ThE II/1*, §1396. "I obtain my self-consciousness by engaging with the world" (*Mensch*, 35). C. S. Lewis invalidates a "pure God-man relationalism" by showing the necessity of nature/matter in this regard. See Lewis, *Problem of Pain*, 19–22.

187. See Van Bentum, *Grenzsituationen*, 177.

188. See Althaus, *Luther*, chapter 18.

189. See *EvF II*, 122; *ThE I*, §964.

190. See 1 John 1:5; 3:5. See also Brunner, *Dogmatics II*, 18, 20, 37; and Moltmann, who agrees with Unamuno that a "God who suffers cannot be the cause of suffering" (Moltmann, *Experiences*, 51–52).

191. Moltmann, *Crucified God*, 221. C. S. Lewis agrees: "Pain would be no problem unless, side by side with our daily experience of this painful world, we had received what we think a good assurance that ultimate reality is righteous and loving [i.e., *personal*]" (Lewis, *Problem of Pain*, 14). See also Trillhaas's assertion: "Belief in God's personhood is required for the problem [of theodicy]" (Trillhaas, *Dogmatik*, 173).

Chapter 7

The Crucified God

Borderline Situations and the Cross of Christ

IN THE LAST CHAPTER, I presented two central pillars of Thielicke's thought: God being (tri-)personal (part one) and the impossibility of man's "three great problems" originating from the same (part two). Thus, the ground is now laid for an analysis of Thielicke's christological conviction as to the (tri-)personal God reaching out to man and his self-inflicted dilemma via Christ the Son. It is the *crucified* God that almost exclusively represents Thielicke's answer to the problem of evil. In part III, I will concentrate on the *horizontal* consequences of his emphasis on the *Deus crucifixus*, viz., his homiletical and pastoral outworking of the said focus. In this chapter, however, it is my aim to carve out the existential basis of Thielicke's *vertical* view of the triune God overcoming man's depths by suffering himself.

Part One: Thielicke's "Insightful Moment"—The Borderline Situation as a Means of Revealing the *Deus crucifixus*

At least since Kant,[1] many have judged that questions in metaphysics and theodicy yield no objectively correct answers. It is therefore not surprising, not only in light of Kant being his favorite philosopher,[2] but also in staunchly Lutheran fashion, that Thielicke refuses to engage in any such undertaking.[3] He considers the question of theodicy to be wrong in

---

1. See Kant, *Über das Mißlingen aller philosophischen Versuche in der Theodizee*.

2. See Röhricht, "Thielicke," 21.

3. See Bayer: "Theology is a *theology of Anfechtung*: it involves trial, testing, and spiritual attack. It renounces the idea of a unity of history and all attempts to offer a theodicy. In other words, it gives up any attempt to justify God and his goodness in the face of radical evil" (Bayer, *Lutheran Way*, 95).

its very essence, since Yahweh "is first known in the immediacy of faith." Therefore, "he cannot be grasped as a principle to which all phenomena [including evil] can be related."[4] Man only recognizes the good demanded from him by God *intra fidem*, and only as he realizes God's ultimate demand, does he gain an understanding of the actuality of evil.[5] Hence not only is good the prime reality, and evil merely its distortion or abuse—i.e., its privation[6]—but a personal God must also be in the paradigm for the problem to make sense.[7]

Moreover, and this time in a Kierkegaardian manner, the whole question of temptation out of which the question of theodicy arises is an existential problem, not an epistemological one: "The believer himself is the field of battle," with the struggle between the spiritual man and the natural man never ending in this aeon.[8] The victory over temptation—and thus, the solution to the problem of theodicy—is likewise not "an epistemological phenomenon," but "an existential event"[9]: "The fixed pole around which everything revolves in Reformation theology is therefore the act through which God wrings faith from us and with it an existence oriented upon God."[10]

On the other hand, following from man's fallen and, as such, constantly tempted nature,[11] "the [epistemological] question of theodicy lurks every-

---

4. *EvF I*, 380. See also *Freedom*, 178; *WiG*, 16: "Mere thinking about the question does not help us to cope with it."

5. See *G&E*, 358–59.

6. See *EvF III*, 452–53. The neoplatonic-Augustinian view of evil having no nature on its own, as *privatio boni*, became official church dogma at the council of Florence (1439–1445). See Adam, *Dogmengeschichte*, 167. C. S. Lewis makes essentially the same point (Lewis, *Mere Christianity*, 35–36). See also Cary, "Classic View," 14–17.

7. See *Freedom*, 175; *ThE I*, §56; *EvF III*, 453; Lewis, *Mere Christianity*, 31; Zacharias, *Can Man Live Without God*, 182–83; Zacharias, *Cries of the Heart*, 66–68. See also Moltmann's citations of Horkheimer and Camus in Moltmann, *Crucified God*, 224n64, 225n68; and Calvert, *Preaching*, 202.

8. *EvF II*, 51. See also *Anfechtung*, 193; *Nihilismus*, 57; *Ernstfall*, 129–30; and *Bilderbuch*, 23. "Rational difficulties . . . are always only a sign that something much more real is not in order, namely, our fellowship with God" (*ZG&S*, 43). "Basically Cartesian theology centers on the question of theodicy." The starting point of Cartesian theology, however, "is man . . . in his givenness and in the givenness of his world. . . . When man begins with himself as a given, God is a problem" (*EvF I*, 221–22).

9. *EvF II*, 55. "Temptation is thus a sign that God refuses to correspond to the image which man's autonomy [autonomous existence] makes of him" (*EvF II*, 52).

10. *Freedom*, 162. Just prior to this, he approvingly quotes Kierkegaard: "Objectively, then, one has only uncertainty; but this is precisely what increases the tension of the infinite passion of inwardness." One wonders how Thielicke would interpret passages like 1 Cor 15:58; Col 1:23; 2:5; 2 Pet 3:17.

11. Due to man's perverted being and reason, the question of theodicy is imposed on God to justify himself. See *EvF I*, 222; *EvF II*, 52.

where at all times."[12] In other words, it cannot be avoided. The question furthermore *does* gain validity under certain *existential* conditions, viz., when man experiences what Thielicke, following Jaspers, calls "the borderline" or "frontier situation" [*Grenzsituation*]:

> As the term indicates, the question of final reality arises *especially* on the horizons of human existence, in suffering, disaster, death, extreme anxiety, and the confrontation with what seems to be meaningless—in short, in situations of trial which usually pose the question of theodicy. *Situations of this kind are crucial points for religion* because they have a special measure of transparency for the final reality.[13]

Thus, whereas Thielicke disdains any objectively binding answer to *the problem of theodicy* in the form of an outworked *philosophical* system, he nonetheless highly welcomes *the question of theodicy* as a *subjective* question typically arising in the borderline situation and ideally serving as a pointer to God. The *Grenzsituation* within which the existentially important questions actualize thereby becomes fundamental to Thielicke's theology[14]—especially to his ethics, for it is "the borderline case and not the normal case [that] poses the actual questions."[15]

We can therefore note a broadening of the concept of "borderline": whilst the notion was "existentially planted" in Thielicke's early life, with specific regard to his literal standing on the border between life and death,[16] in his mature thought, it also covers intellectual scenarios from all kinds of different areas. Agreeing with Tillich, the border is the prolific place for gaining knowledge.[17] Following Jaspers and his individual application of the concept,

---

12. *EvF I*, 380. "The fact that God remains silent and passive . . . constitutes the severest kind of test of faith and confronts us with the full force of the problem of theodicy" (*Freedom*, 175). "Our faith in the father of Jesus Christ is time and again most seriously threatened in times of catastrophe, especially if we are personally involved" (*GldChr*, 451).

13. *EvF III*, 349. Emphasis added. See "EdR," 68; *Lebensangst*, 7–8; and the similarity of this statement to Bromiley's evaluation in chapter 3, part two.

14. This was already recognized and systematically unfolded in the early sixties by Ad van Bentum, who titled his dissertation, "Helmut Thielicke's theology of borderline situations." At that time, of course, van Bentum was not able to take the existential dimension into account. Besides, he concentrates almost exclusively on the first two volumes of *ThE*. See van Bentum, *Grenzsituationen*, 219.

15. *ThE II/1*, §688. The extensive theological usage of "border cases" does not originate with Thielicke. Barth, *Kirchliche Dogmatik III/4*, uses them in his ethics, too.

16. In addition to his illness, Bromiley rightly implies that Thielicke's situation during the Third Reich provided an existential hotbed regarding the "extreme instances of borderline decision" (Bromiley, "Thielicke," 549).

17. See *ThE II/1*, §700; *Mensch*, 21.

it is the borderline situation (i.e., a situation filled with struggle and suffering in which "I inevitably incur guilt" and "have to die"), which theologically and ethically yields promising fruit. Thielicke thus wants to "fertilize" this thought as to this aeon's whole mode of being.[18] He wants to do so because he had experienced its existential power first-hand.

Furthermore, in his eyes, this is not a new idea, but is already present in the Scriptures: "The world and with it man's being . . . is [biblically] revealed from [the standpoint of] its border . . . That is, it [the essence of world and man] is eschatologically revealed."[19] According to van Bentum, Thielicke uses Jaspers's conception only as an approach to elucidate a theological state of affairs, "namely, the irreconcilable, dialectical contrast between God . . . and man."[20] Not necessarily being dependent on him, Thielicke nevertheless resorts to Jaspers's terminology in order to express what he thinks to be the secret of this aeon: its "uncrossable border." By this, he does not so much denote the world's (and man's) chronological, but rather its *qualitative* horizon:

> [In the borderline situation] we . . . are mercilessly confronted with the qualitative borders of our world, forcing us to understand the actual essence of this world: sin and fallenness. The borderline situation thus offers an instructive model by means of which the fact of the fallen world is to be studied and the problem of ethics in its sharpest form is to be put.[21]

Once more, the conceptual connection between Thielicke's central conviction regarding ethical deliberation and his own existential borderline situation (as experienced in his "sickness-unto-death") must be highlighted. It is hereby helpful to recall both Pless's[22] and Speier's evaluation within this specific context: "The impulse emanating from Thielicke's illness and thus affecting his theological work can hardly be overestimated. Thielicke falling

---

18. See *ThE II/1*, §702–4.
19. *ThE II/1*, §705.
20. Van Bentum, *Grenzsituationen*, 43–44.
21. Van Bentum, *Grenzsituationen*, 44. Consequently, on its basis, Thielicke recognizes man's total depravity; for it is not the normal situation but "the utmost possibility, i.e., the borderline situation, which contains the defining statement about our being" (*ThE II/1*, §701, §709). At the same time, in light of what has been explicated in chapter 6, part two, "the borderline situation . . . does not reveal a conflict *in* God, but a conflict *against* God" (*ThE II/1*, §1161). Hence, it is rooted not in God's being but in the depraved nature of this aeon.
22. "Thielicke's existential awareness that human life is always lived on the borderline between life and death permeates both his academic and pastoral work" (Pless, "Thielicke," 441).

ill was for him a borderline situation by which he learned that the border is always a prolific place for gaining knowledge."[23]

At least two Thielickean statements undergird Speier's general assessment, one directly connected to his "existential moment *per se*" and the other indirectly, flowing from it decades later. Regarding the second, forty-two years after his recovery, Thielicke's life was yet again in danger, this time due to a wrong dosage of medication. Without going into more detail (see chapter 3, part three), he describes the low-point of 1975 as follows: "Once again, as so often in my life, I experienced *in borderline situations* mercy and preservation."[24] Is it not a telling conjuncture that he uses the very term he has taken over from Jaspers as a general label for those existential situations in which he was coming close to death?

The same applies all the more to his description of that most fateful event on the evening of Maundy Thursday, 1933, as he evaluates the all-crucial decision of taking the yet untested medicine as "*bordering on attempted suicide.*"[25] Thus, Tillich's theologoumenon that the border is the prolific place for gaining knowledge literally *came into existence* for Thielicke via his reprocessing of the said experience after his miraculous recovery: "*I now knew* what faith meant and everything that had previously only intellectually fascinated me about theology was swept away by completely new impulses."[26]

This initial, existential grounding of the *Grenzsituation* was subsequently further deepened during the war as outlined in chapter 3. Thielicke's manifold experiences with the borderline situations of others strengthened in him the conviction that a "theology in the face of death" cannot tolerate minor matters. It therefore helps to gain the right sense of proportion for both the significant and the irrelevant,[27] as further shown below. Yet, although such theology is *time bound*, it reveals questions and insights that are *timeless*. Thielicke calls this the "insightful moment," that is, the "prolific instant that makes insight possible," thus constituting the essential characteristic of the borderline situation.

---

23. Speier, *Initiator*, 20n4. See also chapter 2, part two.

24. *B&E*, 220. Emphasis added.

25. *Krauss*, 21. Emphasis added. For this and subsequent citations, see chapter 2, part two.

26. *K&K*, 15–16 [*B&E*, 14]. Emphasis added. See also *Wayfarer*, 66 [90]. For one example of ethical insight, in reference to the artificial delaying of death, Thielicke concludes that "here we are walking on borders that never permit clean solutions" (*Sterben*, 35).

27. See *K&K*, 49–50 [*B&E*, 44]; *Lebensangst*, 119–20.

Part Two: *Deus crucifixus*—Thielicke's Personalistic[28] Answer to the Problem of Evil

Thielicke's Personalistic Focus Existentially Embedded

We have just seen that Thielicke, taking his cue from Jaspers, defines the borderline situation (a) as being filled with struggle and suffering; (b) as one in which man inevitably incurs guilt; and (c) as one in which one has to die. Along with Tillich, furthermore, he believes that such a situation ultimately yields promising theological and ethical fruit. Intriguingly, all three elements of this definition are fully met by Thielicke's pivotal encounter with the crucified Christ on the night before Good Friday, 1933.

As parts (a) and (c) have already been addressed above, attention must now briefly shift to the existential embedment of the second factor of the formula: the incurrence of guilt. Thielicke desperately—but nevertheless, willingly—took the risk of suicide. He "wanted to force a decision: either this maximum dose of the medicine would help . . . or the 'poison' would kill."[29] But by taking that suicidal risk, he consciously staked everything on that "one card Christ" in whom forgiveness is to be found; he staked everything on that first personal encounter with the one who, in view of the cross, became his "brother and companion."[30] In other words, Thielicke *personalistically* overcame the threat of death and with it the threat of meaninglessness,[31] and is thus in full accord with his preferred theological schema of thought (see chapter 4). Since the question of meaning, according to Thielicke, is identical with the question of truth[32] and since both meaning and truth are truly personified in the person of Jesus Christ, is it surprising, *in light of* his "Maundy Thursday experience," when he defines the human condition ultimately as a relation to meaning or meaninglessness, either upholding man (in case of the former) or destroying him (if the latter)?[33]

---

28. See chapter 4, part one, for my working definition of this term.

29. *Wayfarer*, 65 [89]. "Tonight your life comes to an end; or you will live entirely anew" (*Krauss*, 23).

30. *Ernstfall*, 150.

31. See Brocher: "As soon as the question of meaning as to one's further life and future arises, the question of death inevitably resurfaces, too" (Brocher, *Wenn Kinder trauern*, 69).

32. See "WuV," 115.

33. See his sermon "Karfreitag 1941" (*NHT*), where he makes the same point. "Death is not life's endpoint but its essence. Consequently, I live only in the truth [or, "meaningful"] if I—in the [constant] knowledge of death—refer my whole life to the acting God, who reveals Himself in [man's] dying" (*Tod*, 161).

This further comes to the fore by considering aspects of his systematic treatment of the "Idea of the Death of God." The death of God entails that "the system of reference is eliminated."[34] Consequently:

> If the God of Descartes does not exist . . . there is no path from the self to the outside world and the result is illusory caricature and deception [meaninglessness]. . . . Polar isolation . . . drives the man who denies God into unsettling solitude. . . . *No one is so alone as the man who denies God*. . . . He is left on his own and has lost the infinite breast on which he used to recline.[35]

"Every understanding of existence that proceeds from self-certainty rather than God-certainty drives the I into radical loneliness."[36] Without reading too much into his emphasis on "the orphaned heart that has lost its higher Father," the similarity to the phraseology of his own existential turn-around is nonetheless there: "Back then [he] was not a Christian, much more a fatalist who had accepted his fate."[37] And when he was finally alone that night, "very much alone" (he emphasizes this in an embedded clause), he "contemplated" the bottle of "AT 10" and, finally, "in an act of desperate determination" gulped its content down,[38] thus "*bordering on attempted suicide.*"[39] Perhaps it is no coincidence that, shortly after writing the indented citation above, Thielicke indeed goes on to elaborate briefly on the issue of self-murder.[40]

Moreover, this emphasis on his being "very much alone"[41] sheds light on another Lutheran lesson, which, at that time, Thielicke seems to have learned "the hard way." In the words of Althaus: "Luther establishes the loneliness of faith by referring to death. In death, each of us is completely alone and must die his own death; no one else can take your place; and no one else . . . can fight the fight of faith in death's great hour of trial and

---

34. *EvF I*, 237. See *Fragen*, 57; *Lebensangst*, 16.

35. *EvF I*, 237–38. Emphasis added. See also *ThE I*, §1958; *Nihilismus*, 156; and *Reden*, 140.

36. *ThE I*, §1956.

37. *Ernstfall*, 149.

38. *Ernstfall*, 149.

39. *Krauss*, 21.

40. See *EvF I*, 238–39; *ThE I*, §1958–62. For Thielicke's engagement with the issues of suicide and euthanasia, see also *ThE I*, §403–12, §1211; *LmdT*, 14, 115–37; *Nihilismus*, 156; the third chapter of *Sterben*; and *Krauss*, 21–22.

41. *Ernstfall*, 149. See *Wayfarer*, 66 [90]: " . . . being restored to life after years of dreadful and demoralizing loneliness."

perplexity."⁴² In light of the closely intertwined relationship of Lutheran thinking and Thielickean experience (see chapter 4), it is not surprising to learn that Luther's focus on man's particular loneliness in death finds a strong echo in Thielicke's later writings.⁴³ Not only in death but also in his sufferings,⁴⁴ as well as quite generally "in the crucial things of life man is lonely and not substitutable."⁴⁵

Thielicke notes that this was borne out for him by "a very trivial experience." Watching a company of soldiers blaring out a song whilst marching down the street, it dawned on him that this "fascinating symbol of the collective" at some point "breaks up again and each man goes back to his family. Then each one leads his own life, each sins in his own way . . . and finally each will also die his own death—alone and with none to accompany him."⁴⁶ But did it really *only then* become clear to Thielicke? Was it not rather on that fateful night when he settled his affairs and was alone, "very much alone,"⁴⁷ that this crucial insight entered his mind?

In any case, quite naturally in view of his relational thought-form (see chapter 4) as well as his understanding of "person" (see chapter 6, part one), the theme of loneliness—in all its different forms—plays a great role

---

42. Althaus, *Luther*, 54. See also Althaus, *Luther*, 53. John Donne called this the "democracy of death": "Death comes equally to us all, and makes us all equal when it comes."

43. "Death is crucially characterized by containing the hour of greatest loneliness" (*ZG&S*, 40). "You can always only die death lonely" (*Lebensangst*, 49). See also *Lebensangst*, 189; *GldChr*, 283. This was Lewis's experience, too: "'Alone into the Alone.' She [Joy Davidman, Lewis's wife] said it felt like that. And how immensely improbable that it should be otherwise!" (Lewis, *Grief Observed*, 15).

44. "Suffering always is an individual issue" (*Sterben*, 122). "My suffering too is always my own, something which I endure in utter loneliness. Though millions of mothers lost their sons in the war . . . each mother bore her pain alone, because she had a unique and unexchangeable relationship of personal love with her boy, which she shared with no one else" (*Freedom*, 213). On the father's side, this is attested to by Thielicke's acquaintance, "the sturdy and popular evangelist Wilhelm Busch" of Essen (*MF&T*, xviii), who concludes upon the death of his two sons: "The hardest things must be fought through alone. No man can help you with that. . . . Many came to console. Back then I realized that a man cannot console another. Everything people said to me did not even reach the depths of pain" (Busch, *Plaudereien*, 175–76). Again, Lewis agrees: "I find it hard to take in what anyone says. Or perhaps, hard to want to take it in. It is so uninteresting" (Lewis, *A Grief Observed*, 1).

45. *Lebensangst*, 50–51.

46. *Freedom*, 213–14. "Every one of them marching there lives in a dimension in which he is not substitutable and utterly lonely; everyone bears his guilt, his anxiety, his death" (*Lebensangst*, 50).

47. *Ernstfall*, 149. See *Wayfarer*, 66 [90].

in Thielicke's thought:⁴⁸ "Before God's throne, none will have a 'next man' to march beside him. And yet, he will have a 'next man,' standing close beside him."⁴⁹ For at the same time, "since Christ is our brother, we are not lonely in our temptation. He suffers it with us throughout all depths."⁵⁰

Correspondingly, Rueger, in his research into Thielicke's christological thinking as represented in his sermons, rightly detects an individualistic one-sidedness at the expense of the sacramental and corporate dimension of Christian existence.⁵¹ Rueger does not, however, appreciate the crucial existential hotbed in which this emphasis flourished. In spite of Thielicke's explicitly relational mode of thought and understanding of "person," and despite his explanation that his notion of the individual must not be confused with individualism,⁵² he seems to apply both primarily (and probably subconsciously, due to his early experiences of life) to the vertical relationship between the individual and Christ. In contrast to other "relational thinkers," such as Ratzinger (whose emphasis on "the we-structure of faith" presents one of the main tenets of his theology), Thielicke thereby neglects to draw similar consequences horizontally, viz., as to the Christian's relationship to the church and her members.

Returning to the issue of meaninglessness, although the *answer* to the question of meaning might have been silenced with the death of God, "the question itself remains and is the source of unrest or madness. In face of this persistent question, there can be *no refuge* in self-resting finitude."⁵³ The question certainly remained for Thielicke that night. Yet in the face of the crucified, in envisioning Christ's own and fellow-suffering, in the midst of the most intense borderline situation possible, he "recognized him as a

---

48. See his definition of hell as "utmost loneliness" (*Woran*, 157); his underlining the fact of Jesus's loneliness during his temptation in the desert (*ZG&S*, 28–29, 115) and Jesus's loneliness in general (*GldChr*, 183); the general threat of loneliness (*ZG&S*, 35, 37–41; *Ernstfall*, 27); the "thou-less loneliness of Fichte's I" (*ThE I*, §424); sin making man lonely (*ThE I*, §1435; *Welt*, 171); the loneliness of the I and of reason without God (*ThE I*, §1935–56, §1980–2009, §2170); loneliness as a characteristic of modern society (*Schweigen*, 72–73; *Krauss*, 77; *Welt*, 248; and *GldChr*, 31); faith potentially leading into loneliness (*Welt*, 244; *GldChr*, 190); etc. This list could easily be continued.

49. *Freedom*, 214.

50. *ZG&S*, 117. For his existential blueprint, see *Reden*, 55, 60; *Ernstfall*, 69–71, 99; *Lebensangst*, 82–83, 150; and *GldChr*, 300. "In that picture of the cross I recognized his own and his fellow-suffering. I recognized him as a brother.... It meant a lot to me that he, too, was in mortal danger" (*Ernstfall*, 150).

51. See Rueger, *Individualism*, chapter 1, esp. 59.

52. See *Tod*, 122.

53. *EvF I*, 248. Emphasis added. "But the question itself has not been silenced. It has an indelible character. This is why it causes fear" (*EvF I*, 240). See also *EvF I*, 245.

brother and companion and talked to him."[54] He thus overcame meaninglessness and entered a relationship with ultimate meaning—indeed, with crucified meaning.[55]

It is thereby important *not* to make Thielicke's overcoming of death and meaninglessness dependent on that night's "happy ending," namely, his miraculous recovery. For "truth, enquired about in the question of meaning, decides *whether we can stand reality*."[56] That is, whether man has *the inner means* at his disposal to overcome, not whether he apparently conquers life's challenges successfully.[57] His account now testifies to the fact that, on that night, he acquired the former by way of personal encounter with the one who *is* the truth, who *is* meaning—i.e., the crucified one—irrespective of any subsequent physical healing because of this encounter.[58]

In a sermon titled, "When Nothing Makes Sense,"[59] his basic view that "the overcoming of death in Christianity is . . . personalistic"[60] finds classic elaboration.[61] Taking Matthew 11:2-6 and the imprisonment of John the Baptist as his point of departure,[62] Thielicke uses John the Baptist and the

---

54. *Ernstfall*, 150.

55. The title of Thiede's book, *Der gekreuzigte Sinn*, gains momentum in this light.

56. "WuV," 115. Emphasis added. Truth "would thus be reality's absolute carrying principle."

57. Thielicke reports on his encounter with the national-socialist mother of a dying twenty-year-old SS-soldier, rendering her words: "'Perhaps I do have a courageous attitude. But please don't probe any deeper; it has no substance behind it whatsoever.' I was thunderstruck by these words. . . . After the war . . . I kept taking up this distinction between attitude and substance" (*Wayfarer*, 139 [183–84]). "Terror at the dream . . . of the loss of transcendence . . . remains the last word. When there is no halting, one can only try to hold out" (*EvF I*, 248).

58. This is in accordance with his statement that "the relation to faith came much later when I was healed after a number of years" (*Krauss*, 17). For without his initial encounter with the crucified one: no subsequent relation to faith. Without an embryo: no fully fledged man! Applied to the current context: even embryonic faith can overcome meaninglessness. See chapter 2, part two.

59. Contained in *Reden*, 227–40 [*How to Believe Again*, 182–93].

60. *Mensch*, 392.

61. Thielicke thus serves as an example of his own verdict on Schleiermacher; namely, that the systematician cannot be understood apart from his sermons. See *MF&T*, 178; *EvF I*, 365; and *EvF II*, 330–31.

62. He uses this passage as a starting point for at least two other sermons. One is titled, "Thy Kingdom Come," contained in *Gebet*, 54–67 [*Our Heavenly Father*, 55–67]; and the other is called, "How Does One Cope with Unresolved Questions?," in *Abenteuer*, 181–92 [*Faith the Great Adventure*, 108–15]. Whereas the first deals more with the collective dimension of human kingdoms as against God's kingdom, the latter is rather similar to "When Nothing Makes Sense" in its pastoral focus on the individual.

black slave Rufus, from James Baldwin's novel *Another Country*, to exemplify Christ's personalistic overcoming of despair and death.

According to Thielicke, Christ's death cry on the cross ("My God, my God, why hast thou forsaken me?"), which depicts "the utmost suffering there is,"[63] provides the key to the question of theodicy. For "if we are threatened with madness in view of our despair of God . . . then we can only make progress by turning with the question to God *himself*."[64] This personalistic key to the problem of evil is provided by Christ, who does not simply bray his distress out into the night of Golgotha but rather turns directly to his Father. He addresses his Father as a "Thou," saying "My God": "He does not charge against somebody unknown, but flings himself at his heart. . . . He trusts that this heart *nevertheless* beats for him."[65]

John the Baptist and Rufus hereby serve as an image of Christ's personalistic overcoming. It is relevant that the way Thielicke presents both characters and their respective historical and fictional scenarios looks like an adaptation of his own existential drama for the stage or, more precisely, for his sermons.

John the Baptist finds himself in a desperate situation: whilst imprisoned and waiting for his executioner, God remains silent: "How is one expected to believe in such a situation?" Moreover, "Does this pondering, doubting, protesting John not live . . . in us?"[66] Yet, John does not begin to speculate,[67] he is not interested in the theoretical question of theodicy,[68] for "in such situations, only the elementary questions remain, [questions] concerning your own being or nonbeing."[69] Calvert aptly comments on this passage:

---

63. "Karfreitag 1941" (*NHT*).

64. *Abenteuer*, 184. See *Ernstfall*, 97–98.

65. *Reden*, 234. Emphasis added. See also *Abenteuer*, 183–84; *Bergpredigt*, 113. For Thielicke's emphasis on faith as the great nevertheless, see chapter 9, part one.

66. *Reden*, 230. See also *Abenteuer*, 182. Identification is one (if not *the*) outstanding characteristic of Thielicke's use of sermonic illustrations—as Dirks highlights: "They are chosen and told in such a way that it is possible for the listener to identify with the persons or action in the illustrations" (Dirks, *Laymen*, 179). Especially in the case of biblical characters and narratives, the means of identification helps to contemporize their meaning. See Dirks, *Laymen*, 220–21. For this specific feature of Thielicke's preaching, see also Langsam, *Konkretion*, 191–202. This homiletical characteristic likewise originates in a particular experience. See *Wayfarer*, 132 [174–75].

67. See *Reden*, 231. However, Thielicke's conviction that "you cannot any longer afford intellectual curiosity when you are waiting for the executioner in your prison cell" is rebutted by Helmuth James von Moltke's mental activities during his internment.

68. *Abenteuer*, 182.

69. *Reden*, 231.

> John's inquiry, voiced indirectly to Jesus, expresses the fundamental issue faced *"by anyone who feels the earth shake beneath his feet while his heart shrinks from the ugly face of meaninglessness"* (186). Thielicke wants his audience to understand that, in the first place, John's personal tribulations plunged him to a much deeper level of inquiry.[70]

Thielicke's direct words (those emphasized above) mirror his own situation, and the "much deeper level of inquiry" can likewise be traced back to Thielicke's own proximity to death.[71] But this is only the starting point for substantial inquiry. As outlined at the beginning of this chapter, it is the *subjective* question of theodicy typically arising in the borderline situation that Thielicke highly welcomes since it contains, as he himself experienced, the great potential of serving as a pointer to God.

The next, decisive step immediately follows: "After I had finished the bottle I looked at the crucifix."[72] In that very moment, Thielicke was faced with the choice between meaning and meaninglessness; the first providing the inner means (*Halt*), the second only offering a desperate stance in the face of nothingness (*Haltung*), as symbolized by Spengler's soldier of Pompeii—a figure he loves to refer to.[73] At this specific point, the dynamics of personalistic overcoming crystallize: John the Baptist does not choose *Haltung*, but *Halt*—that is, "despairing confidence in Jesus": "John does not direct his question into empty space but addresses Jesus himself. . . . He addresses him with a 'Thou,' turning directly to him."[74] Thielicke himself did the very same that night: "I recognized him as a brother and companion and talked to him. . . . It meant a lot to me that he too was in mortal danger."[75]

In the sermon, almost apologizing to his listeners ("It may appear bewildering"), he adds the following remark: "This very question . . . in the death cell . . . brought John closer to the mystery of Jesus than [he ever was] during the greatest moments of his 'publicity.'"[76] Might it be possible that,

---

70. Calvert, *Preaching*, 319. Emphasis added.

71. The second and third reflective outcome of this proximity is outlined in chapter 3, part two: *theological substance* and *existential yearning for profundity*.

72. *Ernstfall*, 150.

73. See *Reden*, 233; *Nihilismus*, 54; *Tod*, 177, 199; *LmdT*, 46–47, 250; "EdR," 75; *Fragen*, 26; *Lebensangst*, 44; *GldChr*, 138, 285; and *Freiheit*, 26.

74. *Reden*, 233.

75. *Ernstfall*, 150.

76. *Reden*, 233. He makes the same point in reference to desperate times during the war. See *Tod*, 27 (fully cited in chapter 10, part two); *Man in God's World*, 10. Bonhoeffer also states that "personal suffering is a more fitting key . . . to the reflective . . . opening of the world than personal fortune" (Bonhoeffer, *Widerstand*, 26).

in this very interpretation, Thielicke looks back on and reappraises his own "Maundy Thursday experience"? Simply exchanging the subject and location of his sermonic statement prompts such a conclusion: "This very address . . . in the hospital room . . . brought Thielicke closer to the mystery of Jesus than [he ever was] during the previous moments of his lifetime."

The second figure of a black slave, Rufus, additionally augments this observation. Baldwin's literary character commits suicide by jumping off a bridge in New York. But just before Rufus does so, a final thought flashes through his mind: whilst also turning to God directly, he now—in stark contrast to John the Baptist—begins to abuse the Almighty verbally, thereby exasperatedly concluding: "Am I not your child also? Now I am coming to you!" Thielicke annotates: "Did he not, after all, still address God as a Thou, albeit gruesomely swathed in a curse . . . ? Was he not a desperate child who wanted to fling himself into eternal arms? As long as I can still say: 'My father,' or 'Your child is coming to you,' I am not left alone."[77]

Once more, the obvious existential blueprint of this sermonic illustration is difficult to ignore. Thielicke refers to Baldwin's Rufus in at least two other contexts. On one occasion, he connects this illustration with Christmas, assuring his readers that "Christmas tells us: God meets us, no matter where we are. And when everything seems to be over, then God's possibilities just begin."[78] In the other context, he lists Rufus (or is it himself?) amongst a range of different characters who all have one thing in common: they all exemplify "the gospel's greatest miracle," namely, that Christ follows each and every one of them into their specific "foreign land": "They are all secured in him, embraced by him . . . Christ is there and died even for those . . . who sigh at the absurdity of being . . . and who, like the dead Christ of Jean Paul, shout desperately: 'Father, where is thine eternal breast at which I can rest?'"[79]

Again, both times Thielicke's phraseology strongly reverberates with his own crucial experience and could easily be applied to describe his momentous encounter with Christ on the evening of Maundy Thursday, 1933. Yet Rufus and John the Baptist are just faint images of the unspeakable despair of the Christ. For it is Christ who "is banished into even more dreadful abysses than his mentally distressed disciple in the cell."[80]

---

77. *Reden*, 234–35.

78. *Ernstfall*, 90.

79. *ThDvGl*, 43. Jean Paul, who had "the first modern vision of the death of God" (*EvF I*, 236), appears so frequently in Thielicke's writings that I refrain from listing all the references here.

80. *Reden*, 234.

Thus, Thielicke closes the circle and turns to speak about that very person whose despair Rufus and the Baptist merely illustrate—namely, the crucified God:

> God is not to be found in lofty speculations but at the very opposite end: in the depths of human misery and in the utmost abandonment, at the stake of the cross. That is where his love drove him. Only the one who looks for him in this ungodly wretchedness will find him. Only the one who takes on Jesus's cross will hold his hand.[81]

Thielicke's Personalistic Focus Systematically Unfolded

Historically, this focus on the *Deus crucifixus* can be traced back to Luther's Heidelberg Disputation in 1518.[82] Whereas, until then, it had more or less been taken for granted to assume God's *apatheia*,[83] Luther's seminal juxtaposing of a *theologia gloriae* with a *theologia crucis* in Heidelberg laid the foundation for later developments (in particular, the rising of a "new orthodoxy" in the late twentieth century, with a strong focus on the suffering God).[84] Church historians, such as McGrath, highlight with the rise of protest-atheism after the First World War, the rediscovery of Luther's works from 1883 onwards, and the growing influence of the *Dogmengeschichte*

---

81. *ThDvGl*, 44. See Hengel's gripping descriptions of the cross: "[The cross] was an utterly offensive affair, 'obscene' in the original sense of the word" (Hengel, *Crucifixion*, 22). "In the death of Jesus of Nazareth, God identified himself with the extreme of human wretchedness" (Hengel, *Crucifixion*, 89). For the "folly of the cross" in the ancient world, see Hengel's excellent little study in general. For example, see his rendered verdicts of Josephus ("the most wretched of deaths") and Cicero ("that plague"; "the very word 'cross' should be far removed not only from the person of a Roman citizen but from his thoughts, his eyes and his ears"; and "the terror of the cross") in Hengel, *Crucifixion*, 8, 37, 42, 44.

82. The *Disputatio Heidelbergensis* was convoked by Luther's fatherly mentor, Johann von Staupitz, at the University of Heidelberg and took place from April 25 until April 27, 1518. Martin Bucer and Johannes Brenz were amongst the many listeners who were won over by Luther for the case of the Reformation. See Forde, *On Being a Theologian of the Cross*.

83. See Moltmann, *Crucified God*, 227–31; Pannenberg, *Basic Questions II*, chapter 5. Pannenberg states: "The concept of a God who is by nature immutable necessarily obstructs the theological understanding of his historical action, and it has done so to an extent that can hardly be exaggerated. It indeed constitutes the background for the idea of the impassibility of God which so fatefully determined the Christology of the early church" (Pannenberg, *Basic Questions II*, 162).

84. See Thiede, *Gekreuzigte[r] Sinn*, 171.

[history of dogma] three developments in response to which the *theologia crucis* was reappraised. Three additional factors furthering the advance of this focus were the rise of process theology, Old Testament studies focusing on God's participation in Israel's suffering, and the renewed psychological— as well as theological—interest in the essence of "love."[85]

Moltmann, one key proponent of this process, points out that "the Greek philosophical concept of the 'God incapable of suffering' by the early church led to difficulties in Christology, *which only more recent theology has set out to overcome*."[86] Although the nineteenth century had already yielded some interesting attempts at rethinking the kenosis of the second person of the Trinity—specifically in protective reaction to David Friedrich Strauss's radical demolition of the conventional Christology of the day[87]—the twentieth century, without a doubt, is primarily indebted to Moltmann's *Crucified God* for putting the *Deus crucifixus* back on the theological agenda.[88]

In light of these modern systematic explorations—as well as Thielicke's own personal involvement with the crucified Christ—it might come as a surprise not to find him amongst those theologians who have explicitly taken up the task of developing a *theologia crucis*. But Thielicke does not

85. McGrath, *Christian Theology*, s.v. "Suffering God." Regarding protest-atheism, see Moltmann, *Crucified God*, 219–27.

86. Moltmann, *Crucified God*, 267. Emphasis added. Thiede, *Gekreuzigte[r] Sinn*, 21, even suggests that the "axiom of God's apparent immutability" has quickened the process of secularization. In reply to major proponents of the *Dogmengeschichte*—like Adolf von Harnack, who considers metaphysics as the "arch evil" of Christendom— Pannenberg rightly states that "it is now necessary to avoid the mistake of demanding that metaphysical elements in the Christian doctrine of God simply be done away with, for that would compel theology to give up the universal claim of God upon all men. It remains the task of theology, however, to rework every remnant that has not been recast" (Pannenberg, *Basic Questions II*, 182–83). See also Ratzinger's speech at Regensburg University. Ratzinger detects three waves of de-Hellenization, beginning with the Reformation, whose "avowed intention" it was to separate Greek speculation from biblical faith (see Hamilton, *Revolt Against Heaven*, 65). Thielicke, in his anti-metaphysical stance (see, for example, *EvF I*, 366; *ThE II/1*, §1347; *Reden*, 260, 271–72; *GldChr*, 288; and esp. *Abenteuer*, 202), must be included in this criticism. In addition to philosophical reasons, his seeing "modern man's dwindling of metaphysical substance" (*Fragen*, 12) might be a pastoral one since he apparently does not think to reach his contemporaries with issues of such sort anymore. See also *EvF II*, xii; *Suche*, 69; *Gespräche*, 70–71.

87. See Thiede, *Gekreuzigte[r] Sinn*, chapter VIII. Thiede discusses the concepts of Ebrard, Gess, Liebner, and Thomasius in this regard. For Strauss's life and work, see *MF&T*, 424–40.

88. Moltmann, *Crucified God*, 201–4, lists Rahner, von Balthasar, Mühlen, and Küng (on the Roman Catholic side) and Schlatter, Althaus, Barth, Jüngel, and Geyer (on the Protestant side) as having developed a *theologia crucis*. Thiede's *Gekreuzigte[r] Sinn* is to be mentioned as a rewarding contemporary contribution. For a criticism of this so-called "new orthodoxy," see Weinandy, *Does God Suffer?*, and his essay with the same title.

seem to be overly interested in explicating the dogmatic subtleties that followed in the wake of the death of the second person of the Trinity. Rather, he states that one of his "constantly recurring theological tasks [is] to reveal *the dogmas' existential relevance.*"[89] This finds confirmation in his response to Krauss's question as to why Thielicke, in contrast to Barth, was not interested in "dogmatic subtleties." Thielicke replies that occasionally he is concerned with subtleties, but his entire basic attitude is different: "The most fascinating [thing] about the gospel, to me, was that it makes life re-emerge in all its dimensions. The world looks different if you have faith."[90]

In the same context, he reaffirms that he "was less interested in dogmas or a doctrine of God but rather in the question: what does faith in God imply for our relation to reality, to the world, to fellow man?"[91] That is also why Thielicke is convinced that "the actual difficulty of dogmatic issues [and of all ethical considerations, by the way[92]] always arises in concreto."[93] As early as 1945, Walther Schönfeld's assessment of Thielicke's theology confirms this overall tendency. Schönfeld speaks of Thielicke's "somewhat one-sided existentialism . . . with its much stronger focus on the practical-pastoral side of truth rather than the theoretical-scholarly [side of truth], [the latter] in the sense of historical-systematic coherences, which are therefore not fully brought to bear [in Thielicke's theology]."[94] This tendency—also

---

89. *Suche*, 150. Emphasis added. "The most beautiful truths turn into lies if they cannot be practiced and if I cannot 'be' in them (John 18:37)" (*Bergpredigt*, 89). "The dogma is the liveliest matter in the world since it makes the question of the whole of existence its own" (*GldChr*, 20).

90. *Krauss*, 24–25. See also *K&K*, 16 [*B&E*, 15]. "I cannot emphasize enough that I do not want to get rid of the conventional theological vocabulary. . . . Those dogmatic words and terms are indispensable . . . But as such . . . they are only suitable in the theological laboratories" (*Suche*, 74). See also Zahrnt, *Sache*, 204, 214.

91. *Krauss*, 55. "To be sure, one cannot do without dogmatic subtleties; but it must be inquired about their status. If one starts with them, all goes wrong" (*Krauss*, 61). See also *K&K*, 16, 235 [*B&E*, 14–15, 232]. Accordingly, Thielicke proclaims that his *Theological Ethics* "is about the much more fundamental task of explicating the theological theme of being-in-the-world in all its varieties" (*ThE I*, vii).

92. See *Freedom*, 153.

93. *ThE II/1*, 10. To Luther, as to Thielicke, the discipline of ethics is in itself an inseparable part of dogmatics (see Althaus, *Luther*, 27). See *ThE I*, Part One, IV., esp. subsection (b) The Unity of Ethics and Dogmatics (§81–97), and V., subsection (d) Consequences for the Relationship between Dogmatics and Ethics (§170–81), esp. §172, §176. See also Speier, *Initiator*, 193n424.

94. Schönfeld, "Gutachten für Senat Uni Tübingen, den 16. Juli 1945" (*NHT*).

noted by Carl F. H. Henry[95] and Matthew Rueger[96]—is decisively rooted in Thielicke's existential encounter with the crucified Christ on the brink of death in April, 1933.

Consequently, not only does Thielicke conclude his sermon, "When Nothing Makes Sense," by reassuring his listeners that "[Christ] does not want to impose a dogma on us but he wants to touch our heart,"[97] but one can also find general signs of disdain as to dogmatic subtleties, which for him are "not discussable,"[98] especially in his pastoral writings and sermons.[99]

95. "None of Thielicke's hearers or readers will doubt his vibrant personal faith... But many... doubt that the truth of God holds adequate place in his system" (Henry, "Thielicke Speaks," 33).

96. "By relying on a 'principle of homeopathy,' Thielicke is purposely connecting the emotions and feelings of Christ to those of his hearers. This is consistent with his idea of the overall spiritual Christ encounter. He is not concerned with the objective fact of Christ's presence in Word and Sacrament, as classic Lutheranism is, but with the subjective impact of Christ's spiritual presence on the emotions and psyche of his hearers" (Rueger, *Individualism*, 50). For the "principle of homeopathy," see also chapter 9, part two.

97. *Reden*, 239.

98. In *Fragen*, 32–33, he equates the adjective "dogmatic" with "not discussable." What a contrast to Schlatter's empirical "theology of facts." For Schlatter, *Dogma*, 580n136, everything that goes beyond the empirical is to be kept away from the area of dogmatics "since that insight that unifies us as a church is not achieved by thoughts about the unexplorable." See also his *Einführung*, 200; Neuer, *Schlatter: Ein Leben*, 166–68, 402, 488.

99. See his youthful attack on Barth, who "transferred his doctrinal endeavors to remote metaphysical spheres, expending his intellectual energy in speculation on the Holy Trinity and other 'heavenly' themes" (*Wayfarer*, 69 [94]), and his note that "my theological work acquired from the outset a motif which freed it from becoming esoteric and dogmatic, and gave it the character of a dialogue" (*Wayfarer*, 79 [107]; *K&K*, 17; *B&E*, 15]). See *Bilderbuch*, 123–24; *EvF I*, 362–63: "We build them [our theological conceptions] like children playing with bricks." They have "only heuristic and not dogmatic rank." See also *Fragen*, 234; and *K&K*, 218, where he states that originally he wanted to call his lay dogmatics not *Woran* [*I Believe*], but *Das langweilige Dogma* ["The Boring Dogma"]. "We neither look for doctrine nor for dogma, but we look for the figure of the Lord Himself" (*Reden*, 31). "Whoever is mournful and tries to find his salvation in a teaching or a Christian theological dogma is sold down the river.... For mourning and insight, grief and thinking, are two different things" (*Reden*, 37). For this conviction, which is seriously questioned by the experience of Gary Habermas as rendered in Strobel, *Case for Christ*, 241–42, see further: "If I want to know what faith is... then I should not ask for dogma" (*Reden*, 164). "The truth... is not about the correctness of some dogmatic statement, but a fact of our life" (*Ernstfall*, 29. See also *Ernstfall*, 105–6). "This faith is not about accepting something as true or about some dogmatic capacity, but it is about a struggle, about a conversation with God" (*Lebensangst*, 57). "It was not a dogma at all... that impressed you.... What has impressed you is the message of the companion Jesus of Nazareth, who suffers like us, who is tempted like us, who dies like us, to be our brother in this, too" (*Lebensangst*, 177). "We do not want to

In the eyes of Thielicke, "the value of dogmatics depends on whether it can be preached."[100] He is convinced that "every dogmatic statement can only be made within the scope of liturgy. Dogmatics itself is proclamation.... It is worship... by means of thinking." [101]

Thus, although Thielicke and, for example, Moltmann both recognize the death cry of the dying Christ as central to the Christian faith, the latter thinks of it primarily (though not exclusively) in systematic terms,[102] whilst the former—even in his systematic treatment—perceives the same mainly pastorally:[103]

> His bitter cry from the depths: "My God, my God, why hast thou forsaken me?" ... bears witness that the very thing which plunges him into these depths of humanity and distance from God is also the sign of his most intimate relation to the Father: he is not complaining about God but speaking to God, so that even in his dereliction God is the Thou with whom he communicates.[104]

Thielicke's prime concern of existential relevance, as indicated in the first paragraphs (especially the third) of chapter 7, part one, is similarly expressed in his "public dogmatics":

> Truly, the riddle of suffering cries out for an answer . . . The dogma . . . better: the gospel . . . knows about this riddle and

---

discuss with them but want to try to show them a bit of Jesus's glory . . . And we should [thereby] not be anxious about every word being . . . of chemically pure Orthodoxy. For the one we address is not to sign a dogma" (*Woran*, 234). "In the New Testament, Jesus is actually not encountering us as a teacher who stimulates our intellect . . . He is not our mind's mentor but the Lord of our life" (*GldChr*, 22). Besides the last curious fact of Thielicke polemically trivializing the mind (not to mention the plainly incorrect statement that Jesus is not depicted as a *rabbi* in the NT; for this, see the seminal work of Riesner, *Jesus als Lehrer*), the striking parallels of some statements to the description of his own "Maundy Thursday experience" should not be missed.

100. *EvF I*, 378.

101. *K&K*, 41 [*B&E*, 36]. See chapter 8.

102. See Moltmann, *Crucified God*, 252; McGrath, *Christian Theology*, s.v. "Suffering God."

103. In passing, pastoral care was also the "basic tendency" in and "final motivation" for the theological works of Karl Rahner. See Rahner, *Erinnerungen*, 18–19, 50.

104. *EvF II*, 371. "He complains of his affliction to God himself. He addresses him as Thou. In spite of the dereliction he thus counts on his presence. But above all . . . he complains with a quotation from Holy Scripture [Psalm 22], that is, with a saying of God himself, so that the circle in the relation with the Father closes again" (*EvF III*, 171). "Even in this utmost *Anfechtung*, the crucified still addresses his Father prayerfully: 'My God, my God'. . . . He talks to his Father with the Father's own words [Psalm 22]. Even here he still is on his side—even in this utmost night" (*Bergpredigt*, 113).

its backgrounds. When Jesus cries on the cross: "My God, my God, why hast thou forsaken me?" he takes the whole mysteriousness of suffering upon himself, making it his own case and plight, providing it with meaning through his death, through the "doctrine of the cross."[105]

Thielicke now gathers up his theological resources to point pastorally to the suffering, since essentially loving, God. This is in stark contrast to the God of Aristotle, for "who loves must suffer for the sake of that which befalls the beloved."[106] Only by keeping this in mind can one truly begin to grasp the suffering dimension of the dying Christ. Due to his supreme love, weighing him down with the whole burden of his clueless and unfortunate human brothers, Christ is always the defeated, for (citing Thomas Mann) "whoever loves the most is always the defeated."[107] Thus, suffering is the "punchline" and "keynote" of Christ's human life from the very beginning.[108]

This is also the reason why Christmas and Good Friday still have such an appeal and a special place in liturgical life, since the suffering humanity and solidarity of the Redeemer strike and claim man here.[109]

---

105. *GldChr*, 18.

106. *Woran*, 42. See Moltmann: "In the surrender of the Son the Father also surrenders himself, though not in the same way. . . . The Father who abandons him and delivers him up suffers the death of the Son in the infinite grief of love. . . . The suffering and dying of the Son . . . is a different kind of suffering from the suffering of the Father in the death of the Son. . . . The Son suffers dying, the Father suffers the death of the Son. The grief of the Father here is just as important as the death of the Son" (Moltmann, *Crucified God*, 243).

107. *Woran*, 42-43; *Bilderbuch*, 139. "He literally loved himself to death" (*Woran*, 111); "He suffered from the way he loved" (*Woran*, 128); "He who endlessly loved and therefore endlessly suffered" ("Jesus Christus im vordersten Graben" (*NHT*)). Compare this with the assertion of von Hildebrand: "Who never truly loved in his life . . . does not know anything about the abysmal dread of death" (von Hildebrand, *Tod*, 14). Moltmann agrees: "A man . . . always suffers only to the degree that he loves" (Moltmann, *Crucified God*, 222). Thielicke somewhat dramatically applies the same formula (i.e., the more love the more suffering) to himself when he speaks of his "suffering from the church" [*Leiden an der Kirche*] due to his love for it (Thielicke, *Woran*, 287). See the German title of his book *Leiden*, in English changed to *Trouble*.

108. *Woran*, 125-26. According to Moltmann: "Jesus is born to face his passion. His mission is fulfilled once he has been abandoned on the cross" (Moltmann, *Crucified God*, 205).

109. See *EvF II*, 270. "Anyone who understands the miracle of Christmas understands that human and earthly matters, guilt, suffering, and death, tears and laughter . . . are taken that seriously by God that he himself entered all of these, that he carried the burden of life and death" (*ThE II/1*, §1966). He especially unfolds this further in his brief sermon, "Jesus Christus im vordersten Graben" (*NHT*) ["Jesus Christ in the Front-Line Trenches," in *Christ and the Meaning of Life*], held during the season of Advent. See *Woran*, 126; *Anfechtung*, 161; and *Ernstfall*, 89: "Crib and cross are made of the same wood."

Therefore, Thielicke pleads "that men should be led to the suffering creature called Jesus."[110] Accordingly, in a most likely fictional letter from a former prisoner of war whom he renders his correspondent, the latter's thoughts surprisingly resemble Thielicke's own "Maundy Thursday experience":[111] "If he [Christ] cannot bring you the father because he [the father] perhaps does not exist, then he still wants to bring you the brother who carries this fatherlessness with you and suffers your depths . . . with you. Look: that is how he came close to me."[112]

Consequently, his pastoral advice for those ministering to dying non-Christians is that they should not lead those entrusted to them to the resurrection-dogma, but rather to the cross; for it is the cross that can most easily be grasped in such situations.[113] Yet, Thielicke must be asked how he imagines the cross to be of any help without the resurrection. To be sure, by pleading "that men should be led to the suffering creature called Jesus," Thielicke hopes that "meditating on his creaturely suffering will itself disclose a dimension of this suffering . . . which leads us to the true heart of the matter."[114] Nonetheless, both Bonhoeffer[115] and Moltmann object in this regard, the latter rightly emphasizing that "without the resurrection, the cross really is quite simply a tragedy and nothing more than that."[116] This is impressively illustrated by philosopher Gary Habermas, who very personally shares about his wife's slow death from cancer: "It was a horribly emotional

---

110. *EvF II*, 386.

111. His correspondent's phrases and expressions, which are rendered by Thielicke in citation form, are very much "Thielickean style" and several contentual points certainly are. If the letter is real, then Thielicke has most likely sandpapered the passages to his purposes.

112. *Lebensangst*, 179 [contained in *Out of the Depths*]. His own "Maundy Thursday experience," as well as one of his favorite references—namely, Jean Paul's focus on man's and the world's fatherlessness in his "Sermon of the Dead Christ"—are reflected in these lines.

113. See *LmdT*, 92–95; *Fragen*, 225–26.

114. *EvF II*, 386. Since "the actual knowledge of [man's] lostness only emerges in light of Christmas and Good Friday. For the entire depth of this lostness only conveys itself by the effort God had to put in the balance to help us" (*ThE I*, §1681).

115. "To cope with dying does not mean that one gets over death. Overcoming dying is within the reach of man; overcoming death is the resurrection. Not by means of the ars moriendi, but by Christ's resurrection a new, purifying wind can blow in the present world" (Bonhoeffer, *Widerstand*, 131–32).

116. Moltmann, *Experiences*, 53. See also Moltmann, *Experiences*, 82n14. Of interest in this respect is also the advice of Father Vladimir Sorokin for Billy Graham. See *Just As I Am*, 520. For a forceful statement of West Germany's first chancellor Konrad Adenauer regarding the significance of the resurrection, see *Just As I Am*, 689. For Thielicke's encounter with Adenauer, see *Wayfarer*, 340–44 [436–40].

time for me, but I couldn't get around the fact that the Resurrection *is* the answer for her suffering.... Losing my wife was the most painful experience I've ever had to face, but if the Resurrection could get me through that, it can get me through anything."[117]

Therefore, according to Moltmann, "we must not isolate the cross, let alone make it something absolute in itself."[118] In any case, Thielicke's advice reflects once more his own momentous encounter with the crucified in April 1933. At that time, he himself was a dying non-Christian, and for him personally it was beneath the crucifix, not in front of the empty tomb, that he settled his affairs. That years later he turns this experience into a debatable piece of general advice without wanting to discredit the importance of the resurrection[119] is just one of many mosaic pieces showing how Thielicke's experiences influenced his theological thinking. From his own experience of suffering and loneliness grows Thielicke's pastoral rather than systematic desire, that is, to stress that Christ's suffering testifies to his being a knowing witness:

> Whoever suffers from now on can say to him or herself: this crucified one suffered more deeply. Whoever is lonely from now on may know: this crucified one crossed zones of separation from man and from God which no man has borne.... By crying out his God-forsakenness he was man per se, the man most weighed down, the man most afflicted with suffering and death. And yet he is the Son of God.[120]

---

117. Cited in Strobel, *Case for Christ*, 242.

118. For "the experience of suffering ... is far surpassed by ... the joy of God's coming glory [as represented through the resurrection]" (Moltmann, *Experiences*, 53). "Easter is God's protest against death. Easter is the feast of freedom from death" (Moltmann, *Experiences*, 33). Thiede underlines this: "Although it [the crucified meaning] has got its place in the absolute, it must not be absolutized.... Cross and resurrection belong together" (Thiede, *Gekreuzigte[r] Sinn*, 60).

119. For example: "The central significance [of the resurrection] ... is beyond question in the NT writings" (*EvF II*, 424). In the resurrection, "Christ ... lets his people participate in his overcoming of death" (*ThE II/1*, §679). See also his echoing of the Apostle Paul (1 Cor 15:13–20): "If Christ is not risen, then his life and work is refuted" (*Ernstfall*, 106). However, "the resurrection of Christ ... is certain only to faith" (*EvF III*, 32). "Only he who is in the truth ... hears the voice of the empty tomb" (*EvF II*, 431). For Thielicke's general conviction as to the historical non-verifiability of the resurrection, it being a "suprasensory event" (*EvF II*, 433), see *EvF II*, chapter XXX. Moltmann agrees (see Moltmann, *Experiences*, 29) and Pannenberg strongly disagrees (see chapter 5, part one).

120. *Ernstfall*, 99. See *EvF II*, 383–84. "We believe Christ for the sake of his vicarious suffering" (*Fragen*, 225).

Golgotha proves that God's love is not cheap love, but pain: "God himself suffers at the very place where the crucified hangs."[121] He undergoes the same temptation, suffering, and judgment as human existence, descending to the very depths where humanity is to be found. The tri-personal God's very essence of love unfolds within Christ's free choice to come under the burden of human existence. His entry into humanity is entirely motivated by his very own initiative, which, in turn, rests upon "the impelling motive of a more than human love."[122]

At the same time, this is one of the decisive differences between the man Jesus and the rest of humanity. For whereas man's freedom of choice arises only on the level of human givenness (i.e., a human being cannot decide whether or not to be human), Christ "*is* asked whether he will be who he is."[123] The very depth of Christ's humanity, into which he was not thrown but freely chose to enter, is his very dignity. For Thielicke, this fact is expressed especially well by Roman Catholic crucifixes, his precise highlighting of such most likely being no coincidence, but being once again existentially rooted.[124] The crucifix provides "the humbled man with a crown even in the very depths."[125] For "in the very depths in which he is so close to us . . . he is also distant from us in uncompromising majesty and remoteness."[126] "How

---

121. *Woran*, 148. This rather undifferentiated statement that "God himself suffers" confirms the observation made above—namely, that Thielicke, at least in his sermons, was not too concerned with dogmatic subtleties. At face value, the statement could suggest *patripassianism*; a heresy which Thielicke, in spite of his more famous saying that one must risk heresies in order to gain the truth (see *K&K*, 180; *SdA*, 25; *Mensch*, 500; and *Suche*, 63, 131), rejects. For "we 'have' the Father in the Son . . . but it cannot be said . . . that the Father 'is' the Son" (*EvF II*, 159).

122. *EvF II*, 381. The Word made flesh can thereby be denoted only by active verbs, not ontic nouns; another reason for Thielicke's preferential schema of thought. Brunner agrees: "The decisive word-form in the . . . Bible is . . . the verb, the word of action" (Brunner, *Divine-Human Encounter*, 32). See also Wilson, *Father Abraham*, 136–38.

123. *EvF I*, 367-68. According to Moltmann: "Jesus consciously and willingly walked the way of the cross and was not overtaken by death as by an evil, unfortunate fate. It is theologically important to note that the formula in Paul [Gal 2:20] occurs with both Father and Son as subject, since it expresses a deep conformity between the will of the Father and the will of the Son in the event of the cross" (Moltmann, *Crucified God*, 243).

124. Recalling chapter 2, in his hospital room, which was run by Roman Catholic nuns—and where he thought he would spend his final night—hung a crucifix. He used this as a visual aid "to straighten out" his life. He further reports that he was allowed to take this crucifix home after his recovery and henceforth had it placed above his office desk (*Wayfarer*, 65 [89]; *Krauss*, 22–23).

125. *EvF II*, 368. See *EvF III*, 435; *Woran*, 55. For Ratzinger describing the cross as God's throne, *regnavit a ligno Deus*, see Ratzinger, *Jesus I*, 370, 388–90.

126. *EvF II*, 371.

else should the cross of Golgotha be understood but as God's holiness [as symbolized by his crown] here struggling with his mercy [as symbolized by his wounds]?"[127] It is about God's self-conquest, his struggle with himself:[128] "[Christ's] true suffering, however, is not that he just suffers at men's hands but that, in a mysterious way, he suffers at God's hands. The older dogmatic tradition has this in view when it says that he bore and suffered the wrath and judgement of God in our place."[129] According to Thielicke, "this hour of Golgotha comprises . . . all the secrets of life and our heart like in a curved mirror. For everything that rises here up against Christ is also inside of us."[130] Hence, "the cross is a dreadful accusation. It is an unprecedented token of catastrophe on the path of humanity."[131]

But in Christ, God gives up his distance from the prodigal son, entering the zone between God and Satan, participating in suffering and death. Through "the Son of God incognito" (Kierkegaard), God "extorts his 'accommodation' from himself: his love is stronger than his justice; mercy overcomes the law of retaliation." That is why this very accommodation is "a miracle 'in' God, a victory in God's struggle with himself, the triumph of the heart over holiness."[132]

In section 607 of his *ThE I*, Thielicke reaffirms that Christ overcame his suffering at God's hands by approaching the Father himself, by "fleeing to God": "In view of the dark, divine judge [*dunkle Richtergott*], the terrified state of mind unload[s] itself in the Why-question and find[s] its aim of overcoming . . . expressed in the personal address." Herein Thielicke recognizes the unity of law and gospel, which can only be an object of faith: "Only the Holy Spirit knows about this tension and unity . . . yet, we only have this unity as we have the Holy Spirit. . . . But whoever turns this unity, in a direct sense, into a theological issue, searches for God . . . per se."[133]

---

127. *Gespräche*, 17.

128. See *Gespräche*, 17; *Offenbarung*, 154; and *Welt*, 274–75: "God the Judge struggles with himself as Father. That is the great miracle . . . the miracle by which God's love defeats the ira dei." See also Moltmann, *Experiences*, 46: "[Gethsemane] was Christ's struggle with God."

129. *EvF II*, 387. See "Karfreitag 1941" (*NHT*).

130. "Karfreitag 1941" (*NHT*).

131. "Karfreitag 1941" (*NHT*).

132. *ThE II/1*, §671–74. This divine struggle, according to Thielicke, is non-existent in Barth's theology.

133. It must be noted that, in this context, Thielicke does *not* use the phrase "we have the Holy Spirit" in the possessive form. This phrase is not only never used in the Bible (*EvF I*, 178), but "the Holy Spirit is [also] spoken of in personal terms. . . . He can encounter me. . . . From this we can see . . . that the phrase . . . is erroneous if it denotes possession" (*EvF I*, 181). See *EvF II*, 48; *EvF III*, 75; and *Gespräche*, 131.

Echoing Luther, he therefore admonishes that "we are not to fix our gaze upon the naked majesty of God. We are to flee from the *Deus absconditus* to the *Deus revelatus*."[134] The *Deus revelatus*, however, is to be found in the crucified Christ: "God's sovereignty is hidden in the cross; and only he who affirms the cross may have knowledge of it."[135]

This passage (*ThE I*, §607) endorses not only Thielicke's pneumatological focus (see chapter 5, part two), but also his dogmatic wariness with penetrating too deeply into the trinitarian mystery surrounding the death of the second person of the Godhead. His prime interest in this regard is pastoral, not dogmatic. But most importantly, his personalistic solution finds its systematic "rounding off" in this paragraph.

Finally—as already indicated in the introductory paragraph on the historical development above—Thielicke is once more truly Lutheran in his focus on God being an *ens miserrimum*. For in response to the God of Aristotelian metaphysics, who "does not love and therefore neither . . . suffer[s]," Luther counters: "If God were really like that, he would consider only himself and would not see the misery of the world outside him; but *if he did worry about it, he would then be the most miserable being*."[136] This great *mysterium tremendum* of the almighty God's powerlessness in this aeon, of his being "the most miserable being," the *ens miserrimum*, ultimately reveals itself in the suffering Christ on the cross. In the words of Althaus, "the cross hides God himself. For it reveals not the might but the helplessness of God. God's power appears not directly but paradoxically under helplessness and lowliness."[137]

---

134. *EvF II*, 126. See *WiG*, 44.

135. *Gebet*, 66. In brackets he adds: "What should we have done with the bomb crater without the cross?" See *EvF II*, 59: "He conceals himself in the suffering form of the Crucified." "The glory of God is concealed under its opposite in the form of a servant (*sub contrario absconditus*)" (*EvF III*, 32). See also the programmatic statements by Althaus, Moltmann, and Hengel: "'He who has seen me has seen the Father.' For this reason true theology and knowledge of God are to be found in the crucified Christ" (Althaus, *Luther*, 26); "Christ the crucified alone is 'man's true theology and knowledge of God'" (Moltmann, *Crucified God*, 212); and "Any genuine theology will have to be measured against the test of this scandal" (Hengel, *Crucifixion*, 89).

136. Cited in Bayer, *Lutheran Way*, 32. Emphasis added. Compare Moltmann: "But the one who cannot suffer cannot love either" (Moltmann, *Crucified God*, 222). "Were God incapable of suffering in any respect . . . then he would also be incapable of love" (Moltmann, *Crucified God*, 230). After having rendered an account of the Auschwitz-survivor Eli Wiesel as "a shattering expression of the *theologia crucis*," Moltmann concludes that "to speak here of a God who could not suffer would make God a demon" (see Moltmann, *Crucified God*, 253, 273–74).

137. Althaus, *Luther*, 30. "God shows that he is God precisely in the fact that he is mighty in weakness, glorious in lowliness" (Althaus, *Luther*, 34). See also the fifth chapter in general for Althaus's explication of Luther's theology of the cross.

Accordingly, Bonhoeffer, writing from prison, can state that "God allows himself to be forced out of this world onto the cross, God is powerless and weak in this world and precisely and only in this he is with us and helps us. . . . Christ does not help us in virtue of his omnipotence, but by virtue of his weakness, in his suffering! . . . Only the suffering God can help."[138]

In turn, in the book that, *inter alia*, led the Nazis to seek his removal and which "helped [him] and some other people to strike the right balance in the confusion of the times,"[139] Thielicke adopts the very same focus on God's this-worldly weakness:

> Do you realize what God's defenselessness means in this world? Do you realize that it is a symbol of his love, of his brotherhood with you? . . . He gives himself up to you, and what you made out of him is shown by the cross. But is the cross . . . for that very reason not his greatest token of love? . . . God has to die for man so that [man] . . . might experience God's heart. . . . That is the secret of God's defenselessness. . . . God's grace is defenselessness and not power; it is the cross and not glory.[140]

Thielicke goes on to interpret this paradoxical helplessness of the divine as an interim of mercy,[141] with God's true nature being eschatologically revealed in the end.[142] The intimidating undertone of his enunciation

---

138. Bonhoeffer, *Widerstand*, 191–92. On a personal note, I initially read this precise passage in Oświęcim, Poland, on the evening of July 10, 2016, just after returning from a three-hour guided tour through the main camp of *Auschwitz I*. That night, Bonhoeffer's words just made perfect sense emotionally. But does this sentiment stand up to rational orthodox scrutiny? Thomas G. Weinandy, "Does God Suffer?," for example, is not convinced that it does: it is not the God who suffers *in his divine nature* who can help, but the omnipotent God who suffers vicariously *in his human nature*. Ratzinger, citing St. Bernard of Clairvaux's *impassibilis est Deus, sed non incompassibilis*, likewise negates a radical kenosis by stressing that "God cannot suffer [per se], but he can suffer vicariously [*nicht leiden, aber . . . mit-leiden*]" (Ratzinger, *Jesus I*, 117–18). Ratzinger stresses God's this-worldly powerlessness whilst maintaining that Christ only suffered in his human nature, but not as a divine person (see Ratzinger, *Jesus I*, 96–97, 101–4, 346, 370, 388–90). In paradigmatic contrast, see Thiede—who, without mentioning Ratzinger, calls such a view "seemingly docetic" (Thiede, *Gekreuzigte[r] Sinn*, 188n57)—and Moltmann: "He was not only assailed . . . in his human nature . . . He was assailed in his very essence" (Moltmann, *Experiences*, 46).

139. *Wayfarer*, 91 [123].

140. *ZG&S*, 111–12. "The cross of Christ was raised in this aeon because it [this aeon] did not bear God's unconditionality" (*ThE II/1*, §259). This is also the reason why God hides himself; for this sick world cannot cope with him in any other way. See *ThE II/1*, §656.

141. See Ezek 33:11; 1 John 4:9–10; 2 Pet 3:9.

142. For Thielicke hinting at the final eschaton as the ultimate solution, see chapter 10, part one.

is certainly further intensified by the historical context within which he existentially found himself: "God's grace is an inquiry to the world.... And then the day of the Lord will come, then the inquiring is over.... The defenseless will reveal himself to the world as the almighty, as the almighty that he has always been."[143]

All three Lutherans, Althaus, Bonhoeffer, and Thielicke, continuing to build on the *theologia crucis*-foundation laid by their confessional forefather, are strongly unified in their conviction as to the centrality of suffering within Christian thought.[144] This centrality is tantamount to Christ's centrality, for the Son of God is the crucified, suffering Christ in whom "is true theology and knowledge of God":[145]

> The cross represents God's extreme absence.... There is here no theology of glory which can depict God at the heart of reality. There is instead a theology of the cross in which God is concealed.... "My God, my God, why hast thou forsaken me?" ... He goes down to this depth and despairs with the despairing.... The complaint of Jesus, his cry of dereliction, is not a shriek in the void. It does not proclaim the death of God. This confession of God's remoteness is an assurance of his nearness.[146] Jesus is not speaking about God and his absence. He addresses him as Thou.... He uses the Word of God [Psalm 22] to cry to the remote and absent God. This brings nearness and peace.... In the praying of this prayer ... the absence of God becomes a vanishing dream and the death of God becomes a vanquished illusion.[147]

---

143. *ZG&S*, 113. See also *Gebet*, where he employs the same contrasting device: "Now God's sovereignty is hidden in the cross ... But one day it will become manifest and [then] every knee must bow either ... worshipping ... [or] forced" (*Gebet*, 66).

144. For the centrality of suffering, see Lewis, *Problem of Pain*, 4–5; Thiede, *Gekreuzigte[r] Sinn*, 174; and Cockshut, *Unbelievers*, 170–71: "Historical Christianity ... cannot be accused of not paying attention to the fact of suffering. [Orthodox Christianity] ... place[s] suffering in the centre of the picture."

145. *EvF II*, 59. In footnote 91, he adds Luther's words that "all wisdom and truth shine forth in the suffering and dying Christ." See Moltmann: "The nucleus of everything that Christian theology says about 'God' is to be found in this Christ event [the cross]" (Moltmann, *Crucified God*, 205).

146. According to Moltmann, "This deep community of will between Jesus and his God and Father is now expressed precisely at the point of their deepest separation ... This event contains community between Jesus and his Father in separation, and separation in community" (Moltmann, *Crucified God*, 243–44).

147. *EvF I*, 229–30. "The only way past protest-atheism is through a theology of the cross which understands God as the suffering God in the suffering of Christ and which cries out with the godforsaken God, 'My God, why have you forsaken me?' For

As central as the doctrine of Christ is to Christianity in general and Lutheranism in particular,[148] so is Thielicke's personalistic solution to the problem of evil unilateral. Encountered by the crucified in his life's most crucial moment, he could conclude with C. S. Lewis's character, Orual: "I know now, Lord, why you utter no answer. You are yourself the answer. Before your face, questions die away. What other answer would suffice?"[149]

---

this theology, God and suffering are no longer contradictions . . . but God's being is in suffering and the suffering is in God's being itself, because God is love" (Moltmann, *Crucified God*, 227). The systematic task of showing that suffering is a part of God's being is taken up by Thiede in *Gekreuzigte[r] Sinn*; his counterpart can be found in Weinandy, *Does God Suffer?*

148. See Althaus, *Luther*, 225.

149. Lewis, *Till We Have Faces*, 308. See Aslan's tears in Lewis's Narniad, *Magician's Nephew*, 131–32. As already pointed out, Moltmann, standing on behalf of many contemporary theologians and philosophers, goes one crucial step further when he ascribes suffering to the *divine* nature: "A God who suffers cannot be the cause of suffering, he contains suffering in himself. That is the solution to the problem of evil" (Moltmann, *Experiences*, 51–52). Thiede, who shares this view, nonetheless criticizes Moltmann of a "firm panentheism": "Moltmann actually does not see the suffering Son . . . Rather, Christ's passion is . . . a matter of the Spirit" (Thiede, *Gekreuzigte[r] Sinn*, 172–73). Fifteen years earlier, Grenz and Olson already pointed to that potential danger in Moltmann's theology (Grenz and Olson, *Twentieth-Century Theology*, 184). But does the danger of panentheism only befall Moltmann? According to Weinandy, this danger is made a reality by any thinker (including Thiede) who regards suffering to be an intrinsic part of the divine nature: "It must be remembered, in accordance with the biblical notion of God, that while God is intimately related to creation as its Creator, He exists in His own distinct ontological order as the Creator. Therefore, the sin and evil that deprive human beings of some good and so cause them to suffer is contained wholly within the created ontological order and *cannot reverberate or wash back into the uncreated order where God alone exists as absolutely good*. If the sin and evil of the created order caused God to suffer, it would demand that God and all else would exist in the same ontological order, for only if He existed in the same ontological order in which the evil was enacted could He then suffer. This is why most of the theologians who espouse a suffering God intentionally advocate a panentheistic notion of God—that is, that while God is potentially more than the cosmos, the cosmos is constitutive of His very being. (Those theologians who espouse a suffering God but deny panentheism fail to grasp the logic of their own position.)" (Weinandy, "Does God Suffer?") Emphasis added.

Part III—Proclamation

The Lord has comforted his people
and will have compassion on his afflicted.

—Isaiah 49:13 (ESV)

Chapter 8

Orator sub specie existentiae

The Making of a Preacher Man in a Culture of Death

JUST AFTER THIELICKE'S PIVOTAL statement regarding the "existential drive" in his thought, which provided us with our point of departure, he continues: "This relation between life and thought was later to reveal itself more immediately and openly in my sermons than it did in my systematic thought."[1] It is therefore only consistent to conclude this study with that area where Thielicke considered himself to be at his strongest, "namely in the proclamation of the Gospel."[2]

Since Thielicke's prominent status as a preacher is reflected in the high number of dissertations and articles[3] dedicated to his preferred area of activity,[4] it suffices to commence part III with a brief yet original out-

---

1. *Wayfarer*, 85 [115].

2. According to the "most loyal" of his "loyal supporters," Jochen Rothert, rendered in *Wayfarer*, 390 [500]. Both in the German and English-speaking contexts, Thielicke has featured most prominently as a preacher, a fact he was not happy about (see Bromiley's remark in *EvF I*, 5). In the German television news (*ARD*) on March 6, 1986, the concluding line of Thielicke's obituary as rendered in Langsam, *Konkretion*, 5, states: "Thielicke became widely known by his sermons in Hamburg's Michaelis Church." Already in 1955, the left-leaning journal *SPIEGEL* highlighted Thielicke's success as a preacher in its front-page story, "Wohin mit dem Evangelium?" ["Whither Goest the Gospel?"]. Finally, Haas and Haug, *Prediger*, titled their publication on Thielicke: *Preacher for our times*. For the English context, see Bromiley's comments in *EvF I*, 5; "Thielicke," 545. See also Anderson, "Foreword," in *Wayfarer*, xv, xxi; Pless, "Thielicke," 457; and Cardwell, "Preaching from Bultmann and Thielicke," 234.

3. For one paradigmatic article, see Cox, "'Eloquent . . . , Mighty in the Scriptures,'" 189–201. See also the dissertations of Calvert, *Preaching*; Speier, *Initiator*; Rueger, *Individualism*; Langsam, *Konkretion*; Richter-Böhne, *Schuld*; and Dirks, *Laymen*. All dedicated their research to different aspects of Thielicke's preaching.

4. "Even in dogmatics, Thielicke never loses his primary interest in proclamation" (Bromiley, "Thielicke," 555). Intriguingly, amongst Thielicke's vast written output, there

line regarding the crucial impact that Thielicke's "eschatological existence" exerted upon his view on the central importance of the kerygma. Both Thielicke's homiletical and pastoral zeal arose during his enforced parish ministry in Swabia, lasting from 1940 until 1942. As will be shown below, the passionate *preacher* came into being due to the oppression of a dictatorship. In the ordeals of war, moreover, a *pastoral heart* was born. And whilst the origin of Thielicke's pastoral heart is rooted in that period, it was further and decisively deepened by the final years of the war as the German downfall was closing in. At this point, it is also worth recalling that Thielicke, prior to his sickness, did not want to become a pastor because he did not consider himself to be a Christian (see chapter 2, part two). Now, after recovery and deprived of academic profession in the middle of the war, he became a pastor with all his heart.

In general, it is quite natural that the pastoral heart is mainly expressed via the passionate preacher, but it is especially true in the case of Thielicke, who regards a homily as an "ongoing pastoral dialogue with the audience."[5] He is further convinced that a sermon must be shaped by the preacher's personal life story, since to preach means to confess God. To confess God, however, means to confess a story, "a story into which I myself am called."[6] We should therefore expect an intensified homiletical and pastoral engagement with those issues that shaped Thielicke himself. How proclamation gained theological center stage by way of his existential context is the focus of this concise but significant chapter.

"By No Means Fit for the Pastoral Ministry": Thielicke's Material Prioritizing of Proclamation Existentially Enforced

The twofold influence of Thielickean life experience and Lutheran thought naturally resurfaces when it comes to Luther's second rule of *meditatio* (see chapter 4) as expressed in the form of a sermon. For Thielicke, a sermon constitutes "the greatest intellectual achievement that can be demanded of a theologian."[7] As to the existential shaping, he proclaims that only truth that one

---

is not one book that specifically deals with homiletics *per se*. Closest to such an undertaking is perhaps his publication on Charles H. Spurgeon, whom he held in high regard, and *Suche*, published in the year of his death.

5. *Fragen*, 228.

6. *Fragen*, 228. With his focus on the preacher's existential context, Thielicke explicitly dissociates himself in the same passage from "some Barthians."

7. *Wayfarer*, 291 [372–73]. See also *Suche*, 38; *Bilderbuch*, 8. For his reasons as to why, see *Wayfarer*, 291–92 [372–74]; *Suche*, 38–45. See also *Wayfarer*, 131–33 [173–76].

has acquired through personal experience can be confessed and preached.⁸ As to the Lutheran frame of mind, especially with regard to his conviction that "wounds must heal wounds" (see chapter 9, part two), Thielicke the preacher truly meets Luther's definition of a theologian "who lets himself or herself be interpreted by it [Holy Scripture] and who, having been interpreted by it, interprets it for other troubled and afflicted people."⁹

Indeed, Thielicke's early and dismal life experiences, which undoubtedly impacted the thematic choice and tone of his sermons, are certainly one reason why he ranks among the famous Christian preachers of the twentieth century, with his reputation as an orator outshining his contributions as a systematic theologian and ethicist: "It may be that the congregation sensed this [relation between life and thought] and, as a result, listened more intensely and were more affected by my sermons."¹⁰ Albeit reluctant to give reasons for his acclaimed success in the pulpit,¹¹ he reveals another important factor as to why he thinks he appealed to his listeners. Since young Thielicke was in the habit of expressing himself rather abstractly and incomprehensibly for the common man,¹² he set out to perfect the art of communicating abstract issues pictorially and vividly. He did so by training himself to observe and collect the "narrative moment" whenever he watched a film or read a novel, thereby beginning to utilize all those moments in the pulpit.¹³

This passage, along with his autobiographical remarks,¹⁴ thus corrects the assumption of Langsam, who wrongly concludes that concretization in preaching is neither teachable nor learnable, but rather the result of "spiritually processed experience." "Such preaching," notes Langsam further, "becomes solely possible against the backdrop of a spiritual existence which is interwoven with one's personal biography."¹⁵ Whereas Langsam rightly

---

8. See *GldChr*, 44.

9. Bayer, *Lutheran Way*, 36. "The Holy Ghost must here be our only master and tutor. . . . When I find myself assailed by temptation, I forthwith lay hold of some text of the Bible" (Bayer, *Luther's Theology*, 33n11). For Luther, one cannot have the Spirit without the external Word.

10. *Wayfarer*, 85 [115].

11. "I was often asked to explain the effect of a sermon, but as a rule, I avoided giving an answer. There is no 'human' interpretation of the 'effect' of a sermon" (*Wayfarer*, 85 [115]). The last line did not prevent the emergence of a number of dissertations analyzing his sermons anyway.

12. See *Wayfarer*, 131 [173].

13. See *Krauss*, 14.

14. See *Wayfarer*, 132 [174–75], 291–92 [373–74].

15. Langsam, *Konkretion*, 239.

implies that Thielicke's art of concretization must not be separated from his crucial experiences during his coerced parish ministry, he is clearly misled when he suggests that this art cannot be acquired by training. Thielicke not only disagrees, but is further convinced that *all* proclamation must aim in a concrete way at the hearer: "Proclamation is actual proclamation or it is not proclamation at all."[16]

Ironically, had it not been for the Nazis and the friendship of a bishop, Thielicke would probably never have experienced that key moment that led him to this insight. Subsequently, it initiated his lifelong training and radically changed the course of his theological development. This becomes clear by bringing to mind his strong convictions prior to his enforced move. In a letter to "Dekan Prof. D. Hans Schmidt" of Halle on November 16, 1939, Thielicke assures the addressee that he considers it to be "in every way impossible" to save his chair by combining it with a pastorate:

> First of all, because I am an academic and by no means fit for the practical ministry. Further, because a coexistence of both professions makes the academic work as I understand it . . . unmanageable. And finally, because I have three big literary hopes which I want to realize over the next years . . . Therefore, I could never voluntarily make myself choose to do that [take on a pastorate].[17]

After his dismissal from Heidelberg in April 1940, however, the time of autonomous decision-making was over. With a still "abstract" Thielicke desperately looking for a livelihood, Swabian Bishop Theophil Wurm finally brought an end to his unemployment by assigning him a parish ministry in the rural area of Ravensburg. In retrospect, Thielicke regards this enforced change of profession as "setting the course" [*Weichenstellung*]:

> Up until that time, I had lived under the foolish illusion that I could only set foot in the pulpit when I had got the theological theory completely clear in my mind. It was for this reason that I had always avoided preaching whenever possible. It was only after I *had* to preach because of my job that I gradually realized how false my previous conception had been. . . . I learned to understand that faith comes from preaching and that theology is merely the result of later reflection on this faith. Thus theology

---

16. *EvF III*, 9. If Langsam is right, then all those preachers are to be pitied who have not had the "right" experiences leading them to the art of concretization. Indeed, if he is right, and if Thielicke's verdict as to "actual proclamation" is also true, then there has not been much proclamation in church history at all.

17. (*NHT*).

does not, as I had previously imagined, *precede* preaching but *follows* it. In retrospect, I now know that I could not have written the eight volumes of my systematic theology . . . if I had not had the spiritual experiences I owe to my preaching duties.[18]

In the same context, Thielicke mentions a specific letter from Emil Brunner, who drew his attention to these dangers of "pure intellectuality" and abstruseness in his thinking: "His critique of my esoteric and academic style caused me to worry whether I would be able to preach in a way that would be intelligible to ordinary people. I resolved to concentrate all my intellectual energies on this task."[19] The context and immediate sentence following this citation strongly suggest that Brunner's letter reached and initiated a change of thinking at the beginning of Thielicke's parish ministry in 1940. Brunner's message, however, dates from September 25, 1947,[20] when Thielicke already held a chair at the University of Tübingen and had experienced popularity amongst several thousand listeners over the years.[21]

At any rate, before taking up the pastorate, Thielicke was a "pure only-academic," but by means of his initially loathed pastoral office, he learned the significance of proclamation for the theological task: "This exercitation I needed badly."[22] Many years later, as the founding dean of the newly established theological faculty at the University of Hamburg, Thielicke implemented the custom for all his teaching staff of regularly ascending the pulpit: "We wanted our students to witness a personal demonstration by their teachers of how all theology develops from and leads back to the preaching of the Gospel."[23] Eduard Thurneysen probably voices the senti-

---

18. *Wayfarer*, 131 [173]. See *Kanzel*, 46–47. In the German original, the eight volumes of Thielicke's systematic theology comprise four volumes of his *Theological Ethics*, three volumes of *The Evangelical Faith*, and his anthropology, *Being Human—Becoming Human*.

19. *Wayfarer*, 132 [174]. This statement, along with other remarks in the same context, confirms my critique of Langsam footnoted earlier.

20. (*NHT*).

21. That he apparently made some theological progress in accordance with Brunner's wishes is disclosed in another letter dated July 25, 1964 (*NHT*), in which Brunner almost enthusiastically praises Thielicke's latest volume of *Theological Ethics*: "What a gigantic performance! But above all: What a concentration of thought, what an abundance of knowledge and ability."

22. *Krauss*, 34.

23. *Wayfarer*, 269 [344]. See *Suche*, 50; *Krauss*, 34. At the same time, missionary proclamation is a task not confined to the teacher of theology, but something concerning every single believer: "Wherever faith is vital, it also proclaims itself to the outside world" ("Church and Atheism," 109). See *Reden*, 40–41. For proclamation being the duty of every believer, not just the teacher's, see *EvF I*, 223; *EvF II*, 396; *Lebensangst*, 55, 143; and esp. *Woran*, 183, 247. For the church as a whole, see *Freedom*, 204.

ment of many in the first line of the following statement, written in a letter to Thielicke on August 6, 1968:

> By preaching yourself, by betting on this horse time and again, you encourage [others] to preach. And not like Tillich, who in his religious orating . . . tried to address the famous "modern man" in a rather complicated, not to say intricate and sophisticated way, after all. Has he really reached him? I doubt it! Even though, I remember him [Tillich] thankfully.[24]

Mutatis mutandis, one might say that what John Calvin's stay in the city of Strasbourg did for him (1538-1541),[25] Thielicke's time in and around Ravensburg (1940-1942) likewise did for Thielicke. Without Nazi coercion to accept a position he initially abhorred, Thielicke very likely would not have become the esteemed preacher that he turned out to be.

The most significant theological consequence that followed from this particular experience, existentially embedded within his earlier and foundational call to conversion, is Thielicke's conviction of the priority of proclamation, and with it, faith, over theology.[26] This very order—and therefore, the location from where the theological question is asked—represents *the* crucial problem for Thielicke.[27] The misery rooted in the wrongly ordered: theology *then* proclamation, is because it excludes the application of the Spirit's power: "We do not let ourselves be convinced by the exertion of proclamation anymore; that it is possible and that the testimonium Spiritus Sancti becomes an actual event."[28]

---

24. (*NHT*). In general, the correspondence between Thielicke and Barth's close friend, Thurneysen, reveals a rather intimate friendship. See, for example, Thurneysen's following comments in letters dating from January 21, 1967 (*NHT*): "Of course, I took note of Zahrnt's 'Sache mit Gott' and noticed—not without satisfaction—that he presents your Ethics next to Barth's Dogmatics as the most important theological work of our century"; from January 29, 1969 (*NHT*): "For I am always not only your friend but also someone learning and receiving from you. I must thank you for both: for friendship and teaching"; from April 15, 1969 (*NHT*): "And now I want to thank you once more for your great dogmatic work [*EvF I-III*]. It has all been simply clear to me. It is brilliantly written. And I cannot think of anything where I would have to object"; and from September 13, 1969 (*NHT*): "You accompany my thinking and life more than you can imagine. Again and again I turn to your books." See also *Wayfarer*, 72 [98].

25. See McGrath, *Calvin*, 135–38.

26. For his detailed unfolding, see the subsection titled: "Relation of Proclamation and Theology," in *EvF I*, 196–202. See also Forde, *Theology is for Proclamation*, highlighting the enabling of proclamation as the true purpose of theology.

27. See *K&K*, 235 [*B&E*, 232].

28. *Kanzel*, 47. "Whilst proclaiming . . . I began to realize what proclamation is: that the Word . . . was present with its witnessing power and pneumatic efficacy . . . Why, now the revaluation of the hitherto relationship between theology and proclamation

He illustrates this by stating that as a pastor, he was suddenly and undesirably forced to stop thinking about *how* one can talk about God, and instead—by way of experiment—found out *if* God really talks. Only if and as God's Spirit addresses the hearer does the question of "how" ensue. That is why theology needs to be under the auspices of proclamation: "Only by looking back at enacted proclamation does theology become possible."[29] On the kerygmatic basis of a transforming encounter with the Holy Spirit, personal *fiducia*-faith as the controlling factor for "doing" theology emerges (see chapter 5).[30] Yet, at the same time, there is no proclamation without theological reflection:

> Pure proclamation—proclamation in itself—does not exist. From the very beginning it is permeated by theological reflection.... For anyone who proclaims has already ... acquired the message for himself.... What I mean by the primacy of proclamation cannot be dissected chronologically ... It is merely about the factual emphasis, which is crucial.[31]

Thielicke's concern does not touch on a chronological ordering. Rather, proclamation's priority over theology is by nature, and not in time, with proclamation being the *qualifier* of theology.[32] In other words, he is primarily concerned with the kerygmatic, pneumatic dimension within which the theological task must take place. The latter cannot *in principle* precede the former:[33] "Faith is always greater than our theology."[34]

---

dawned on me.... Is our misery not rooted in the fact that generally we do *not* ask for proclamation's foundations on the basis of a carried out proclamation ... because personally we did not ... draw from the real presence of the Holy Spirit?" (*Kanzel*, 46–47). See also Bromiley, "Thielicke," 546, 549.

29. *K&K*, 235–36 [*B&E*, 232–33]. For the "if-case" and the self-authenticating Word, see also *Kanzel*, 48, 56, 57, 63.

30. See *EvF I*, 172. "Theology puts its question on the basis of encounter with the proclaimed Word and exposure to it. Hermeneutics then investigates the question and its modalities and conditions. It is the epilogue in a process which is effected by the creative Word in the miracle of the Spirit. It is never a prologue" (*EvF I*, 198).

31. *ThDvGl*, 25 [*Kanzel*, 86–87]. See *EvF I*, 199; *Kanzel*, 54, 64.

32. See Barth: "Without the *precedence* of the creative Word, there can be not only no proper theology but, in fact, no evangelical theology at all! ... What is at stake is the fundamental theological act that contains and determines everything else" (Barth, *Introduction*, 18). Schlatter also agrees, see Neuer, *Schlatter: Ein Leben*, 26, 34, 426.

33. See *EvF I*, 196. Thielicke recognizes Karl Rahner as an ally (*EvF I*, 196n4).

34. *Gespräche*, 59. "Faith is more than its formulation" (*Gespräche*, 92). "The confessor is more than his confession. The thinker's existence is greater than the reflection of his thinking. That is why the Christian is never fully absorbed by his theology" (*Offenbarung*, 169).

This essential arrangement of proclamation over theology also leads him, as already delineated (see chapter 7, part two), to a rather pragmatic approach as to the worth of the dogmatic task: "The value of a dogmatics depends on whether it can be preached. . . . We have defined theology as a process of reflection which arises out of faith, i.e., out of proclamation already heard. It is thus subordinate to proclamation and yet also continually related to it."[35] In his early autobiographical "work report," Thielicke goes even further, not only relating but indeed *equating* one with the other: since "dogmatics in itself *is* proclamation," it follows that "it is worship . . . by means of thinking."[36] According to Thielicke, "you can only think about God on your knees."[37]

Cox's evaluation that "Thielicke recognized the significance of the preaching task . . . by relating it to the more generally recognized 'scholarly' task"[38] therefore does not go far enough. Rather, the theological scholar is not to be had without preaching, that is, the theologian *is* a preacher or he is not a theologian at all. Once again, this specific and essential view is deeply entrenched in Thielicke's life circumstances, specifically in what he experienced between 1940 and 1942. Without Nazi harassment, he most likely would not have arrived at this insight.

---

35. *EvF I*, 378. "A theology must be proclaimable, for theology itself arises from proclamation" (*ThDvGl*, 26 [*Kanzel*, 87]). "A theology which cannot be preached must be judged as poor theology" (*Kanzel*, 45). For his pastoral reasons, see *Kanzel*, 13–14, 27–28 [*Exercise*, 4–5, 25–26].

36. *K&K*, 41 [*B&E*, 36]. Emphasis added. See Schlatter's similar attitude: "[Karl] Steffensen [one of Schlatter's teachers when he was a student in Basel] showed me that thinking is worship" (Schlatter, *Rückblick*, 40).

37. *Bilderbuch*, 71; *K&K*, 40–41 [*B&E*, 36].

38. Cox, "Biblical Preachers," 200.

Chapter 9

Homo sub specie malis

Pastoral Challenges in the Face of Death

How does Thielicke exhort, comfort, and strengthen his audience with regard to death and suffering in light of his own experiences? In the final two chapters, I attempt to provide an answer by moving our attention to four main pastoral loci which can be seen as the "cardinal points" of Thielicke's pastoral engagement with the problems of suffering and death.

Since he regards kerygma and theology as indissoluble (see chapter 8), this concentration cannot be limited to his sermonic material alone. The procedure of drawing from all primary sources equally, as applied thus far, will also be maintained for the remaining course of this work. In doing so, I methodologically go one significant step further than other studies on Thielicke's pastoral thinking, which mainly concentrate on its homiletical expressions. By explicitly including his systematic works, I aim to do justice to his own theological persuasion, at the same time endeavoring to contribute originally to the specific area at hand.

Part One: "Nevertheless I am continually with Thee"—*Anfechtung,* the "faith against," and personalistic overcoming

Thielicke's pastoral orientation, which essentially informs his systematics (see chapter 7), naturally comes to full expression when he addresses man's three great problems of guilt, suffering, and death[1] as a Christian counsellor. His systematic focus on Christ's personalistic overcoming of suffering at God's hands by addressing the Father himself[2] thereby unsurprisingly translates into his pastoral approach.

---

1. For Thielicke's tripartite formula, "sin/guilt, suffering, and death," see chapter 6.
2. See chapter 7, part two, esp. the passage on *ThE I*, §607.

One example for this is his introduction to his eighth sermon on the Sermon on the Mount, "Talking About God or With God?" Here, he introduces his audience to the famous initiator of the Bethel-foundations, "Father" Friedrich von Bodelschwingh, and how he lost his four children within two weeks (!) to diphtheria.[3] In spite of his uttermost pain, Bodelschwingh does not ask "How could God let this happen?" or "Why is God doing this to me?" He does not talk *about* God but, rather, by turning with his grief directly *to* God, he transforms his suffering into intense prayer.[4] In addressing God himself, he neither loses contact with God in this "nightmarish *Anfechtung*," nor does he allow "his childlike conversations with the father in heaven" to be destroyed by his most terrible moments. In doing so, Bodelschwingh follows the example of the crucified Christ who, in his own utmost *Anfechtung*, addresses the father prayerfully: "My God, my God . . ."[5]

Luther's first rule for studying theology, the all-crucial role of *oratio* (prayer; see chapter 4), presents the very heart of such personalistic overcoming. For Thielicke, prayer, by definition, presupposes a *personal counterpart*. His arrival at this insight is firmly entrenched in his existential circumstances[6] and directly translates to his pastoral application of Psalm 73, exemplified by a specific sermon on this key passage during the war in 1941:

> This psalm shows us how the believer, by struggling through severe *Anfechtung*, brings himself to appropriate this tenet [of the nevertheless]. The problem is not solved theologically or theoretically, but is overcome by divine pastoring. Such faith in God's faithfulness we can only obtain—and maintain in the face

---

3. See *Bergpredigt*, 112. The American "equivalent" to Bodelschwingh might be found in Horatio Spafford, who tragically lost all four of his daughters in a disaster at sea in November 1873. In his direct turning to God, Spafford resembles Bodelschwingh. See Rusten and Rusten, *Christian History*, 672–73.

4. Bonhoeffer states that "our fears for the other must be transformed into prayers" (Bonhoeffer, *Widerstand*, 102). See also Bonhoeffer, *Widerstand*, 211. Thielicke makes the same point: "As soon as fears arise they must be turned into prayer" (*Bergpredigt*, 165).

5. *Bergpredigt*, 113.

6. Despite the risk of repetition, Tillich's telling response to the question of whether he prays will be restated at this point. Without any personal notion of God, Tillich is reported to have answered: "No, but I meditate." As outlined in chapter 6, part one, Thielicke found himself in similar danger until his momentous encounter with the crucified Christ initiated a process of maturation in this regard.

of every *Anfechtung*—by praying. In the act of praying, we are being led to real knowledge of faith.[7]

Especially, but not exclusively, in the face of utter pointlessness and meaninglessness (as in the case of Bodelschwingh), the decisive task of prayer becomes problematic, however, for it requires "a reading/interpretation of the situation."[8] It is therefore possible that "I may ask for something . . . which *I think* I need." Yet, "my [apparent] needs may rest on a misinterpretation of my situation and thus on false hopes and fears."[9] Yet, "if God's thoughts are higher than my thoughts, then this does not imply a quantitative increase . . . but . . . their entire otherness, their qualitative difference."[10]

It follows that "I only know the [general] theme of such thoughts, namely, that they are thoughts of peace and not of sorrow; but the relation of this theme to concrete events is hidden in the heart of God so that I am related to them . . . in a venture of trust."[11] This venture, in turn, constitutes a pneumatic action as "God's Spirit himself intervenes on our behalf, standing in for ourselves."[12] That is why man must constantly be prepared to let his prayerful asking be corrected by God's answers,[13] according to the Lord's Prayer: "*Thy* Will Be Done."

However, this is also why man cannot know meaning *per se*, since it is personalistically grounded and not ontologically deducible: "We do not know meaning; we believe in him who knows meaning. Hence meaning does not manifest itself with demonstrable evidence. It remains under the cover of the cross . . . It is grasped only in a faith which is immediate to him who fixes our destiny but only mediate, in a relation of Nevertheless, to destiny itself."[14] Not only does his own personalistic overcoming of mean-

---

7. "Predigt während der Bibelwoche 1941/42. 5. Abend Psalm 73" (*NHT*). See also his sermon on overcoming fear (based on Matt 6:19–34) in *Bergpredigt*, esp. 159–64. For the existential blueprint, see *Krauss*, 22–23: "The night I took the medicine, I kind of set my life in order. I prayed. In my [hospital] room hung a crucifix. . . . In the face of the crucified, I thought of the forgiveness of sins, simply to straighten my life out."

8. *ThE II/1*, §1138.

9. *ThE II/1*, §1139. Emphasis added. See also *Bergpredigt*, 147. A classic example of such misinterpretation might be found in Matt 20:20–23 and Mark 10:35–40.

10. *ThE II/1*, §1140.

11. *ThE II/1*, §1140. "The foundation of the world is friendly and fatherly. So the Christian . . . rather says, 'Nevertheless, I am continually with thee' (Psalm 73:23)" (*Freedom*, 178).

12. *ThE II/1*, §1136.

13. See *ThE II/1*, §1141. See also *Bergpredigt*, 148.

14. *EvF II*, 33. See also *Welt*, 197.

inglessness (see chapter 7, part two) shine through in these lines, but this quotation also leads to the second important facet of this subsection, i.e., Thielicke's recurring emphasis on faith being a "faith against":

> The experience of meaninglessness . . . discredits all individual experiences of meaning. . . . The whole in its total sweep and compass remains hidden from view [contra the *analogia entis*]. *Of a piece with this* is the fact that faith in God is also faith against appearances. We are theologians of the cross and not of glory.[15] . . . Faith is not an insight into the nexus of meaning which enables us to speak in terms of a Because . . . Instead, it finds itself referred to a Nevertheless. "Nevertheless I am continually with thee . . . " (Psalm 73:23).[16]

Since Christ is truth and meaning *in person*, the crisis of meaninglessness—as specifically experienced in the face of personal tragedies—can only be overcome by relating to the truth and meaning incarnated in Christ. This can be all the more so since in the crucified Christ, in *suffering*, man finds truth and meaning; Christ meets the sufferer in the very depths which are individually and concretely faced by each human.

Thielicke's own initial experience in this regard was soon substantiated by his parish ministry during the war, as he now also experienced the gloom of others. Ministering at the deathbeds and in the rooms of those who received death notices from the battlefields, he found out "in a way he could not have dreamt of" that the gospel could help and provide comfort in the darkest moments of life.[17] In the ordeals of war, a pastoral heart was born.

Yet, correspondingly, with Thielicke's strict rejection of the analogy of being, it also follows that faith can *only* be found in the "nevertheless." It is therefore no coincidence that Thielicke titled his first major systematic work (after his doctoral dissertation), which was written during the war: *Theologie der Anfechtung* [*Theology of Contestation*], for it mirrors his basic conviction of faith being essentially and always a contested faith.

Faith is not something one possesses as a constant but rather an event which has to gain control over the believer daily.[18] Faith is not only faith in God but also and especially faith against evil reality; a faith *against appearances*.[19] Indeed, by its very nature, faith is always under assault: "It is achieved

---

15. Here Thielicke footnotes the fifth chapter of Althaus's *Luther*, referred to above.
16. *EvF II*, 33. Emphasis added.
17. *K&K*, 26 [*B&E*, 23–24]. See also *ThDvGl*, 51.
18. See *Anfechtung*, III–IV; *ThDvGl*, 112 [*Kanzel*, 133]; and *WiG*, 17: "One never has the nevertheless, no Christian ever possessed it, one always only could pray for it."
19. See *EvF I*, 228.

only as the enduring of trial."[20] Faith is "an act of contested [in the sense of *Anfechtung*] trust," which literally lives in protest against appearances even when everything argues against it:[21] "The one in whom faith believes reveals himself in the midst of what faith believes against: anxiety, fear, *Anfechtung* precisely become the material out of which faith is formed. Uncontested man would never be able to grasp what faith is. A man never calling out of the depths would never experience what prayer is."[22]

Both the specifically Lutheran frame of mind and Thielicke's own experiences clearly resurface in this specific definition of faith—the former grounding the latter theologically and the latter confirming the former existentially. According to Luther, "the cross and *Anfechtung* must come so that one's faith might grow and become strong.... Faith is never stronger than in the strongest *Anfechtungen*."[23] On this basis, we begin to understand why, in the eyes of Luther, "faith is the art of comprehending God in his opposite."[24] Wengert comments that "'the revelation [of God] under the appearance of the opposite ... is Luther's traditional definition of the theology of the cross; it is finding God in the last place we could reasonably look."[25] Correspondingly, Thielicke not only accepts *Anfechtung* in the form of ungodly suffering, pain, and death, but also, moreover, turns it into a constituent part of faith.

In terms of the second experiential facet, with regard to Matthew's account of Peter walking on the water and finally sinking before Jesus's eyes, Thielicke makes the following insightful comment: "That is why precisely in those critical moments, whilst being threatened by a deadly sickness, in the air-raid shelter, in the slowly tightening net of human

---

20. *EvF I*, 25.

21. *Mensch*, 493–94.

22. *ThE I*, §534. See also *ThE III*, §1784. Van Bentum may be right when he states that this sort of faith obtains its intellectual object—if at all—from the "against" (Van Bentum, *Grenzsituationen*, 85). Whereas Thielicke certainly also tries to explicate the positive "for/in," nonetheless, his focus on the negative "nevertheless" dominates (see Thielicke stating his primary interest in *EvF I*, 15, or his changing the title from *Ich glaube* ["I Believe," first and second edition] to *Woran ich glaube* ["What I Believe," third edition] and his rationale for this move in the preface of *Woran*, 7–8). Since for Thielicke, the positive object of faith clarifies itself by opposing *Anfechtung*, the latter serves as an epistemological *via*, without which the core cannot be had.

23. As rendered in Rieger, *Luthers theologische Grundbegriffe*, 22.

24. Althaus, *Luther*, 32.

25. Wengert, "Peace, Peace," 205n32. See Wengert, "Peace, Peace," 200, where he equates suffering with "God's alien work." See also Bayer, *Luther's Theology*, 17, 20–22, 35–36, where Bayer unfolds the role of agonizing struggle (*tentatio*) and experience (*experientia*) within Luther's thinking.

intrigues, we have to realize whom we trust to have power over us."[26] Intriguingly, Thielicke lists exactly three examples which he himself painfully experienced (deadly sickness, air-raids, intrigues; see part I), hereby showing that, for him, faith in those particular moments is a faith against, i.e., a "nevertheless." In this account, according to Thielicke, Matthew highlights the nature of faith by making it clear that faith is not to be confused with sight. Faith is demanded of the disciples, just as it was of him,[27] in the midst of chaos and in spite of not being able to see (that is, they see nothing but desperation).[28] It is a faith against appearances, *not because of* some criteria, *but in spite of* the circumstances:

> All who have experienced God testify with overwhelming unanimity: The reason why we believe is not "because . . . ," "because" it pays off and "because" we see substantial evidence as to God's actions so that we do not buy a pig in a poke if we believe. Rather, all adjust their confession of faith to this tone: "Nevertheless I am continually with thee"—*although* we only see furious elements in force, *although* the power of darkness seems to have the last word . . . That is why we can only confess and announce in the midst of menace who or what God is for us.[29]

Ignoring for a moment Thielicke's apparent self-contradiction[30]—as well as the obvious experiential[31] and epistemological shortcomings (see the following subsection) of his statement—the existential-Lutheran echo resonating from the theological conviction uttered here appears yet again striking. Seeing this Lutheran double feature of personalistic overcoming and "nevertheless" already prefigured in Christ,[32] Thielicke concludes the

---

26. *ThDvGl*, 88 [*Kanzel*, 115–16].

27. *Initially* on Maundy Thursday, 1933, and *continually* afterwards, especially during World War II.

28. *ThDvGl*, 89 [*Kanzel*, 116–17]. This is attested to by Horatio Spafford. After the death of his four daughters, he finished a poem with a synonym of "nevertheless": "Even so—it is well with my soul" (Rusten and Rusten, *Christian History*, 673).

29. *ThDvGl*, 89. See also *WiG*, 17; *Freedom*, 178.

30. Elsewhere, Thielicke describes two ways of arriving at final reality, i.e., God: "the ecstasis of experiencing the absolute" and "the rationality of metaphysical reflection" ("EdR," 65). In this context, Thielicke grants both ways validity.

31. One only has to think of the intellectual coming to faith (or, in Thielicke's words, through "the rationality of metaphysical reflection") of individuals like G. K. Chesterton, C. S. Lewis, or Alister E. McGrath, to recognize the shortcoming of his conviction in this particular instance.

32. See Moltmann: "It is only in the 'nevertheless' which is in such total contradiction to what he desires that Christ [in Gethsemane] holds fast to the fellowship with the God who as a Father withdraws from him: 'Nevertheless not as I will, but as Thou wilt'" (Moltmann, *Experiences*, 45).

homily touched upon at the beginning of this subsection with *his* definition of prayer and faith: "We are called by our names . . . Answering this call that has reached us: that is 'praying.' And to trust with all your heart that it is the Father who has called whilst bravely walking into the dark, [nonetheless] constantly calling back, perhaps like Peter, who shrieked as he was about to sink: that is believing."[33]

The nature of faith is of utmost importance both for man in general and for the Christian theologian in particular. Moreover, Thielicke's specific understanding of the nature of faith is deeply connected with his own experiences, especially with his "sickness-unto-death." Third, Thielicke's understanding is open to criticism. Hence, I shall discuss it in the following subsection before returning to his pastoral handling of the problem of theodicy.

Thielicke's Understanding of "Faith as Nevertheless" Appraised: *fiducia* as Blind Trust?

Thielicke's strong epistemological emphasis on "faith as nevertheless" is rooted in his understanding of *fiducia* as being opposite to sight; not only to eschatological sight and thus to final immediacy,[34] but—and here it is getting problematic—also to sensory sight and thus to empirical data: "Noetic renunciation of sensory knowledge goes hand in hand with the confession of faith."[35] His strong emphasis on Christian faith being a faith against phenomenal appearances[36] apparently makes him throw out the baby with the bathwater. He separates the mental/rational act of insight (*notitia/assensus*) from the spiritual act of faith (*fiducia*)[37] and stands herein, like Schleiermacher,[38] under the influence of Kant, his favorite philosopher, who infamously had to remove knowledge in order to make room for faith.

For Thielicke, faith is the confession of an absolute certainty that cannot be proven or supported by verifiable information.[39] He even goes so

---

33. *Bergpredigt*, 124.

34. See *EvF I*, 391; *EvF III*, 168.

35. *EvF II*, 82. See also *EvF I*, 210; *EvF III*, 29, 40, 152.

36. See *Woran*, 85; *EvF I*, 291; *EvF III*, 23; and *Gespräche*, 132.

37. See *EvF III*, 297, 337. "For this fundamental decision [whether Christ is authorized by God or not] there are no cognitive criteria" (*EvF II*, 289). "The relation of trust does not arise out of the causative reasoning of a Therefore. It is in the venture of a Nevertheless that 'I am continually with thee' (Psalm 73:23)" (*EvF III*, 362).

38. See Heron, *Century of Protestant Theology*, 24.

39. See *Woran*, 19 [*I believe*, 3]; *ThDvGl*, 89 [*Kanzel*, 116–17]; and *Weltanschauung*,

far as to state that the smaller the initial guiding light becomes, the greater the trust that is provoked.[40] The impact of Occam,[41] Luther,[42] and especially Kierkegaard[43] clearly comes to the fore here. But if Thielicke really is serious about this, then it logically follows that it would be best to have as little cognitive light as possible.

Accordingly, and strongly reminiscent of his own borderline situation, culminating on the night he took the medicine,[44] he comments on the passage where Abraham, the father of faith, sacrifices his son Isaac: "He throws himself into the arms of God, blind and without a clue as to how God will catch him, but certain that God's arms will catch him."[45] Thielicke concludes: "Thus, faith has a noetic function. But it [the noetic function] is not prior to faith. . . . Rather, the noetic moment comes after faith: By trusting God . . . I will, like Abraham, know him . . . "[46] Hence, Thielicke bases the *notitia/assensus* elements of faith on *fiducia*, instead of the other way round. Consequently, and in full consensus with kerygma theology, he can brand the seeking of historical facticity as an "evading the faith," for "the Word is a truth which creates the conditions under which it discloses itself, namely, the being in the truth."[47]

However, that Abraham might have trusted God on this special occasion precisely *because* he had already got to know the divine nature in the past, that Abraham only acted on the basis of *prior* insight about God, does not seem to be a viable option for Thielicke. Indeed, only in light of what the

---

31, where he defines faith as "a pre-theoretical stage of insight" and "a non-justifiable presupposition."

40. See *Gespräche*, 118; *Welt*, 261–63.

41. See Sierszyn, *2000 Jahre Kirchengeschichte. Band 2*, 224–27.

42. "God's hiddenness and man's faith thus belong together. Yes, Luther can even say that God hides himself and his saving will precisely in order to make room for that faith" (Althaus, *Luther*, 56).

43. See *Offenbarung*, 167–68; Rohde, *Kierkegaard*, 45–69, 101–6.

44. This is further confirmed by his conceptional return to the borderline situation (see chapter 7, part one) in the very next paragraphs (*ThE II/1*, §1160–63), after his discussion of Abraham's sacrifice.

45. *ThE II/1*, §1157.

46. *ThE II/1*, §1159.

47. *EvF II*, 37–38. See also *EvF II*, 430–38, esp. 434–35; *Offenbarung*, 160–70, esp. 161, 165. For two critical voices, see Pannenberg, *Basic Questions I*, 85; and Craig, "Leaping Lessing's Ugly, Broad Ditch," who *inter alia* responds to the "strongest reason for [Lessing's] historical skepticism" as rendered by Thielicke in *Offenbarung*, 158–59. For Pannenberg's theological counter-project in this regard, see esp. Pannenberg, *Systematic Theology III*, 136–55.

patriarch had already *assented* to as *notitia* beforehand, did God's claim to sacrifice Isaac appear as contradictory to his divine being.

The same can be said of Thielicke's curious interpretation of the woman with the flow of blood (Matt 9:20-22; Mark 5:25-34; Luke 8:43-48). The woman's motivation in touching the edge of Jesus's cloak is regarded by him as superstitious, instead of his evaluating her actions in light of the prophetic promises of the Tanakh, as underlined, for example, by Ray Vander Laan: "This wasn't simply a desperate plea for healing [*fiducia* without *notitia/assensus*] . . . this was her affirmation that she recognized the messianic character of Jesus and His work. She believed He was the Messiah [*fiducia* on the basis of *notitia/assensus*]."[48] It is rather regrettable that, from such a questionable exegesis, Thielicke repeatedly draws the pastoral conclusion that it does not really matter whether one has conceptually grasped the truth as long as one is willing to trust and to love.[49]

Likewise, according to Thielicke, Anselm "does not want to understand in order to believe, which would put understanding before belief. He believes in order to understand." Anselm does not prove in order to pray, but "prays before he 'proves.' . . . Believing and understanding do not synchronize. They are apart. Believing is ahead of understanding. In faith, we know more than we do with reason."[50] Thielicke's whole project of prioritizing proclamation over theological reflection (see chapter 8) must be seen in this dubious epistemological light.

In stark contrast to Thielicke's Kantian isolation of the *fiducia*-aspect of faith, Schlatter, for instance, is convinced that "Schleiermacher's repeating of Anselm's formula credo ut intelligam as a guiding rule for his dogmatics was a disaster [*Unglück*] for the German theology and church. Already Baader corrected this by rightly observing [that] 'every faith stands in the midst of a given and assigned knowledge.'"[51] Schlatter regards both the *credo ut intelligam* and the *intelligo ut credam* as elementary, not only in order to render the relationship between insight and faith correctly, but also to avoid that sort of irrational faith which considers the elementary task of justifying

---

48. Vander Laan, *Echoes of His Presence*, 74. For the prophetic passages in the Tanakh, see Vander Laan, *Echoes of His Presence*, 72.

49. See esp. *Woran*, 30-31; *Reden*, 270; and *Suche*, 125-26. See also *EvF III*, 351, 364; *Woran*, 13, 119-20, 233; *Ernstfall*, 104, 150; *Gespräche*, 117; *Lebensangst*, 185; and his sermon "How Faith Begins," in *Reden*, esp. 64-65.

50. *EvF I*, 280. See also *EvF II*, 174-75.

51. Schlatter, *Dogma*, 569n77. See also Schlatter, *Einführung*, 58-60.

itself as obsolete.[52] According to Schlatter, "every act of faith is also an act of understanding."[53]

William Lane Craig has taken up Schlatter's admonition that both *credo ut intelligam* and *intelligo ut credam* are needed for a healthy—and thus missionary—expression of Christianity. Craig differentiates between *knowing* that Christianity is true and *showing* it to be true. The first happens through the inner witness of the Holy Spirit, possibly but not necessarily drawing from external evidence (thus, evidence is not the basis of faith but supports and confirms it). The second should happen methodologically in such a way that Christianity's truth claims are displayed rationally, hence open for the non-believer to engage with it accordingly.[54]

Ignoring such counsel might entail serious consequences for the Christian believer since "an ungrounded belief is easily swayed and abandoned, *even though it might be correct*. Only when we have provided warrant for our beliefs can we avoid changing our minds irrationally or believing irresponsibly."[55] But it also puts the non-Christian seeker at a disadvantage, because "to protect one's interpretive scheme from criticism is to rob it of the only way it can display its claims to truth."[56] In such a case, the Christian message makes itself inaccessible to anyone *extra fidem*; and thus puts up barriers in the wrong place. For the sake of God's kingdom, in its individual and corporate dimension, both dire states must be avoided.

A lot more would have to be said about Thielicke's dubious interpretation of this central theological locus, but space and thematic concentration prevent any deeper pursuit here. Besides the philosophical rudiments that he presents for his view, for the present purpose, it must suffice to highlight the strongly existential undertones in the said persuasion.[57] Thielicke might

---

52. See Schlatter, *Einführung*, 112. For a similar analysis, see Pannenberg, *Systematic Theology III*, 136–55.

53. Schlatter, *Glaube und Wirklichkeit*, 178.

54. See Craig, *Reasonable Faith*, 43–60.

55. Wolfe, *Epistemology*, 15. Emphasis added. Although there is no consensus among epistemologists as to exactly what constitutes justification of true belief, it can nonetheless be stated that justification or warrant is the generic difference between knowledge (justified, true belief) and mere belief (see Craig, *Only Wise God*, 123–25; von Wachter, *Kausale Struktur*, 234, 248; Plantinga, *Warranted Christian Belief*). In the words of Austrian composer, Schubert, "Reason is nothing but faith analyzed" (cited in Kavanaugh, *Great Composers*, 69).

56. Wolfe, *Epistemology*, 65.

57. This impression becomes particularly strong in *Woran*, 85: "The darker the mantling gets, the stronger this faith must become. We have all experienced it ourselves how especially in the darkest hours of our life, when no man was able to help and the greatest agony of loneliness attacked our heart, the miracle of the nevertheless was

have arrived at this conviction without his "sickness-unto-death." Against the existential backdrop of his illness, however, the mere fact that he does hold to it so convincingly acquires contextual meaning, especially in view of his own programmatic statement driving this study.[58]

Part Two: "In the Front-Line Trenches" and Yet "in Control" —Christ's Solidarity and God's Omnipotence

"In the Front-Line Trenches": Christ's Solidarity

In a brief sermon titled, "Jesus Christ in the Front-Line Trenches," Thielicke presents his pastoral approach to the problem of suffering in a nutshell: "Wounds must heal wounds. Those who are wounded seek comfort from fellow-sufferers."[59] Whilst obviously pointing to Christ "[becoming] one of the wounded because he [freely] wanted to be one of us,"[60] Thielicke, with this specific formula that "wounds must heal wounds," at the same time also hints at his own life-story through which he arrived at this understanding. He himself can console his wounded listeners as he understands their suffering due to his own manifold experiences. Conversely, "when one is not being subjected to the same trials with them, one naturally hesitates to say anything."[61]

---

experienced and God rose His stars above us." For a similar emphasis, see *Bilderbuch*, 38–39.

58. See *Wayfarer*, 85 [115].

59. "Jesus Christus im vordersten Graben" (*NHT*) ["Jesus Christ in the Front-Line Trenches," in *Christ and the Meaning of Life*]. See also *Woran*, 222; "EdR," 73–74; *Krauss*, 20. For Thielicke's ethical application of what he calls an "act of higher homeopathy" (by which God sustains this fallen world with its own fallen means), see *ThE II/1*, §655–56, §1130: a *justum in re* does not exist in this aeon due to its totally depraved nature. But God wants to take the de facto imperfect into his own hands. Thielicke's "theology of compromise" is to be located within this conceptual context. See also *GldChr*, 160, where he proclaims "the secret of this world: namely, that the good . . . can only exist in revolt against itself: indeed, that even love . . . may be forced to employ lovelessness and brutal force as its means . . . The world calls this tragic; the Christian talks of the fallen world." See also *GldChr*, 443: "In a world of injustice . . . the good can only live cased in armor." For his phrase, "higher homeopathy," see *EvF I*, 91; *Freedom*, 23–24, 151; and *Bergpredigt*, 151.

60. "Jesus Christus im vordersten Graben" (*NHT*). *Lebensangst*, 40: "Wounds must heal wounds. Hence, man's actual helpers have always only been the greatly wounded . . . Only thus was Jesus able to become the counsellor . . . for he himself had to resist the powers of guilt, suffering, and death."

61. *Freedom*, 201. In this specific case, he talks about the brethren behind the iron curtain in the East, continuing: "However, we too once lived under the burden of ideologies . . . and only in view of this do I dare even to try . . . a helpful answer."

It is therefore only natural that he introduces this particular sermon with a personal account of looking for shelter, together with his family, in a peaceful little village after having lost their Stuttgart home in the bombings during the summer of 1944. Contrary to Calvert's assumption that the village merely serves as an imaginary device,[62] the place, illustration, and sermon are once again firmly rooted in Thielicke's personal circumstances.[63] But Calvert is right in observing that, through this story, Thielicke wants to convey to his listeners the existentially learned insight that "the people . . . most qualified to come to the aid of the afflicted are those who have been sorely afflicted themselves."[64]

Yet, Thielicke did not initially gain this specific understanding by way of his Korntal-experience, even though he uses it as a sermonic illustration. Rather, his decisive insight that "wounds must heal wounds" can ultimately be traced back once more to Maundy Thursday, 1933: "After I had finished the bottle I looked at the crucifix. . . . At that time, Christ was still foreign to me, but in that picture of the cross, I recognized his own and *his fellow-suffering. I recognized him as a brother and companion* and talked to him. . . . *It meant a lot to me that he too was in mortal danger.*"[65]

However, in this specific homily, Thielicke does not focus on the cross but instead, in appropriate accordance with the season of Advent, concentrates on Christ's incarnation. Christ did not remain in "the safe base of heaven," "he did not call us from a distance with a few encouraging words. No, he . . . came to us in the front-line trenches,"[66] illustrating this by contrasting "the village of 'religion' far beyond the mountains of this evil world" with the eyes of the one who "knows about the ruins of our lives."[67] Even in death,[68] Christ has become man's "companion" [*Kamerad*], the very same term Thielicke uses for his own crucial encounter in 1933. "Can there be a more fervent backing and fellow suffering than in the cry:

---

62. See Calvert, *Preaching*, 288.

63. The Thielickes lived in the village of Korntal as refugees from 1944 to 1945. In *Wayfarer*, 182–83 [236–37], he describes his search in the village for a new home, providing the starting point for this specific sermon.

64. Calvert, *Preaching*, 288.

65. *Ernstfall*, 150. Emphasis added.

66. "He transfers himself from the shelter of his Logos home to the abyss of guilt, pain, and death" (*EvF II*, 384).

67. "Jesus Christus im vordersten Graben" (*NHT*).

68. "He not only suffers because of men, but he suffers with men. . . . Jesus has become our companion in death. He experienced the final distress first-hand" ("Karfreitag 1941" (*NHT*)).

'My God'? Thus, he is our brother. Thus, he is the archetype of the pastor who goes with us in the front-line trenches."[69]

Now, Thielicke does not merely end by highlighting Christ's solidarity, but decisively concludes his thoughts with an emphasis on God's omnipotence. As pointed out previously, mere solidarity could be received from fellow man and does not help on its own.[70] Therefore, after having stressed that God is fully man in Christ, solidly united in every aspect of manhood, Thielicke goes on to underline that in the deep comforting knowledge of God's son being a knowing witness, one can "accept everything from his hand *because this hand is in control of all things*."[71]

God "in Control": Thielicke's Christological Reason for Divine Omnipotence

This bold claim is again rooted in his own existential circumstances. For in correspondence with the twin basis of Lutheran mind and personal experience, Thielicke gives a *christological* as well as an *existential* reason to augment his assertion.

As to the first, christological reason, everything depends on the *Deus crucifixus*. The cross of Christ, his blood and justice, does not dissolve sin, suffering, and death, but sorrow is "changed in the depths"; it is intrinsically transformed. Evil entities are still existent but robbed of their *exousia* and autonomy. *Simul justus et peccator*: the justified sinner still sins but is not bound by sin anymore. Its spell is broken, so to say. The same as with death and suffering: they still exist but cannot reach their victorious end any longer. They are defeated powers, robbed of their authority, overcome by (quoting Luther) man "crawling into Christ."[72]

Accordingly, hell "can already, in the here and now, draw us into its demonic force field; for it means separation from God in all of its forms. It means utmost loneliness." But in light of the cross, the whole perspective changes:

> The loss of a beloved one, the final agonies of multiple sclerosis, the sight of a brutally murdered child: all this does not yet have to be hell *as long as I hold the father's hand stretching out into my*

69. "Karfreitag 1941" (*NHT*).
70. See *EvF II*, 325.
71. "Jesus Christus im vordersten Graben" (*NHT*). Emphasis added. The togetherness of divine solidarity and omnipotence is especially well-illustrated in *Bilderbuch*, 113–14, where he lists both next to each other.
72. *ThE I*, §527–28.

darkness. But if I neither recognize meaning in my suffering nor hold the hand of the one who knows the meaning of all this . . . then . . . hell is not far off.[73]

The most terrible aspect of suffering is not so much its physical aspect, as tormenting as this can be. Rather, it consists in the psychological aspect—the meaninglessness encountered when God is not in the paradigm (see chapter 7, part one). Out of this follows the (wholly) other, substantiated by Thielicke's personalistic thought-form: that is, he stakes everything on the one card, Christ.[74] By saying "yes" to him, one does not *give up* in the face of fate but rather *gives in* to the Father's will.[75]

This is the major difference between "with and without God": suffering and death gain new significance "with God" in the paradigm by being transformed from absurdity into the secret of "higher thoughts."[76] In light of Christ's cross and his future reign,[77] man's current suffering is transformed from meaningless pain into pains of labor, "and these are different from disc pain or toothache . . . for pains of labor are overshadowed by the joy and expectation of the great moment lying ahead."[78]

Consequently, "even in times of bestiality, Christians can still praise God. . . . The utopian, however, suffers a terrible shock when human

---

73. *Woran*, 157. Emphasis added. See also *Bilderbuch*, 55–56; *Bergpredigt*, 26, 162.

74. This finds classic expression in the final lines of *Wayfarer*, 419 [536]: "The land to which we are called is a *terra incognita* . . . There is only one voice that we will recognize there because it is already familiar to us here: the voice of the Good Shepherd." See also *EvF III*, 407, 410; *Woran*, 312; *Schweigen*, 75; *Mensch*, 393; and "Kurze Antwort auf die Frage, warum ich Christ bin" (*NHT*).

75. See *Woran*, 40. For the demarcation of man's will by God's will, see *Woran*, 43; *Anfechtung*, 205–8.

76. *Woran*, 246. Regarding his own experience of this insight, see *Wayfarer*, 120 [159].

77. Moltmann prefers the Lutheran translation "future of Jesus Christ" rather than "second coming," since the latter "implies that Christ is not there at the moment," thus "not correspond[ing] to the experience of his presence in the Spirit" (Moltmann, *Experiences*, 33–34).

78. *ThDvGl*, 111. "But what about death? . . . Painful and difficult though our end may be through cancer or multiple sclerosis or earthquakes or air crashes, even these most bitter things can be only a visitation, a taking home. We are expected" (*EvF III*, 408). See also his sermon, given in September 1939, on John 16:33 (on September 1, 1939, Germany started the Second World War by invading Poland): "'I have overcome.' That does not mean: . . . I have abolished death. It does not mean: There shall be no war anymore. Rather, it means: You may know that all this cannot harm you anymore, because it cannot separate you from my love. All pains are nothing but a visitation. . . . Everything is visitation and question. Yes: also a question; a question which can be negated all the same" (*NHT*).

bestiality destroys his confidence in man."⁷⁹ Both adherents do not know what "the letter of life" brings, but "with God" one knows the sender via Jesus Christ, "and I know what He means for me."⁸⁰ Because of "the horn of salvation," there is deliverance from fear. No matter whether surrounded by prison walls, threatened by cancer, or fatally belied by others: "with Dietrich Bonhoeffer we can say [that we are] wonderfully safeguarded by good powers [*Von guten Mächten wunderbar geborgen*]."⁸¹ But this fundamental truth must prove itself in the deepest depths. It is true even in that place which has become the symbol of humanity's utter low point: Auschwitz-Birkenau.⁸²

God "in Control"? Divine Omnipotence Challenged in View of Auschwitz-Birkenau

How can one praise God's omnipotence after Auschwitz? According to Thielicke, in spite of all the justified subjective, "existential frustration"⁸³ stored up in this question, the objective side of the protest nonetheless misfires. To begin with, in view of Auschwitz, it would be better for the questioner not to become disillusioned with God, but rather with man, in whose evil heart all these atrocities are rooted.⁸⁴ But what is more, the view that after Auschwitz it is no longer possible to praise God makes the moment absolute.⁸⁵ In wholly Cartesian manner,⁸⁶ it endows the "I" and the present with absolute significance. Everything else pales in the eyes of the modern individual "which so focuses on the self-consciousness of the moment that

---

79. *EvF I*, 394; *Freedom*, 43.

80. *Woran*, 41. "Ahead of the nihilist lies nothingness; but the Christian knows that the Father of Jesus Christ strides through the firestorms in judgement and mercy" (*K&K*, 46 [*B&E*, 40]).

81. *Reden*, 224. The translation of Bonhoeffer's hymn is taken from *Wayfarer*, 391 [500].

82. The term "theology after Auschwitz" goes back to Johann Baptist Metz. For a brief overview of the impact of Auschwitz upon christological developments, see Ruhstorfer, "Christologie nach Auschwitz," 237–41.

83. For the term "existential frustration," see Frankl, *Man's Search for Meaning*, 100.

84. See *Gebet*, 57; *ThDvGl*, 118–19; and *WiG*, 32: "The horrors of a degenerate humanity are awfully well, and with frightening realism, recorded in this book [the Bible]. . . . To me, it is a comfort to see that the biblical view of man and the world envisages all this and that the faith demanded from me is not demanded by an authority living off illusions." For the latter, see *EvF II*, 255; *EvF III*, 64; and chapter 6, part two.

85. In a different context, Bonhoeffer also warns not to make the moment absolute (Bonhoeffer, *Widerstand*, 208).

86. See chapter 7, part one, esp. *EvF I*, 221–22: "Basically Cartesian theology centers on the question of theodicy."

it loses all sense of history."[87] Yet, to regard the experience of God's absence as specifically modern amounts to an illusion: "The absence and hiddenness of God are not just a modern problem. They are a problem in every age. Each age has its own experience of them. Fundamentally, their history runs parallel to that of faith. It is its alter ego."[88]

Thus, by clinging to such a view, the adherent implicitly empties *every suffering prior to Auschwitz* of its qualitative dimension, of its abysmal depth, of its very own tragedy and horror. Is it only after Auschwitz that it is no longer possible to praise God? If so, was it then still feasible to praise him, for example, after 560 Jewish men, women, and children were burnt at the stake outside Nuremberg in 1349? If at all, it was no longer possible to praise God after the very first murder committed by Cain. Cain, however, just like Auschwitz, is "in all of us."[89] Man is the problem, not God. And God is the questioner, not man. The problem of evil did not just turn up at Auschwitz. What Auschwitz did was intensify man's subjective awareness of it; putting it back on the (theological) agenda.[90]

To be sure, Auschwitz, as *the* symbol for the Shoah, represents a quantitative dimension never reached before in the history of mankind. As such, it has led to certain "painful revisions" of christological thinking.[91] But it adds nothing to the objective, qualitative dimension of the problem of evil *per se*. The problem has been there ever since the fall, and orthodox Christianity has always been gravely aware of it.[92] Thiede is therefore right when he states that Christian theology should not let itself be silenced by such fallacious reasoning, as if there had been no other atrocities in human history; as if natural disasters had not always, and even more so, put the heavenly reign of an omnipotent deity into question.[93] Rather, the important question is whether the "nevertheless" of faith proves itself *in* Auschwitz; whether the suffering and yet omnipotent God can preserve man *in* the midst of hell. Only if Christ's followers *in* Auschwitz were silenced *by* Auschwitz would it be legitimate to give up praise *after* Auschwitz. But this, clearly,

---

87. *EvF I*, 228.

88. *EvF I*, 228. That is why, for Thielicke, faith by nature is a faith against reality.

89. For "The Cain Within Us," see esp. *Welt*; for Auschwitz "within us," see *ThDvGl*, 118–19.

90. Metz observes that one specific characteristic of christological thinking after Auschwitz is its "sensitivity for the question of theodicy" (Ruhstorfer, "Christologie nach Auschwitz," 238).

91. Ruhstorfer, "Christologie nach Auschwitz," 238.

92. A fact rightly highlighted by Cockshut, *Unbelievers*, 169–72; and Lewis, *Problem of Pain*, 4–5, 14.

93. See Thiede, *Gekreuzigte[r] Sinn*, 59.

is not the case. In reply to his own rhetorical question as to whether there has ever been worship in the midst of hell, Thielicke lists several historical examples—from Stephen in Acts to exemplary heroes of the faith in various concentration camps: God's rainbow and their praise did not cease in times of terror; so why should both stop *after* Auschwitz?[94] The very same emphasis is laid by Moltmann: "There would be no 'theology after Auschwitz' ... had there been no 'theology in Auschwitz.' Anyone who later comes up against insoluble problems and despair must remember that the Shema of Israel and the Lord's Prayer were prayed in Auschwitz. It is necessary to remember the martyrs, so as not to become abstract."[95]

Moltmann's call to remember is expressed by Thielicke as follows: "I believe that especially the case of crisis [*der Ernstfall*] reveals the actual depth of truth contained in our faith. Auschwitz and Ravensbrück were tragedies. And there, God was praised. We ought to listen to those who witness to the crisis."[96]

How were these martyrs able to persevere in those outermost borderline situations? Because of the love of Christ—who is stronger than any suffering—one is called to endure. For Christ's love, proven in the lowest depths, is echoed in a question formulated by Zinzendorf: "This I did for you—what will you do for me?" Thus, for the one who loves, suffering can never be the final word. Instead, the final word is the praise of God.[97]

God "in Control": Thielicke's Existential Reason for Divine Omnipotence

This christological emphasis on praising God in the midst of suffering can only sustain itself on the basis of Thielicke's very own experience that God's hand is in control. On this basis, he poses a challenge to his listeners and readers: whoever "finds himself between a rock and a hard place shall praise ... for a start. ... Nothing changes us like worship of God, especially in the darkest moments of our life,"[98] for "gratitude and praise blaze the trail to God's heart ... even in hours of trial, terror, and *Anfechtung*."[99] Indeed, it is

---

94. See *Reden*, 263–66; *Abenteuer*, 154–56; and *EvF II*, 256–57.
95. Moltmann, *Crucified God*, 278.
96. *Reden*, 266.
97. See *Abenteuer*, 156, 179.
98. *Gebet*, 165.
99. *Abenteuer*, 155–56. See *Bilderbuch*, 36–37. For "the power of gratitude," see also Bonhoeffer, *Widerstand*, 52, 61, 73, 87, 101, 109, 169, 208. See also C. S. Lewis's crucial insight gained towards the end of his account of his spiritual struggle: "Praise

conspicuous how repeatedly in his pastoral writings and sermons Thielicke explicitly encourages his audiences *to try faith out*. With his view of faith being an "experiment," Thielicke puts himself in the line of Schleiermacher and in direct contrast to C. S. Lewis.[100] Trust, which is always a risk, can only be gained through testing: "We can only find out who Christ really is . . . if we get involved with him, if we take a chance with him."[101]

This stance of "I-dare-you" appears to be firmly rooted, yet again, in his deeply personal encounter beneath the crucifix that night in 1933. Thielicke so confidently proclaiming that "faith proves itself in the midst of risks"[102] makes sense in light of his own borderline situation. Not only was he initially attracted to theology because martyrs were prepared to "risk" their lives for their beliefs, but he also "risked" suicide himself by taking the whole bottle of yet untested medicine (see chapter 2, part two). In this personally grounded challenge he sees himself confirmed by Scripture:

> When we put ourselves under Jesus, we rise above things; when we put ourselves above Jesus, things rise above us. Again and again, Christians have put it to the test . . . They have tested this freedom [of God's children] even in prisons, concentration camps, and penitentiaries, and it was precisely in these places of extreme constraint that it proved itself.[103]

The divine attributes of omnipresence,[104] omniscience, and omnipotence[105] are the reasons why he thinks this to be the case. This is expressed in the penultimate sermon of his "public dogmatics" during the war:

---

is the mode of love which always has some element of joy in it. . . . Don't we in praise somehow enjoy what we praise, however far we are from it?" (Lewis, *Grief Observed*, 72). Bonhoeffer makes the same point (Bonhoeffer, *Widerstand*, 73, 101). The central importance of gratitude and worship, especially during times of suffering, is furthermore revealed in a deeply moving way by the testimony of Corrie ten Boom as retold by Metaxas, *Seven Women*, chapter 5. See also Zacharias, *Cries of the Heart*, chapter 6.

100. For Schleiermacher, see, for example, Otto, "Introduction," in *On Religion*, esp. xix. For the opposite view of C. S. Lewis see, for instance, Lewis, *God in the Dock*, 27: "The belief in such a supernatural reality itself can neither be proved nor disproved by experience. The arguments for its existence are metaphysical, and to me conclusive."

101. *Abenteuer*, 224. See his problematic prioritization of *fiducia*, appraised in chapter 9, part one. See also his sermon, "How Faith Begins: Trying out Christ," in *Abenteuer*, 189–92.

102. *EvF I*, 361. Moltmann similarly states that "the raising of Christ is proved by our courage to rise against death" (Moltmann, *Experiences*, 32).

103. *Freedom*, 197.

104. "First . . . their radius of action reduced to a minimum, but yet access to the above remained open" (*Freedom*, 197).

105. "Second, they knew . . . : 'Nothing can befall me, save what thou has foreseen and what is good for me.' . . . They also knew . . . that he holds judges, hangmen, spies

Not everything is from God. But everything must pass ... his censorship before it may hit us. ('Jesus Christ stands between me and every darkness.') In passing God's eyes it is transformed.... It is given a purpose which it must serve: it must work for our good (Romans 8:28); ... sorrows now turn into touchstones [*Prüfsteine*] and occasions of trust; the world's anxieties and the fear of life must direct us to the one who has overcome the world.[106]

It is precisely because of the three divine attributes listed above that a new perspective now emerges for all those who put their trust in Christ. It is an essentially transformed perspective of man *sub specie aeternitatis*, for "to praise God really means nothing else but to see history from the perspective of its end, that is, from the throne of God where all the tribulations will be ended."[107]

In conclusion, Christ's solidarity, God's omnipotence, and dialogical prayer have come to light as the three major components in Thielicke's pastoral handling of the question of theodicy. Drawing on the New Testament account of the *proskynesis* of the Magi to the newborn Christ, with gold, myrrh, and frankincense having traditionally been interpreted as standing for the Savior's kingship (omnipotence), passion (solidarity), and dialogical priesthood (prayer), respectively,[108] we can also say that by way of illustration, these three tokens of homage symbolize Thielicke's theological focal point as he deals with sin, guilt, and death pastorally.

... in his hand like marionettes ... that he also ordained this lot and kept it in his power. For even the forces of oppression are in his hand" (*Freedom*, 197). See also *Woran*, 254; *Bergpredigt*, 166–67. "God is not only lord of the hearts ... but he is lord of the whole world. Not only Francis of Assisi and Bodelschwingh belong to those whose lord he is, but Cyrus and Nebuchadnezzar and Stalin and Mao Zedong, too" (*Suche*, 233); "God is the crucial factor of history.... God is not a factor of our inwardness" (*GldChr*, 212–13); "Although we now hear the dark minor-note: what is played is still God's symphony ... The kingdoms of this world are about to go; but the kingdom of God is about to come" (*Welt*, 314); and "Even the powerful rulers of this world ... are not able to spoil God's plan but, unknowingly, are a part of it" (*Reden*, 224). See also Lutzer's interpretation of divine providence in the case of Nazi Germany (Lutzer, *Hitler's Cross*, 48–54).

106. *GldChr*, 452. See also *Woran*, 176; *Bergpredigt*, 27; *Ernstfall*, 85–86; *Welt*, 197–98; *Reden*, 41. Bonhoeffer agrees: "Not everything that happens is simply 'God's will.' But nothing actually happens without God's will (Matt 10:29), i.e., every event, however ungodly it may be, offers access to God" (Bonhoeffer, *Widerstand*, 93).

107. *Freedom*, 198; *Bergpredigt*, 167. See also 2 Cor 4:16–8. Thielicke applies one of his favorite quotes by Joseph Wittig, namely, that "a biography really should not begin with a man's birth, but with his death ... for only there can one see the whole of his life in its fulfillment," to history. If one views the writing of history "as a kind of biography of the world, one arrives at a similar thesis" (*Freedom*, 167).

108. See Ratzinger, *Jesus: Prolog*, 115.

Chapter 10

Homo sub specie aeternitatis

The Pastoral Commission
in the Face of Death

Part One: The Cosmic Eschaton as the Believer's Ultimate Hope

As we have just seen in the previous chapter, the *cosmic* dimension of God's ultimate justice reaching out to all men and to the whole of creation, the *supra-individual* level of the eschaton, when "he will be all in all," is firmly and only rooted in God's omnipotence and fundamental goodness.[1] Yet, at this point Thielicke intriguingly—since implicitly and unintentionally—contradicts his own problematic words rendered earlier, namely, that "whoever is mournful and tries to find his salvation in a teaching or a Christian theological dogma is sold down the river . . . For mourning and insight, grief and thinking are two different things."[2] Indeed, the very opposite is true, as he himself states: "No matter how harshly they [the powers of oppression] may deal with us, they are conquered powers. And *because* these powers are under the control and subject to the triumph of God, *there will always be* grounds for praise and thanksgiving."[3] Contrary to his own declaration, Thielicke precisely does "find salvation . . . in a Christian theological dogma," that is, in the teaching of divine goodness and omnipotence.

---

1. See *ThE I*, §1306, §1351; *ThE II/1*, §2200. Grudem reiterates Berkhof's classification that "Lutheran scholars have emphasized the fact that it [the new earth] will be an entirely new creation, while Reformed scholars have tended to emphasize those verses that say simply that this present creation will be renewed" (Grudem, *Systematic Theology*, 1160–61). While Grudem prefers the Reformed position, Thielicke, unsurprisingly, falls into the Lutheran category. See *EvF III*, 424, 435.

2. *Reden*, 37. See also chapter 7, part two.

3. *Freedom*, 198. Emphasis added.

Thielicke establishes a direct connection between the believer's daily practical life and his theoretical idea of God. It is *because* of what he or she thinks of God that man can rejoice. It is *because* of his knowledge that the Apostle Paul can—indeed *must*—sing at midnight, in spite of his fears.[4] It is *because* of man's specific doctrine that his or her perspective on current circumstances is changed. It is *because* of Christ's resurrection that the pious are again and again provided with certitude in the midst of greatest agony.[5] Consequently, there is no praise without contentual anchorage, no doxology without orthodoxy; a truth *inter alia* made explicit by Carl Trueman, who, in reference to John Henry Newman, underlines that "the identity of whom we praise actually informs the content of how we praise him."[6] Hence, contradicting his own statement, Thielicke concedes that knowledge in the form of doctrinal insight and the mastering of grief *does* go hand in hand with the latter being firmly rooted in the former, which, in turn, must correspond to reality.[7]

Nevertheless, according to Thielicke, without cosmic eschatology, there is no hope for individual, personal eschatology. As against Schiller and Goethe, the history of the world is *not* the judgement of the world.[8] Rather, the problem of theodicy can only be solved eschatologically:

> One can know the significance of the individual part only when one knows the whole to which it belongs and in which it has its proper rank. This is why it is only in eschatological "sight," in which the panorama of the whole will present itself, that the point will be disclosed of that which now in its obscurity

---

4. See *Gebet*, 165. This praise, in turn, takes away his fears by consciously placing him right into God's kingdom even whilst confined to a damp prison cell. See also Romans 11:33–36, where the Apostle's doxology firmly rests on his orthodoxy. For sanctification being based on obedience to the truth, see 1 Peter 1:22.

5. See *Abenteuer*, 221.

6. Trueman, *Creedal Imperative*, 142. See also Bonhoeffer, *Widerstand*, 98; and Sproul et al., *Classical Apologetics*, 21, pointing to the same truth.

7. Thielicke implicitly criticizes the postmodern understanding of knowledge and language in *Welt*, 42, 112, 302–3. For the ambiguity of language, see *Mensch*, 64–69. This ambiguity is rooted in language being "the verbal medium of sinners" (*EvF III*, 414), "involv[ing] brokenness and indirectness for anything transcendent it seeks to express" (*EvF I*, 78). See also *Woran*, 115, 118, 148. Only the Holy Spirit can restore this brokenness (see chapter 5, part two), as "perhaps" symbolically expressed in the speaking of tongues (see *EvF I*, 78).

8. See *Freedom*, 172–73; *ThE I*, §2118; *ThE II/1*, §2114, §2137, §2213; *GldChr*, 246, 394; *Woran*, 145, 255; *Ernstfall*, 72; and *WiG*, 26.

> demands of us the Nevertheless of faith and, in this way, grants victory over the problem of the hiddenness of God.[9]

Indeed, it is this very tension between the "already" and the "not yet" that gives rise to the task of ethics, making it necessary in the first place: "The theme of ethics consists in the 'wayfaring between two worlds'. . . . It lives under the law of the 'not yet' and under the peace of the 'soon I come' (Acts 22:20). *Theological Ethics is eschatological or it is nothing.*"[10] Accordingly, Thielicke not only lived an "eschatological existence" in the individual sense, but was also strongly aware of the eschaton's cosmic dimension, letting the essential hope of Christianity for ultimate justice and peace in God's future reign sustain him in the here and now:

> Both with the Nazis and later the student revolt, people like me who sought the truth in this ancient and eternally young book . . . were constantly cursed as representatives of the past tense. I, on the other hand, felt myself through this ancient book to be already facing the future, namely that period in the future that would make clear the futility of the gods of the day and testify to the eternity of the one God.[11]

Moltmann, in response to Horkheimer, hereby aptly encapsulates the central importance of such eschatological hope in light of the world's current state:

> "In view of the suffering in this world, in view of the injustice, it is impossible to believe the dogma of the existence of an omnipotent, all-gracious God" [says Horkheimer against optimistic theism]. . . . In view of the suffering in this world, in view of

---

9. *EvF III*, 168. See also *ThE I*, §503, §2118; *ThE II/1*, §252n1. In the words of Trillhaas, "No theodicy without eschatology" (Trillhaas, *Dogmatik*, 176). This factum was not only generally ignored in the modern era—particularly by two of its representative thinkers, Leibniz and Kant (see Thiede, *Gekreuzigte[r] Sinn*, 22, 24, 132; Pannenberg, *Systematische Theologie. Band II*, 192)—but the danger of a "disappearance of eschatological expectancy" under different metaphysical presuppositions is, for Thielicke, also present in Barth's theology (see *ThE I*, §596m–x, esp. §596r). For this danger in Barth, see further chapter 6, part two.

10. *ThE I*, §212. Emphasis added. The task of *Theological Ethics* "is essentially determined by the still pending, by the delayed Parousia" (*ThE I*, §195). "Ethics' appropriate zone is . . . the area of tension between the old and the new aeon" (*ThE I*, §198).

11. *Wayfarer*, 417 [533]. See also *Krauss*, 69; *Notwendigkeit*, 23; *Mensch*, 367; and *K&K*, 43 [*B&E*, 38]. "We don't know what comes [in the future]. But we know who comes" (*Woran*, 266). "We live in the name of that which has been promised to us and which is still to come. Christians are people who do not live according to the 'still' of the past perfect tense, but who live according to the 'already' of the future tense" (*Reden*, 23).

the injustice, however, it is also impossible not to hope for truth and righteousness and that which provides them.[12]

Moltmann's observation is existentially enlarged by the dictum of Holocaust survivor, Viktor E. Frankl: "We all said to each other in the camp that there could be no earthly happiness which could compensate for all we had suffered."[13] Amidst the uttermost perverse circumstances, the prisoner's psyche had to develop, and it made many more bestial and hate-filled by the day.[14] Frankl calls this process "depersonalization."[15] And yet, in light of a naturalistic worldview, this world not only is unjust and brutish to the extreme but there will also never be any final, eschatological justice.[16] Thus, Thielicke not only disagrees with Horkheimer's first premise but furthermore also regards it as fundamental for the realization of Moltmann's second premise. Taking the "Nevertheless-Psalm 73" as his basis, Thielicke concludes that the problem of evil is only finally solved *sub specie aeternitatis*: "The dictatorship of the moment ends when its end is perceived (verse 17)."[17]

Indeed, this eschatological view of time obviously emerges as the essential difference with the naturalistic understanding based on chance: "Chance is actually a category of the 'moment.' That is . . . [it] implies a very definite *point of view* from which I approach the event, namely, the point of view of the moment. The moment is therefore also the time-area in which the question of theodicy becomes especially acute."[18] The writer of Psalm 73, in contrast, changes the aspect of the accidental in two senses: "First, the psalmist surmounts the moment by viewing 'the whole' of their [the mighty, the rich, and the wicked] lives, by . . . looking backward; and second, he surmounts the moment by going into the 'sanctuary' and thus viewing the success of the moment *sub specie aeternitatis*."[19] This cosmic dimension of Thielicke's eschatological hope is aptly summarized by a well-known syllogism:

12. Moltmann, *Crucified God*, 224–25.
13. Frankl, *Man's Search for Meaning*, 93.
14. A process testified, for example, in Zywulska, *Ich überlebte Auschwitz*, 81.
15. Frankl, *Man's Search for Meaning*, 88.
16. See Lutzer, *Hitler's Cross*, 55. One of many commendable points of the beautiful film, *The Mission* (1986), directed by Roland Joffé, is that it leaves the viewer with a strong inner urge for ultimate justice. See also the parable at the end of Walter Nigg's historical survey of chiliasm in Nigg, *Das ewige Reich*, 370–71.
17. *Mensch*, 331. See 1 Peter 5:10–11. This eschatological hope is eventually also expressed by C. S. Lewis in his own spiritual struggle. See Lewis, *Grief Observed*, 83.
18. *Freedom*, 168.
19. *Freedom*, 168.

1. If God is all-good, he will defeat evil.
2. If God is all-powerful, he can defeat evil.
3. Evil is not yet defeated.
4. Therefore, God can and will one day defeat evil.[20]

In accordance with his christocentric-experiential approach, Thielicke is certain that Christ will return to judge the living and the dead, for already he has stretched his hand into man's minuscule life; right now, the first rate of his glory is to be experienced.[21] Furthermore, on the basis of God's omnipotence, Thielicke states that suffering "only submits to me the question of trust and wants to teach me the art of saying: 'Nevertheless, I am continually with Thee.' . . . Whoever can truly believe that in the end God's triumph will wait, this person could live differently."[22] *Sub specie aeternitatis*, with Christ's resurrection in the paradigm, the absoluteness of suffering is broken and relativized, as practically expressed in the believer's "serenity of faith."[23]

By emphasizing divine solidarity and omnipotence, the messianic personages of *the suffering servant* and *the heavenly son of man*, as revealed in the Tanakh, implicitly shine through.[24] True to his salvation-historical [*heilsgeschichtliche*] understanding (see chapter 5, part one), the two great events in God's conquest of the powers of evil, *the incarnation* and *the Parousia*, his suffering and his future glory, are fundamental for the church and man's victorious overcoming in the end.[25] To illustrate this, Thielicke uses two analogies from World War II: the decisive battle of Stalingrad and Victory Day, the former inspired by Carl F. Goerdeler[26] and the latter taken

---

20. See also Payne, *Older Testament*, 200–4. "The Old Testament is committed to the fundamental position of divine retribution [as is the New Testament]" (Payne, *Older Testament*, 200). For an opposite view concerning the role of retribution in the New Testament, see Moule, "Punishment and Retribution."

21. See *Woran*, 260, 264–66. By "first rate," Thielicke means the spiritual gifts (*charismata*).

22. *Woran*, 254–55.

23. *Woran*, 254, 265. See also Moltmann, *Crucified God*, 278. For their emphasis on the *risus paschalis*, see *Woran*, 46; Haas and Haug, *Thielicke*, 24–25; and Moltmann, *Experiences*, 32–33. For Thielicke's "eschatological laughter," see chapter 1, part three.

24. See Ladd, *Last Things*, 12–18, 46. "The Son of Man must appear on earth before he comes in glory, and his earthly mission was to fill the role of the Suffering Servant" (Ladd, *Last Things*, 17).

25. See Cullmann: "The preexistent one, the one crucified yesterday, the one ruling in hiddenness today, the one returning at the turn of the aeons: they are all one; it is the same Christ, yet in the exercise of chronologically successive, salvation-historical [*heilsgeschichtliche*] functions" (Cullmann, *Christus und die Zeit*, 94–95).

26. Had the July 20 plot been successful, Goerdeler, the former senior mayor of

from Oscar Cullmann: "The essential point is that in the war between God and Satan, the decisive battle has already been fought. The anti-godly forces have already been overcome in Christ's resurrection. . . . The final Victory Day will bring the hidden but already operative triumph of God to the whole world and present it to sight as well as faith."[27]

In the meantime, however, and in spite of looming victory, Christian existence essentially remains contested. The Christian finds himself in constant battle. The hour of affliction is always near.

Part Two: "The Hour of Affliction"—Divine Judgement (*krisis*), Salvific Chance (*soteria*), and Ethical Suffering

"The Hour of Affliction" as Divine Judgement (*krisis*)

In chapter 9, part one, I outlined that Thielicke not only accepts *Anfechtung*, but, in truly Lutheran manner, makes it a constituent part of faith:

> Fundamentally, on every page, the New Testament is aware that we men are *always* under stress; but it also knows that God wants to turn the very thing that oppresses us into the material of faith . . . The man who lives only in the sunshine . . . never has a chance to learn the "Nevertheless" of faith at all. That is why God *blesses* us with stresses, strains, and trials . . . The depths are the very nurseries where the vital germs of our faith grow and prosper.[28]

By this he does not mean that suffering automatically leads to God, though, for "misery not only teaches you to pray, it also teaches you to curse."[29]

Leipzig, would have become the first German chancellor of a post-Hitler government. Leaving a strong impression on Thielicke (*Wayfarer*, 175 [227]), he was one of the leading civil figures of the German resistance against Hitler. For Thielicke's portrayal, see *Wayfarer*, 174–78 [226–31]; *Krauss*, 9, 37; and *K&K*, 43–44 [*B&E*, 38]. In a personal letter to Goerdeler on June 16, 1944 (*NHT*), written about a month before the failed assassination plot, Thielicke states: "I am sure that an inner rising of our nation is only possible if it learns again to respect and honor *that figure* . . . that brought about the turn of the eras and gave the occidental culture its deepest character." This might be the letter referred to in *Wayfarer*, 177 [230]. After severe torture, the Nazis hanged Goerdeler on February 2, 1945.

27. *EvF III*, 169. See *EvF III*, 428–30, 432; *ThE I*, §1706–7; *Mensch*, 356; *Abenteuer*, 165–67; Cullmann, *Christus und die Zeit*, 72–73, 124; and Ladd, *Last Things*, 47–48.

28. *Freedom*, 198–99. Emphasis his. See his citation of Luther in the context of the role of prayer discussed earlier: "Not to be contested can be the greatest contestation [*Anfechtung*]" (*ThE II/1*, §1146).

29. *K&K*, 45–46 [*B&E*, 40]; *ThE I*, §2193; *Fragen*, 218; *Welt*, 59; *Bilderbuch*, 54.

Rather, it leads to the potentially fruitful borderline or frontier situation outlined above (see chapter 7, part one): "Man in suffering and death is much closer to the secret of his life than in joy.... In joy, one can forget God because the moment is already taken, but in suffering, one can, at most, doubt him... That is why there is something like hospital chaplaincy, but nothing like carnival chaplaincy."[30]

At the same time, Thielicke does not negate Bonhoeffer's thesis that God can also be found in the middle of life's goodness, although he utters concerns that Bonhoeffer's radical demand to seek God at the center of life "throw[s] out the baby with the bath water."[31] Thielicke's own experiences as to the "religious potential" of such extreme moments make him recognize, however, that "that which I do not suffer, I also do not take seriously."[32] Consequently, he disdains those too common prayers for relief or removal of "suffering and catastrophes which really are only much needed visitations and fires of catharsis."[33]

In a sermon on Moses's encounter with God in the burning bush, he further expands on this: "If we would only experience his love and goodness as conceived by us... then he would be homely close, then we would not fear him."[34] But this is not how God deals with mankind. Thousands of people die in earthquakes, airplanes crash, and children are abused by sex offenders. In such events, God remains inconceivable and enigmatic. And "when Bodelschwingh lost his four children to diphtheria... he uttered the abysmal statement: 'Only now I understand how hard God can be.'"[35]

Hence, God can very well meet man in pain and suffering, at least when the latter takes him seriously, when God is reckoned with. In this specific context, discussing God's alienness [*Fremdheit*], Thielicke also very briefly touches on the idea of God as *genius malignus*, the belief of God being all-powerful but evil. C. S. Lewis greatly struggled with this view after the death of his beloved wife, Joy Davidman;[36] in the wake of

---

30. *Tod*, 27.

31. *EvF III*, 349n13. For Thielicke's further engagement with Bonhoeffer's thesis (as expressed in *Widerstand*, 141–42), see *EvF II*, 65, 100–1; *EvF III*, 332–33; and "EdR."

32. *Woran*, 140.

33. *Anfechtung*, 206.

34. *Abenteuer*, 195. According to C. S. Lewis, "If God's goodness is inconsistent with hurting us, then either God is not good or there is no God: for in the only life we know He hurts us beyond our worst fears and beyond all we can imagine" (Lewis, *Grief Observed*, 31).

35. *Abenteuer*, 195.

36. See Lewis, *Grief Observed*, 5, 33–39.

Descartes,[37] the notion of a Dionysian demon of deception passionately occupied the mind of Nietzsche;[38] and the concept of a cunning God is undeniably present in the Quran.[39]

But here, Thielicke only uses it as a short, sermonic illustration, assuring his listeners that it is no surprise when people turn their backs on God in view of the above-listed sufferings. For in light of all this, it is more bearable to assume chance and blind fate instead of living with "the nightmarish idea" of "a sadistic God."[40] From this, he moves on to share briefly his conviction that God cannot easily—if at all—be found in the historical Jesus (see chapter 5), before he drives his main point home that everything comes down to *being* recognized by God: "How many men of God therefore [because of their being met by God] stated that they were hit by one [divine] word . . . Thus—perhaps during an air-raid, whilst the cellar is quaking and it is burning above—one word can suddenly lead into freedom: 'Don't be afraid, I am with you!'"[41]

Thielicke's own Lutheran conversion experience is reflected once again in these lines: the passive voice, forlorn circumstances, and one decisive call from the consequently personal God. Without a doubt, Thielicke regards himself as being among those "many men of God" who "were hit by one word."

"The Hour of Affliction" as Salvific Chance (*soteria*)

The important point to be clarified for our present purpose is the observation that, by subtly shifting the focus from God's foreignness as disclosed through the burning bush to God's calling out from the very same bush,

37. Descartes, *Meditationen über die erste Philosophie*, 42.

38. That Nietzsche was not really an atheist but an "atheistic theologian"—indeed, that he was "a theologian with his whole existence" propagating a "diabolic pantheism"—is the thesis of Thiede in his third chapter on Nietzsche in *Gekreuzigte[r] Gott*, 71–92.

39. See Surahs 8:30 and 13:13. Of course, Islamic monotheism differs from Nietzsche's pantheism.

40. *Abenteuer*, 195. "If all this [suffering] actually comes from God, then we are faced with the following alternative of dread: we can either accept a blind force of fate . . . or, if we dare to assume a personal God, we can only see him as a sadist. Then the assumption of a non-personal, blind, accidental force would be the more merciful one since it would save us from bitterness and the hatred of God (Luther)" (*GldChr*, 451). He thus implicitly chimes in with Camus's thought (as rendered in Moltmann, *Crucified God*, 221), that the very "concept of the personal God" as derived from the Bible intensifies the "metaphysical rebellion" in light of this world's miserable state.

41. *Abenteuer*, 199.

Thielicke transforms the hour of judgement (*krisis*) into an hour of chance (*soteria*). He stresses the dual nature of divine judgement, not only recognizing the more obvious *krisis*-character of the "hour of affliction" [*Katastrophenstunde*; literally: "hour of catastrophe"],[42] but also appreciating its *soteria*-potential, i.e., suffering as a salvific chance: "Whilst his earthly foundations break apart, man is called to ask for those foundations of *stable* value; whilst his past life, traditions, and former [supra-individual] world statuses . . . descend into blood and dread, he has to bear the question whether this really is the end or whether there is something before him that contains a future."[43]

This is vividly brought to life by a previously mentioned evangelist and companion of Thielicke, Wilhelm Busch of Essen, who, after the tragic deaths of his two sons, was forced to the realization that "in such times, you are faced entirely anew with the question as to whether you really want to be serious about the hope Jesus gives."[44] Hence, "the Advent-hour of *soteria* always forces a *decision*."[45] "The hour of affliction is always a divine *inquiry*—no more, but truly no less either."[46]

---

42. In light of the Christian still being a part of this fallen world and his solidarity with it, "He stops . . . asking: 'Why me?' and asks instead: 'Why not me? Why shall I belong to the survivors?' He knows that judgement rightly hits him, too; indeed, that it will even begin 'at the house of God' (1 Pet 4:17)" (*ThE II/1*, §2190). Thielicke's stance is grippingly applied to real life in a pastoral letter to a young woman who was raped by occupiers after Germany's downfall in 1945 (see *Lebensangst*, 148–49 ["In the Depths," in *Out of the Depths*]). Again, it is Thielicke's decisive conclusion that "the secret of judgement . . . is disclosed . . . only on the basis of faith" (*Freedom*, 175).

43. *ThE II/1*, §2191. In this particular context, he puts the emphasis more on the supra-individual, historical judgement within which the individual finds himself. The *soteria*-dimension of suffering especially recurs throughout *Lebensangst*, 27, 41, 84, 130–31, 147, 151, and in his sermon on John 16:33, given at the beginning of the war in September 1939 (*NHT*): "By means of our text . . . we immediately recognize that God only wants to bless us with all those pains and all that fear [in the manuscript, the word "bless" is underlined twice]. Or is it not mercy to get roused like that for once and to look at the world in the cold light of day and to adapt therefore to the reality of God's existence, who suddenly becomes visible in that very light; into whom we might have sleepwalked otherwise . . . For is there anything worse than bumping into God unprepared?"

44. Busch, *Plaudereien*, 176.

45. *ThE II/1*, §2193. Again, the potential existential connection should not be missed, for in that night, he "wanted to *force a decision*: either this maximum dose of the medicine would help me or the 'poison' would kill me" (*Wayfarer*, 65 [89]). Emphasis added.

46. *ThE II/1*, §2195.

Accordingly, Thielicke's interpretation of Germany's war-disaster focuses on the positive implications, viz., the educative purpose it has for the theological discipline:

> Our theology getting constantly healthier and more central is owed to the experience, made under terrors and visitations, that it is a liturgical discipline. . . . Every other theology will be buried on the bleak steppes of Russia and under the rubble of the homeland. God needs these graves so that there can be a resurrection. . . . We humans in the church were at the end of our tether. But now God has spoken. Let us not dare right now to see merely the negative in the great pains and breakdowns! . . . Our time is not only an epoch of tears but also one of divine seeds: those who sow with tears will reap with joy.[47]

Thielicke does not interpret Germany's sufferings causally, but appreciates them teleologically: in light of God's educative purposes.[48] Schlatter, in passing, uttered a similar hope as to the spiritual effects of the First World War. Being devastated by the enormous atrocities and loss of human life, he was at the same time without doubt that God would effect a new devotion among the German people by means of it.[49] Like Thielicke, Schlatter was convinced that theology must be renewed by restoring its confessing character, sensing the enormous responsibility of theology towards the church.[50] Both, however, were eventually disappointed by the practical outcomes of their hopes regarding a possible reform of church and theology, as well as the potential reawakening of faith in the wake of national disaster.[51]

Thielicke's view of the *soteria*-potential of affliction is expressed in at least one other place. In the final chapter of his book on his travels and experiences in the USA, he renders a journalist's question as to what he "regards as being America's most important issue." Thielicke replies: "How the American understands suffering."[52] He explains that it belongs inextricably to the being of humanity that there is suffering that lasts, that cannot be overcome

---

47. *K&K*, 42–43 [*B&E*, 38]. "The Christian knows that the father of Jesus Christ strides through the firestorms in judgement *and* mercy" (*K&K*, 46 [*B&E*, 40]). Emphasis added.

48. See also *Freedom*, 174–75; Bromiley, "Thielicke," 546; and chapter 10, part three.

49. See Neuer, *Schlatter: Ein Leben*, 566–67.

50. Neuer, *Schlatter: Ein Leben*, 162.

51. For Thielicke, see *Anfechtung*, chapter XII, esp. 257 ["Religion in Germany," 144–45]. For Schlatter, see Neuer, *Schlatter: Ein Leben*, 579. See also Bonhoeffer, who shared a similar hope: "Perhaps it is a largely unconscious knowledge that, in the hour of ultimate danger, prompts everything that wants to escape the Antichrist to seek refuge in Christ" (Bonhoeffer, *Ethics*, 341). Thanks to Stephen N. Williams for this reference.

52. *Gespräche*, 253.

in this world. It is not only about eliminating but also about accepting it.[53] In the States, however, Thielicke notices a tendency towards suppression of essentially human topics such as death and aging:[54] "The American has no relation to suffering."[55] That is why knowledge of the purpose, meaning, and task of suffering, of the fact that man can "suffer ethically," must be regained by the American people: "We have to try to gain a new understanding that suffering also must be accepted . . . Here our proclamation should have one of its main emphases. . . . Nevertheless, I am continually with thee."[56]

"The Hour of Affliction": Ethical Suffering as Meaningful Outcome

Amid suffering, to ask self-consciously for the meaning of it all puts man in direct contrast with the animal world, lifting him above the level of unquestioning vegetating.[57] But self-awareness not only characterizes humanness,[58]

---

53. *Gespräche*, 254.

54. *Gespräche*, 253-54. See also *K&K*, 112-15 [*B&E*, 81-82] (in this instance, an abbreviated version of *K&K*). The alarming proliferation of the so-called "prosperity gospel/teaching"—with its roots in the USA—attests to this.

55. *Sterben*, 118-19. See the following statements by Bonhoeffer: "Most possible painlessness was one of the subconscious principles of our life. . . . Your generation, by bearing deprivations, pains, and heavy ordeals from an early age, will be harder and truer-to-life. 'It is good for a man that he bear the yoke in his youth' [Lam 3:27]" (Bonhoeffer, *Widerstand*, 154); "Apropos, even in the Old Testament, the blessed one had to suffer a lot . . . but nowhere does it follow (just as little as in the New Testament) that happiness and suffering, blessing and cross, are juxtaposed in absolute opposition. . . . Suffering, too, is a road to freedom" (Bonhoeffer, *Widerstand*, 200). See also Moreland: "Happiness involves suffering, endurance, and patience because these are important means to becoming a good person who lives the good life" (Moreland, *Kingdom Triangle*, 94).

56. *Gespräche*, 257. See also his general admonition as to this in *K&K*, 75-76 [*B&E*, 64-65] (fully cited in chapter 3, part three).

57. *EvF I*, 48; *Ernstfall*, 64. "The knowledge of death . . . distinguishes man from animals. Animals live for the moment with no future in view. . . . Man looks ahead to the future" (*EvF III*, 389).

58. Not "establishes," since if self-consciousness were to *determine* humanness, then what about the embryo, fetus, people in a coma, or the mentally handicapped? True to his relational understanding, Thielicke negates any ontological grounding of personhood (see *Mensch*, 101-2), instead asserting the "relation to the Creator as the decisive nub of humanness" (*Mensch*, 102). Accordingly, it is not man who defines the unformed embryo as human life, but God who sees life from the very first moment (he refers to Psalm 139 in this regard). Thielicke can even grant man's pre-existence *insofar* as man already imaginarily exists prior to his conception in the mind of God. See *Mensch*, 103. Regarding the end of man's life, see *Mensch*, 103-9. For the alien dignity of the unborn, see *ThE III*, §2740-43. As truthful and appealing as this might

it also enables man to "suffer ethically." This specifically human quality means that the person can seize and transfer suffering into a productive task of self-realization,[59] at the same time excluding any form of a *coup de grâce* for human beings.[60]

In relation to self-consciousness being an essential human feature, Roman Catholic philosopher von Hildebrand—also calling it "being awakened"—highlights the fundamental significance of vigilance [*Wachheit*]: "The more vigilant someone is, the more his personhood is actualized." In the Kierkegaardian sense, the more man is self, an individual; the more, in turn, he or she is opposed to the herd mentality; the more capable he or she is of true fellowship; the richer his or her personhood; the deeper his or her understanding of values; and the livelier his or her conscience.[61]

Thielicke, without referring to von Hildebrand, intriguingly adds to this line of thought as follows: "The more highly organized a man is and the more sublime his constitution in mind and soul, the more sensitive he will be and the broader his capacity for suffering."[62] He then applies this to the suffering of Christ. As Christ is the prototype of true humanness, the only whole man that ever lived, he suffers both "differently and more fully than [we do]."

---

seem from a Christian point of view, it must nevertheless be asked whether this line of arguing is successfully applicable in the secular public square, as it *presupposes* a Christian view of man. In general—and with regard to the abortion debate in particular—it is therefore more advisable to argue philosophically and thus comprehensibly for the sake of the non-Christian. Two excellent examples of such an approach are the presentations of Roman Catholic philosophers, Francis J. Beckwith (at that time still an evangelical), *Politically Correct Death*, and Peter Kreeft, "Pro-Life Logic." Intriguingly, Thielicke himself argues for the preservation of natural law for the sake of the common good: even if put *extra fidem*, the question regarding the last norms constitutes "antitoxin for the wildest consequences of [man's] hubris" (*ThE I*, §2129). See also *ThE I*, §2128–37, esp. §2133 and §2136.

59. See *Mensch*, 105; *Gespräche*, 257; *Krauss*, 58; *Sterben*, 31, 120; and *LmdT*, 75–76. "Only on the ground of self-awareness can man suffer ethically, can he make something out of his suffering" (*LmdT*, 133).

60. See *ThE III*, §2870; *Ernstfall*, 123; *LmdT*, 75–76; *Krauss*, 58; and *Sterben*, 120. "Applied to man it would be iniquity for this shot would destroy the chance of meaningful being" (*Sterben*, 31).

61. See von Hildebrand, *Tod*, 7–8. See also *MF&T*, 516.

62. *EvF II*, 387. "It belongs to the status of a marked individuality that the humanum is more vulnerable . . . since it provides much greater targets. . . . Everybody knows that a highly cultured and therefore 'sensitive' man is disparately more susceptible to undertones . . . in a social relation or even in a polemic than an uncomplicated nature-boy" (*ThE III*, §2340–41). This trait is also displayed in highly sensitive persons (*HSP*), making them both more prone to external stimuli, and yet equally more ingenious with regard to their cognitive and emotional abilities. See Aron, *Highly Sensitive Child*.

Without Thielicke explicitly stating the next point, this line of thinking might nonetheless be continued in the following way: Christ's suffering is not only far worse than any other human suffering due to his pure sensitivity, flowing from fully aware vigilant *love*, but he is also, consequently, man's perfect exemplar regarding "ethical suffering," because he transferred his utmost capacity for suffering into the very task he came to accomplish. This most painful task was man's redemption, Christ thereby realizing his true self, his true destiny, by being a personal savior. But even he asked the question of meaning, that is, the God question,[63] in the midst of his greatest suffering. How much more, then, does the same question arise on the basis of fallen human self-consciousness?[64]

In dealing with this question, the key figure for Thielicke comes in the biblical character of Job. What increasingly afflicts Job is not so much the physical pain of his suffering but rather his gradually losing sight of any meaning or purpose in it, "the abyss of emptiness opening up before him."[65] Whereas at the beginning, Job still tries to make sense out of his suffering,[66] the enemy, "being the good psychologist that he is," adds two factors that crush Job's attempt at rationalization. The first factor is the *degree* of pain, the second its *duration*. As to the former, by suffering "torments of hell," one gets so "filled out" that the question of meaning simply does not arise anymore. As to the latter, suffering goes on beyond the accepted timeframe one sets oneself (e.g., "I can cope with one or two years . . . ").[67] The tempter makes one's suffering continue beyond the frame man can accept as meaningful.[68]

Once more, Thielicke's own "sickness-unto-death" is mirrored in these reflections. He claims that any of his readers who have experienced heavy and endless agonies know what he is talking about: "This destiny, at which end one renounces God because no more meaning can be recognized, because faith in a God allowing the meaningless, the brutally

---

63. See Gollwitzer, *Krummes Holz–aufrechter Gang*, 176.

64. For Thielicke's engagement with Freud, who discards the question of meaning, see *Mensch*, 443–45.

65. *ThDvGl*, 108. See also *Anfechtung*, 191; *ZG&S*, 18.

66. See *Woran*, 38; *ZG&S*, 18.

67. *WiG*, 23–25; *ThDvGl*, 113–14; and *Woran*, 38–39.

68. See *WiG*, 23; *ZG&S*, 18–19. For Job, see *ZG&S* [*Between God and Satan*], esp. chapters 3 and 4.

idiotic, shatters."[69] This is the most extreme, the most serious thing that can happen to faith.[70]

And yet, *without* a (tri-)personal God, at best nothing remains but a stoic *amor fati*: one's surrender to destiny.[71] Into what kind of abyss, into what absurdity would mankind plunge without God—and therefore suffering being robbed of any meaning at all?[72] That is why he recurrently renders Jean Paul's "Sermon of the Dead Christ," later worked out in all its logic by Nietzsche,[73] for the true terror lies in the extinction of everything valid, beautiful, meaningful, and truthful that any man has ever lived for. In short, it lies in the *nihil*.[74]

Correspondingly, it is simply not comprehensible for man to cease in his apparently meaningful existence.[75] On the basis of a specific experience on May 1, 1931,[76] almost two years before his sickness reached its near-fatal climax, Thielicke picks up a thought of the highly controversial psychiatrist, Alfred E. Hoche,[77] in order to give voice to the "intolerable thought that the

---

69. *Woran*, 39. Moltmann notes that, according to Camus, "the metaphysical rebellion . . . [derives] from the Bible, with its concept of the personal God" (Moltmann, *Crucified God*, 221).

70. See *ThDvGl*, 114; *Freedom*, 175. "Meaninglessness is the strongest objection to God" (*ZG&S*, 19).

71. See *Woran*, 39. This stance is best illustrated for Thielicke in Spengler's soldier of Pompeii (see chapter 7, part two).

72. See *ThDvGl*, 107.

73. See *EvF I*, 236–42. For his engagement with Wetzel, Jacobsen, and Nietzsche, see *EvF I*, 242–59.

74. See *ThDvGl*, 109.

75. This is the dilemma of the naturalistic worldview which cannot offer consistency *and* happiness at the same time. For either there is no objective meaning and the naturalist lives accordingly, that is, "unhappily"; or there is no objective meaning and he still lives as if there were meaning, namely, inconsistently. *Inter alia*, this has been pointed out by Craig, "The Absurdity of Life Without God." Thielicke, *LmdT*, 50, observes this in Camus, who "has his pores wide open to be secretly infiltrated with meaningful consolations [*Sinntröstungen*]," an observation confirmed by Mumma's somewhat controversial book, *Albert Camus and the Minister*. See Sire, "Camus the Christian?"

76. See *Krauss*, 19.

77. Thielicke does not mention this, but Hoche, born to a pastor in 1865, was one of the first to develop the concept of systematically murdering invalids [*Krankenmord*], which was later adopted by the Nazi-regime. In 1920, the Social Darwinist co-authored the booklet, *Die Freigabe der Vernichtung lebensunwerten Lebens: Ihr Maß und ihre Form* ["Permitting the Destruction of Life Unworthy of Life: Its Measure and Shape"], propagating the killing of so-called *Ballastexistenzen*—people whose lives would constitute a "burden" for the rest of society. Hoche died on May 16, 1943, in Baden-Baden. See Klee, *Personenlexikon zum Dritten Reich*, 260; Weikart, "Darwinism and Death," 330–32.

huge subjective world within us should be wiped out while others go on boastfully as if nothing had happened."[78] Thielicke thus concretely illustrates the fundamental good of man existing as a personal being *and of man* (at least subconsciously) *perceiving it to be so*. In the words of von Hildebrand, "existence as a personal being is such an unheard of, fundamental, taken-for-granted good that we are usually not fully aware of its value."[79] Consequently, "the loss of this fundamental good, the descent into nothingness, would be a terrible evil."[80] For being a person is "the precondition for all happiness": "To lose it means the greatest loss. . . . It is false to believe that only suffering is an evil. The objective loss of being is a terrible evil."[81]

Indeed, according to von Hildebrand, the loss of personal existence is the "greatest evil."[82] That is why Augustine prefers being a sentient, albeit pain-filled creature over being a stone, sensing no pain at all.[83] For "whatever things exist are good."[84] In other words, being-in-suffering is far better than non-being since, "despite the reality of the *vallis lacrimarum*, we can proclaim: how beautiful thou art, world! How sweet the life!"[85] Likewise, for Thielicke, "the totality of our existence is a gift."[86]

---

78. *EvF II*, 28. See also *EvF III*, 391; *Woran*, 171; and *LmdT*, 63, 100–1. One is reminded of what Paul Tillich called the "threat of non-being" in this regard.

79. See Chesterton's brilliant chapter, "Ethics of Elfland," in *Orthodoxy*, unfolding this further.

80. Von Hildebrand, *Tod*, 21.

81. Von Hildebrand, *Tod*, 23. See also von Hildebrand, *Tod*, 90. Here, I can merely hint at the critical implications this infinite value of personal being entails for the eschatological teaching of annihilationism.

82. Von Hildebrand, *Tod*, 38.

83. Von Hildebrand, *Tod*, 21n13.

84. Augustine, *Confessions*, VII.12.18.

85. Von Hildebrand, *Tod*, 53. This view thus implies an answer to the question as to whether the world's non-existence would have been better than this suffering one. According to Moreland and Craig: "The person who knows God, no matter what he suffers, no matter how awful his pain, can still truly say, 'God is good to me!' simply in virtue of the fact that he knows God, an incommensurable good" (Moreland and Craig, *Philosophical Foundations*, 550).

86. *GldChr*, 251. Not many have worded this insight as eloquently as Chesterton: "The test of all happiness is gratitude . . . Children are grateful when Santa Claus puts in their stockings gifts of toys or sweets. Could I not be grateful to Santa Claus when he put in my stockings the gift of two miraculous legs? We thank people for birthday presents of cigars and slippers. Can I thank no one for the birthday present of birth?" (Chesterton, *Orthodoxy*, 47–48).

Yet, in view of this aeon's "pallid twilight," there have always been "many atheists and other depressed groups"[87] who preferred not to be.[88] But such "world-despairing pessimism . . . knows nothing of . . . God still having his hand in this world of darkness and that he has got his rainbow of mercy placed above this world of flood and downfalls. Even the darkest world still rests in the hands of God."[89] Again, this strong pastoral encouragement for his listeners during the air raids in World War II can only be made because Thielicke himself has "encountered no darkness above which it [the rainbow] does not shine and no valley, no matter how gloomy, which some of God's greetings have not reached."[90]

If God *really* became incarnated in Christ, if the ultimate meaning expressed Himself meaningfully within man's world, thus infinitely upgrading man's own being, "then this would change our lives. . . . Then everything [*suffering included*] in my life would gain another meaning, another significance."[91] In short, it would make *the* decisive difference:

> If we were not allowed to know . . . that Jesus Christ is enthroned in the midst of . . . the abyss . . . [then] we would face hopeless disaster. Nietzsche did not know that and it became his nightmare . . . He perished because he wanted to have the truth without grace. Yet, such truth no man can bear. . . . That is the greatness of Christ . . . that he suffered man's deepest miseries himself. Here and only here God is to be found.[92]

What a striking parallel to Luther's christological focus in the midst of gloom, as encapsulated by Althaus: "Consideration of Christ's own anguished death and of the grievous doubts and temptations of the crucified helps faith to attain that end, to endure the most difficult troubles and anxieties without succumbing to despair. Only if Christ is with us, can we bear the worst troubles and anxieties without falling into despair."[93]

---

87. *EvF III*, 409.

88. Such as Sophocles, Arthur Schopenhauer, or, in present times, one of Germany's leading atheists, Ansgar Beckermann, expressing this view in a public debate with William Lane Craig in Munich on October 29, 2015.

89. *GldChr*, 161.

90. *Wayfarer*, 419 [535]. For Thielicke's emphasis on the symbolic force of the rainbow, see the introduction.

91. *Woran*, 107–8. See Lewis, *Problem of Pain*, 36–39.

92. *GldChr*, 124–25. See *EvF I*, 259.

93. Althaus, *Luther*, 59. And yet, this was not of immediate help to C. S. Lewis: "[C.] reminded me that the same thing seems to have happened to Christ: 'Why hast thou forsaken me?' I know. Does that make it easier to understand?" (Lewis, *Grief Observed*, 5). What might Thielicke reply? Perhaps that, according to his notion of faith as the

Once more, the double helix of his experiential-Lutheran shaping is clearly enunciated in these lines. The Lutheran Thielicke, quite in accordance with his character trait (as outlined in chapter 1, part three), experienced both extremes of nihilistic meaninglessness and personified meaning in his own life, culminating in this momentous night in 1933.[94]

Since faith is always in the face of and against evil reality, Thielicke asks himself, "whether the contradiction between reality and God . . . is not in fact a contradiction between reality and ideas of God rather than God himself." For God has fully revealed himself in his Son; therefore, "the contradiction between reality and God is never overcome by perception,"[95] but only christologically.

As God himself shares the deepest human suffering in Christ and suffers whenever man suffers, man can rest assured that his suffering is known and borne by Christ, the "fellow-sufferer."[96] Indeed, for Thielicke, it is God's very suffering in Christ that is the only definitive reason why man can believe and trust God.[97] It is his answer to the subtitle of his lay-dogmatics, *Woran ich glaube: Der Grund christlicher Gewissheit* [*What I believe: The basis of Christian certitude*].[98] The otherwise unknown Father becomes known by giving his dearest Son, part of himself, and in so doing, he "suffers for my sake, more than I could ever suffer myself."[99]

By relating to God's suffering initiative in trust (*fiducia*), in turn, man can now know the one who knows him. By getting to know "God's heart" in trusting faith, man does not find out why things happen,[100] but man knows that whatever hardship crosses his path, it comes from someone who car-

---

great "nevertheless" (see chapter 9, part one), man is not really meant to understand anyway. Shall this be the final answer?

94. Regarding "personified meaning," see also Ratzinger (*End of Time?*, 21) cited in Gallagher, *Faith Maps*, 144, who speaks of "the Logos itself, the eternal Word, the eternal meaning of the cosmos that dwells in the Son of Man." Correspondingly, see the title of Thiede's book, *Gekreuzigte[r] Sinn* (*Crucified Meaning*).

95. *EvF I*, 229. See also *EvF II*, 74.

96. *Woran*, 134. See Bonhoeffer: "Christ does not help us in virtue of his omnipotence, but by virtue of his weakness, in his suffering! . . . Only the suffering God can help" (Bonhoeffer, *Widerstand*, 191–92).

97. A view also shared by Stott, who could never believe in God if it were not for the cross (Stott, *Cross of Christ*, 210).

98. *Woran*, 112, 128. On logical certainty [*Sicherheit*] and psychological certitude [*Gewissheit*], see also Tennant, *Nature of Belief*, 3–14.

99. *Woran*, 41–42.

100. "I don't know why suffering hits me and why there is suffering . . . in the world in the first place. But through Christ I look into the heart of the one who gives thought to it and whose thoughts are higher than our thoughts" ("Kurze Antwort auf die Frage, warum ich Christ bin" (*NHT*))

ried it himself,[101] its last meaning thus consisting of "a love bled away by a heart which suffered itself to death because of it."[102]

The words of Holocaust survivor Viktor Frankl thus aptly encapsulate Thielicke's own conviction: if there is meaning in life at all, then there must be meaning in suffering.[103] Thielicke therefore appreciatively engages with Frankl's position in his anthropology, *Mensch*, contrasting the logotherapeutic approach with that of Freud, whilst also unfolding his own notion of "ethical suffering" in the same context once more.[104] This fact that man can "suffer ethically" *due to* his experience of concrete meaning in suffering *by virtue of* the personified truth and meaning, viz., the suffering Christ, leads to our final subsection, which looks into Thielicke's focus on suffering as a productive task.

Part Three: Not "Why" but "What for"—Suffering as the "Great Commission" of Mankind

We have seen that Thielicke regards faith essentially to be not a "because," but a "nevertheless, in spite of" (see chapter 9, part one). This conviction is dually rooted in his Lutheran frame of mind and his own life circumstances. Such a faith against appearances, however, is only sustained in the twin light of divine solidarity and omnipotence, for without the former, there is neither understanding nor comfort; but without the latter, there is no hope regarding ultimate victory and justice, no hope that man's tears will one day truly be wiped away (see part one of this chapter). Thus, it is only on the basis of a personal relationship that the constitutive factor of *Anfechtung* is transformed from an hour of *krisis* into one of *soteria*. The hour of affliction can only be overcome personalistically, namely, by man relating himself to the personified truth and meaning, thereby fully seizing his or her human potential of ethical suffering (see part two of this chapter).

---

101. *Woran*, 107.

102. *Woran*, 244–45. "He literally loved himself to death" (*Woran*, 111).

103. Viktor Frankl, as rendered by Thielicke in *Reden*, 3.

104. See *Mensch*, 464–65; *Sterben*, 125–26, where he praises Frankl's logotherapeutic approach. For a brief introduction to logotherapy, see the second part of Frankl's *Man's Search for Meaning*.

Horizontal Suffering Vertically Illuminated: A Change of Perspective in Light of Ultimate Meaning

Under this threefold perspective of divine personal being, divine goodness, and divine omnipotence—which reflects itself in the person of Jesus Christ—suffering is ultimately bestowed with meaning. The question of meaning, therefore, cannot be answered by pointing to immanent ends, for meaning *per definitionem* is an intrinsically transcending entity. It naturally goes beyond man's horizon.[105] That is why it eventually turns out to be the God question,[106] making the great Western crisis of meaning in the wake of Nietzsche, which was unswervingly followed by the Death-of-God movement in the sixties, understandable.[107]

Central to the legacy of Nietzsche's attack on the whole Western tradition, of his "deplatonizing rather than dechristianizing,"[108] is the abdication of meaning as apprehended in his transcendent-less perception of death.[109] The Nietzschean divinization of man goes hand in hand with a loss of divine purpose, with a loss of a hand from which both the good and the bad can be accepted, and with it an absolutization of man's needs and desires[110]—i.e., an absolutization of the "I," an absolutization of the moment, and an absolutization of Auschwitz.

In view of this identity crisis, it is only consistent that Western man finds himself helpless in the face of suffering: "It does not prompt any other question but how it can be reduced in the cheapest possible manner."[111] If man's will and claim to well-being become the new dogma, however, then suffering can objectively only be understood as a minus, a loss.[112] But then it also follows that any life that does not meet this new standard may be liquidated,[113] assisted in suicide, or not even allowed into this world.

---

105. See *LmdT*, 11.

106. See Gollwitzer, *Krummes Holz*, 176; *Anfechtung*, 193.

107. See the dictum of Nietzsche's biographer, Frenzel: "[Nietzsche] is one of the few great thinkers of the nineteenth century . . . without which the twentieth century would not have become what it is" (Frenzel, *Nietzsche*, 7). For Thielicke's engagement with the Death-of-God movement, see the second part of *EvF I*. For a concise overview, see also Grenz and Olson, *Twentieth-Century Theology*, 156–69.

108. *EvF I*, 250.

109. See *Tod*, 35–38.

110. See *Tod*, 37–38.

111. *Sterben*, 119.

112. For a closer look at Western man's detrimental move "from human flourishing to satisfaction of desire," see Moreland, *Kingdom Triangle*, 94–96; Moreland and Issler, *Lost Virtue of Happiness*, esp. chapter 1.

113. See *Sterben*, 120–21.

If, however, man's horizontal perspective is fundamentally transformed by conscious implantation into the divine vertical dimension, then the "why"-question of suffering changes accordingly. Then it also becomes possible that man, even though his or her *suum* most likely consists in health and well-being, might nonetheless arrive at maturity (i.e., actual identity) via suffering.[114] In a sermon at the end of the war with a rather pre-deterministic undertone, Thielicke highlights the crucial consequence that follows from this transformation of perspective:

> Only God's will comes to pass in the end. And that is why it becomes uninteresting (it is very easy to say what I say now; I know that it is very difficult to live out) for a Christian to ask "Why" was this allowed to happen to me? Rather, the question must be put as follows: "What for" does God let this happen? Without a doubt only . . . to realize his and no other plans.[115]

Divinely illuminated, man's whole outlook on life essentially changes. The biblical message proclaims deliverance in the face of this undecipherable problem of meaning, by transforming the question "Why?" into "Whither? To what end?" And on the basis of the story of the man born blind in John 9, the answer can only be: "That the works of God might be made manifest."[116] Whereas the question "Why?" is looking for metaphysical causes, only prompting untenable answers beginning with "Because," the question "What for?" rests assured in the loving foundation of this world, established by a Father in whose counsel all answers remain hidden: "Nevertheless, I am continually with Thee (Ps 73:23)."[117]

Thielicke's pastoral priority over his metaphysical wariness (see chapter 7, part two) as well as his solely non-Cartesian starting point resurface here: God is the questioner, not man. Christ, as personified truth

---

114. See *ThE I*, §2110. He goes on to add: "Not to mention, the actual theological question how health and suffering impact our standing to eternity." C. S. Lewis, before the death of his beloved wife, recognized in suffering a means to "the perfecting of the beloved" (Lewis, *Problem of Pain*, 38). Thielicke, in contrast, albeit convinced that "everything that befalls man becomes a task," also thinks that there are limits; for with certain forms of suffering, man cannot acquire maturity anymore. See *Krauss*, 58.

115. *GldChr*, 449–50. "God even uses the elements of this fallen world (death, guilt, and suffering) to let them mysteriously serve his ends. It is the alien (Luther), the indirect will of God which can use such detours for his purposes and aims. The geometric formula that the direct line is the shortest distance between two points does not apply in God's kingdom. The people in the Bible know about the devious routes, via depth and byways, leading them to goals which they would never have reached by the direct lines as desired by them" (*GldChr*, 452).

116. *Freedom*, 178.

117. *Freedom*, 178.

and meaning, is subject to no criterion but is himself the criterion, making himself manifest in the process of proclamation.[118] Whereas Cartesian theology, with self-conscious man as its starting point, centers on the "why"-question of theodicy,[119] the "whither"-question starts with God, thereby providing everything else with meaning. God, however, questions man: "Adam, where art thou?"[120]

The pastoral application of this changed view of perspective is expressed paradigmatically in Thielicke's letter to a young woman who was raped by members of the occupying forces after the downfall of the Third Reich in 1945.[121] Indeed, this letter encapsulates all the aspects we have looked at thus far in this chapter.

Thielicke begins by emphasizing his understanding, based on his experiences during the war, where he encountered and spoke words of comfort to many other women who had shared a similar fate. Moreover, he experienced first-hand that anyone who opens up in the hour of deepest affliction, in the very borderline situation, can experience Christ's nearness more than in any other moment—even the greatest spiritual bliss. Apparently confronted by the victim with Romans 8:28, he then exhorts her to nourish hope by adopting an eschatological point of view. For not only will this hour dissipate when seen from the perspective of eternity—it will be a "moment," nothing more—but it also may well be that the good that God will bring about by way of her suffering can only be recognized on the day of judgement.

He further cautions her to leave the egocentric (Cartesian) perspective (on which the question of theodicy rests) behind, since it may also be possible that in this most terrible moment of her life, God has deeply joined her with the guilt of the German people.[122] But this hour of affliction is not only marked by *krisis*, it also contains chances and opportunities. In addition to its great *soteria*-potential of experiencing Christ's nearness like never before, through this heavy burden, God has also set her with a task and everything now comes down to what she does with it. Yet, in this very letter, Thielicke also stresses *Anfechtung* and suffering as essential characteristics of faith, since only in those depths can God get a chance to pour out all his blessings.

---

118. See *EvF III*, 362. For God as the questioner, see *EvF II*, 31, 96, 271, 288; and Speier, *Initiator*, who dedicated his dissertation to this particular theme.

119. See *EvF I*, 222.

120. *Lebensangst*, 156. According to Ebeling: "The *coram*-relationship reveals that the fundamental situation of man is that of a person on trial" (Ebeling, *Luther*, 197).

121. See *Lebensangst*, 147–51 ["In the Depths," in *Out of the Depths*]. See also *Wayfarer*, 188–89 [244–45].

122. For this emphasis, see also *Freiheit*, 15.

At the same time, he directs her attention to the fellow suffering of Christ, whose body was likewise abased and who called out: "My God, my God, why hast thou forsaken me?" Staying true to his personalistic answer to the problem of evil, he thus closes the letter by reminding his addressee once more that her life is truly filled with plenty of rewarding tasks.

In short, in an attempt to sharpen his listeners' hearts for the manifold tasks and blessings that might come out of such circumstances, here and elsewhere, Thielicke commissions the suffering individual not to ignore all the potential that is contained in the unpleasant and the horrific. Gaining such perspective is no easy task but takes "holy inner disciplining." Yet, the difficulty of the task does not diminish its existence, no matter how deep the abyss. Therefore, Thielicke "solemnly proclaim[s] in the name of [John 9:1–3] that in the midst of all your pain a task is put to you." For "God is always positive . . . he did it 'for' a reason."[123]

Out of this divine goodness,[124] as well as Thielicke's relationalism,[125] flows his focus on the potential of everything, including suffering, in relation to man's personal growth. Quite in accordance with Trillhaas's and Pannenberg's definition of "personality" outlined earlier (see chapter 6, part one), human character develops by taking on and solving tasks set for man in the course of his encountering the world. Man grows with "his higher purposes." By "purposes" Thielicke means the goals to which man relates and the tasks he takes on.[126] He can do so by virtue of his capacity for volitional decision, by being given self-consciousness, which essentially differentiates him from the brute and thus makes the "task" possible. It enables him not to be delivered up to natural processes, but to unfold

---

123. *Lebensangst*, 40–41.

124. That is, God's love, combined with his omnipotence. "We ought to be certain that he also rules *this* world, that he sets us tasks of love . . . and that everywhere along the way his greetings are waiting for us, reassuring us that he thinks of us" (*Woran*, 290). For the existential anchorage, see *Wayfarer*, 419 [535]: "Indeed, I have encountered no darkness above which it [the rainbow] does not shine and no valley, no matter how gloomy, which some of God's greetings have not reached."

125. "I always only experience myself in my attribute of being a partner and member of this world; I always only experience myself in my relations, in my 'being-towards-something' [*Sein zu etwas*] and 'being-for-something' [*Sein auf etwas hin*]" (*ThE II/1*, §1375). In addition to what was said in chapter 4, see the following footnote.

126. See *ThE II/1*, §1384. "I become 'I myself' by encounter. Man comes into being and grows with his tasks, his goals, his encounters and also by 'turning-away from himself' [*Weg-gewandt-sein von sich selbst*]" (*ThE II/1*, §1611–12). "Character always emerges by means of a task, i.e., not of his own accord but by virtue of that which encounters him, of what is assigned to him; he solely comes into being through encounter" (*Fragen*, 77).

himself, and to objectify himself whilst doing so.[127] Consequently, man is given the task of reacting to suffering: he can "suffer ethically," "suffering can turn into a productive task."[128]

In commissioning the believer thus, Thielicke joins the ranks once more with the imprisoned Bonhoeffer, who not only held to the conviction that "every event, however ungodly it may be, offers access to God,"[129] but who also considered his present circumstances in confinement—albeit running counter to his own wishes—as a divine commission by which he was to be prepared and made mature for tremendous future tasks: "That is why we should not shake off our experiences but rather have to preserve and process them, [thereby] letting them become fruitful. Never before have we experienced the furious God so violently, and this is grace, too. . . . Don't harden your hearts."[130] Likewise, according to Bonhoeffer, the moment of *krisis* contains the promise and potential to turn into the moment of *soteria*.

A Regenerate Heart Regenerates Structures: the Task of Preventing Future Wounds

Finally, Thielicke's great commission for the sufferer, arising out of his above-mentioned stances on divine goodness, man's essential relationality, and wounds having to heal wounds, does not restrict itself to the individual act of charity. Rather, "love has the task not merely of binding up wounds but of preventing them, i.e., creating circumstances which, as far as possible, will rule out the wicked acts of the thieves."[131] He paradigmatically expresses his conviction of "love in structures" by freely extending the parable of the Good Samaritan, asking his audience to imagine the Samaritan

---

127. See *ThE II/1*, §1595–96. Thielicke does not use the term, but his position bears resemblance to the so-called "soul-making theodicy" as advocated by Hick, who, in turn, builds on the thought of Irenaeus (see Hick, *Evil and the God of Love*).

128. *Sterben*, 31. See also *Krauss*, 58; and chapter 10, part two. This theorem finds paradigmatic application in the concrete case of his commemorative address on the occasion of a freighter disaster, where he exhorted his listeners to consider that they can only cope with their grief if thinking of their dead becomes a task—if it gives their lives a new direction. See *Schweigen*, 77. See also his "Vorwort zum Totenbuch der Erlanger Uttenreuther," May 24, 1964 (*NHT*), where he lays the same emphasis.

129. Bonhoeffer, *Widerstand*, 93.

130. Bonhoeffer, *Widerstand*, 84, 146. Contrary to Thielicke, however, Bonhoeffer does not negate the question "why," but considers it important, especially when the "what for" appears dubious. See Bonhoeffer, *Widerstand*, 157.

131. *EvF III*, 62. See Schlatter's similar emphasis in *Einführung*, 194–95. Schlatter, like Thielicke further down, claims that Luther and the Reformation left these issues unaddressed.

as the mayor of a town. His next step, after having dropped the victim off at the inn, would have been to think about how to prevent such crimes systematically and prophylactically in the future.[132] Hence, the Christian love for the neighbor carries with it a suprapersonal dimension, becoming concretized in political, economic, or social action. It is here that Christians, who have always been highly commendable in caring for the wounded, can learn from antagonists such as Karl Marx, who recognized that the fault lies in the system: "This insight should lead Christians to the point where love takes up the task of working at the system."[133]

This is all the more so since the structures of this aeon are perverted by man's fall. Thus, restored man, by being "ordered to fight . . . against those powers of disruption which God does not want," follows his exemplar, Christ, whose life was dedicated to this struggle in suffering and on the cross. Even if this struggle turns out to fail, it must still work together for the good according to God's universal governance.[134]

However, one of two extremes to be avoided here is the illusion, as entertained, for example, by Herbert Marcuse, that changing the world can change the human heart, which, theologically speaking, is only a new form of works righteousness.[135] The other momentous mistake, according to Thielicke, consists in the assumption that by changing the center of the world, viz., the human heart, the world will *automatically* change itself, too. But although this conclusion seems to be a natural one, especially in Thielicke's view of man being this fallen world,[136] to him it is wrong all the same. For the message of love may lack credibility if "proclaimed by those who represent a loveless world of exploitation and who do nothing to promote change": "How wrong it can be to begin with a message of love in a loveless world which is left unchanged, and to entertain the illusion that a disordered world will soon be set to rights once the human heart is affected and changed by this message."[137]

But in his exposé of the two extremes, is Thielicke not merely pointing towards the two fundamental postures of a faith without works and works without faith? His own position—that every change has to start

132. For Thielicke's detailed unfolding, see his essay, "Strukturen," esp. 111–12; *EvF III*, 62–65; *EvF II*, 249–58; *Mensch*, 288–91; *Reden*, 151–65, esp. 159–64; *Suche*, 219–24; *Notwendigkeit*, 10–15; and *Krauss*, 61.

133. *EvF II*, 251. See *Wayfarer*, 397–98 [509]; *Notwendigkeit*, 10–11.

134. See *ThE II/1*, §896–98.

135. See *EvF II*, 253. For Thielicke's criticism of Marcuse, see *Kulturkritik*, 40–48; *Mensch*, 53–56; and *Wayfarer*, 399 [510–11].

136. See chapter 6, part two; *EvF I*, 384; and *EvF II*, 257.

137. *EvF II*, 253.

with a person's heart and not with structures—is made abundantly clear numerous times, especially in his essay, "Strukturen" ["Can structures be proselytized?"].[138] Thus, his proposed third option of "draw[ing] alongside the people of this world as brothers,"[139] of letting the motive of *agape*-love direct every concept of world change,[140] is not really a third option at all, but rather the practical consequence of a changed human heart, a change expressing itself in holistic thinking which is followed, in turn, by action; in other words—a faith followed by works.

This observation is confirmed by Thielicke's delineation of the same theme elsewhere, such as in his anthropology and in a specific sermon dedicated to this theme, where he omits the third option altogether.[141] Moreover, it is also expressed in one of those rare moments when he levels criticism against his own Lutheran tradition. Although Luther's Reformation rightly started with the human heart, it subsequently ignored the question as to whether the renewed heart now also consistently pumps blood into the extremities,[142] whether and how personal saving *fiducia*-faith makes itself (ethically) felt in all the different spheres of life. Thielicke understood his own massive project—especially his *Theological Ethics*—to transcend these "limitations of Reformation insight,"[143] which partly explains his wariness with regard to dogmatic subtleties (as outlined in chapter 7, part two).

To be sure, by putting his emphasis as such, Thielicke apparently wants to protect himself from the accusation of propagating a merely subjective version of private religion.[144] Yet, a closer look reveals that his third option is nothing more than his first alternative brought to its natural conclusion:

138. See, for example, his conclusion in "Strukturen," 114: "The microcosm of the heart is the source from which every renewal flows." See also *Bergpredigt*, 154–55, 159; *Reden*, 162–63; *Suche*, 225; Bromiley, "Thielicke," 553; and Ratzinger, *Licht der Welt*, 193.

139. *EvF II*, 253.

140. *EvF II*, 254.

141. See *Mensch*, 291; *Reden*, 163–64.

142. See *Mensch*, 292–95; *Suche*, 223–24; *Notwendigkeit*, 13–15; and Bromiley, "Thielicke," 550. Schlatter articulates similar concerns. See Neuer, *Schlatter: Ein Leben*, 789–92.

143. *Suche*, 223. See *Suche*, 109; *Krauss*, 24–25; and *Wayfarer*, 85 [115]: "The main aim of these [theological] reflections was to interpret the totality of human historical existence . . . in light of its ambivalent position between creation and fall." Obviously, a mistranslation occurred at this point, for how can there be an ambivalent position *between* both; that is, *before* the fall? My own correction: "in its ambivalence between creation and fallen world [*gefallener Welt*]."

144. See, for example, *Bilderbuch*, 68–70. For an analysis of the concept of "private religion," see Hornig, "Die Freiheit der christlichen Privatreligion," 198–211. Hornig traces its origin back to the thought of Johann Salomo Semler.

a converted heart which steadily pumps new blood into every part of the body, a process also known as "sanctification."[145] Thielicke is convinced that changing the world can only come about by a *real* change of heart that does not find atrophy in scanty subjectivism but rather objectifies itself in the structures over which it can exercise some impact.[146]

At any rate, "all acts of God are creative and positive. They want to be turned into a task and bring us closer to him."[147] By Jesus proposing the question "What for?," he provides man with a productive task.[148] In the end, the only legitimate question is not: "Why did God let this happen?" but rather: "What task and impetus does God want to give us with all of this?"[149] Somewhat ironically, though, Thielicke implicitly seems to answer the much-discarded why question nonetheless. In one of his sermons during the sixties, it is telling that he asks his audience: "Why does God leave us alone with all those riddles? Why does he make it so difficult?" He replies: "*So that* he sets us a positive task."[150] Ultimately, even Thielicke cannot help but respond to the "Why?"—although he vehemently tries to do so as unmetaphysically as possible, answering teleologically: "What for?" Man's full grasp of the said teleological dimension, however, is "an eschatological act."[151] Trillhaas's conclusion—namely, that "the problem [of theodicy] shows that faith is hardly able to break away from metaphysical reflections"[152]—is thus intriguingly confirmed by such a self-confessed anti-metaphysical thinker as Thielicke.[153]

---

145. This becomes especially clear in his sermon on the parable of the mustard seed (see *Bilderbuch*, 82, 88).

146. Thus, by taking only *EvF I* and *II* into account in his review, Klann is misled in his judgement that "Thielicke argues against the inference that changes in the human heart will produce corresponding changes in the world" (Klann, "Helmut Thielicke Appraised," 157).

147. *Lebensangst*, 138.

148. See *Lebensangst*, 39.

149. *GldChr*, 378.

150. *Welt*, 261. Emphasis added. He goes on to try to augment this with Kierkegaard's dictum that precisely when no objective certainty is given, the "infinite passion of inwardness awakens."

151. *ThE II/1*, §891.

152. Trillhaas, *Dogmatik*, 172.

153. I use "anti-metaphysical" in the contemporary sense of the term as defined by van Inwagen and Sullivan, "Metaphysics," subsection 2.1. As shown earlier, Thielicke can be classified as such not because he denies the metaphysical subject matter, which he does not, but on the basis of his questioning its legitimacy as well as utility.

Conclusion

LIFE AND THOUGHT CANNOT be separated. Thinking flows from living. Human living, in turn, is navigated via self-conscious thinking. Accordingly, Thielicke was not only enabled to "suffer ethically," but his whole theological work "was always only a superstructure placed upon the experiences and sufferings of [his] life."[1] To explicate the "existential drive at work in [Thielicke's] thought"—or, more precisely, to carve out the particularly eschatologically motivated aspects of his theology planted in the face of death—was the purpose of this book. Let me conclude by summarizing some of my central findings, followed by a final synopsis as to what I believe to be one major strength and weakness of his theology.

In part I, one of the first things we noticed with regard to Thielicke's "eschatological existence" was his antipodean nature, swinging between melancholy and sanguinity, misery and joviality. Predisposed by the "crass difference" in his parents' tempers, he was especially inclined towards exhausting both extremes of the human psyche.

Second, this specific personality type made Thielicke particularly sensitive and prone to experiences of finitude from an early age, either explicitly triggered, as in the event of his grandfather's death, or implicitly, as in the case of the ladder-wagon.

Third, this already strong awareness of mortality was considerably heightened by Thielicke's "sickness-unto-death," lasting from 1929 until 1933. The importance of those four years, culminating in his completely unexpected healing, cannot be overestimated.

Fourth, although Thielicke did not consider himself to be a committed Christian as a young man, his miraculous recovery on Good Friday, 1933, proved to be the turning point in this regard. By all available accounts, it

---

1. *Wayfarer*, 85 [115]. See *Wayfarer*, 84 [113], for the same remark regarding his theological ethics.

CONCLUSION 233

must be concluded that this occasion initiated his conversion to Christ. As shown in parts II and III, that momentous encounter with the crucified God directed his theological thinking into new channels.

Fifth, this first-person experience of immediate death and suffering prepared Thielicke for the depths of the Third Reich. Both the threat from the regime and the burden of the air raids additionally deepened his orientation towards a "theology in the face of death."

Sixth, in the context of the former, the threat from the regime, Thielicke's mind-set and behavior in terms of actively opposing Nazism were examined and reappraised. Whereas the fact that Thielicke opposed the Nazis cannot be denied, the way he struggled for his lectureship undermines Thielicke's perceived role as a resistance fighter. Certain documents furthermore revealed a partly problematic lack of critical distance to Germany's darkest era after 1945.

Seventh, Thielicke's encounters with death and suffering did not cease with the downfall of the Nazi regime in May 1945 but continued beyond the war. These encounters, however, would never regain the unique combination of intensity and longevity that they displayed in the theologically formative years between 1929 and 1945.

In conclusion, I established Thielicke's existence as a decisively "eschatological" one by virtue of his manifold encounters with death and suffering throughout the formative years of his life. The culmination of his "sickness-unto-death" on the night of Maundy Thursday, 1933, in combination with his miraculous recovery from the next morning onwards, initiated his personal and salvific *fiducia*-turn to the *crucified* Christ. The question of *how* his tragic life experiences (prior and subsequent to Thielicke's existential climax) further impacted and recurred in his theological system was pursued in parts II and III.

I began part II by showing in chapter 4 that his strongly contested [in the sense of *Anfechtung*] coming to faith, as well as the basic tenets of his relational thought-form, clearly matched the convictions of his confessional forefather, Martin Luther. This laid the groundwork for a systematic analysis of different theological loci in light of his experiences. By concentrating on particular aspects of soteriology and pneumatology (chapter 5), the way was paved for a closer look at the trinitarian heart of Thielicke's theology in light of his "eschatological existence" (chapters 5–7). In this process, Thielicke's deeply *personal* understanding of the Godhead and his unilaterally *personalistic* answer to the problem of evil were elucidated. At the same time, it became obvious that both convictions must be seen as rooted in his own existential circumstances—namely, a *personal fiducia*-encounter with the *Deus crucifixus*, which was consolidated by his pastoral experiences during the war.

The line of argumentation then naturally segued into part III, where I analyzed Thielicke's role as a preacher (chapter 8) and pastor (chapters 9–10) under the specific perspectives of both suffering and eternity. In chapter 8, I concluded that Thielicke would very likely never have become an esteemed orator had he not been enforced by the Nazis to give up his beloved academic position at the University of Heidelberg. In the final two chapters, I had a close look at the four "cardinal points" in Thielicke's pastoral engagement with suffering and death. In chapter 9, I critically examined his conception of faith as "nevertheless" and highlighted his emphasis on Christ's solidarity, God's omnipotence, and man's prayer. In chapter 10, moreover, I focused on the importance the ultimate eschaton occupies in Thielicke's thinking as well as the potential he ascribes to the hour of affliction. Accordingly, for Thielicke, the central question arising out of our misery is not "why," but "what for": suffering is mankind's "great commission."

By covering the main areas of his theology, I attempted to demonstrate in detail that his early life, saturated with death and affliction, was the—occasionally explicit and, at other times, implicit—driving force in the essential fields of his theological expertise. Without the former, his existential *pathei mathos*, the latter, at least in the pronounced manifestations as presented, would not have come into being.

Whilst I primarily focused on an exegetical presentation of Thielicke's thinking in view of a life constantly lived on the borderline, certain facets were nonetheless also appraised along the way. As contrast is the mother of clarity, this was often done by comparing Thielicke's persuasions with that of other more or less noted thinkers in and outside his field.

All in all, it is without a doubt one of the strong points—if not *the* strength—of Thielicke's theology and proclamation, to have made the Christian message accessible and real for both the specialized as well as the lay people of his day. This powerful aspect is rooted in his own concrete experiences and existential witness, which, in turn, are intrinsically connected with the phenomena of death and suffering. Consequently, such existential grounding provided both his theology and sermons with an "eschatological edge" that captured his hearers' imaginations by setting their own lives in the context of eternity.[2]

On the other hand, an existential interpretation of faith as trust (*fiducia*) can remain one-sided. That, indeed, is one of the dangers suggested strongly in the case of Thielicke. As Ratzinger, for example, has time and

---

2. As aptly phrased by Pless, "Thielicke," 442.

again emphasized, the distinction between the God of philosophy and the God of faith—or the difference between rationality and relationship—should not be exaggerated. But such exaggeration, resulting from Thielicke's twin-foundation of philosophical predisposition and existential intensification, is just what happens in his thinking. By placing a heavy emphasis on the individual's personal, subjective experience,[3] by concentrating on the encounter with Christ on the experiential basis of "trying faith out," Thielicke apparently commits one mistake he himself warns against: he endows the "I" with absolute significance. By making the experiential moment absolute (see chapter 9, part two), he presents it as *the* key to faith.

As previously shown, the strongest answer to why he does so is more likely than not to be found in his *Sitz im Leben*. By means of Thielicke's paradigmatic case, we can see the benefits and dangers of the impact of the existential context upon the theological task, of the subject(ive) upon the object(ive). That both cannot entirely be separated goes without saying, especially with regard to theology (as outlined in chapter 1, part two), where God, as the object of reflection, ideally transforms the subject. By "doing" theology, the theologian ideally becomes the actual subject him- or herself. But in the case of Thielicke, we can come under the impression that his specific experiences turn into the main source of his theological thought.

This is specifically and intriguingly confirmed by Richter-Böhne's critical and accurate verdict on Thielicke's (in)famous "Good Friday Sermon" [*Karfreitagspredigt*], delivered in 1947, in which he publicly attacked the Allies for their program of denazification. Of that particular sermon, Richter-Böhne concludes that "today's dominating experiences of suffering and death *become conditions* for the speech about the cross. Insofar, Thielicke's sermon moves along the lines of *anthroponomous subordination* [*der anthroponomen Subordination*]."[4] This apt expression does not just appear to be applicable in terms of the said sermon. More importantly, it also applies to broader areas of Thielicke's theology as presented throughout this work—most notably, his understanding of the essence of faith, but also his subscription to the twentieth century's "new orthodoxy" of an intrinsically suffering God. Hence, by relating the four main sources of theology (i.e., Scripture, reason, tradition, and experience) to the Thielickean enterprise,

---

3. Rueger arrives at a similar conclusion: "It has been noted repeatedly how spiritual wrestling bespeaks that side of faith that is highly personal and private. For Thielicke, personal faith belongs less to the realm of certain knowing than it does to the realm of wrestling . . . Drawing attention to this inner conflict within the human heart is to focus on the side of faith that involves one's emotions and inner psyche" (Rueger, *Individualism*, 82).

4. Richter-Böhne, *Politische Predigt*, 109. Emphasis added.

we can be led to the conclusion that experience turns into the "powerhouse" implicitly dominating the other three repositories.

It was my aim to make this tacit dominance of a specifically "eschatological existence" explicit by showing the potential where and how of its surfacing. After all, Thielicke leaves no doubt that virtually all of his "theological problems have emerged not as the result of purely intellectual processes, but have grown from situations in [his] life—mainly from conflicts."[5] His existentially laden theology, which is more interested in the function of theological statements in life than in their independent truth-value, is firmly connected to both the Kantian and *thanatos*-imbued roots of his formative years. While such a predominantly experience-based way of thinking certainly has its drawbacks, we are at the same time indebted to Thielicke for also leaving a many-sidedly meritorious theological legacy, not least precisely because of his down-to-earth focus, which is driven, overall, by a desire to honor the Lord Jesus Christ. Thielicke thus deserves to be rediscovered in this day and age.

---

5. *Wayfarer*, 84 [113].

Bibliography

a) Primary Sources: Unpublished Letters and Manuscripts[1]

Thielicke, Helmut Friedrich Wilhelm. "Antiautoritäre Erziehung." In *NHT:Acb:5*.
———. "Ariernachweis." In *NHT:Z:C:6.3*.
———. "Bin ich blöd, wenn ich glaube?" In *NHT:Abd:11*.
———. "Der Glaube kommt vom Lesen." In *NHT:Acb:45*.
———. "Freundesbrief, Korntal bei Stuttgart, Mitte November 1944." In *NHT:Bce2:1 (1)*.
———. "Gespräch mit dem Reichsdozentenführer am 24. Mai 1940." In *NHT:Bce1:1*.
———. "Jesus Christus im vordersten Graben." In *NHT:Aca:11*.
———. "Karfreitag 1941." In *NHT:Ada:18*.
———. "Kurze Antwort auf die Frage, warum ich ein Christ bin." In *NHT:Acb:66*.
———. "Letter to Althaus, Paul. October 3, 1939." In *NHT:Bce1:1*.
———. "Letter to Althaus, Paul. March 13, 1940." In *NHT:Bce1:1*.
———. "Letter to Althaus, Paul. March 7, 1945." In *NHT:Ba:2a*.
———. "Letter to Althaus, Paul. March 27, 1945." In *NHT:Ba:2a*.
———. "Letter to Althaus, Paul. November 27, 1953." In *NHT:Bca4:1*.
———. "Letter to Augstein, Rudolf. October 15, 1968." In *NHT:Ba:4a*.
———. "Letter to Bechtold, [no first name given]. April 7, 1940." In *NHT:Bce1:1*.
———. "Letter to Bechtold, [no first name given]. May 15, 1940." In *NHT:Bce1:1*.
———. "Letter to Dibelius, D. October 1, 1939." In *NHT:Bce1:1*.
———. "Letter to Dibelius, Otto. January 19, 1952." *NHT:Bca 3:1-2*.
———. "Letter to Elert, Werner. October 4, 1939." In *NHT:Bce1:1*.
———. "Letter to Goerdeler, Carl F. June 16, 1944." In *NHT:Ba:27*.
———. "Letter to Handrich, Karl. February 7, 1950." *NHT:Bca2:1-12*.
———. "Letter to Heinemann, Gustav W. February 17, 1968." In *NHT:Bca16:3a*.
———. "Letter to Heinemann, Gustav W. September 14, 1968." In *NHT:Bca18:1*.
———. "Letter to Herrigel, Eugen. April 2, 1940." In *NHT:Bce1:1*.
———. "Letter to Herrigel, Eugen. April 15, 1940." In *NHT:Bce1:1*.
———. "Letter to Herrmann, Mrs. January 16, 1941." In *NHT:Bce1:1*.

1. Archived at the Handschriftenlesesaal der Staats- und Universitätsbibliothek Hamburg Carl von Ossietzky, Von-Melle-Park 3, 20146 Hamburg, Germany.

———. "Letter to Mackensen, Eberhard von (Generaloberst). February 14, 1946." In *NHT:Ba:52*.

———. "Letter to Niemöller, Martin. April 5, 1950." *NHT:Bca2:1-12*.

———. "Letter to Scheel, Gustav Adolf. April 4, 1940." In *NHT:Bce1:1*.

———. "Letter to Schmidt, D. Hans. November 16, 1939." In *NHT:Bce1:1*.

———. "Letter to Schultz, W. (Landesbischof). August 18, 1943." In *NHT:Ba:73a*.

———. "Letter to Weizsäcker, Viktor von. March 16, 1940." In *NHT:Bce1:1*.

———. "Letter to Wulff, [no first name given]. June 12, 1968." In *NHT:Bca16:2*.

———. "Letter to Schultze, Walter. May 27, 1940." In *NHT:Bce1:1*.

———. "Letter to Thurneysen, Eduard. January 25, 1967." In *NHT:Ba:82*.

———. "Offizielle Habilitationsurkunde vom 9. Juli 1935, Erlangen." In *NHT:Z:C:5.1*.

———. "Offizielle Zuweisung für die Dozentur für das Fach Systematische Theologie nach Erlangen am 31. August 1936." In *NHT:Z:C:5.1*.

———. "Predigt am Totensonntag 21.11.1943." In *NHT:Ada:21a*.

———. "Predigt über Joh. 16, 33ff. September 1939." In *NHT:Ada:5*.

———. "Predigt während der Bibelwoche 1941/42. 5. Abend Psalm 73." In *NHT:Ada:10.3 (Ada:10 (2))*.

———. "Prüfungszeugnis für den Kandidaten der Theologie Dr. phil. Helmut Thielicke. Koblenz, den 11. Oktober 1932." In *NHT:Z:C:5.1*.

———. "Traueransprache für Marineleutnant Hans Erich Leschke. July [no day given], 1944." In *NHT:Adc:1*.

———. "Traum vom gnädigen Ende." In *NHT:Acb:98a*.

———. "Über die Religionsphilosophie. November 23, 1929." In *NHT:Aea:14.8*.

———. "Über die Tübinger Theologie." In *NHT:Abe:7*.

———. "Vergeben." In *NHT:Acb:103*.

———. "Vorwort zum Totenbuch der Erlanger Uttenreuther. May 24, 1964." In *NHT:Acc:5*.

———. "Wie man sich das Paradoxe im Christentum erklären und vorstellen kann. November 20, 1928." In *NHT:Aea:14.2*.

———. "Zum Fall Wenke. WamS, March 28, 1965." In *NHT:Acb:129*.

———. "Zwischenruf bei der Rektorfeier. [No month and day given], 1967." In *NHT:Acb:141*.

b) Primary Sources: Published

Thielicke, Helmut Friedrich Wilhelm. *Auf dem Weg zur Kanzel. Sendschreiben an junge Theologen und ihre älteren Freunde*. Stuttgart: Quell, 1983.

———. *Auf der Suche nach dem verlorenen Wort. Gedanken zur Zukunft des Christentums*. Bergisch Gladbach: Gustav Lübbe Verlag, 1988.

———. *Auf Kanzel und Katheder. Aufzeichnungen aus Arbeit und Leben*. Hamburg: Furche, 1965.

———. *Begegnungen und Erfahrungen*. Wuppertal: Brockhaus, 1977.

———. "Can the Church and Atheism Coexist?" Translated by John C. Holden. *Theology Today* 21.1 (1964) 108–11.

———. *Christliche Verantwortung im Atomzeitalter. Ethisch-politischer Traktat über einige Zeitfragen*. Stuttgart: Evangelisches Verlagswerk, 1957.

———. *Das Bilderbuch Gottes. Reden über die Gleichnisse Jesu*. Stuttgart: Quell, 1982.

———. "Das Ende der Religion. Überlegungen zur Theologie Dietrich Bonhoeffers." In *"Religionsloses Christentum" und "Nicht-Religiöse Interpretation" bei Dietrich Bonhoeffer*, edited by Peter H. A. Neumann, 65–100. Darmstadt: Wissenschaftliche Buchgesellschaft, 1990.

———. *Das Gebet das die Welt umspannt. Reden über das Vaterunser aus den Jahren 1944/45*. Stuttgart: Quell, 1991.

———. *Das Lachen der Heiligen und Narren. Nachdenkliches über Witz und Humor*. Stuttgart: Quell, 1988.

———. *Das Leben kann noch einmal beginnen. Ein Gang durch die Bergpredigt*. Stuttgart: Quell, 1990.

———. *Das Schweigen Gottes. Glauben im Ernstfall*. Stuttgart: Quell, 1988.

———. *Das Verhältnis zwischen dem Ethischen und dem Ästhetischen*. Leipzig: Felix Meiner, 1932.

———. *Das Wunder. Eine Untersuchung über den theologischen Begriff des Wunders*. Leipzig: J. C. Hinrichs Verlag, 1939.

———. *Der Christ im Ernstfall. Das kleine Buch der Hoffnung*. Freiburg: Herder, 1981.

———. *Der Einzelne und der Apparat. Von der Freiheit des Menschen im technischen Zeitalter*. Hamburg: Furche, 1964.

———. *Der Glaube der Christenheit. Unsere Welt vor Jesus Christus*. Göttingen: Vandenhoeck & Ruprecht, 1955.

———. *Der Nihilismus. Entstehung—Wesen—Überwindung*. Pfullingen: Verlag Günther Neske, 1951.

———. "Der Sexus ist kein Sündenpfuhl. SPIEGEL-Gespräch mit Professor D. Dr. Helmut Thielicke (Universität Hamburg) über Moral und Kirche." *SPIEGEL* 49 (1966) 68–87.

———. *Deutschland: Demokratie oder Vaterland. Die Rede an die Deutschen und eine Analyse ihrer Wirkung von Ekkehard Othmer*. Tübingen: Rainer Wunderlich Verlag, 1964.

———. *Die Evangelische Kirche und die Politik. Ethisch-politischer Traktat über einige Zeitfragen*. Stuttgart: Evangelisches Verlagswerk, 1953.

———. "Die Frage nach dem Sinn unseres Lebens." http://www.uebersee-club.de/vortrag/vortrag-1955-04-05.pdf.

———. *Die geheime Frage nach Gott. Hintergründe unserer geistigen Situation*. Freiburg: Herder, 1976.

———. *Die Lebensangst und ihre Überwindung*. Gütersloh: Bertelsmann, 1957.

———. *Die Schuld der Anderen. Ein Briefwechsel zwischen Helmut Thielicke und Hermann Diem*. Göttingen: Vandenhoeck & Ruprecht, 1948.

———. "Eine Rede im Dritten Reich vor Heidelberger Studenten zur Eröffnung der Vorlesung am 15. Juni 1939." In *Zeugnis und Dienst. Beiträge zu Theologie und Kirche in Geschichte und Gegenwart*, edited by Gottfried Sprondel. Bremen: Schünemann Universitätsverlag, 1974.

———. *Einführung in die christliche Ethik*. München: Piper, 1963.

———. *The Evangelical Faith I. Prolegomena: The Relation of Theology to Modern Thought-Forms*. Translated and edited by Geoffrey W. Bromiley. Grand Rapids: Eerdmans, 1974.

———. *The Evangelical Faith II. The Doctrine of God and of Christ*. Translated and edited by Geoffrey W. Bromiley. Grand Rapids: Eerdmans, 1977.

———. *The Evangelical Faith III. Theology of the Spirit*. Translated and edited by Geoffrey W. Bromiley. Grand Rapids: Eerdmans, 1982.

———. Foreword to *Man in God's World*, by Helmut Thielicke. London: James Clarke, 1967.

———. *Fragen des Christentums an die moderne Welt. Untersuchungen zur geistigen und religiösen Krise des Abendlandes*. Tübingen: Mohr/Siebeck, 1948.

———. *The Freedom of the Christian Man. A Christian Confrontation with the Secular Gods*. Translated by John W. Doberstein. New York: Harper & Row, 1963.

———. *Geschichte und Existenz. Grundlegung einer evangelischen Geschichtstheologie*. Gütersloh: Gütersloher Verlagshaus, 1964.

———. *Gespräche über Himmel und Erde. Begegnungen in Amerika*. Stuttgart: Quell, 1964.

———. *Glauben als Abenteuer. Unsere Lebensfragen im Lichte biblischer Texte*. Stuttgart: Quell, 1983.

———. *Goethe und das Christentum*. München: Piper, 1982.

———. *Helmut Thielicke im Gespräch mit Meinold Krauss. In Zusammenarbeit mit dem ZDF*. Stuttgart: J. F. Steinkopf Verlag, 1988.

———. *Jesus Christus am Scheidewege*. Berlin: Furche, 1938.

———. *Kirche und Öffentlichkeit. Zur Grundlegung einer lutherischen Kulturethik*. Tübingen: Furche, 1947.

———. "Können sich Strukturen bekehren? Zu einem Grundproblem aktueller Sozialethik." *Zeitschrift für Theologie und Kirche* 66.1 (1969) 98–114.

———. *Kulturkritik der studentischen Rebellion*. Tübingen: Mohr/Siebeck, 1969.

———. *Leben mit dem Tod*. Tübingen: Mohr/Siebeck, 1980.

———. *A Little Exercise for Young Theologians*. Carlisle: Paternoster, 1996.

———. *Man in God's World*. Translated and edited by John W. Doberstein. London: James Clarke, 1967.

———. *Mensch sein—Mensch werden. Entwurf einer christlichen Anthropologie*. München: Piper, 1976.

———. "Michael von Jung. Der Mann und seine Zeit." In *Fröhliche Grablieder zur Laute*, by Michael von Jung, 134–60. Freiburg: Herder, 1977.

———. *Modern Faith and Thought*. Translated by Geoffrey W. Bromiley. Grand Rapids: Eerdmans, 1990.

———. *Notes from a Wayfarer: The Autobiography of Helmut Thielicke*. Translated by David R. Law. Cambridge: James Clarke, 1995.

———. *Notwendigkeit und Begrenzung des politischen Auftrags der Kirche*. Tübingen: Mohr/Siebeck, 1974.

———. *Offenbarung, Vernunft und Existenz. Studien zur Religionsphilosophie Lessings*. Gütersloh: Bertelsmann, 1957.

———. "Reflections on Bultmann's Hermeneutic—I." Translated by John Macquarrie. *The Expository Times* 67.5 (1956) 154–57.

———. "Reflections on Bultmann's Hermeneutic—II." Translated by John Macquarrie. *The Expository Times* 67.6 (1956) 175–77.

———. "Religion in Germany." *Annals of the American Academy of Political and Social Science* 260 (1948) 144–54.

———. *Schuld und Schicksal. Gedanken eines Christen über das Tragische*. Berlin: Furche, 1935.

———. *So sah ich Afrika. Tagebuch einer Schiffsreise*. Stuttgart: Quell, 1986.

———. *Theologie der Anfechtung.* Tübingen: Mohr/Siebeck, 1949.
———. *Theologie und Zeitgenossenschaft. Gesammelte Aufsätze.* Tübingen: Rainer Wunderlich Verlag, 1967.
———. *Theologische Ethik. I. Band: Prinzipienlehre. Dogmatische, philosophische und kontroverstheologische Grundlegung.* Tübingen: Mohr/Siebeck, 1965.
———. *Theologische Ethik. II. Band: Entfaltung. 1. Teil: Mensch und Welt.* Tübingen: Mohr/Siebeck, 1965.
———. *Theologische Ethik. II. Band: Entfaltung. 2. Teil: Ethik des Politischen.* Tübingen: Mohr/Siebeck, 1966.
———. *Theologische Ethik. III. Band: Entfaltung. 3. Teil: Ethik der Gesellschaft, des Rechtes, der Sexualität und der Kunst.* Tübingen: Mohr/Siebeck, 1968.
———. *Theologisches Denken und verunsicherter Glaube. Eine Hinführung zur „modernen" Theologie.* Freiburg: Herder, 1974.
———. *Tod und Leben. Studien zur christlichen Anthropologie.* Genf: Editions Oikumene, n.d.
———. *The Trouble with the Church: A Call for Renewal.* Translated and edited by John W. Doberstein. London: Hodder and Stoughton, 1966.
———. *Über uns leuchtet der Bogen. Ein Bibel-Lesebuch.* Bergisch Gladbach: Gustav Lübbe Verlag, 1999.
———. *Und wenn Gott wäre . . . Reden über die Frage nach Gott.* Stuttgart: Quell, 1983.
———. *Von der Freiheit, ein Mensch zu sein. Orientierungen und Entscheidungshilfen.* Freiburg: Herder, 1981.
———. "Wahrheit und Verstehen." *Zeitschrift für Theologie und Kirche* 62.1 (1965) 114–35.
———. "Warum ich als Christ Weihnachten feiere." *Die Zeit.* 25 December 1958. http://www.zeit.de/1958/52/warum-ich-als-christ-weihnachten-feiere/komplettansicht.
———. *Weltanschauung und Glaube.* Stuttgart: Deutsche Verlags-Anstalt, 1946.
———. *Wer darf leben? Ethische Probleme der modernen Medizin.* München: Goldmann, 1970.
———. *Wer darf sterben? Grenzfragen der modernen Medizin.* Freiburg: Herder, 1979.
———. *Wie die Welt begann: Der Mensch in der Urgeschichte der Bibel.* Stuttgart: Quell, 1960.
———. *Wo ist Gott? Aus einem Briefwechsel.* Göttingen: Vandenhoeck & Ruprecht, 1940.
———. *Woran ich glaube. Der Grund christlicher Gewissheit.* Stuttgart: Quell, 1980.
———. *Zwischen Gott und Satan. Die Versuchung Jesu und die Versuchlichkeit des Menschen.* Wuppertal: Brockhaus, 1978.

c) Secondary Sources: Unpublished Letters and Manuscripts[2]

Althaus, Paul. "Letter to Helmut Thielicke. December 6, 1953." In *NHT:Bca4:1.*
———. "Letter to Helmut Thielicke. January 29, 1955." In *NHT:Bca5:1–7.*
———. "Letter to Helmut Thielicke. March 7, 1945." In *NHT:Ba:2a.*

---

2. Archived at the Handschriftenlesesaal der Staats- und Universitätsbibliothek Hamburg Carl von Ossietzky, Von-Melle-Park 3, 20146 Hamburg, Germany.

———. "Letter to Helmut Thielicke. March 14, 1940." In *NHT:Bce1:1*.
———. "Zeugnis über cand.theol.Dr.phil.Helmut Thielicke. Erlangen, 1. Febr. 1933." In *NHT:Z:C:5.3*.
Barth, Karl. "Letter to Helmut Thielicke. April 1, 1950." In *NHT:Bca2:1-12*.
———. "Letter to Helmut Thielicke. April 22, 1956." In *NHT:Ba:5*.
———. "Letter to Helmut Thielicke. November 7, 1967." In *NHT:Ba:5*.
———. "Letter to Wolfhart Pannenberg. December 7, 1964." In *NHT:Ba:5*.
Brunner, Emil. "Letter to Helmut Thielicke. July 25, 1964." In *NHT : Ba : 9*.
———. "Letter to Helmut Thielicke. September 25, 1947." In *NHT:Ba:6-11*; *NHT:Z:C:5.3*.
Campenhausen, Hans von. "Letter to Helmut Thielicke. January 29, 1968." In *NHT:Bca16:2*.
———. "Letter to Helmut Thielicke. November 8, 1968." In *NHT:Ba:12*.
Carter, Jimmy. "Letter to Helmut Thielicke. May 17, 1982." In *NHT:Ba:12*.
Erhard, Ludwig. "Letter to Helmut Thielicke. April 8, 1964." In *NHT:Ba:23*.
Handrich, Karl. "Letter to Helmut Thielicke. February 3, 1950." In *NHT:Bca2:1-12*.
Haselmayr, Friedrich. "Letter to Helmut Thielicke. March 28, 1940." In *NHT:Bce1:1*.
Heinemann, Gustav W. "Letter to Helmut Thielicke. January 8, 1968." In *NHT:Bca16:3 + 3a*.
———. "Letter to Helmut Thielicke. June 15, 1964." In *NHT:Ba:35*.
Heisenberg, Werner. "Letter to Helmut Thielicke. January 27, 1965." In *NHT:Ba:36*.
Herrigel, Eugen. "Referenz für akademische Laufbahn." In *NHT:Z:C:5.3*.
Hirsch, Emanuel. "Letter to Schultz, W. (Landesbischof). August 9, 1943." In *NHT:Ba:73a*.
Jetter, Hartmut. "Letter to Helmut Thielicke. January 23, 1968." In *NHT:Ba:43*.
Mackensen, Eberhard von. "Letter to Helmut Thielicke. January 29, 1946." In *NHT:Ba:52*.
Martini, Paul. "Gutachten der Medizinischen Klinik in Bonn." In *NHT:Z:C:5.3*.
Niemöller, Martin. "Letter to Helmut Thielicke. October 11, 1935." In *NHT:Ba:61*.
Preuss, Johann Sebastian. "Die latente Tetanie (relative Nebenschilddrüseninsuffizienz): Ihre Erkennung und Behandlung." In *NHT:Z:C:5.8.2*.
Rad, Gerhard von. "Letter to Helmut Thielicke. March 14, 1940." In *NHT:Ba:63*.
Rahner, Karl. "Letter to Helmut Thielicke. July 27, 1964." In *NHT:Bca10:18*.
"Reichsdozentenführer." "Letter to Helmut Thielicke. July 15, 1940." In *NHT:Bce1:1*.
Scheel, Gustav Adolf. "Letter to Helmut Thielicke. April 24, 1940." In *NHT:Bce1:1*.
Scheel, W. (father of Gustav Adolf Scheel). "Letter to Helmut Thielicke. April 1, 1940." In *NHT:Bce1:1*.
———. "Letter to Helmut Thielicke. April 3, 1940." In *NHT:Bce1:1*.
———. "Letter to Helmut Thielicke. April 17, 1940." In *NHT:Bce1:1*.
———. "Letter to Helmut Thielicke. July 25, 1940." In *NHT:Bce1:1*.
Schönfeld, Walther. "Gutachten für Senat Uni Tübingen, den 16. Juli 1945." In *NHT:Z:C:5.3*.
Seiler, [no first name given] ("Kreisleiter"). "Letter to Helmut Thielicke. June 1940." In *NHT:Bce1:1*.
Thielicke, Marieluise. "Freundesbrief Februar 1982." In *NHT:Bce2:1 (1)*.
———. "Freundesbrief Februar 1984." In *NHT:Bce2:1 (1)*.
———. "Freundesbrief Juni 1985." In *NHT:Bce2:1 (1)*.
———. "Freundesbrief März 1981." In *NHT:Bce2:1 (1)*.

Thurneysen, Eduard. "Letter to Helmut Thielicke. April 15, 1969." In *NHT:Ba:82*.
———. "Letter to Helmut Thielicke. August 6, 1968." In *NHT:Ba:82*.
———. "Letter to Helmut Thielicke. February 19, 1967." In *NHT:Ba:82*.
———. "Letter to Helmut Thielicke. January 21, 1967." In *NHT:Ba:82*.
———. "Letter to Helmut Thielicke. January 29, 1969." In *NHT:Ba:82*.
———. "Letter to Helmut Thielicke. September 13, 1969." In *NHT:Ba:82*.
Tügel, Franz. "Letter to Helmut Thielicke. May 24, 1940." In *NHT:Bce1:1*.
Wurm, Theophil. "Letter to Helmut Thielicke. January 10, 1950." *NHT:Bca2:1–12*.

d) Secondary Sources: Published

Adam, Alfred. *Lehrbuch der Dogmengeschichte. Band 2: Mittelalter und Reformationszeit*. Gütersloh: Gerd Mohn, 1981.
Agee, Chris. *Next to Nothing*. Cambridge: Salt, 2009.
———. "On *A Grief Observed*." Paper presented at the C. S. Lewis Festival. Belfast, NI. 22 November 2015.
Althaus, Paul. *The Theology of Martin Luther*. Translated by Robert C. Schultz. Philadelphia: Fortress, 1981.
Anderson, H. George. Foreword to *Notes from a Wayfarer: The Autobiography of Helmut Thielicke*, by Helmut Thielicke, xiii–xxi. Cambridge: James Clarke, 1995.
Aron, Elaine N. *The Highly Sensitive Child*. New York: Broadway, 2002.
Audi, Robert. *Epistemology: A Contemporary Introduction to the Theory of Knowledge*. London: Routledge, 2007.
Augustine. *Confessions*. Translated by R. S. Pine-Coffin. London: Penguin, 2002.
Baggett, David, and Jerry L. Walls. *Good God: The Theistic Foundations of Morality*. Oxford: Oxford University Press, 2011.
Baillie, John. *Our Knowledge of God*. London: Oxford University Press, 1949.
Barth, Karl. *Der Römerbrief*. München: Kaiser, 1924.
———. *Die Kirchliche Dogmatik. Band I.1: Die Lehre vom Worte Gottes*. Zürich: Theologischer Verlag, 1980.
———. *Die Kirchliche Dogmatik. Band I.2: Die Lehre vom Worte Gottes*. Zürich: Theologischer Verlag, 1980.
———. *Die Kirchliche Dogmatik. Band II.1: Die Lehre von Gott*. Zürich: Theologischer Verlag, 1980.
———. *Die Kirchliche Dogmatik. Band II.2: Die Lehre von Gott*. Zürich: Theologischer Verlag, 1980.
———. *Die Kirchliche Dogmatik. Band III.1: Die Lehre von der Schöpfung*. Zürich: Theologischer Verlag, 1980.
———. *Die Kirchliche Dogmatik. Band III.2: Die Lehre von der Schöpfung*. Zürich: Theologischer Verlag, 1980.
———. *Die Kirchliche Dogmatik. Band III.3: Die Lehre von der Schöpfung*. Zürich: Theologischer Verlag, 1980.
———. *Die Kirchliche Dogmatik. Band III.4: Die Lehre von der Schöpfung*. Zürich: Theologischer Verlag, 1980.
———. *Evangelical Theology: An Introduction*. Translated by Grover Foley. London: Weidenfeld and Nicolson, 1968.

Bauckham, Richard J. "Universalism: A Historical Survey." *Evangelical Review of Theology* 15.1 (1991) 22–35.

Bayer, Oswald. *Martin Luther's Theology: A Contemporary Interpretation*. Translated by Thomas H. Trapp. Grand Rapids: Eerdmans, 2008.

———. *Theology the Lutheran Way*. Translated and edited by Jeffrey G. Silcock and Mark C. Mattes. Grand Rapids: Eerdmans, 2007.

Becker, Ernest. *The Denial of Death*. New York: Free Press, 1973.

Beckwith, Francis J. *Politically Correct Death*. Grand Rapids: Baker, 1993.

Bentum, Ad van. *Helmut Thielickes Theologie der Grenzsituationen*. Paderborn: Bonifacius, 1965.

Bernstein, Leonard. *The Unanswered Question: Six Talks at Harvard*. Cambridge: Harvard University Press, 1976.

Besier, Gerhard, and Gerhard Sauter. *Wie Christen ihre Schuld bekennen: Die Stuttgarter Erklärung 1945*. Göttingen: Vandenhoeck & Ruprecht, 1985.

Bloesch, Donald G. *Essentials of Evangelical Theology*. 2 vols. Peabody, MA: Hendrickson, 2006.

———. "Thielicke's Ethics: A Review Article." *Lutheran Quarterly* 20.3 (1968) 309–13.

Boa, Kenneth, and Robert M. Bowman Jr. *Faith Has Its Reasons: An Integrative Approach to Defending Christianity*. Milton Keynes: Paternoster, 2006.

Bockmühl, Klaus, ed. *Die Aktualität der Theologie Adolf Schlatters*. Gießen: Brunnen, 1988.

Bonhoeffer, Dietrich. *Ethics*. Dietrich Bonhoeffer Works 6. Translated by Reinhard Krauss, et al. Minneapolis: Fortress, 2009.

———. *Nachfolge*. Gütersloh: Gütersloher Verlagshaus, 2013.

———. *Widerstand und Ergebung*. München: Kaiser, 1990.

Brandenburg, Albert. "Thielickes Neue Dogmatik." *Catholica* 4.67 (1968) 304–13.

Brocher, Tobias. *Wenn Kinder trauern: Wie sprechen wir über den Tod?* Zürich: Kreuz Verlag, 1980.

Bromiley, Geoffrey W. "Church Members First, Citizens Second." *Christianity Today* 30.8 (1986) 26–29.

———. "Helmut Thielicke." In *A Handbook of Christian Theologians*, edited by Martin E. Marty and Dean G. Peerman, 543–60. Cambridge: Lutterworth, 1984.

Broszat, Martin. "Resistenz und Widerstand." In *Bayern in der NS-Zeit: Herrschaft und Gesellschaft im Konflikt. Teil C*, edited by Martin Broszat, et al., 697–99. München: Oldenbourg, 1981.

Brown, Dale. *Understanding Pietism*. Nappanee, IN: Evangel, 1996.

Brunner, Emil. *Die Christliche Lehre von Schöpfung und Erlösung: Dogmatik Band II*. Zürich: Theologischer Verlag, 1972.

———. *The Divine-Human Encounter*. Translated by Amandus W. Loos. London: SCM, 1944.

———. *Dogmatics*. Vol. 1. Translated by Olive Wyon. London: Lutterworth, 1949.

———. *Dogmatics*. Vol. 2. Translated by Olive Wyon. London: Lutterworth, 1952.

———. *The Letter to the Romans: A Commentary*. Translated by H. A. Kennedy. London: Lutterworth, 1959.

———. *Man in Revolt. A Christian Anthropology*. Translated by Olive Wyon. London: Lutterworth, 1937.

Busch, Wilhelm. *Plaudereien in meinem Studierzimmer*. Gladbeck: Schriftenmissions-Verlag, 1976.

Butler, Joseph. *The Analogy of Religion*. London: George Bell and Sons, 1886.
Byrne, James M. *Religion and the Enlightenment*. Louisville: Westminster John Knox, 1997.
Calvert, Michael. "Preaching and the problem of evil: a case study in the published sermons of Helmut Thielicke." PhD diss., North-West University, 2014. http://dspace.nwu.ac.za/handle/10394/17579.
Cardwell, Walter D. "Preaching from Bultmann and Thielicke." *Encounter* 24.2 (1963) 234–36.
Carnell, Edward J. *An Introduction to Christian Apologetics*. Grand Rapids: Eerdmans, 1966.
Cary, Phillip. "A Classic View." In *God and the Problem of Evil*, edited by Chad Meister and James K. Dew Jr., 13–36. Downers Grove, IL: InterVarsity, 2017.
Chesterton, G. K. *Orthodoxy*. Rockville, MD: Serenity, 2009.
Clark, David K. *To Know and Love God: Method for Theology*. Wheaton, IL: Crossway, 2003.
Clark, J. C. D. "Thomas Paine: The English Dimension." In *Selected Writings of Thomas Paine*, edited by Ian Shapiro and Jane E. Calvert, 579–601. New Haven: Yale University Press, 2014.
Clements, Keith W., ed. *Friedrich Schleiermacher: Pioneer of Modern Theology*. London: Collins, 1987.
Cockshut, A. O. J. *The Unbelievers. English Agnostic Thought 1840–1890*. London: Collins, 1964.
Collins, Francis S. *The Language of God: A Scientist Presents Evidence for Belief*. London: Simon & Schuster, 2007.
Coren, Michael. *C. S. Lewis—der Mann, der Narnia schuf*. Translated by Barbara Trebing. Moers: Brendow, 2005.
Cornelius, Nadja. *Genese und Wandel von Festbräuchen und Ritualen in Deutschland von 1933 bis 1945*. Köln: Institut für Völkerkunde, 2003.
Cox, James W. "'Eloquent . . . Mighty in the Scriptures': Biblical Preachers from Chrysostom to Thielicke." *Review and Expositor* 72.2 (1975) 189–201.
Craig, William Lane. "The Absurdity of Life Without God." Reasonable Faith. http://www.reasonablefaith.org/the-absurdity-of-life-without-god.
———. "Concept of God in Islam and Christianity." Reasonable Faith. http://www.reasonablefaith.org/concept-of-god-in-islam-and-christianity.
———. "Defenders—Doctrine of God: Excursus on Natural Theology, part 3: The Role of Arguments and Evidence." Reasonable Faith. http://www.reasonablefaith.org/defenders-3-podcast/s4.
———. "Defenders—Doctrine of God: Excursus on Natural Theology, part 11: Scientific Confirmation of the Beginning of the Universe." Reasonable Faith. http://www.reasonablefaith.org/defenders-3-podcast/s4.
———. "Defenders—Doctrine of Man, part 15: Original Sin." YouTube. https://www.youtube.com/watch?v=MCUJ77wAXHw.
———. "How Can Christ Be the Only Way to God?" Reasonable Faith. http://www.reasonablefaith.org/how-can-christ-be-the-only-way-to-god.
———. "Leaping Lessing's Ugly, Broad Ditch." Reasonable Faith. http://www.reasonablefaith.org/leaping-lessings-ugly-broad-ditch.
———. "The Mind-Boggling Trinity." Reasonable Faith. http://www.reasonablefaith.org/the-mind-boggling-trinity.

———. *The Only Wise God*. Eugene, OR: Wipf & Stock, 2000.

———. *Reasonable Faith: Christian Truth and Apologetics*. Wheaton, IL: Crossway, 2008.

Craig, William Lane, and Kai Nielsen. "Does God Exist?" Reasonable Faith. http://www.reasonablefaith.org/does-god-exist-the-craig-nielsen-debate.

Cullmann, Oscar. *Christus und die Zeit*. Zürich: Evangelischer Verlag, 1946.

Dawood, N. J., trans. *The Koran*. London: Penguin, 2003.

Descartes, René. *Meditationen über die erste Philosophie*. Stuttgart: Reclam, 1971.

Dirks, Marvin. *Laymen Look at Preaching: Lay Expectation Factors in Relation to the Preaching of Helmut Thielicke*. North Quincy, MA: Christopher, 1972.

Dyrness, William A. "The Pietistic Heritage of Schleiermacher." *Christianity Today* 23.6 (1978) 15–17.

———. *Themes in Old Testament Theology*. Carlisle: Paternoster, 1998.

Ebeling, Gerhard. "Des Todes Tod: Luthers Theologie der Konfrontation mit dem Tode." In *Zum Gedenken an Helmut Thielicke*, edited by Jörg Lippert, 31–46. Hamburg: Pressestelle der Universität Hamburg, 1987.

———. *Luther: An Introduction to his Thought*. Translated by R. A. Wilson. London: Collins, 1970.

Edgar, William. "Adam, History, and Theodicy." In *Adam, the Fall, and Original Sin: Theological, Biblical, and Scientific Perspectives*, edited by Hans Madueme and Michael Reeves, 307–21. Grand Rapids: Baker Academic, 2014.

Emery, Gilles. *The Trinity: An Introduction to Catholic Doctrine on the Triune God*. Translated by Matthew Levering. Washington DC: Catholic University of America Press, 2011.

Ericksen, Robert P. *Theologians under Hitler*. New Haven: Yale University Press, 1985.

Fichte, Johann Gottlieb. "Über den Grund unseres Glaubens an eine göttliche Weltregierung." In *Atheismus: Profile und Positionen der Neuzeit. Dargestellt an Hand ausgewählter Texte*, edited by Albert Esser, 57–69. Köln: Hegner, 1971.

Flint, Thomas P. *Divine Providence: The Molinist Account*. Ithaca, NY: Cornell University Press, 1998.

Forberg, Friedrich Karl. "Entwicklung des Begriffs der Religion." In *Atheismus: Profile und Positionen der Neuzeit. Dargestellt an Hand ausgewählter Texte*, edited by Albert Esser, 70–84. Köln: Hegner, 1971.

Forde, Gerhard O. *On Being a Theologian of the Cross: Reflections on Luther's Heidelberg Disputation, 1518*. Grand Rapids: Eerdmans, 1997.

———. *Theology is for Proclamation*. Minneapolis: Fortress, 1990.

Frankl, Viktor E. *Man's Search for Meaning: An Introduction to Logotherapy*. Translated by Ilse Lasch. New York: Touchstone, 1984.

Frazier, Claude A. *Theologians and their Faith*. No bibliographical information available.

Frenzel, Ivo. *Nietzsche*. Reinbek/Hamburg: Rowohlt, 1996.

Friedländer, Saul. *Kurt Gerstein oder die Zwiespältigkeit des Guten*. München: C. H. Beck, 2007.

Gallagher, Michael P. *Faith Maps: Ten Religious Explorers from Newman to Joseph Ratzinger*. Mahwah, NJ: Paulist, 2010.

Geier, Manfred. *Kants Welt: Eine Biographie*. Reinbek/Hamburg: Rowohlt, 2005.

Girgis, Sherif, et al. *What is Marriage? Man and Woman: A Defense*. New York: Encounter, 2012.

Gloege, Gerhard. "Der theologische Personalismus als dogmatisches Problem." *Kerygma und Dogma* 1.1 (1955) 23–41.

———. "Zur Prädestinationslehre Karl Barths: Fragmentarische Erwägungen über den Ansatz ihrer Neufassung." *Kerygma und Dogma* 2.3 (1956) 193–217.

———. "Zur Prädestinationslehre Karl Barths: Fortsetzung und Schluß." *Kerygma und Dogma* 2.4 (1956) 233–55.

Goffar, Janine, ed. *C. S. Lewis Index: Rumours from the Sculptor's Shop*. Carlisle: Solway, 1997.

Gollwitzer, Helmut. *Krummes Holz—aufrechter Gang: Zur Frage nach dem Sinn des Lebens*. München: Kaiser, 1971.

———. *Von der Stellvertretung Gottes: Christlicher Glaube in der Erfahrung der Verborgenheit Gottes*. München: Kaiser, 1967.

Gollwitzer, Helmut, et al., eds. *Du hast mich heimgesucht bei Nacht: Abschiedsbriefe und Aufzeichnungen des Widerstandes 1933-1945*. München: Kaiser, 1960.

Graham, Billy. *Just As I Am: The Autobiography of Billy Graham*. New York: HarperCollins, 1997.

Grenz, Stanley J., and Roger E. Olson. *Twentieth-Century Theology: God and the World in a Transitional Age*. Carlisle: Paternoster, 1992.

Greschat, Martin, ed. *Die Schuld der Kirche: Dokumente und Reflexionen zur Stuttgarter Schulderklärung vom 18/19 Oktober 1945*. München: Kaiser, 1982.

———, ed. *Personenlexikon Religion und Theologie*. Göttingen: Vandenhoeck & Ruprecht, 1998.

Gross, Raphael. *Anständig Geblieben: Nationalsozialistische Moral*. Frankfurt/Main: Fischer, 2010.

Grudem, Wayne. *Systematic Theology: An Introduction to Biblical Doctrine*. Leicester: InterVarsity, 1994.

Haas, Rudolf, and Martin Haug. *Helmut Thielicke—Prediger in unserer Zeit*. Stuttgart: Quell, 1968.

Hamann, Brigitte. *Hitlers Wien: Lehrjahre eines Diktators*. München: Piper, 2010.

Hamilton, Kenneth. *Revolt Against Heaven*. Exeter: Paternoster, 1965.

Hedinger, Ulrich. "Kritische Bemerkungen zur Protologie." *Theologische Zeitschrift* 31.2 (1975) 84–94.

Hengel, Martin. *Crucifixion: In the Ancient World and the Folly of the Message of the Cross*. Philadelphia: Fortress, 1977.

Henry, Carl F. H. "Thielicke Speaks to the Fundamentalists." *Christianity Today* 9.12 (1965) 33–35.

Heron, Alasdair I. C. *A Century of Protestant Theology*. Cambridge: Lutterworth, 1980.

Herz, Gerhard. "Bach's Religion." *Journal of Renaissance and Baroque Music* 1.2 (1946) 124–38.

Hick, John. *Evil and the God of Love*. Basingstoke: Palgrave Macmillan, 2010.

———. "Theology and Ethics." *The Expository Times* 80.1 (1968) 23.

Higginson, Richard. "Thielicke: Preacher and Theologian." *The Churchman* 90.3 (1976) 178–92.

Hildebrand, Dietrich von. *Über den Tod*. St. Ottilien: EOS Verlag, 1980.

Hollon, Ellis W. "The Heart of Christian Ethics." *Christianity Today* 11.10 (1967) 36–37.

Holthaus, Stephan. *Konfessionskunde*. Hammerbrücke: Jota-Publikationen, 2008.

Horn, Christoph. "Augustinus." In *Klassiker der Religionsphilosophie. Von Platon bis Kierkegaard*, edited by Friedrich Niewöhner, 69–83. München: C. H. Beck, 1995.

Hornig, Gottfried. "Die Freiheit der christlichen Privatreligion." *Neue Zeitschrift für systematische Theologie und Religionsphilosophie* 21.2 (1979) 198–211.
Hütter, Reinhard. *Suffering Divine Things: Theology as Church Practice*. Translated by Doug Stott. Grand Rapids: Eerdmans, 2000.
Jewett, Paul. *Emil Brunner's Concept of Revelation*. London: James Clarke, 1954.
Johnson, Thomas K. "The Moral Crisis of the West: Reflections from Helmut Thielicke and Francis Schaeffer." *Presbyterion* 17.2 (1991) 119–24.
Kantzenbach, Friedrich Wilhelm. *Programme der Theologie: Denker, Schulen, Wirkungen. Von Schleiermacher bis Moltmann*. München: Claudius Verlag, 1984.
Kavanaugh, Patrick. *Spiritual Lives of the Great Composers*. Grand Rapids: Zondervan, 1996.
Keathley, Kenneth. *Salvation and Sovereignty: A Molinist Approach*. Nashville: Broadman & Holman, 2010.
Kierkegaard, Søren. *Fear and Trembling*. Translated by Alastair Hannay. London: Penguin, 2005.
Kitwood, T. M. *What is Human?* London: InterVarsity, 1970.
Klann, Richard. "Helmut Thielicke Appraised." *Concordia Journal* 6.4 (1980) 155–63.
Klee, Ernst. *Das Personenlexikon zum Dritten Reich: Wer war was vor und nach 1945*. Frankfurt/Main: Fischer, 2005.
———. *Persilscheine und falsche Pässe: Wie die Kirchen den Nazis halfen*. Frankfurt/Main: Fischer, 1992.
Kraft, Charles H. *Defeating Dark Angels: Breaking Demonic Oppression in the Believer's Life*. Kent: Sovereign World, 1993.
Kraus, Hans-Joachim. "Julius Schniewind." In *Tendenzen der Theologie im 20. Jahrhundert*, edited by Hans Jürgen Schultz, 219–24. Stuttgart: Kreuz-Verlag, 1967.
Kreeft, Peter. *The Journey: A Spiritual Roadmap for Modern Pilgrims*. Downers Grove: InterVarsity, 1996.
———. "Pro-Life Logic." YouTube. 14 March 2013. https://www.youtube.com/watch?v=zfotAcvsMbg.
Ladd, George E. *The Last Things*. Grand Rapids: Eerdmans, 1982.
Langsam, Friedrich. *Helmut Thielicke. Konkretion in Predigt und Theologie*. Stuttgart: Calwer, 1996.
Lenz, Johann Maria. *Christus in Dachau*. St. Gabriel/Mödling: Missionsdruckerei, 1960.
Lewis, C. S. *The Four Loves*. New York: Harcourt, 1960.
———. *God in the Dock: Essays on Theology and Ethics*. Edited by Walter Hooper. Grand Rapids: Eerdmans, 1974.
———. *The Great Divorce*. Glasgow: Collins Fontana, 1974.
———. *A Grief Observed*. New York: Bantam, 1976.
———. *The Last Battle*. London: HarperCollins, 2010.
———. *Letters to Malcolm*. New York: Harcourt, 1964.
———. *The Magician's Nephew*. London: HarperCollins, 2010.
———. *Mere Christianity*. New York: Macmillan, 1958.
———. *Out of the Silent Planet*. London: HarperCollins, 2005.
———. *The Pilgrim's Regress*. Glasgow: Collins, 1984.
———. *The Problem of Pain*. London: HarperCollins, 2002.
———. *The Screwtape Letters*. London: HarperCollins, 2002.
———. *Till We Have Faces*. Grand Rapids: Eerdmans, 1964.

Lewis, Warren H. "Memoir by Warren Lewis." In *Letters of C. S. Lewis: Revised and Enlarged Edition*, edited by Walter Hooper, 21–46. Orlando: Harvest, 1993.
Lindner, Wulf-Volker. "Eröffnung durch den Sprecher des Fachbereichs Evangelische Theologie." In *Zum Gedenken an Helmut Thielicke*, edited by Jörg Lippert, 9–13. Hamburg: Pressestelle der Universität Hamburg, 1987.
Lippert, Jörg, ed. *Zum Gedenken an Helmut Thielicke*. Hamburg: Pressestelle der Universität Hamburg, 1987.
Lohse, Bernhard. "Martin Kähler." In *Tendenzen der Theologie im 20. Jahrhundert*, edited by Hans Jürgen Schultz, 19–23. Stuttgart: Kreuz-Verlag, 1967.
Lohse, Bernhard, and Hans P. Schmidt, ed. *Leben angesichts des Todes: Beiträge zum theologischen Problem des Todes. Helmut Thielicke zum 60. Geburtstag*. Tübingen: Mohr/Siebeck, 1968.
Lorenzmeier, Theodor. "Herbert Braun." In *Tendenzen der Theologie im 20. Jahrhundert*, edited by Hans Jürgen Schultz, 500–4. Stuttgart: Kreuz-Verlag, 1967.
Lundin, Roger. *The Culture of Interpretation: Christian Faith and the Postmodern World*. Grand Rapids: Eerdmans, 1993.
———. "Helmut Thielicke Is Dead at 77." *Christianity Today* 30.7 (1986) 42.
Lütgert, Wilhelm. *Die theologische Krisis der Gegenwart und ihr geistesgeschichtlicher Ursprung*. Gütersloh: Bertelsmann, 1936.
Lütz, Manfred. *Gott. Eine kleine Geschichte des Größten*. München: Pattloch, 2007.
Lutzer, Erwin W. *Hitler's Cross*. Chicago: Moody Publishers, 1995.
Macaulay, Ranald, and Jerram Barrs. *Being Human: The Nature of Spiritual Experience*. Downers Grove: InterVarsity, 1978.
MacDonald, Gordon. "Speaking into Crisis: Pastors Bonhoeffer and Thielicke Show Us How to Address Terrible Times." *Leadership* 4 (2002) 62–66.
MacGregor, Kirk R. *Luis de Molina*. Grand Rapids: Zondervan, 2015.
Mackie, J. L. *The Miracle of Theism*. Oxford: Clarendon, 1982.
Macquarrie, John. "The Evangelical Faith, Volume I: Prolegomena." *Journal of Theological Studies* 30.2 (1979) 594–96.
———. *Martin Heidegger*. London: Lutterworth, 1968.
Madueme, Hans, and Michael Reeves, ed. *Adam, the Fall, and Original Sin: Theological, Biblical, and Scientific Perspectives*. Grand Rapids: Baker Academic, 2014.
Maier, Hans. *Welt ohne Christentum—was wäre anders?* Freiburg: Herder, 2009.
Marquardt, Friedrich-Wilhelm. "Helmut Gollwitzer." In *Tendenzen der Theologie im 20. Jahrhundert*, edited by Hans Jürgen Schultz, 556–64. Stuttgart: Kreuz-Verlag, 1967.
"Martin Heidegger—Ein Porträt." 1 July 2012. YouTube. https://www.youtube.com/watch?v=WxjjgGcx608.
McGrath, Alister E. *Christian Theology: An Introduction*. Malden: Wiley-Blackwell, 2011. Kindle edition.
———. "C. S. Lewis: Reluctant Prophet." Lecture delivered at St. Paul's Cathedral. London, UK. 7 April 2013. https://www.youtube.com/watch?v=9jPPfHVncYg.
———. *Der Weg der christlichen Theologie*. Translated by Christian Wiese. Gießen: Brunnen, 2007.
———. *From the Beginnings to 1500*. Vol. 1 of *Iustitia Dei: A History of the Christian Doctrine of Justification*. Cambridge: Cambridge University Press, 1986.
———. *Johann Calvin: Eine Biographie*. Translated by Gabriele Burkhardt. Zürich: Benziger, 1991.

———. *Luther's Theology of the Cross: Martin Luther's Theological Breakthrough.* Oxford: Blackwell, 2000.

Metaxas, Eric. *Seven Women and the Secret of Their Greatness.* Nashville, TN: Nelson Books, 2015.

Moltke, Helmuth James von, and Freya von Moltke. *Abschiedsbriefe Gefängnis Tegel: September 1944–Januar 1945.* München: C. H. Beck, 2011.

McKenna, Michael, and D. Justin Coates. "Compatibilism." Stanford Encyclopedia of Philosophy. 25 February 2015. https://plato.stanford.edu/entries/compatibilism.

Moltmann, Jürgen. *The Crucified God.* Translated by R. A. Wilson and John Bowden. London: SCM, 1974.

———. *Experiences of God.* Translated by Margaret Kohl. Philadelphia: Fortress, 1981.

———. "Look Forward! An Interview with Simon Jenkins." Third Way. June 2012. http://www.thirdwaymagazine.co.uk/editions/jun-2012/high-profile/look-forward!.aspx.

Montgomery, John Warwick. "Thielicke On Trial." *Christianity Today* 22.12 (1978) 57.

Moreland, J. P. *Kingdom Triangle.* Grand Rapids: Zondervan, 2007.

———. *Love Your God with All Your Mind: The Role of Reason in the Life of the Soul.* Colorado Springs: NavPress, 1997.

———. *Scaling the Secular City: A Defense of Christianity.* Grand Rapids: Baker, 1987.

———. "Truth, Contemporary Philosophy, and the Postmodern Turn." *JETS* 48.1 (2005) 77–88.

Moreland J. P., and Klaus Issler. *The Lost Virtue of Happiness.* Colorado Springs: NavPress, 2006.

Moreland J. P., and William Lane Craig. *Philosophical Foundations for a Christian Worldview.* Downers Grove: InterVarsity, 2017.

Moule, C. F. D. "Punishment and Retribution: An Attempt to Delimit Their Scope in New Testament Thought." *SEA* 30 (1965) 21–36.

Mumma, Howard. *Albert Camus and the Minister.* Brewster, MA: Paraclete, 2000.

Neuer, Werner. *Adolf Schlatter: A Biography of Germany's Premier Biblical Theologian.* Translated by Robert W. Yarbrough. Grand Rapids: Baker, 1995.

———. *Adolf Schlatter: Ein Leben für Theologie und Kirche.* Stuttgart: Calwer, 1996.

Newman, John Henry. *Apologia Pro Vita Sua.* London: Longmans/Green,1900.

Ngien, Dennis. "The God Who Suffers. If God does not grieve, then can he love at all? An argument for God's emotions." Christianity Today. 3 February 1997. http://www.christianitytoday.com/ct/1997/february3/7t2038.html?start=1.

Nigg, Walter. *Das ewige Reich: Geschichte einer Hoffnung.* Zürich: Diogenes, 1996.

Nitsche, Bernhard. "Der Heilige Geist als trinitarische Person?" In *Dogmatik heute*, edited by Thomas Marschler and Thomas Schärtl, 333–39. Regensburg: Pustet, 2014.

Nordlander, Agne. *Die Gottebenbildlichkeit in der Theologie Helmut Thielickes.* Stockholm: Almqvist & Wiksell, 1973.

Olson, Roger E. *God in Dispute: "Conversations" among Great Christian Thinkers.* Grand Rapids: Baker Academic, 2009.

Otto, Rudolf. Introduction to *On Religion: Speeches to Its Cultured Despisers*, by Friedrich Schleiermacher, viii–xxvii. New York: Harper and Row, 1958.

Packer, J. I. *Evangelism & the Sovereignty of God.* Downers Grove: InterVarsity, 1991.

Pannenberg, Wolfhart. *Anthropology in Theological Perspective.* Translated by Matthew O'Connell. Philadelphia: Westminster, 1985.

———. *Basic Questions in Theology.* Vol. 1. Translated by George H. Kehm. London: SCM, 1970.

---——. *Basic Questions in Theology.* Vol. 2. Translated by George H. Kehm. London: SCM, 1971.
———. *Christentum in einer säkularisierten Welt.* Freiburg: Herder, 1988.
———. "God's Presence in History." *Christian Century* 98.8 (1981) 260–63.
———. "How to Think About Secularism." First Things. October 2007. http://www.firstthings.com/article/2007/10/002-how-to-think-about-secularism-39.
———. "Person." In *Religion in Geschichte und Gegenwart*, Vol. 5, 230–35. Tübingen: Mohr/Siebeck, 1961.
———. *Systematic Theology.* Vol. 2. Translated by Geoffrey W. Bromiley. Edinburgh: T&T Clark, 1994.
———. *Systematic Theology.* Vol. 3. Translated by Geoffrey W. Bromiley. Edinburgh: T&T Clark, 1998.
———. *Systematische Theologie. Band I.* Göttingen: Vandenhoeck & Ruprecht, 1988.
———. *Systematische Theologie. Band II.* Göttingen: Vandenhoeck & Ruprecht, 1991.
———. *Theologie und Reich Gottes.* Gütersloh: Gerd Mohn, 1971.
Payne, J. Barton. *The Theology of the Older Testament.* Grand Rapids: Zondervan, 1978.
Pearcey, Nancy. *Total Truth: Liberating Christianity from Its Cultural Captivity.* Wheaton, IL: Crossway, 2008.
Plantinga, Alvin. *God, Freedom, and Evil.* London: Allen & Unwin, 1975.
———. *The Nature of Necessity.* Oxford: Clarendon, 1974.
———. *Warranted Christian Belief.* Oxford: Oxford University Press, 2000.
Pless, John T. "Helmut Thielicke (1908-1986)." *Lutheran Quarterly* 23.4 (2009) 439–64.
Polanyi, Michael. *Personal Knowledge.* Chicago: University of Chicago Press, 1958.
Presbyterian Report. "Presbyterian Report of the Creation Study Committee." June 2000. http://pcahistory.org/creation/report.pdf.
Preuss, Johann Sebastian. *Die latente Tetanie (relative Nebenschilddrüseninsuffizienz): Ihre Erkennung und Behandlung.* Zirndorf: Bollmann-Verlag, 1937.
Professors of Germany. "To the Civilized World." *The North American Review* 210.765 (1919) 284–87.
Putz, Erna. *Franz Jägerstätter.* Grünbach: Edition Geschichte der Heimat, 1997.
Quest, Hans-Jürgen. "Helmut Thielicke." In *Tendenzen der Theologie im 20. Jahrhundert*, edited by Hans Jürgen Schultz, 549–55. Stuttgart: Kreuz-Verlag, 1967.
Rahner, Karl. "Erbsünde und Monogenismus." In *Theologie der Erbsünde*, by Karl-Heinz Weger. Freiburg: Herder, 1970.
———. *Erinnerungen.* Freiburg: Herder, 1984.
Raimbault, Ginette. *Kinder sprechen vom Tod. Klinische Probleme der Trauer.* Translated by Rainer Harnisch. Frankfurt/Main: Suhrkamp, 1980.
Ratzinger, Joseph. "Einführende Worte zum 3. Tag des Newman-Symposiums." In John Henry Newman. *Apologia Pro Vita Sua.* Translated by Maria Knoepfler. Illertissen: Media Maria, 2010.
———. *Einführung in das Christentum.* München: Kösel, 2000.
———. *Eschatologie—Tod und ewiges Leben.* Regensburg: Pustet, 2017.
———. *Introduction to Christianity.* Translated by J. R. Foster. San Francisco, CA: Ignatius, 1990.
———. "Glaube, Vernunft und Universität. Erinnerungen und Reflexionen." Speech at Regensburg University. Regensburg, Germany. 12 September 2006. http://www.vatican.va/holy_father/benedict_xvi/speeches/2006/september/documents/hf_ben-xvi_spe_20060912_university-regensburg_ge.html.

———. *Jesus von Nazareth. Band I*. Freiburg: Herder, 2007.
———. *Jesus von Nazareth. Band II*. Freiburg: Herder, 2011.
———. *Jesus von Nazareth. Prolog: Die Kindheitsgeschichten*. Freiburg: Herder, 2014.
———. *Licht der Welt. Der Papst, die Kirche und die Zeichen der Zeit. Ein Gespräch mit Peter Seewald*. Freiburg: Herder, 2012.
Rees, Laurence. *Auschwitz: Geschichte eines Verbrechens*. Translated by Petra Post et al. Augsburg: Weltbild, 2008.
Rhodes, Ron. "Tough Questions about Evil." In *Who Made God?*, edited by Ravi Zacharias and Norman Geisler, 33-48. Grand Rapids: Zondervan, 2003.
Richter-Böhne, Andreas. *Unbekannte Schuld: Politische Predigt unter alliierter Besatzung*. Stuttgart: Calwer, 1989.
Rieger, Reinhold. *Martin Luthers theologische Grundbegriffe*. Tübingen: Mohr/Siebeck, 2017.
Riesner, Rainer. *Jesus als Lehrer*. Tübingen: Mohr/Siebeck, 1981.
Rissmann, Michael. *Hitlers Gott. Vorsehungsglaube und Sendungsbewusstsein des deutschen Diktators*. Zürich: Pendo, 2001.
Rohde, Peter P. *Kierkegaard*. Reinbek/Hamburg: Rowohlt, 1959.
Röhricht, Rainer. "Der Name 'Gott.'" In *Leben angesichts des Todes: Helmut Thielicke zum 60. Geburtstag*, edited by Bernhard Lohse and Hans P. Schmidt, 171-90. Tübingen: Mohr/Siebeck, 1968.
———. "Helmut Thielicke. Parteiliche Gedanken zu Person und Werk." In *Zum Gedenken an Helmut Thielicke*, edited by Jörg Lippert, 19-29. Hamburg: Pressestelle der Universität Hamburg, 1987.
Römisch Katholischer Katechismus. *Katechismus der Katholischen Kirche*. München: R. Oldenbourg Verlag, 1993.
Rueger, Matthew. "Individualism in the Christology of Helmut Thielicke's sermons: analysis and response." PhD diss., Durham University, 2003. http://etheses.dur.ac.uk/3713.
Ruhstorfer, Karlheinz. "Christologie nach Auschwitz." In *Dogmatik heute*, edited by Thomas Marschler and Thomas Schärtl, 237-41. Regensburg: Pustet, 2014.
Rusten, E. Michael, and Sharon Rusten. *The One Year Christian History*. Wheaton, IL: Tyndale House, 2003.
Sacks, Jonathan. *The Persistence of Faith. Religion, Morality, and Society in a Secular Age*. London: Continuum, 2005.
Schaeffer, Francis A. *How Should We Then Live?* Wheaton, IL: Crossway, 1983.
Schirrmacher, Christine. *Der Islam: Eine Einführung*. Lahr: Johannis, 2009.
———. *The Islamic View of Major Christian Teachings*. Bonn: Culture and Science Publication, 2008.
Schirrmacher, Thomas. "Zur religiösen Sprache Adolf Hitlers: Zusammenfassende Thesen des Buches *Hitlers Kriegsreligion*." International Institute for Religious Freedom. http://www.iirf.eu/fileadmin/user_upload/IIRF_Reports/iirf_bulletin_10.pdf.
Schlatter, Adolf. *Das christliche Dogma*. Stuttgart: Calwer, 1923.
———. *Die philosophische Arbeit seit Cartesius*. Gießen: Brunnen, 1981.
———. *Einführung in die Theologie*. Stuttgart: Calwer, 2013.
———. *Glaube und Wirklichkeit: Beiträge zur Wahrnehmung Gottes*. Stuttgart: Calwer, 2002.
———. *Gottes Gerechtigkeit: Ein Kommentar zum Römerbrief*. Stuttgart: Calwer, 1975.

———. *Rückblick auf meine Lebensarbeit*. Stuttgart: Calwer, 1977.
Schleiermacher, Friedrich Daniel Ernst. *Der Christliche Glaube. Nach den Grundsätzen der Evangelischen Kirche im Zusammenhange dargestellt. Band I*. Berlin: Walter de Gruyter, 1960.
———. *On Religion: Speeches to Its Cultured Despisers*. Translated by John Oman. New York: Harper and Row, 1958.
Scott, David A. "The Trinity and Ethics: The Thought of Helmut Thielicke." *Lutheran Quarterly* 29.1 (1977) 3–12.
Siddiqui, Mona. "Islam and the Question of a Loving God." In *Religion, Society, and God: Public Theology in Action*, edited by Richard Noake and Nicholas Buxton, 32–48. London: SCM, 2013.
Siedentop, Larry. *Inventing the Individual: The Origins of Western Liberalism*. Milton Keynes: Penguin, 2015.
Siegele-Wenschkewitz, Leonore. "Die Theologische Fakultät im Dritten Reich. Bollwerk gegen Basel." In *Semper Apertus: Sechshundert Jahre Ruprecht-Karls-Universität Heidelberg 1386–1986. Festschrift in sechs Bänden. Band III: Das zwanzigste Jahrhundert 1918–1985*, edited by Wilhelm Doerr, 504–43. Berlin: Springer-Verlag, 1985.
Sierszyn, Armin. *2000 Jahre Kirchengeschichte. Das Mittelalter. Band 2*. Holzgerlingen: Hänssler, 2006.
———. *2000 Jahre Kirchengeschichte. Reformation und Gegenreformation. Band 3*. Holzgerlingen: Hänssler, 2007.
Simpson, D. P. *Cassell's Latin Dictionary*. London: Cassell & Company, 1982.
Sire, James W. "Camus the Christian?" Christianity Today. 23 October 2000. http://www.christianitytoday.com/ct/2000/october23/39.121.html.
Smith, R. Scott. "Post-Conservatives, Foundationalism, and Theological Truth: A Critical Evaluation." *JETS* 48.2 (2005) 351–63.
Speier, Holger. *Gott als Initiator des Fragens. Helmut Thielickes Apologetik im theologie- und zeitgeschichtlichen Kontext*. Marburg: Tectum, 2009.
Spener, Philip Jacob. *Pia Desideria*. Translated and edited by Theodore Tappert. Eugene, OR: Wipf & Stock, 2002.
Sproul, R. C., et al. *Classical Apologetics*. Grand Rapids: Zondervan, 1984.
Stott, John. *The Cross of Christ*. Leicester: InterVarsity, 1986.
Strauss, David Friedrich. *Die christliche Glaubenslehre. Band I*. Darmstadt: Wissenschaftliche Buchgesellschaft, 2009.
Strobel, Lee. *The Case for Christ*. Grand Rapids: Zondervan, 1998.
———. *The Case for Faith*. Grand Rapids: Zondervan, 2000.
Strong, Augustus Hopkins. *Systematic Theology*. Rochester: E. R. Andrews, 1886.
Swinburne, Richard. *Responsibility and Atonement*. Oxford: Clarendon, 1989.
———. "The Social Theory of the Trinity." *Religious Studies* 54.3 (2018): 419–37.
Tennant, F. R. *The Nature of Belief*. London: Centenary, 1943.
Thiede, Werner. *Der gekreuzigte Sinn. Eine trinitarische Theodizee*. Gütersloh: Gütersloher Verlagshaus, 2007.
Thielicke, Berthold. Foreword to *Das Schweigen Gottes: Glauben im Ernstfall*, by Helmut Thielicke, 7. Stuttgart: Quell, 1988.
Thielicke, Marieluise. *Aus meiner Kinderzeit*. Stuttgart: Quell, 1994.
———. Foreword to *Das Lachen der Heiligen und Narren: Nachdenkliches über Witz und Humor*, by Helmut Thielicke, 7–8. Stuttgart: Quell, 1988.

Tillich, Paul. *Systematic Theology.* Vol. 1. London: SCM, 1988.
Torrance, Alan J. "Christian Experience and Divine Revelation in the Theologies of Friedrich Schleiermacher and Karl Barth." In *Christian Experience in Theology and Life: Papers Read at the 1984 Conference of the Fellowship of European Evangelical Theologians,* edited by I. Howard Marshall, 83–113. Edinburgh: Rutherford House, 1988.
Trillhaas, Wolfgang. *Dogmatik.* Berlin: Walter de Gruyter, 1972.
———. "Persönlichkeit." In *Religion in Geschichte und Gegenwart,* Vol. 5, 227–30. Tübingen: Mohr/Siebeck, 1961.
Trueman, Carl R. *The Creedal Imperative.* Wheaton, IL: Crossway, 2012.
———. "Original Sin and Modern Theology." In *Adam, the Fall, and Original Sin: Theological, Biblical, and Scientific Perspectives,* edited by Hans Madueme and Michael Reeves, 167–86. Grand Rapids: Baker Academic, 2014.
Vander Laan, Ray. *Echoes of His Presence.* Colorado Springs: Focus on the Family, 1996.
Van Inwagen, Peter, and Meghan Sullivan. "Metaphysics." Stanford Encyclopedia of Philosophy. 31 October 2014. https://plato.stanford.edu/archives/fall2017/entries/metaphysics.
Vine, William E. *Vine's Expository Dictionary of Old & New Testament Words.* Nashville: Thomas Nelson, 1997.
Volk, Hermann. *Emil Brunners Lehre von dem Sünder.* Münster: Regensbergsche Verlagsbuchhandlung, 1950.
Vonholdt, Christl R. "Beziehungsraum Mutterleib: Einblick in die Entwicklung des vorgeburtlichen Kindes." Deutsches Institut für Jugend und Gesellschaft. http://www.dijg.de/ehe-familie/bindung/mutterleib-vorgeburtliche-entwicklung.
Wachter, Daniel von. "Der Mythos der Aufklärung. Teil 1: Eigenlob stinkt." Vonwachter.de 17 February 2014. http://www.von-wachter.de/papers/Wachter-Aufklaerung-01.pdf.
———. *Die kausale Struktur der Welt.* Freiburg: Karl Alber, 2009.
Walker, Theodore Jr. "Living with Death." *Journal of the American Academy of Religion* 52.2 (1984) 413–14.
Walldorf, Jochen. *Realistische Philosophie: Der philosophische Entwurf Adolf Schlatters.* Göttingen: Vandenhoeck & Ruprecht, 1999.
Walters, Orville S. "Thielicke's Ethics: The Ethics of Sex." *Christianity Today* 8.16 (1964) 39–40.
Ward, Keith. *God: A Guide for the Perplexed.* Oxford: Oneworld, 2003.
Ward, Michael. *Planet Narnia: The Seven Heavens in the Imagination of C. S. Lewis.* Oxford: Oxford University Press, 2008.
Ward, Wayne E. "Apostles' Creed Comes Alive." *Christianity Today* 13.8 (1969) 16.
Weger, Karl-Heinz. *Theologie der Erbsünde.* Freiburg: Herder, 1970.
Weikart, Richard. "Darwinism and Death: Devaluing Human Life in Germany 1859–1920." *Journal of the History of Ideas* 63.2 (2002) 323–40.
Weinandy, Thomas G. "Does God Suffer?" First Things. November 2001. https://www.firstthings.com/article/2001/11/does-god-suffer.
———. *Does God Suffer?* Edinburgh: T&T Clark, 2000.
Wengert, Timothy J. "'Peace, Peace . . . Cross, Cross,' Reflections on How Martin Luther Relates the Theology of the Cross to Suffering." *Theology Today* 59.2 (2002) 190–205.

Willard, Dallas. "Jesus the Logician." http://www.dwillard.org/articles/artview.asp?artID=39.

Williams, Stephen N. "Reason, law and religious freedom." *Ethics in Brief* 20.5 (2015) http://klice.co.uk/uploads/Ethics%20in%20Brief/EiB_Williams_20_5_WEB.pdf.

Williams, Thomas D., and Jan Olof Bengtsson. "Personalism." Stanford Encyclopedia of Philosophy. 2 December 2013. https://plato.stanford.edu/archives/sum2016/entries/personalism.

Wilson, Marvin R. *Our Father Abraham: Jewish Roots of the Christian Faith*. Grand Rapids: Eerdmans, 1989.

Wolfe, David L. *Epistemology*. Downers Grove: InterVarsity, 1982.

Wright, N. T. *Surprised by Hope*. London: SPCK, 2007.

Young, Brad H. *Jesus the Jewish Theologian*. Peabody, MA: Hendrickson, 1999.

Zacharias, Ravi. *Can Man Live Without God*. Dallas: Word, 1994.

———. *Cries of the Heart*. Nashville: Word, 1998.

Zahrnt, Heinz. *Die Sache mit Gott*. München: Piper, 1996.

Zizioulas, John D. *Being as Communion: Studies in Personhood and the Church*. Crestwood, NY: St. Vladimir's Seminary, 2000.

Zywulska, Krystyna. *Ich überlebte Auschwitz*. Translated by Przezylam Oswiecim. Warszawa: tCHu, 2011.

Index of Names

Abraham (Biblical Character), 194, 194n44
Adam (Biblical Character), 135, 135n110, 138–43, 226
Adam, Alfred, 85n80, 106n119, 120n20, 122n31, 150n6
Adenauer, Konrad, 168n116
Althaus, Paul, 4–5, 6n13, 13n55, 23, 23n33, 25, 26, 26n52, 26n53, 38, 41n26, 74n4, 80n48, 80n51, 83, 83n69, 83n71, 83n72, 84, 84n77, 85n80, 86, 86n87, 86n89, 86n90, 87n93, 89n5, 97, 97n58, 97n64, 99n75, 108n138, 113n168, 133n97, 140n139, 146, 147, 148, 148n188, 155, 156n42, 163n88, 164n93, 172, 172n135, 172n137, 175n148, 190n15, 191n24, 194n42, 221, 221n93
Anderson, H. George, 33, 33n97, 179n2
Anselm of Canterbury, 103n103, 195
Aquinas, Thomas, 134n104
Aristotle, 105, 119n9, 123, 123n36, 167
Aron, Elaine N., 217n62
Augstein, Rudolf, 12n51
Augustine of Hippo, 19n21, 77, 80, 89, 105, 106n119, 133, 220, 220n84

Baader, Franz von, 195
Bach, Johann Sebastian, 8, 8n30
Bacon, Francis, 113n167
Baggett, David, 109n145
Baillie, John, 95n48

Baldwin, James, 159, 161
Balthasar, Hans Urs von, 163n88
Barrs, Jerram, 109n144
Barth, Karl, 7n15, 8, 9, 9n33, 13, 13n55, 14n62, 28, 28n71, 41, 41n27, 44n37, 47, 53n76, 75, 79n39, 80n53, 82n62, 82n63, 92, 93, 94n39, 95, 95n44, 95n48, 96n57, 100, 100n82, 101, 101n89, 102n93, 105n115, 130n84, 131n86, 134, 134n101, 136, 136n118, 137n127, 138n128, 142, 143n161, 147n184, 151n15, 163n88, 164, 165n99, 171n132, 184n24, 185n32, 208n9
Bauckham, Richard J., 136n118
Bayer, Oswald, 54n82, 76, 76n15, 81n57, 81n58, 82, 82n63, 82n64, 82n65, 82n67, 82n68, 84, 84n78, 84n79, 85, 85n80, 85n82, 85n85, 87n94, 88n1, 89n5, 103n97, 112n162, 114n172, 149n3, 172n136, 181n9, 191n25
Bechtold, [no first name given], 42n28, 47n46
Becker, Ernest, 20n24
Beckermann, Ansgar, 221n88
Beckwith, Francis J., 216n58
Bengtsson, Jan Olof, 76n17
Bentum, Ad van, 38n13, 148, 148n187, 151n14, 152, 152n20, 152n21, 191n22
Berkhof, Louis, 206n1

257

INDEX OF NAMES

Bernard of Clairvaux, 173n138
Bernstein, Leonard, 6, 6n11, 8n29, 16, 16n2
Besier, Gerhard, 9n33
Bingen, Hildegard von, 146
Bloesch, Donald, 9n35, 96, 96n56, 99n75, 137n127
Boa, Kenneth, 9n35
Bockmühl, Klaus, 138n129
Bonhoeffer, Dietrich, 7, 7n18, 13, 13n57, 29, 37, 37n8, 49n56, 56, 56n91, 56n92, 56n93, 56n94, 57n97, 57n98, 59n105, 81n61, 107n129, 123, 124n42, 124n45, 129n74, 144n166, 160n76, 168, 168n115, 173, 173n138, 174, 188n4, 201, 201n81, 201n85, 203n99, 205n106, 207n6, 212, 212n31, 215n51, 216n55, 222n96, 228, 228n129, 228n130
Bodelschwingh, Friedrich von, 107n129, 188, 188n3, 189, 204n105, 212
Boom, Corrie ten, 203n99
Bowman, Robert M. Jr., 9n35
Braun, Herbert, 119, 119n14
Brenz, Johannes, 162n82
Brocher, Tobias, 17n9, 17n13, 21n26, 154n31
Bromiley, Geoffrey W., xxv, 59, 59n107, 80n51, 96n57, 101n90, 110n146, 111n159, 151n13, 151n16, 179n2, 179n4, 184n28, 215n48, 230n138, 230n142
Broszat, Martin, 43–44, 44n35, 46n42
Brown, Dale, 74n7
Brunner, Emil, 9, 9n33, 14n62, 62n125, 77n24, 80, 80n53, 80n55, 81n56, 83n72, 90, 90n16, 94n39, 97n58, 100n79, 102n93, 106, 107n128, 111n158, 113n167, 113n169, 122, 122n29, 133, 133n97, 133n98, 137n127, 138n128, 139, 139n134, 140n143, 141, 141n146, 142n154, 148n190, 170n122, 183, 183n21
Buber, Martin, 147, 148
Bucer, Martin, 162n82

Bultmann, Rudolf, 92, 97, 97n62, 100n81, 102, 102n91, 142, 142n155
Bunyan, John, 1
Buonarroti, Michelangelo, 133, 140
Busch, Wilhelm, 156n44, 214, 214n40
Butler, Joseph, xxiin3
Byrne, James M., 143n160

Cain (Biblical Character), 202, 202n89
Campenhausen, Hans von, 12, 12n50, 12n52
Camus, Albert, 121n24, 148, 150n7, 213n40, 219n69, 219n75
Calvert, Michael, xxiv, xxivn12, 34, 34n99, 34n100, 59, 60, 61n114, 137, 137n120, 139, 139n136, 150n7, 159, 160n70, 179n3, 198, 198n62, 198n64
Calvin, John, xxii, xxiin4, 108, 108n137, 110n150, 145n170, 184
Cardwell, Walter D., 179n2
Carlyle, Thomas, 78
Carnell, Edward J., 127n62
Cary, Phillip, 150n6
Chemnitz, Martin, 89, 89n8
Chesterton, Gilbert K., 12n46, 122n33, 141n149, 192n31, 220n79, 220n86
Christians, Emil, 48, 48n51, 65
Cicero, 162n81
Clark, David K., 8n23
Clark, Jonathan C. D., 120n17
Clements, Keith W., 75n9
Coates, D. Justin, 134n103
Cockshut, Anthony O. J., 174n144, 202n92
Collins, Francis C., 81n61
Coren, Michael, 20n25
Cornelius, Nadja, 47n45
Cox, James W., 179n3, 186, 186n38
Craig, William Lane, xxi–xxii, xxiin2, 95n48, 126, 127n58, 137n126, 141n150, 144n166, 145n171, 194n47, 196, 196n54, 196n55, 219n75, 220n85, 221n88
Cullmann, Oscar, 210n25, 211, 211n27
Cyrus (Biblical Character), 204n105

INDEX OF NAMES

Davidman, Helen Joy, 109n145, 121n24, 156n43, 212
Descartes, René, 155, 213, 213n37
Dibelius, D., 41n26
Diem, Hermann, 9, 45n38
Dilthey, Wilhelm, xxi
Dirks, Marvin, 19n19, 22n31, 33, 33n95, 33n96, 34, 36n2, 40n23, 60, 60n110, 159n66, 179n3
Donne, John, 123, 156n42
Dummett, Michael A. E., 144n166
Duns Scotus, John, 120n20
Dyrness, William A., 75n9

Ebeling, Gerhard, 62–63, 62n125, 63n126, 75, 75n14, 76, 76n18, 76n19, 77n21, 77n22, 77n23, 79n42, 81n58, 83n70, 85n80, 118, 118n4, 122n28, 136n114, 147, 147n184, 226n120
Ebner, Ferdinand, 147, 148
Ebrard, Johann Heinrich August, 163n87
Elert, Werner, 41n26
Emery, Gilles, 103n104, 109n145, 114n174, 120n20, 129n77
Eppinger, Hans, 24, 24n42, 26n55
Erbslöh, Horst, 48–49
Ericksen, Robert P., 26n52
Esser, Albert, 119n10
Eusebius of Caesarea, 108n137
Eve (Biblical Character), 133, 141, 145n169
Ezekiel (Biblical Character), 113

Feuerbach, Ludwig, 93, 121, 122n34, 128n70
Fichte, Johann Gottlieb, 119, 119n9, 119n10, 120, 157n48
Flint, Thomas P., 141n150
Forberg, Friedrich Karl, 119n10
Forde, Gerhard O., 83n71, 162n82, 184n26
Francis of Assisi, 204n105
Frankl, Viktor E., 122n34, 128, 128n66, 201n83, 209, 209n13, 209n15, 223, 223n103, 223n104
Frazier, Claude A., 18n17

Freisler, Roland, 40n24
Frenzel, Ivo, 224n107
Freud, Sigmund, 77n27, 218n64, 223
Frick, Heinrich, 26n54
Friedländer, Saul, 43, 43n34
Friedrich II (Holy Roman Emperor), 124

Galilei, Galileo, 111n159
Gallagher, Michael P., 222n94
Geier, Manfred, 75n9
Gess, Wolfgang Friedrich, 163n87
Geyer, Hans-Georg, 163n88
Girgis, Sherif, 124n47
Gloege, Gerhard, 77, 77n25, 78n29, 80n47, 80n55, 122, 122n28, 134n101
Goerdeler, Carl F., 44, 44n36, 210, 210n26
Goethe, Johann Wolfgang von, 123, 123n36, 207
Goffar, Janine, 56–57, 57n95
Gogarten, Friedrich, 97n62
Gollwitzer, Helmut, 7, 8n23, 68n153, 97, 97n65, 128n67, 218n63, 224n106
Graham, Billy, 58n104, 137n127, 168n116
Grenz, Stanley J., 97n62, 102n91, 124n43, 175n149, 224n107
Grudem, Wayne, 206n1

Haas, Rudolf, 12, 12n51, 13n54, 58n101, 58n102, 179n2, 210n23
Habermas, Gary, 165n99, 168
Hamann, Brigitte, 8n29, 47n45
Hamilton, Kenneth, 163n86
Handrich, Karl, 28n71
Harnack, Adolf von, 163n86
Haselmayr, Friedrich, 41n27
Haug, Martin, 12n51, 13n54, 58, 58n101, 58n102, 179n2, 210n23
Haydn, Joseph, 8, 10n36
Hegel, Georg Wilhelm Friedrich, 119n12
Heidegger, Martin, 77, 81n60, 103
Heinemann, Gustav, 11n42, 44n37
Hengel, Martin, 162n81, 172n135

INDEX OF NAMES

Henry, Carl F. H., 165, 165n95
Herder, Johann Gottfried, 135n108
Hermann, D., 26n54
Heron, Alasdair I., 193n38
Herrigel, Eugen, 22, 22n32, 23, 25, 25n49, 25n50, 26
Herz, Gerhard, 8n30
Heschel, Abraham, 119n7
Hess, Rudolf, 40
Hick, John, 138n130, 228n127
Higginson, Richard, 59, 60, 60n108, 100n83
Hildebrand, Dietrich von, 21, 21n28, 33, 73, 73n1, 85, 121n24, 122n33, 127n64, 167n107, 217, 217n61, 220, 220n80, 220n81, 220n82, 220n83, 220n85
Hitler, Adolf, 8n29, 37, 41n25, 42, 45–46, 47n45, 48, 210n26
Hoche, Alfred E., 219, 219n77
Holthaus, Stephan, 16n3, 134n102
Horkheimer, Max, 150n7, 208, 209
Horn, Christoph, 106n119
Hornig, Gottfried, 230n144
Hütter, Reinhard, 54n81, 84n79

Inwagen, Peter van, 231n153
Irenaeus of Lyons, 228n127
Isaac (Biblical Character), 194–95
Issler, Klaus, 224n112

Jacobsen, Jens Peter, 219n73
Jägerstätter, Franz, 20n25, 36n1, 46n44, 49n55
Jaspers, Karl, 111n159, 151, 152, 153, 154
Jeremiah (Biblical Character), 113
Jewett, Paul, 142n154
Job (Biblical Character), 218, 218n68
Joffé, Roland, 209n16
John (the Baptist), 57n98, 158, 159–62
Josephus, Flavius, 162n81
Jüngel, Eberhard, 163n88
Justin Martyr, 122n26

Kähler, Martin, 97n62, 98, 98n66, 98n71, 99, 99n74, 100, 113, 113n169

Kant, Immanuel, xxi, 75n9, 96, 100, 100n79, 120, 120n17, 138n129, 149, 149n1, 193, 208n9
Kantzenbach, Friedrich Wilhelm, 98n67
Kavanaugh, Patrick, 10n36, 196n55
Kennedy, John F., 64
Kierkegaard, Søren, xxi, 6, 80, 80n47, 91n19, 93, 93n33, 95, 100, 100n79, 105, 111n158, 113, 133n97, 150n10, 171, 194, 217, 231n150
Klann, Richard, 231n146
Klee, Ernst, 24n42, 41n25, 45n39, 46n43, 219n77
Kraft, Charles H., 135n110
Krauss, Meinold, 4, 13n56, 19, 30, 31, 33, 36, 53n76, 60, 68n151, 98n72, 164
Kreeft, Peter, 216n58
Küng, Hans, 119, 119n15, 163n88

Ladd, George E., 210n24, 211n27
Langsam, Friedrich, 3n2, 14, 14n62, 14n64, 14n65, 22n31, 23, 23n35, 34, 34n101, 35, 59, 103, 103n98, 103n99, 147, 147n183, 159n66, 179n2, 179n3, 181, 181n15, 182n16, 183n19
Law, David R., 17n6, 42n31
Leibniz, Gottfried Wilhelm, 123, 123n36, 208n9
Lenz, Johann, 14, 14n59
Leontius of Byzantium, 120n20
Lessing, Gotthold Ephraim, 100n81, 111, 112
Lewis, Clive Staples, 16n2, 19, 19n21, 20, 20n23, 20n25, 56, 90n11, 106, 106n123, 106n125, 106n126, 107n129, 109n144, 109n145, 119n7, 121n24, 122n34, 123n37, 124n45, 126, 126n54, 127n60, 128, 128n69, 129n75, 131n86, 133, 133n95, 133n99, 135n110, 141, 141n149, 143n161, 144n163, 148n186, 148n191, 150n6, 150n7, 156n43, 156n44, 174n144, 175, 175n149, 192n31, 202n92, 203n99, 204,

INDEX OF NAMES

204n100, 209n17, 212, 212n34, 212n36, 221n91, 221n93, 225n114
Liebner, Karl Theodor August, 163n87
Lindenschmidt, [no first name given], 67
Lindner, Wulf-Volker, 62, 62n121
Lippert, Jörg, 5n10
Loewenich, Elisabeth von [née Thielicke], 12n52, 17, 23
Löfgren, David, 141n145
Lohse, Bernhard, 60, 98n71
Lorenzmeier, Theodor, 119n14
Lundin, Roger, 69n154, 111n154
Lütgert, Wilhelm, 110n151
Luther, Martin, 7, 7n14, 29n76, 32, 53, 54, 62, 74, 75, 76, 76n18, 77, 77n25, 78n29, 79, 80, 80n46, 80n51, 81, 82, 83, 83n71, 84, 84n79, 85, 86n87, 87, 87n93, 88, 89, 89n5, 92n26, 100, 103n97, 107, 111, 112, 114, 115, 116, 116n180, 122n28, 123n35, 131n88, 134, 139, 140n139, 141, 145n170, 147, 155, 156, 162, 162n82, 164n93, 172, 172n137, 174n145, 180, 181, 181n9, 188, 191, 191n25, 194, 194n42, 199, 211n28, 213n40, 221, 225n115, 228n131, 230, 233
Lütz, Manfred, 124, 124n47
Lutzer, Erwin W., 204n105, 209n16

Macaulay, Ranald, 109n144
Mackensen, Eberhard von, 44n37
Mackie, John L., 119n15
Macquarrie, John, 81n60
Madueme, Hans, 142n156
Mahler, Gustav, 6, 8, 8n29
Maier, Hans, 121n25
Mann, Thomas, 167
Mao, Zedong, 204n105
Marcuse, Herbert, 229, 229n135
Marquardt, Friedrich-Wilhelm, 8n23, 97n65
Martini, Paul, 22, 22n30, 23n36, 24, 24n39, 24n43, 25, 25n46, 25n47, 25n48, 26, 26n56, 27

Marx, Karl, 229
McGrath, Alister E., xxiin4, 83n71, 101n86, 108n137, 110n150, 119n9, 144n166, 145n170, 162, 163n85, 166n102, 184n25, 192n31
McKenna, Michael, 134n103
Melanchthon, Philipp, 79n42, 89, 89n5, 89n8, 108, 108n138, 130
Metaxas, Eric, 203n99
Metz, Johann Baptist, 201n82, 202n90
Meyer-Erlach, Wolf, 41n26
Molina, Luis de, 141n150
Moltke, Helmuth James von, 40n24, 56, 56n94, 159n67
Moltmann, Jürgen, 7, 7n20, 8, 8n27, 55, 55n85, 80n46, 85n81, 108n137, 108n138, 113n167, 121n23, 125n51, 127n64, 128n68, 133n97, 148, 148n190, 148n191, 150n7, 162n83, 163, 163n85, 163n86, 163n88, 166, 166n102, 167n106, 167n107, 167n108, 168, 168n116, 169, 169n118, 169n119, 170n123, 171n128, 172n135, 172n136, 173n138, 174n145, 174n146, 174n147, 175n149, 192n32, 200n77, 203, 203n95, 204n102, 208, 209, 209n12, 210n23, 213n40, 219n69
Montgomery, John Warwick, 44n37
Moreland, James P., xxiin2, 95n48, 109n144, 126, 127n58, 216n55, 220n85, 224n112
Moses (Biblical Character), 212
Moule, Charles F. D., 210n20
Mozart, Wolfgang Amadeus, 8
Mühlen, Heribert, 163n88
Mumma, Howard, 219n75

Nebuchadnezzar (Biblical Character), 204n105
Nesbit, John, 13n53
Neuer, Werner, 66n142, 79n41, 105n115, 109n144, 110n151, 165n98, 185n32, 215n49, 215n50, 215n51, 230n142

INDEX OF NAMES

Newman, John Henry, xxii*n*3, 207
Nicholas of Cusa, 122
Niemöller, Martin, 28n71
Nietzsche, Friedrich, 49n55, 114n174, 213, 213n38, 213n39, 219, 219n73, 221, 224, 224n107 Nigg, Walter, 209n16
Nordlander, Agne, 79n40, 79n45, 80n55, 100n79, 138, 138n128, 139n131, 141, 141n145, 142, 142n153, 142n154, 142n155, 143, 143n157

Occam, William of, 194
Oettingen, Alexander von, 133n97
Olson, Roger E., 97n62, 102n91, 102n93, 124n43, 175n149, 224n107
Origen, 120n20
Otto, Rudolf, 204n100

Packer, James I., 144n165, 145n171
Pannenberg, Wolfhart, 19n21, 81n60, 89n5, 89n9, 92, 93, 93n31, 97, 97n62, 97n64, 97n65, 98n66, 102, 102n91, 108n140, 108n141, 110, 110n147, 110n149, 113n168, 113n169, 119n9, 119n11, 120n20, 121, 121n22, 121n24, 121n25, 122, 122n26, 123, 123n37, 124n45, 125, 125n49, 126n54, 126n55, 128n70, 129n73, 134n105, 139n135, 162n83, 163n86, 169n119, 194n47, 196n52, 208n9, 227
Pascal, Blaise, 80, 80n47
Paul (Apostle), 13, 19, 95, 169n119, 170n123, 207
Paul, Jean, 161, 161n79, 168n112, 219
Payne, J. Barton, 130n81, 130n82, 210n20
Pearcey, Nancy, 126, 126n56
Peter (Apostle), 91, 115, 191, 193
Plantinga, Alvin, 196n55
Plato, 77, 78

Pless, John T., 61–62, 61n115, 61n117, 61n118, 61n119, 152, 152n22, 179n2, 234n2
Polanyi, Michael, 8n23
Preuss, Johann Sebastian, 24, 24n44, 27, 27n60, 27n63, 27n65
Putz, Erna, 20n25, 36n1, 49n55

Quest, Hans-Jürgen, 9n33

Rahner, Karl, xxii, xxii*n*5, 7, 7n21, 8, 8n28, 142n156, 145n171, 163n88, 166n103, 185n33
Raimbault, Ginette, 17n7, 17n8, 17n10, 17n12
Ratzinger, Joseph (Pope Benedict XVI.), 7, 7n22, 13, 13n58, 55n88, 78n33, 80, 80n54, 83n72, 91, 91n21, 94n42, 96n57, 103n104, 105, 106, 106n119, 106n120, 106n124, 106n125, 107, 113n167, 114n170, 123, 123n39, 123n40, 123n41, 129n77, 130, 130n83, 135n110, 146n175, 157, 163n86, 170n125, 173n138, 205n108, 222n94, 230n138, 234
Reeves, Michael, 142n156
Richard of Saint Victor, 123n37
Richter-Böhne, Andreas, 9n33, 45n38, 46n43, 179n3, 235, 235n4
Rieger, Reinhold, 82n68, 84n79, 92n26, 106n122, 116n180, 116n181, 116n183, 122n28, 191n23
Riesner, Rainer, 165n99
Rilke, Rainer Maria, 73n2
Rissmann, Michael, 47n45
Robinson, John A. T., 129n75
Roessler, Roman, 80n55
Rohde, Peter P., 91n19, 194n43
Röhricht, Rainer, 8, 8n25, 9n31, 10, 10n36, 14, 14n64, 14n66, 62, 62n122, 62n123, 86, 86n88, 100n79, 118, 118n5, 129n77, 149n2
Rothert, Jochen, 179n2
Rousseau, Jean-Jacques, 143
Rueger, Matthew, 89n7, 157, 157n51, 165, 165n96, 179n3, 235n3

Ruhstorfer, Karlheinz, 201n82, 202n90, 202n91
Rusten, E. Michael, 13n53, 188n3, 192n28
Rusten, Sharon, 13n53, 188n3, 192n28

Sacks, Jonathan, 124n47
Sauter, Gerhard, 9n33
Schaeffer, Francis, 119n7
Scheel, Gustav Adolf, 41n27
Schiller, Johann Christoph Friedrich, 135n108, 136, 138, 207
Schirrmacher, Christine, 126n57, 134n100
Schirrmacher, Thomas, 47n45
Schlatter, Adolf, 7, 7n19, 66n142, 79, 79n41, 89, 90, 90n12, 90n13, 96n52, 97n58, 100, 100n82, 105n115, 109n144, 122, 122n27, 124, 124n45, 128, 128n69, 139n135, 141, 141n148, 163n88, 165n98, 185n32, 186n36, 195–96, 195n51, 196n52, 196n53, 215, 215n51, 228n131, 230n142
Schlatter, Susanna, 66n142
Schleiermacher, Friedrich, xxi, xxiii, 75n9, 100n81, 110, 131n88, 142, 158n61, 193, 195, 204, 204n100
Schlink, Edmund, 141n146
Schmalenbach, Marie, 54n79
Schmidt, Hans, 39, 39n22, 182
Schmidt, Hans P., 60, 65, 65n137
Schniewind, Julius Daniel, 98, 98n72, 99
Scholl, Sophie, 49n55
Schönfeld, Walther, 164, 164n94
Schopenhauer, Arthur, 221n88
Schubert, Franz Peter, 196n55
Schultze, Walter, 40, 41, 41n26, 42, 42n28, 44n37
Schwinn, Wilhelm, 146, 147, 147n180
Scott, David A., 129, 129n76
Seiler, [no first name given], 42n28
Semler, Johann Salomo, 230n144
Siddiqui, Mona, 126n57, 127n64
Siedentop, Larry, 121n25
Siegele-Wenschkewitz, Leonore, 40n24
Sierszyn, Armin, 145n170, 194n41
Simpson, D. P., 89n9

Sire, James W., 219n75
Sölle, Dorothee, 128n67
Sophocles, 221n88
Sorokin, Vladimir, 168n116
Spafford, Horatio, 188n3, 192n28
Speier, Holger, 5, 5n9, 11n43, 14n64, 30, 30n79, 34, 34n98, 39n19, 39n22, 41n26, 43, 43n32, 44, 44n37, 45, 45n38, 59, 62n124, 101, 101n88, 103n99, 110, 110n148, 114, 114n171, 152, 153, 153n23, 164n93, 179n3, 226n118
Spener, Philip Jacob, 74n7, 100n81
Spengler, Oswald, 160, 219n71
Spinoza, Baruch, 119n9
Spranger, Eduard, 65
Sproul, Robert C., 90, 90n14, 207n6
Spurgeon, Charles H., 179n4
Stalin, Josef, 204n105
Staupitz, Johann von, 145n170, 162n82
Steffensen, Karl, 186n36
Stephen (Biblical Character), 203
Stott, John, 222n97
Strauss, David Friedrich, 119, 119n12, 163, 163n87
Streicher, Julius, 39, 39n22
Strobel, Lee, 165n99, 169n117
Strong, Augustus H., 89, 89n10, 90
Sullivan, Meghan, 231n153
Swinburne, Richard, 123n37, 142n156

Tennant, Frederick R., 222n98
Tertullian, 120n20
Thiede, Werner, xxii n2, 49n55, 83, 83n75, 119n7, 122n34, 124, 124n44, 125, 125n51, 133n96, 133n97, 134n105, 158n55, 162n84, 163n86, 163n87, 163n88, 169n118, 173n138, 174n144, 174n147, 175n149, 202, 202n93, 208n9, 213n38, 222n94
Thielicke, Berthold, 11, 12, 12n52
Thielicke, Karina, 12n52
Thielicke, Marieluise, 4n5, 4n6, 12n52, 48n49, 59, 59n106, 65, 65n135, 66, 66n140, 66n143, 66n144, 67, 67n149, 68n150

Thielicke, Rainer, 12n52
Thielicke, Wolfram, 5, 11, 11n44, 12n52, 13, 13n53, 13n54, 48n50
Thomasius, Gottfried, 163n87
Thompson, Francis, 146
Thurneysen, Eduard, 28n71, 183, 184n24
Tillich, Paul, 100n81, 119, 119n7, 119n13, 120, 120n18, 131, 132, 151, 153, 154, 184, 188n6, 220n78
Torrance, Alan, 8, 8n26
Trillhaas, Wolfgang, 125, 125n49, 148n191, 208n9, 227, 231, 231n152
Trueman, Carl R., 140n144, 142n152, 207, 207n6
Tügel, Franz, 41n27

Unamuno, Miguel de, 148n190

Vander Laan, Ray, 195, 195n48
Vine, William E., 75n12, 82n68
Volk, Hermann, 140n143, 141, 141n147, 142n154
Vonholdt, Christl R., 125n48

Wachter, Daniel von, 119n15, 120n17, 134n104, 196n55
Walker, Theodore Jr., 73n3
Walldorf, Jochen, 90n13, 122n27
Walls, Jerry L. 109n145
Walters, Orville S., 142n155
Ward, Keith, 120n18, 128n71, 145n168, 146, 146n173

Ward, Michael, 109n144
Warfield, Benjamin, 140
Weger, Heinz, 142n156
Weikart, Richard, 219n77
Weinandy, Thomas G., 133n96, 163n88, 173n138, 174n147, 175n149
Weizsäcker, Viktor von, 47n46
Wengert, Timothy J., 32, 32n92, 83n70, 84, 84n78, 85, 85n84, 86, 86n91, 89n8, 191, 191n25
Wetzel, Friedrich Gottlieb, 219n73
Wiesel, Eli, 172n136
Williams, Stephen N., 8n26, 215n51
Williams, Thomas D., 76n17
Wilson, Marvin R., 113n167, 128n71, 170n122
Wittig, Joseph, 14, 15, 205n107
Wolfe, David L., 196n55, 196n56
Woodrow, James, 140
Wright, Nicholas T., 101n87
Wulff, [no first name given], 11n42
Wurm, Theophil, 51, 182

Young, Brad H., 119n7

Zacharias, Ravi, 150n7, 203n99
Zahrnt, Heinz, 13n55, 35n102, 38n13, 44n37, 97n62, 100n79, 101n86, 101n89, 108n136, 119n14, 122n29, 136n118, 164n90, 184n24
Zinzendorf, Nikolaus von, 74, 203
Zizioulas, John D., 125, 125n50
Zwingli, Huldrych, 134, 144n166
Zywulska, Krystyna, 209n14

Index of Scripture Passages

Psalms

22	166n104, 174
23	115
23:4	vi
33:6	134n105
73	188, 209
73:17	209
73:23	189n11, 190, 193n37, 225
90:12	71
139	216n58

Isaiah

25:8	136n114
49:13	177

Lamentations

3:27	216n55

Ezekiel

33:11	173n141

Matthew

6:19–34	189n7
9:20–22	195
10:17	38
10:29	205n106
10:39	132n94
11:2–6	158
16:13–20	91n20
16:25	132n94
20:20–23	189n9

Mark

5:25–34	31n87, 195
8:27–30	91n20
10:35–40	189n9

Luke

8:43–48	195
9:18–21	91n20
9:24	132n94
17:33	132n94

John

1:3	134n105
8:58	130
9	225
9:1–3	227
14:27	14n61
16:33	200n78, 214n43
18:37	103, 113, 164n89

Acts

22:20	208

Romans

1:18–32	109
4:17	134n105
5:12	142n154
6:23	139
8:28	205, 226
11:33–36	207n4

1 Corinthians

12–14	114
15:13–20	169n119
15:26	136n114
15:58	150n10

2 Corinthians

4:8–10	13n58
4:16–18	205n107
6:8–10	13n58

Galatians

2:20	170n123

Philippians

1:18–26	19n22

Colossians

1:23	150n10
2:5	150n10

Hebrews

11:3	134n105

James

2:19	90n15

1 Peter

1:22	207n4
4:17	214n42
5:10–11	209n16

2 Peter

3:9	173n141
3:17	150n10

1 John

3:16	127n63
4:7–10	127n63
4:9–10	173n141
4:19	127n63
4:16	125n51, 125–26

2 John

9	91n22

Revelation

21:4	136n114

www.ingramcontent.com/pod-product-compliance
Lightning Source LLC
Chambersburg PA
CBHW071238230426
43668CB00011B/1496